国家社科基金重点项目"英语+法律复合型人才培养体系构建与应用研究"阶段性成果（项目编号：18AYY012）

法 律 英 语 教 研 丛 书

丛书主编 张法连 张清

美国商标法
判例研究

张法连 赖清阳 著

中国政法大学出版社

图书在版编目（ＣＩＰ）数据

美国商标法判例研究/张法连，赖清阳著. —北京：中国政法大学出版社，2018.11
ISBN 978-7-5620-8658-1

Ⅰ.①美… Ⅱ.①张…②赖… Ⅲ.①商标法－案例－研究－美国 Ⅳ.①D971.23

中国版本图书馆CIP数据核字(2018)第243131号

书　名	美国商标法判例研究 MEIGUO SHANGBIAOFA PANLI YANJIU
出版者	中国政法大学出版社
地　址	北京市海淀区西土城路 25 号
邮　箱	fadapress@163.com
网　址	http://www.cuplpress.com（网络实名：中国政法大学出版社）
电　话	010-58908466(第七编辑部) 58908334(邮购部)
承　印	固安华明印业有限公司
开　本	720mm×960mm　1/16
印　张	23
字　数	355 千字
版　次	2018 年 11 月第 1 版
印　次	2018 年 11 月第 1 次印刷
定　价	69.00 元

前　言

　　美国是实施知识产权制度最为成功的国家。1870年美国即制定了联邦商标法，现行商标法是颁布于1946年的兰哈姆法，规定了商标使用的在先原则。美国的商标法体系是美国知识产权法律中最完整的一部分，商品外形、声音、颜色、味觉均可以申请注册商标，并分为商品商标、服务商标、证书商标和集体标志四大类。商标注册由位于弗吉尼亚（Virginia）的美国专利商标局（UNITED STATES PATENT AND TRADEMARK OFFICE, USPTO）办理。对侵害商标专用权的行为，美国法律规定侵害人应赔偿商标权人所受的实际损失（actual damage），包括所受损害（例如，商誉受损），所失利益（例如，销售损失）及维权费用，而且特别规定了恶意侵害行为可判定高额赔偿（三倍赔偿）。1996年美国开始实施《美国联邦商标反淡化法》，对著名商标予以更为严格的保护，规定了著名商标的保护和使用的原则，以及混淆、诋毁行为的法律责任等内容，因此较为合理地解决了与互联网域名有关的商标淡化问题。

　　高科技产业的制胜之道在于充分利用知识产权的保护。现代知识经济体系中的成功者，多半在研发、技术进步、产品制造、市场营销中，制定专利、商标攻防战略战术，依靠知识产权法保护其有形和无形资产。现代社会的经济活动，离不开法律的游戏规则。知法，守法，而不犯法，才是正确的做法，才能让天地充满正气及和气。近年来，中国企业的管理能力与水平虽然显著提高，但对专利及商标的保护及知识产权的尊重，仍大有需改进之处。

　　本书作者张法连教授毕业于美国印第安纳大学法学院，获法学博士学位（JD），曾在美国的州司法部、律师事务所工作，对法律语言、知识产权法等颇有研究。张法连教授曾担任美中友好交流促进会主席，为中美之间的法务、教育、经贸等合作交流作出了杰出贡献。张法连教授目前担任中国法律英语教学与测试研究会会长，中国政法大学教授，博士生导师。本书另一位作者赖清阳法学博士（JD）在美国得克萨斯州最高法院、中等法院及地方法院特准执业；在美国华盛顿哥伦比亚特区各级法庭、美国联邦行政法庭及上诉法庭做出庭律师。赖清阳博士担任中美韩律师事务所（LGLC）所长，率领数十位美国、韩国及中国律师，在美国处理大量专利及商标诉讼案件。赖清阳博士对知识产权侵权诉讼案件，久战成军师，清理战场，痛定思痛，并常与职场同仁相互交流探讨，以见贤思齐，免蹈旧辙。在此要特别提及中国台湾地区的冷耀世先生，对本书的编辑出版功不可没，非常感谢冷先生的高度配合。

随着中国加入世界贸易组织以及市场经济的不断发展，知识产权问题日益引起社会各界的关注。同时，制定和实施知识产权战略的呼声也不断提高。在这一时期，研究并分析美国的商标法判例，对中国企业大有裨益。为了便于研究美国案例，作者把美国法院的判决意见原文附录在每个判例解析的后面，以方便对照及比较。

两位作者编撰此书，力求深入浅出，浅显易懂。案例中的企业，也多是一般人耳熟能详的企业，因此读来，更加生动有趣，这也是本书的特色，可以在课堂上，严肃讨论美国商标法及经典判例，也可以在课堂下轻松聊叙，一起雅赏，更是现代知识产权经济体系下，企业及个人处理知识产权问题的必需读物。身为法律人，虽才疏学浅，但能为中美法律交流活动，献上一分努力，深感骄傲。生命有限，但学海无涯，盼学界先进不吝赐教。

让我们一起努力，让中国从代工的生产国，变成知识产权强国，走出低利，迈向品牌营销或专利授权的高报酬区，让中国的高科技产业更上一层楼！加快中国现代化建设的历史进程，成为傲视全球的专利商标大国！

编著者

2018 年 3 月 19 日

目　录

电脑操作界面的霸主之争

微软公司状告林多斯公司案

WINDOWS vs. LINDOWS

判例简介

比尔·盖茨领导的微软公司（Microsoft corp）是世界 PC 机软件开发的先导。微软公司 1981 年为 IBM-PC 机开发的操作系统软件 MS-DOS 曾用在数以亿计的 IBM-PC 机及其兼容机上。但随着微软公司的日益壮大，Microsoft 与 IBM 已在许多方面成为竞争对手。1991 年，IBM 公司和苹果公司解除了与微软公司的合作关系，但实际上 IBM 公司与微软公司的合作关系从未间断过，两个公司保持着既竞争又合作的复杂关系。微软公司的产品包括文件系统软件（MS-DOS 和 Xenix）、操作环境软件（窗口系统 Windows 系列）、应用软件 MS-Office 等，多媒体及计算机游戏，有关计算机的书籍以及 CDROM 产品。1992 年，微软公司买进 Fox 公司，迈进了数据库软件市场，成为个人电脑软件行业的"巨无霸"。

自 20 世纪 80 年代末以来，风靡全球的视窗（Windows）系统奠定了微软公司的行业霸主地位。Windows 随之成为个人电脑操作系统的第一品牌。1991 年，芬兰赫尔辛基大学有位名叫雷诺斯·托瓦兹（Linus Torvalds）的学生，开始在业余时间撰写一套个人电脑操作软件。经过三年努力，雷诺斯终于开发了一个崭新的操作系统，并根据自己的名字将其命名为 Linux。Linux 与微软操作系统的重大区别在于，Linux 的所有原始码都向公众开放，任何人都可以用 Linux 的原始码开发这个操作系统。而微软的大部分原始码都属于商业机

1

密，不向公众开放，所以微软的操作系统独有微软公司一家可以开发。

Linux 一问世，并没有引起微软公司的过多关注。微软公司与软件业的同行大都认为 Linux 不过是一位电脑软件业余爱好者的作品，成不了大气候，可任其自生自灭。事实证明，这种想法是错误的。经历了十年缠斗，Linux 不但没有自生自灭，反倒逐渐壮大，并开始蚕食微软公司的 Windows 市场。

在这一背景之下，林多斯公司（Lindows. com corp）注册成立，正式将 Linux 操作系统市场化。这一举动令微软公司十分不安，因为 Linux 操作系统经过市场化，很有希望成为 Windows 的有力竞争对手，最终是否成为 Windows 的杀手，也难以预料。

微软公司一向以咄咄逼人著称于业界，面对 Linux 的挑战自然不会罢休。在电脑软件业，微软公司对付竞争对手的策略是软硬兼施，或者收购，或者起诉。林多斯公司成立后，微软公司决定以商标侵权和淡化著名商标 Windows 为由起诉林多斯公司。

在商标诉讼战中，商标侵权和淡化著名商标是原告最常用的也是最致命的两大进攻武器。原告一旦得手，被告不但要停止使用有争议的商标，而且还要赔偿原告的经济损失。对于被告来说，一旦输掉商标侵权和淡化著名商标的诉讼，可谓赔了夫人又折兵。不过，与其被动挨打，不如主动出击，如果得手，反倒能化被动为主动。被告这一制胜策略的关键在于证明原告的商标已经成为一种产品的通用名称，因而失去了商标的效力。

在与微软公司的较量中，林多斯公司便运用这一策略，向法院提供了大量的证据，以期证明在微软公司使用 Windows 作为商标以前，Windows 已经成为个人电脑图形操作系统的通用名称。在这种情况下，尽管微软公司使用 Windows 作为商标后，赋予了 Windows 第二层意义，专指微软公司开发的个人电脑视窗操作系统，但是微软公司并不能因此禁止别人使用 Windows 或以近似的词语来描述其他个人电脑图形操作系统。如果林多斯公司这一策略得逞，微软公司指称的两大罪名自然化为乌有，林多斯公司不但可以摆脱微软公司的诉讼，而且可以继续使用林多斯公司的商标和网域名称，与 Windows 在市场上一决高低。

在这场将对软件市场产生重大影响的商标攻防战中，Windows 在被微软公

司用以作为商标时是否已经成为个人电脑图形操作系统的"通用名称",就成
为决定微软公司与林多斯公司胜负的关键。在认定一个商标是否成为一项产
品的通用名称时,法院必须首先确定该产品的种类。在本案中,原告和被告
均同意 Windows 所指的产品是以图形为界面的个人电脑操作系统。

确定了产品的种类后,法院就可以深入到问题的核心,即决定一个商标
是否已经成为某种产品的通用名称。在这一阶段,法院会经由两个问题来决
定一个商标是否已经被通用化为通用名称:第一个问题是"你属于谁";第二
个问题是"你是什么"。如果一个商标可以回答消费者的第一个问题,而不能
回答第二个问题,那么这个商标就还没有成为通用名称。原因在于消费者可
以知道这个商标是指某家具体的产品,而不是指任何一种相同类型的产品。

相反的,如果一个商标可以回答第二个问题,而不能回答第一个问题,
那么这个商标就已经变成通用名称。原因在于,消费者已经把一个商标等同
于相同类型的产品,而无法把这个商标与某一家产品联系起来。例如,"阿司
匹林"可以回答消费者"你是什么",而不能回答消费者"你属于谁",所以
"阿司匹林"这个商标已经成为一个通用名称,不再具有商标的效力。

消费者无法把"阿司匹林"与某一家产品联系起来,而是与一种退烧药
联系起来。与此不同,"柯达"可以回答消费者"你属于谁",而不能回答消
费者"你是什么"。所以,尽管"柯达"是世界上最大的软片品牌,但是消费
者并没有把"柯达"等同于软片,而是把"柯达"与一个软片品牌联系起来。

在本案的较量过程中,林多斯公司辩称,Windows 就像"阿司匹林"一
样,已经成为个人电脑图形界面操作系统的通用名称。微软公司当然不同意这
种说法,称 Widnows 只能回答消费者"你属于谁",而不能回答消费者"你是
什么",所以消费者并没有把 Windows 与个人电脑图形界面操作系统等同起
来,而是把它与微软公司的个人电脑图形界面操作系统联系起来。所以,
Windows 并没有成为个人电脑图形界面操作系统的通用名称,而是专指微软公
司的视窗操作系统。

林多斯公司为了反驳微软公司的说法,便引用微软公司的几个"死对头"
在使用"Windows"一词时的做法。例如"苹果"(APPLE)电脑公司和"施
乐"(XEROX)影印机公司早在几十年前便经常用 Windows 来指称个人电脑

图形界面的操作系统。而且，微软公司自己也经常用"Windows"一词来描述个人电脑图形界面操作系统。为了证明这一点，林多斯公司甚至邀请微软公司几位开发第一代 Windows 的元老出庭作证，并把微软公司自己出版的产品说明书和电脑辞典呈堂作为证据。

面对林多斯公司步步紧逼的证据，微软公司针锋相对，除了正面反驳外，还从杜克大学请来了著名的语言学教授，作为专家澄清"Windows"一词在软件业中的含义。这位专家的确不辱使命，他查阅了 26 部通用英文辞典，在法院上历数各部辞典中对"Windows"一词的解释，得出结论："Windows"一词从来没有成为个人电脑图形界面操作系统的通用名称，也没有成为任何电脑软件的通用名称。

法院内外，双方互不相让，剑拔弩张，加紧准备最后的审判。这起案件不仅引起了无数软件公司的关注，也牵动着无数 Windows 和 Linux 用户的心。世界各地数以亿计的软件开发商和电脑用户均等待这场旷日持久的审判结果。出人意料的是，2004 年 7 月 19 日，微软公司与林多斯公司发表联合声明，称双方已经达成协议，化解了 Windows 商标的侵权之争。协议的大部分内容不为外界所知。不过，按照双方公开的部分条款，林多斯公司同意放弃这个有争议的商标和网域名称。2004 年 8 月 31 日，林多斯公司正式改名为 Linspire. com。至此，这场引起世界关注的微软公司和林多斯公司的商标之争终于画上了一个句号。

虽然这场官司以双方的和解告终，却成为一个商标攻防战的经典案例。如前所述，在本案中原告与被告争执的焦点在于 Windows 是否是一个指称个人电脑图形界面操作系统的通用名称。美国商标法禁止使用产品通用名称作为同类产品的商标，其主要用意之一是为了防止垄断。如果一家电脑公司可以把"电脑"注册成自己产品的商标，那么其他电脑公司就不能再用"电脑"来指称自己的产品。一旦如此，拥有"电脑"商标的这家电脑公司便会轻而易举地垄断电脑市场。

但是，美国商标法并不禁止使用一种产品的通用名称作为另一类产品的商标。例如，"苹果"是一种水果的通用名称，任何一家生产或销售苹果的商家不能注册"苹果"作为自己苹果产品的商标。但是，一家电脑公司却可以注册"苹果"作为自己电脑产品的商标。

本案启示与解析

该案虽然以双方和解收场，却成为一个商标攻防战的经典案例。在本案中，原告与被告争议的焦点在于 Windows 是否是一个指称个人电脑图形界面操作系统的通用名称（generic name）。要理解双方为何在这个问题上纠缠不休，就必须了解美国商标法对商标不同等级的保护。

根据美国商标法和有关法院判例，商标根据受保护力度的不同可分为四个等级。第一个等级是通用名称，完全不受美国商标法的保护，如"Computer"之于电脑产品。商标法禁止使用这类产品的通用名称作为商标，所以任何企业或个人用 Computer 做电脑的商标，都不会受到美国商标法的保护。第二个等级是描述性名称（descriptive name），比如本案中的"Windows"之于"个人电脑图形界面操作系统"。描述性商标必须在消费者中获得第二层意义（secondary meaning）后，才受到商标法保护。当初，微软公司在美国专利商标局注册 Windows 商标时曾经被拒绝，原因就在于这是一个描述性名称，而当时微软公司并没有充分证明 Windows 已经在消费者中获得了第二层意义。此后，为了使 Windows 在消费者中获得第二层意义，微软投入了数以亿计的广告费，在市场上大作宣传，最终成功地注册了 Windows 商标。第三个等级是暗示性名称（suggestive name），比如"Ice"之于薄荷糖。暗示性名称不需要藉由第二层意义的证明即受到法律保护。第四个等级是任意使用或稀奇古怪的名称（arbitrary and fanciful names），比如"Apple"之于电脑，"Kodak"之于胶卷等，这种商标受美国商标法的最高保护。

美国商标法禁止使用产品的通用名称作为同类产品的商标，其主要用意之一是为了防止垄断。如果一家电脑公司可以把"电脑"注册成自己产品的商标，那么其他电脑公司就不能再用"电脑"来指称自己的产品。一旦如此，拥有"电脑"商标的这家电脑公司便会轻而易举地垄断电脑市场。但是，美国商标法并不禁止使用一种产品的通用名称作为另一类产品的商标。比如说，"苹果"是一种水果的通用名称,任何一家生产或销售苹果的商家不能注册"苹果"作为自己苹果产品的商标。但是,一家电脑公司却可以注册"苹果"作为自己电脑产品的商标,比如著名的"苹果"电脑公司,这样做并不会导致垄断。

在本案中,如果法庭认定 Windows 已经成为个人电脑图形界面操作系统的通用名称,微软公司将失去这个已经家喻户晓的商标,其损失将无法估计。而林多斯公司若不能成功证明 Windows 已经被通用化(genericism),就将面临输掉这场官司并支付巨额赔偿的命运。而 Windows 是否已经被通用化的问题在本案中并不明朗。法庭可能会作出有利于任何一方的判决。显然,在这种关键问题悬而未决的情况下,微软公司和林多斯公司均不愿承担败诉的风险,退一步海阔天空,双方终以和解了结了这起官司。从商标侵权诉讼的策略上讲,这可能是双方能够作出的最佳选择了。

引用判决

Microsoft Corp. v. Lindows. com, Inc.

ORDER

On March 15, 2002, the Court issued an Order denying Plaintiff's motion for a preliminary injunction on the grounds that Microsoft had only raised "serious questions" about the merits of its case and the balance of hardships did not tip sharply in its favor (Dkt. No. 64). The Court's preliminary ruling analyzed the validity of Microsoft's "Windows" trademark and concluded that the "roughly equal bodies of evidentiary support" prevented it from granting the preliminary injunction. In the Motion for Reconsideration presently before the Court (Dkt. No. 67), Microsoft contends that the Court applied the wrong test for genericness and further argues that it misapplied the evidence submitted by Lindows. com.

Under the Local Rules of the Western District of Washington, "motions for reconsideration are disfavored" and will ordinarily be denied unless the moving party shows "manifest error in the prior ruling or ... new facts or legal authority which could not have been brought to [the Court's] attention earlier with reasonable diligence." Local Rule CR 7 (h)(1). Microsoft's motion is brought under the rule's "manifest error" standard, as it claims that a "fundamental misapprehension of the test for 'genericness' led the Court" to an incorrect conclusion. Pla.'s Mot., at 1.

I. TEST FOR GENERICNESS

The Court cited to and applied the Ninth Circuit's test for genericness: "A generic term is one that refers to the genus of which the particular product is a species." Order, at 14 [quoting Comm. for Idaho's High Desert, Inc. v. Yost, 92 F.3d 814, 821 (9th Cir. 1996)]. The Order also relied upon several cases from the Seventh Circuit which applied an indistinguishable standard: "in order to be generic ... the word in question must serve to denominate a type, a kind, a genus or a subcategory of goods." Order, at 25 [quoting Henri's Food Prods. Co. v. Tasty Snacks, Inc., 817 F.2d 1303, 1305–06 (7th Cir. 1987)].

Microsoft argues that Lindows.com presented no evidence showing that the consuming public understood "windows" to refer to the class of goods commonly described as operating systems. It also contends that the Court's use of Seventh Circuit case law "conflicts directly with the Ninth Circuit test which requires that the alleged generic term ... be considered as a whole and that genericness turns on consumers' perception of the whole term." Pla.'s Mot., at 2–3. The plaintiff's argument, however, misconstrues the Court's synthesis of the case law from the two circuits.

As demonstrated by the quoted sections above, the Ninth and Seventh Circuits apply a test for genericness that is for all intents and purposes identical. The Seventh Circuit has gone further to explain why an "adjective can be a generic term when that word is part of a common descriptive name of a kind of goods." Henri's Food Prods., 817 F.2d at 1305. Thus, the Seventh Circuit held that "light," and its phonetic equivalent "lite," were generic words when used in reference to beer because "light beer" was a generic name for a type of beer. See Miller Brewing

Co. v. G. Heileman Brewing Co. , 561 F. 2d 75, 80 – 81 （7th Cir. 1977）. The
Seventh Circuit used this analysis again in Henri's Food Prods. when it concluded
that "tasty" was not a generic term because " 'tasty salad dressing' is not a kind,
sort, genus or subcategory of salad dressing. " 817 F. 2d at 1306. By example, the
court contrasted "French dressing," showing that "French," unlike "tasty," did
"serve [ ] to classify the noun to which it is attached. " Id. ; see also Mil–Mar Shoe
Co. v. Shonac Corp. , 75 F. 3d 1153, 1160 （7th Cir. 1996）（finding "warehouse
shoes" to be generic）.

　　Microsoft also contends that the Court should reject the Miller Brewing line of
cases from the Seventh Circuit because they conflict directly with the Ninth Circuit's
approach of determining genericness of composite terms by examining the term as a
whole rather than its constituent parts individually. See Filipino Yellow Pages, 198
F. 3d 1143, 1148–1150 （9th Cir. 1999）（rejecting arguments that a combination of
generic words yields a generic term and discussing cases where the court analyzed the
terms "Committee for Idaho's High Desert," "California Cooler," "Self–Realization
Fellowship Church" and "Filipino Yellow Pages" as a whole to determine whether
they were generic）. The Seventh Circuit adheres to the same approach, as it une-
quivocally stated in Mil–Mar Shoe, 75 F. 3d at 1161 （ "We have recognized in the
past that the genericness of a composite term must be evaluated by looking at the
term as a whole. " ）. All of the Seventh Circuit cases cited by the Court first analyzed the composite terms —— "tasty salad dressing," "French dressing," "warehouse shoes" and "light beer" —— as a whole before concluding that the adjectives
classifying the nouns to which they were attached were also generic terms. In sum, no
direct conflict exists between the two circuits' tests for genericness of composite
terms. Further, the Ninth Circuit has never commented on, let alone rejected, the
Seventh Circuit's genericness evaluation of adjectives that classify nouns, and the
Court believes that it would accept Miller Brewing's reasoning if it were ever
presented with the question.

　　The Court's conclusion regarding the distinctiveness of the " Windows " trademark follows directly from the synthesis of this case law. Pointing to "light beer" and "matchbox toys" as examples consistent with Ninth Circuit law where consumers viewed composite terms as genus names, see Pla. 's Mot. , at 2 n. 2, Microsoft maintains that "Windows" cannot be generic because it is not the name for a class of products. Microsoft's reasoning is flawed because it ignores the Seventh Circuit's case law holding that when a composite term is generic and is made up of an adjective (or other descriptive word) that classifies a noun, the adjective itself can also be a generic term. Microsoft's argument also ignores its own analysis of the Defendant's evidence, which shows repeated references to the composite terms "window manager," "windowing environment," "windows programs" and several others. Microsoft's outline of the evidence in the Declaration of Timothy L. Boller even characterizes each of these composite terms as the genus for a type of product. See Boller Decl. P 16, Exs. 1 – 14 (highlighting trademark references to "Windows" in blue, descriptive references in yellow and genus references in pink/purple).

Through its own use of the evidence, Microsoft essentially admits that these terms refer to the genus of computer software products that have windowing capability. Just as with "light beer" and "matchbox toys," see 2 J. Thomas McCarthy, McCarthy on Trademarks and Unfair Competition § 12: 10 (4th ed. 2001) (citing cases) , it logically follows that the use of "windows," "window" and "windowing" is also generic when used to refer to the same class of products.

II. EVIDENCE OF GENERICNESS

Having clarified the legal analysis relied upon by the Court in its ruling on the motion for a preliminary injunction, it is worth revisiting briefly some of the evidence with a sharper focus.

Several news articles that pre – date the introduction of Microsoft Windows as well as the first attempt to register the trademark include references to "window managers" and specifically point to Microsoft Windows as a product within this genus. In an article describing Microsoft's entry into the "window wars," the author frequently used the term "window managers" to describe Microsoft's first "Windows" product. See John Markoff, Microsoft Does Windows, InfoWorld, Nov. 21, 1983, at 32 ("Microsoft announced Windows, a window manager and graphical-device interface .... ") (Boller Decl. Ex. 2) ; see also A Fierce Battle Brews Over the Simplest Software Yet, Business Week, Nov. 21, 1983, at 114 ("windowing programs are expected to be standard on every personal computer") ; Andrew Pollack, Integrating the Software, N. Y. Times, Dec. 1, 1983, at D2 ("Window packages have been dubbed environments. ") ; Microsoft Philosophy Presages Entry in Window Wars, InfoWorld, Nov. 14, 1983, at 56 ("Given the ammunition, can a Microsoft window manager be far away?").

Advertisements, a key indication of how any industry communicates with its customers, also commonly referred to products by identifying them as a "window manager," "windowing environment" or describing them as compatible with other window managers, such as Microsoft Windows. See, e. g. , Boller Decl. Ex. 8, at MS 000770 ("DESQview. The Multitasking, Windowing Environment") ; MS 000769 ("Unlike many other screen managers, C – scape is a true windowing environment. ") ; MS 000756 ("Runs under most window managers, e. g .... Dec Windows") ; MS 000776 ("Only HDS' X terminals come with a built-in Open Look window manager. ").

Similarly, many dictionaries used these terms to describe a class of computer software products. For example, Alan Freedman's The Computer Glossary defines "Windows," "windows environment" and "windows program" as follows: "*Windows* is a windows program from Microsoft Corporation .... A *windows environment* is a computer that is running under an operating system that provides multiple windows on screen. [e. g.] Microsoft Windows .... A *windows program* is software that adds a windows capability to an existing operating system. " Alan Freedman, The Computer Glossary 751–52 (4th ed. 1989) (Boller Decl. Ex. 4, at MS 000607–08). In another dictionary, "windows environment" is defined as " [a] computing environment characterized by an operating system that allows multiple windows on the display screen. Examples of such environments include DESQview, Microsoft Windows, Presentation Manager, and X Window for the IBM, and Finder or MultiFinder for the Macintosh. " Allen L. Wyatt, Computer Professional's Dictionary 344 (1990) (Boller Decl. Ex. 4, at MS 000629).

Even Microsoft's own computer dictionary includes expansive definitions of "windowing environment" and "windowing software":

windowing environment, An operating system or shell that presents the user with specially delineated areas of the screen called windows. Each window can act independently, as if it were a virtual display device. Windowing environments typically allow windows to be resized and moved around on the display. The Apple Macintosh Finder, Microsoft Windows, and the OS/2 Presentation Manager are all examples of windowing environments.

windowing software Programs, such as Microsoft Windows, that enable users to work with multiple on-screen windows. Windowing software acts as an intermediary between an operating system, such as MS-DOS, and application programs designed to work within a windowing environment. See also graphical user interface.

In addition to consistently coupling the company's name with its various Windows versions, Microsoft also showed that it understood "windows" to denote a class of products by referring to its first Windows product as a "window manager". In a 1983 article discussing the company's introduction of Windows 1.0, the group manager for Microsoft Windows was quoted as saying, "the window manager is actually a small part of this announcement." Microsoft Does Windows, supra. Steve Ballmer, who was then the vice president for marketing, also described Windows using the same terms: "He [Steve Bulmer (sic)] said that after an extended internal debate about the philosophy of designing window managers, Microsoft had settled on ? ." Id.

Finally, there is some evidence that Microsoft's competitors also used the term "window manager" to refer to their system software or graphical user interface. See, e.g., Apple Computer, Inc. v. Microsoft Corp., 799 F. Supp. 1006, 1024

(N. D. Cal. 1992) (listing the "X Consortium Tab Window Manager" in the scenes a faire table); Microsoft Computer Dictionary 482 (4th ed. 1999) ("Macintosh Window Manager"); Kurt W. G. Mathies & Thom Hogan, Managing Multiple Windows, MacUser, June 1990, at 273 ("Macintosh Window Manager").

III. CONCLUSION

Applying the proper Ninth Circuit test for genericness and the Seventh Circuit's gloss regarding adjectives and other descriptive words that classify the noun to which they are attached in composite terms, the evidence shows that the consuming public used the terms "windows," "window" and "windowing" to refer to a type of graphical user interface or other software program, including operating systems, in which overlapping windows are the predominant visual feature. As a result, the Court did not err in either its legal or factual analysis when it denied Microsoft's motion for a preliminary injunction. The Motion for Reconsideration is DENIED.

SO ORDERED this 13 day of May, 2002.

JOHN C. COUGHENOUR, CHIEF UNITED STATES DISTRICT JUDGE

恶意抢注近似的网域名称

可口可乐、麦当劳、百事可乐、华盛顿邮报状告波迪案

drinkcoke.org　　mycoca-cola.com

mymcdonalds.com

mypepsi.org　　my-washingtonpost.com

判例简介

20 世纪 90 年代以来，网络的勃兴在商标领域引发了不少新问题。到底谁有资格拥有某个网域名称呢？是一个花了苦心经营商誉的公司，还是有眼光看准这个名称的非凡价值而抢占的人呢？甚至于只是一个喜欢这个名称的普通使用者呢？传统的商标侵权标准已经不能完全应对网络上的商标侵权现象。例如，在网络兴起之初，许多拥有著名商标的公司没有注册相应的网域名称，建立自己的网站。一些熟悉网络的公司或个人便捷足先登，抢先注册了与著名商标名称相同或相近的网域名称。

当消费者按照某个著名商标的名称在网上查询有关讯息时，便会发现进入的网站与自己要查找的产品毫无关系。这种"恶意抢注网域名称"的情况，令一些大公司头疼不已。在无法可依的情况下，一些公司为了避免麻烦，便出高价收购这些被人"抢注"的网站。如此一来，抢注与某些著名商标名称相同或相近的网域名称就成为某些人一本万利的"生意"。

一些人注册数百甚至上千个与大公司商标名称相同或相近的网域名称，只等着这些公司花重金前来收购。在此同时，抢注网域名称也成了一些人发

泄对某些大公司不满的手段。例如，如果一个人要损害某公司的商业形象，就可以注册了一个与这家公司名称相同或相近的网域名称，并在这个网域名称下建立一个有不良内容的网站或链接。消费者在上网查找这家公司的讯息时，便可能看到这些令人生厌的内容，从而对这家公司的商业形象造成损害。

当然，大部分人抢注网域名称是为了日后出售牟利，也有一部分人是为了损害竞争对手的商业形象，还有一些人是出于政治目的。无论目的与动机如何，20世纪90年代，抢注网域名称已经成为令许多公司深恶痛绝的网络"圈地运动"。

针对这种情况，美国国会在1999年通过了《反抢注消费者保护法》[1]，禁止恶意注册与某个商标名称相同或相近的网域名称牟利，或淡化某个著名商标。这一法案实施后，联邦法院依此判决了几个恶意抢注网域名称的案件。其中影响比较大的案件就有可口可乐、麦当劳、百事可乐和华盛顿邮报联合状告波迪案。

自2002年7月起，波迪开始注册了一系列令人似曾相识的网域名称，其中包括 drinkcoke. org、mycoca-cola. com、mymcdonalds. com、mypepsi. org、my-washingtonpost. com 等。明眼人一看便知，这些网域名称与可口可乐、麦当劳、百事可乐和华盛顿邮报的公司名称或商标名称极其相似。

不过，与许多人抢注网域名称进行牟利的目的不同，波迪这样做主要是出于政治目的，商业牟利尚在其次。原来，波迪是位激进的反堕胎人士，视堕胎为杀人，并在网络上大张旗鼓地展开反堕胎宣传。波迪注册了以上网域名称后，便把这些网域名称链接到一个反堕胎的网站 abortionismurder. com（"堕胎就是杀人网"）。

这个网站不但包含大量的反堕胎言论，而且张贴有一些血淋淋的堕胎图片。这个网站也包含一些向反堕胎组织捐款的讯息以及销售反堕胎宣传品的广告。另外，波迪还把这些网域名称链接到他自己的反堕胎网站，并声称可口可乐、麦当劳、百事可乐和华盛顿邮报等均支持反堕胎。

首先作出反应的是华盛顿邮报。2002年7月8日，华盛顿邮报的律师向

---

[1]　Anticybersquatting Consumer Protection Act（ACPA）。

波迪发函，要求他立即停止抢注并关闭与华盛顿邮报名称相似的网域名称。随之，可口可乐、百事可乐和麦当劳先后向波迪发出了类似的律师函。这些公司采取双管齐下的策略，与波迪的网络提供商取得联系。在几大公司的要求下，波迪的网络提供商停止向波迪提供与前述网域名称相关的服务。但是，波迪并未因此而停止侵权行为，他换了几家网络提供商，继续使用这些网域名称进行反堕胎宣传。

几家大公司警告无效，便诉诸法律，向联邦法院控告波迪违反了《反抢注消费者保护法》，要求法院责令波迪立即关闭这些网站并停止使用这些网域名称。根据《反抢注消费者保护法》的规定，以牟利为目的恶意抢注与某个商标名称相似的网域名称要负民事责任。从技术上而言，原告若想打赢官司，必须在法律上证明两点：第一，被告抢注的网域名称与原告的商标或公司名称相似，容易令消费者混淆；第二，被告抢注该网域名称是以牟利为目的。

波迪对这两条一概否认。首先，他辩称，自己注册的网域名称中虽然包含着"可口可乐""百事可乐""麦当劳""华盛顿邮报"等字样，但自己注册的网域名称与以上公司的网域名称并不相同。消费者在寻找这些公司的网站时不太容易会跑到波迪注册的网站去。尤其是在使用搜索引擎搜寻这些公司的讯息时，消费者会在搜寻结果中找到这些公司的网站，而不至于误把波迪注册的网站当作这些公司的网站。

不过，法院没有接受波迪的这种辩解。法院指出，根据《反抢注消费者保护法》，被告不得抢注与原告商标名称或公司名称相似的网域名称，以混淆消费者的视听。所以，波迪注册的网域名称即使与可口可乐、百事可乐、麦当劳以及华盛顿邮报等公司的网域名称不同，也与本案的问题无关。与本案问题有关的是，波迪注册的那些网域名称是否与可口可乐、百事可乐、麦当劳以及华盛顿邮报的商标名称或公司名称相似，以至于会造成消费者的混淆误认。

事实上，本案中有争议的几个网域名称中均包含"可口可乐""百事可乐""麦当劳"以及"华盛顿邮报"等字样。可口可乐等公司进一步向法院提供证据，证明已经有消费者误入波迪注册的包含可口可乐名称的网站。在此基础上，法院认定，波迪注册的几个有争议的网域名称与可口可乐、百事可乐、麦当劳和华盛顿邮报等公司或商标的名称极其相似，容易混淆消费者的视听。

其次，波迪也否认自己注册这些网域名称是出于牟利，并称自己的做法受到美国宪法第一修正案的保护。在法律上证明"恶意"并不是件容易的事。为了帮助法院确定被告的行为是否出于"恶意"，《反抢注消费者保护法》列出了许多法院要综合考虑的因素。归纳起来，法院必须先检视，被告注册这些网域名称有没有正当理由，例如自己拥有同名的商标或把自己的姓名作为网域名称等。如果法院发现被告具有正当的理由注册和使用有争议的网域名称，就不能认定被告有"恶意"。

在本案中，波迪从未拥有过可口可乐、百事可乐、麦当劳以及华盛顿邮报等商标，自己的名字也与这些商标无关。而且，波迪也找不出其他正当理由来注册和使用这些带有"可口可乐""百事可乐""麦当劳"和"华盛顿邮报"字样的网域名称。不过，没有正当理由并不必然就表示有"恶意"。

要证明"恶意"，还必须考虑其他因素，例如被告有意利用有争议的网域名称误导消费者以牟利，或损害商标拥有者的商业形象或声誉等。在这个关键问题上，波迪否认自己注册这些有争议的网域名称是出于任何商业目的。他辩称，自己注册这些网域名称完全是出于反堕胎的目的，与商业利益没有任何关系，所以应当受美国宪法第一修正案言论自由条款的保护。

但是，法院再度拒绝了波迪的辩解。法院认定，波迪注册这些有争议的网域名称的主要目的是把可口可乐、百事可乐、麦当劳和华盛顿邮报的消费者引到他支持的反堕胎网站去。这里涉及大量的反堕胎的政治言论。不过，法院同时认定，波迪注册的这些有争议的网域名称不完全是非商业性质的。这些网域名称链接的反堕胎网站包含有吸引网络使用者捐款的信息，也包含有出售反堕胎纪念品的信息。虽然波迪没有直接从这些商业活动中牟利，他的行为却因此具有了商业色彩。

此外，波迪把自己注册的包含可口可乐名称的网域名称链接到一个包含令人心理产生不良反应的照片的反堕胎网站，这实际上损害了可口可乐公司的商业形象和声誉。所以，法院进一步认定，波迪抢注包含可口可乐、百事可乐、麦当劳和华盛顿邮报等公司和商标名称的网域名称是出于以牟利为目的的"恶意"。因为其行为涉及商业利益，所以不受美国宪法第一修正案言论自由条款的保护。

基于以上理由，法院依据《反抢注消费者保护法》认定波迪的行为侵害了可口可乐、百事可乐、麦当劳以及华盛顿邮报等公司的商标权，责令波迪立即停止使用有关网域名称，并不得再注册类似的网域名称。

本案启示与解析

近年来，域名与商标的权利冲突越来越严重。这种冲突有多种表现形式并且产生的原因也是多样的。解决这一问题应首先加强国际方面的合作，建立一个国际性的制度框架，然后根据我国网络的发展状况制定相应的国内法。同时，应加强域名制度与现有知识产权制度的衔接，结合网络发展的技术特点构建域名与商标等知识产权的协调机制才是解决域名与知识产权冲突的必由之路。

1999 年，美国国会通过《反抢注消费者保护法》以后，在网络上以营利为目的抢注大公司域名的行为大为收敛。但是，出于非商业目的抢注网络域名的事件却层出不穷，例如可口可乐、麦当劳、百事可乐、华盛顿邮报状告波迪一案。

《反抢注消费者保护法》的立法目的有二。一是为了保护消费者，使消费者不被虚假域名所误导。二是为了保护名牌企业和著名商标所有者的权益。在认定侵权方面，《反抢注消费者保护法》吸纳了商标法中消费者混淆误认的原则。按照这一原则，被告抢注的网络域名与原告的商标或公司名称必须相同或相似，会导致消费者混淆误认。几乎所有抢注网络域名的案件必然符合这一条件，否则，就失去了抢注网络域名的意义。

但是，就如同其他法律一般，《反抢注消费者保护法》也设有例外。如果被告能提出注册与大公司名称相同或相近的网络域名有正当理由，比如说优先使用了与注册网络域名相同的名称，或用自己的姓名作为网络域名等，那么被告就没有违反《反抢注消费者保护法》。

因此，仅仅证明被告注册的域名与原告的商标相同或相近，只是依据《反抢注消费者保护法》诉讼的第一步。最关键的是第二步，即证明被告抢注网络域名是出于以牟利为目的的恶意（bad faith）。在法律上证明"恶意"往往比证明事实更难。不过，《反抢注消费者保护法》和法庭的判例为证明"恶意"提出了一些具体指标。

其中，最重要的一个指标是，被告抢注网络域名是否出于营利的目的。如果被告抢注大公司的网络域名是为了等待被抢注的大公司前来收购，或者是为了与大公司争夺生意，法院基本上可以认定这种抢注是出于恶意。但是，对于那些不涉及营利的网络域名抢注行为，法院经常无法认定被告是否具有恶意，因而无法适用《反抢注消费者保护法》定案。之所以如此，主要原因在于国会不想因《反抢注消费者保护法》而妨碍受美国宪法第一修正案保护的言论自由。

在本案中，波迪败诉的原因有二。一是把抢注的网络域名链接到具有营利色彩的反堕胎网站上。这些网站包含有吸引网友捐款的信息，也包含有出售反堕胎纪念品的信息。尽管这些网站不属于营利性质，但至少它们具有营利的色彩。这使得政治言论与商业言论混杂在一起，令政治言论染上了商业色彩。几家原告大公司正是抓住这一点，破解了波迪基于宪法第一修正案的辩护，成功地说服法院认定波迪抢注网络域名是出于恶意。二是把有争议的域名链接到具有令人心理产生不良反应内容的网站。这样做便涉嫌损害原告的商业声誉。在这种情况下，法院认定波迪抢注域名是出于恶意并不令人意外。

虽然本案的原告可口可乐、麦当劳、百事可乐、华盛顿邮报等公司来自不同的行业，但却有一个共同点：都是全世界著名的大公司。这一案件的判决再次向公众发出一个明确的信息：越是著名的商标享有的保护力度就越大。

引用判决

The Coca-Cola Company, McDonald's Corporation,
Pepsico, Inc. , The Washington Post Company and
Washingtonpost. Newsweek Interactive Company, LLC,
Plaintiffs v. William S. Purdy, Defendants

MEMORANDUM OPINION, ORDER, AND PERMANENT INJUNCTION

I. INTRODUCTION

On January 20, 2005, oral argument before the undersigned United States District Judge was heard on The Coca-Cola Company, ▼McDonald's Corporation, Pepsico, Inc. ▼, The Washington Post ▼Company, and Washingtonpost Newsweek Interactive Company, ▼LLC's (collectively "Plaintiffs") Motion for Summary Judgment [Docket No. 86]. Plaintiffs' Complaint [Docket No. 1] alleged claims against William S. Purdy, Sr. ("Purdy"), Please Don't Kill Your Baby, and Does 1-10 (collectively "Defendants") for: violating the Anticybersquatting Consumer Protection Act (Count I); Trademark Infringement (Count II); Counterfeiting (Count HI); False Representation (Count IV); Federal Trademark Dilution (Count V); Deceptive Trade Practices (Count VI) and Common Law Trademark Infringement (Count VII). At [* 2] oral argument, Plaintiffs consented to dismiss Count ITJ (Counterfeiting) and Count V (Federal Trademark Dilution) without prejudice.

Plaintiffs' motion urges the Court to enter judgment in its favor on the remaining five counts and to issue a permanent injunction preventing Defendants from registering, using, owning, holding in any way, or trafficking in any domain name that (i) incorporates, and is identical or confusingly similar to, Plaintiffs' famous and protected marks Coca-Cola ▼ (R), Coke (R), McDonald's (R), McDonalds. com

(R), MyMcDonalds. com (R), Pepsi-Cola (R), Pepsi (R), The Washington Post ▾ (R), and WashingtonPost. com (R), or any other mark owned by Plaintiffs, and (ii) does not alert the unwary Internet user to the protest or critical commentary nature of the attached website within the language of the domain name itself. Defendants did not file any written response to Plaintiffs' Motion for Summary Judgment, however, William S. Purdy, Sr. did appear and argue at oral argument. For the reasons set forth below, Plaintiffs motion is granted.

II. BACKGROUND

Defendants have registered over 60 Internet domain names that incorporate the trademarks Coca-Cola ▾ (R), Coke (R), McDonald's (R), McDonalds. com (R), MyMcDonalds. com (R), Pepsi-Cola (R), Pepsf, The Washington Post ▾ (R), and WashingtonPost. com (R), and MyWashingtonPost. com (R). The web sites for these domain names display content that does not originate from, is not sponsored by, and is not affiliated with the Plaintiffs, including color pictures that purport to be dismembered aborted fetuses and links to fund-raising appeals.

On July 23, 2002, this Court issued an Order for Emergency Temporary Restraining Order and Preliminary Injunction [Docket No. 12]. On September 5, 2002, after Plaintiffs demonstrated Defendants were engaged in additional activities that violated the July 23, 2002 Order, the Court issued an Amended Order for Emergency Temporary Restraining Order and Preliminary Injunction [Docket No. 19]. After the Court found that Purdy had violated the original injunction by registering more than 60 prohibited domain names, the Court issued an Order on January 28, 2003 finding him in contempt [Docket No. 56]. A supplemental contempt order was also issued on March 10, 2003 [Docket No. 75] after the Court found Defendant had engaged in further violations of the Order. Purdy appealed this Court's preliminary injunction [Docket No. 13], January 28, 2003 contempt order [Docket No. 72] and March 10, 2003 supplemental contempt order [Docket No. 80] to the Eighth Circuit Court of Appeals. After consolidating Purdy's appeals, the Eighth Circuit issued an

Opinion and Judgment affirming this Court's orders granting preliminary injunctive relief and dismissing the appeals of the contempt order and sanctions for lack of jurisdiction [Docket Nos. 84, 85] . *See Coca-Cola Company v. Purdy*, 382 F. 3d 774
(8th Cir. 2004). The matter was remanded to this Court for further proceedings. The
Court now considers whether the preliminary injunction should be made permanent.

III. DISCUSSION

A. Summary Judgment Standard

Federal Rule of Civil Procedure 56 (c) provides that summary judgment shall
issue "if the pleadings, depositions, answers to interrogatories, and admissions on
file, together with the affidavits, if any, show that there is no genuine issue as to any
material fact and that the moving party is entitled to judgment as a matter of law."
Fed. R. Civ. P. 56 (c) ; *see Matsushita Elec. Indus. Co. , Ltd. v. Zenith Radio Corp. ,*
475 U. S. 574, 587, 89 L. Ed. 2d 538, 106 S. Ct. 1348 (1986); *Anderson v. Liberty
Lobby, Inc. ,* 477 U. S. 242, 252, 91 L. Ed. 2d 202, 106 S. Ct. 2505 (1986); *Celotex
Corp. v. Catrett ,* 477 U. S. 317, 323, 91 L. Ed. 2d 265, 106 S. Ct. 2548 (1986). On a motion for summary judgment, the Court views the evidence in the light most favorable to
the nonmoving party. *Ludwig v. Anderson*, 54 F. 3d 465, 470 (8th Cir. L995). The nonmoving party may not "rest on mere allegations or denials, but must demonstrate on
the record the existence of specific facts which create a genuine issue for trial."
Krenik v. County of Le Sueur, 47 F. 3d 953, 957 (8th Cir. 1995).

B. Count I: Anticybersquatting Consumer Protection Act

The July 23, 2002 and September 5, 2002 Orders set forth the Court's
reasoning in granting Plaintiffs' request for a preliminary injunction under the Anticybersquatting Consumer Protection Act ("ACPA") , 15 U. S. C. § 1125 (d). In its
September 1, 2004 Opinion, the Eighth Circuit endorsed this Court's reasoning and
affirmed the orders granting preliminary injunctive relief. For the purposes of the instant matter, the material legal and factual issues remain unchanged. For the reasons

set forth in this Court's Orders granting preliminary injunctive relief and the Court of Appeals' Opinion, Plaintiffs' Motion for Summary Judgment is granted on Count 1.

C. Count II: Trademark Infringement

This Court granted the preliminary injunction and the Court of Appeals affirmed on the grounds that the injunction was warranted under the ACPA. Neither court considered whether such relief could also be granted under a trademark infringement claim. As a result, it is necessary to consider Plaintiffs' allegation of trademark infringement in greater depth.

Plaintiffs argue that Defendants' registration and use of domain names that are identical or confusingly similar to Plaintiffs' marks constitutes trademark infringement. To prevail on a trademark infringement claim, pursuant to 15 U. S. C. § 1114, a plaintiff must show: (1) ownership of a valid trademark; and (2) a likelihood of confusion between the registered mark and the alleged infringing use by the defendant. *See*, *e. g.*, *First Bank v. First Bank Sys.*, *Inc.*, 84 F. 3d 1040, 1044 (8th Cir, 1996).

Possessing a registered trademark is prima facie evidence that the trademark is valid. *Id.*; *see also Aromatique*, *Inc. v. Golden Seal*, *Inc.*, 28 F. 3d 863, 869 (8th 1994) ("registration of a mark creates a rebuttable presumption that the mark is valid"). Since it is undisputed that the trademarks at issue are all federally registered and Defendants have offered no evidence to rebut the resulting presumption, the Court finds that the trademarks are valid.

To determine "whether under all the circumstances there is a likelihood of confusion" between marks, courts evaluate the following six factors:

(1) the strength of the earlier mark; (2) the similarity between the mark at issue and the alleged infringer's mark; (3) the degree to which the products compete with each other; (4) the alleged infringer's intent to pass off its own goods as those of the trademark owner . . . ; (5) incidents of actual confusion; and (6) whether the degree of purchaser care can eliminate any likelihood of confusion which would otherwise exist.

Minnesota Mining & Manufacturing Co. v. Rauh Rubber, *Inc.* 130 F. 3d 1305, 1308 (8th Cir. 1997) (citations omitted); *see also SquirtCo v. Seven－Up Co.* , 628 F. 2d 1086, 1091 (8th Cir. 1980).

As to the initial factor, it is clear that Coca－Cola ▼ (R), Coke (R), McDonald's (R), McDonalds. com (R), MyMcDonalds. com (R), Pepsi－Cola (R), Pepsi (R), The Washington Post ▼ (R), WashingtonPost. com (R), and MyWashingtonPost. com (R) are "indisputably famous and distinctive marks. " *Coca－Cola Company et al.* , 382 F. 3d at 786. With respect to the second factor, Defendants registered domains that are identical or confusingly similar to Plaintiffs' trademarks. Although the parties do not compete for goods or services, the third factor is met because Defendants intended to redirect Plaintiffs' audience and customers to view content of their choosing. *See Planned Parenthood Fed'n of Am.* , *Inc. v. Bucci*, 1997 U. S. Dist. LEXIS 3338, ＊ 21 (S. D. N. Y. Mar. 24, 1997), *aff'd*, 152 F. 3d 920 (2d Cir. 1998) ("defendant's use is classically competitive: he has taken plaintiffs mark as his own in order to purvey his Internet services － his web site － to an audience intending to access plaintiffs services").

The fourth factor is also satisfied as Defendants have registered the domain names with a bad faith intent to profit from them by tarnishing and diluting Plaintiffs' marks and by relying on Plaintiffs' good names and goodwill to achieve the personal gain of promoting their messages, generating publicity and raising money for supported causes. This bad intent is further manifested in that none of the domain names contains or consists of a name by which Defendants are known, and Defendants had not previously used any of the names at issue in connection with the *bona fide* offering of goods or services. In addition, Defendants have continued and expanded their practice of registering identical or confiisingly similar domain names even in the face of a preliminary injunction against that practice.

The fifth factor considers incidents of actual confusion. Although "actual confusion is not essential to a finding of infringement," at least two incidents evidence the existence of such confusion. *WSM* , *Inc. v. Hilton* , 724 F. 2d 1320, 1329 (8th

Cir. 1984). One disgusted Coca−Cola ▼ (R) customer contacted the company and said he could not finish consuming the Coke (R) product he was drinking after viewing the content on one of Defendants' web sites. *See* First Alexandri Decl. [Docket Nos. 4 − 5] Ex. 22. Defendants use of the domain name *wpni. org* also proved confusing after e−mail intended for WashingtonpostNewsweek interactive Company ("WNIC") employees was mistakenly addressed to Defendants' site. *See* Fourth Alexandri Decl. [Docket No. 30] Exs. 182–83; Doherty Decl. [Docket No. 25] PP 3–4; Hong Decl. [Docket No. 26] PP 3–4.

The final factor considers whether the degree of purchaser care can eliminate any likelihood of confusion which would otherwise exist between the products. Several courts have noted that the quick and effortless nature of "surfing" the Internet makes it unlikely that consumers can avoid confusion through the exercise of due care:

In the internet context, in particular, entering a website takes little effort − usually one click from a linked site or a search engine's list; thus, web surfers are more likely to be confused as to the ownership of a web site than traditional patrons of a brick−and−mortar store would be of a store's ownership.

Northern Light Tech. Inc. v. Northern Lights Club, 97 F. Supp. 2d 96, 115 (D. Mass. 2000) aff'd 236 F. 3d 57 (1st Cir. 2001) [quoting *Brookfield Communications, Inc. v. West Coast Entm't Corp.* , 174 F. 3d 1036, 1057 (9th Cir. 1999)]. As a result, "ordinary Internet users do not undergo a highly sophisticated analysis when searching for domain names." *Green Prods. Co. v. Independence Corn By − Products. Co.* , 992 F. Supp. 1070, 1079 (N. D. Iowa 1997).

For the aforementioned reasons, there is sufficient evidence to support a finding that a likelihood of confusion exists between the registered mark and the alleged infringing use by the Defendants. As a result, the Court grants Plaintiffs' Motion for Summary Judgment on Count II.

D. Counts IV, VI and VII: False Representation, Deceptive Trade Practices and Common Law Trademark Infringement

Finally, Plaintiffs assert Defendants' actions amount to false representation, deceptive trade practices and common law trademark infringement. *See* 15 U.S.C. § 1125 (a) and Minn. Stat. § 325D. 44. As noted above, this Court's prior Orders and the Court of Appeals' opinion were analyzed on the strength of Plaintiffs' ACPA claim. Plaintiffs also devoted significant time to supporting their trademark infringement claim in their summary judgment memorandum and at oral argument. However, Plaintiffs provide only a cursory discussion of Counts IV, VI, and VII in their memorandum and did not mention these claims at oral argument. Although Plaintiffs briefly argue that claims such as false representation, deceptive trade practices and common law trademark infringement are governed by the same analysis as federally-registered marks under 15 U.S.C. § 1114, this Court finds Plaintiffs have not sufficiently developed these claims. In addition, Plaintiffs' relief is not dependent on successfully prosecuting these claims. As a result, Counts IV, VI, and VII are dismissed without prejudice.

IV. CONCLUSION

Based on the foregoing, and all the files, records and proceedings herein, IT IS HEREBY ORDERED that:

1. Plaintiffs' Motion for Summary Judgment [Docket No. 86] is GRANTED IN PART AND DENIED IN PART;

2. Plaintiffs' Complaint [Docket No. 1] is GRANTED as to Counts I and II while Counts IV, VI and VII are DISMISSED WITHOUT PREJUDICE;

3. Defendants and their officers, agents, servants, employees, attorneys, and all persons in active concert or participation with them are permanently prohibited and enjoined from registering, using, owning, holding in any way, or trafficking in any domain name that (i) incorporates, and is identical or confusingly similar to, Plaintiffs' famous and protected marks Coca-Cola ▾ (R), Coke (R), McDonald's (R), McDonalds. com (R), Pepsi-Cola (R), Pepsi (R), The Washington Post ▾ (R), and WashingtonPost. com (R), or any other mark owned by Plaintiffs, and (ii) does not alert the unwary Internet user to the protest or critical commentary

nature of the attached website within the language of the domain name itself;

4. Without limiting the generality of the foregoing, Defendants and their officers, agents, servants, employees, attorneys, and all persons in active concert or participation with them are permanently prohibited and enjoined from registering, using, owning, holding in any way, or trafficking in any of the following domain names: *mycoca − cola. com*, *drinkcoke. org*, *mymcdonalds. com*, *pepsisays. com*, *mypepsi. org*, *washmgtonpostsays. com*, *washingtonpost. cc*, *washingtonpost. ws*, *my − washingtonpost. com*, *wpni. org*, *washingtonpost − editorialpage. com*, *washington-postedits. com*, *washingtonpost − federalcourt. com*, *washingtonpost − eightcircuit. com*, *washingtonpost − supremecourt. com*, *the washingtonpostappealcom washingtonpost − consititution. com*, *washingtonpostcourt. com*, *thewashingtonposrjury. com*, *washing-tonpostjudges. com*, *washingtonpoststates. com*, *washingtonpostcitizen. com*, *washing-tonpostfreedom. com*, *washingtonpostspeech. com*, *washingtonpost − freespeech. com*, *thewashingtonpostchristian. com*, *washingtonpostcandidates. com*, *thewashingtonpostb-aby. com*, *thewashingtonpost−mybook. com*, *washingtonpost−oreilly. com*, *thewashing-tonpostfactor. com*, *thewashingtonpost − nospinzone. com*, *washingtonpost − plannedpar-enthood. com ,thewashingtonpostconfession. com*, *thewashingtonpostpostvirus. com*, *the-washingtonpostwatch. com*, *thewashingtonpostnews. com*, *washingtonpostcyberspace. com*, *washingtonpostinternet. com*, *thewashingtonpostbirth. com*, *thewashingtonposteffect. com*, *thewashingtonpostfame. com*, *thewashingtonpostfetus. com*, *thewashingtonpostframe. com*, *thewashingtonpoststillness. com*, *thewashmgtonpostliberal. com*, *thewashingtonpostlife. com*, *thewashingtonpostmission. com*, *thewashingtonpostreign. com*, *thewashingtonpostreli-gion. com*, *thewashingtonpostrescue. com*, *thewashingtonpostsorrows. com*, *thewashing-tonpostspin. com*, *thewashingtonpostsyndrome. com*, *thewashingtonpostwalk. com*, *thewashingtonpostwomb. com*, *washingtonpostcon-fusion. com*, *washingtonposthealth. com*, *washingtonpostsuffering. com*, *thewashing-tonpostoccassion. com*, *thewashingtonpostunderstanding. com*, *thewashingtonpostshare-holder. com*, *yourwashingtonpost. com*, *nocoke−pepsi. com*, *gopepsi. org*, *pepsi−ludac-ris. com*, *pepsi−orelly. cora pepsiheaven. com*, *pepsiright. com*, *thepepsichallenge. org*,

lovemcdonald. com , ilovethewashingtonpost. com. jesuslovesthewashingtonpost. com , thewashingtonpostjesus. com , thewashingtonpostjesus. st. thewashingtonpostjew. com , thewashingtonpostmuslim. com ,thewashingtonpostkoran. com , thewashingtonpostmotherofjesus. com , thewashingtonpostvirginmary. com , thewashingtonpostchildsacrafice. com , thewashingtonpostblessedvirgin. com , thewashingtonpostourladyoffadmima. com , thewashingtonpostwonderfulitalian. com , thewashingtonpostitalianbandit. com , thewashingtonpoststubbomchild. com , thewashingtonpostourladyofguadalupe. com , thewashingtonpostourladyofmedugorje. com , thewashingtonpostspeechjail. com , thewashingtonpost. nu. washingtonpost−christianperspective. com , thewashingtonpost−johnkerryconnection. com , thewashingtonpost−faegrebensonconnection. com , washingtonpost−eighthcircuitruling. com , washingtonpost−shareholder. com , washingtonpost − tencommandents. com , washingtonpost − voteforpresidentbush. com , and washingtonpost−truefacts. com ;

5. The persons enjoined by this Order include, but are not limited to, all persons listed as technical or administrative contacts for any identified website, including but not limited to Mark A. Purdy H and William S. Purdy II;

6. Defendants shall forthwith advise all domain name registrars they have previously or currently employed of this Order and instruct them to take all actions necessary to stop the functioning of all domain names that violate the standards set forth in paragraph 3, including but not limited to all of the domain names listed in paragraph 4, and shall instruct all such domain name registrars to cooperate in the transfer of such domain names to the appropriate Plaintiff as specified in paragraph 7 below;

7. Defendants shall transfer to the appropriate Plaintiff within three days the ownership of any domain name that violates the standards set forth in paragraph 3, including but not limited to all of the domain names listed in paragraph 4 that Defendants have not already so transferred; and,

8. Defendants shall, within ten days from the date of this Order, file a report with the Court and provide a copy to the Plaintiffs, setting forth the manner in which they have complied with the terms of this Order.

何谓商业表征[1]

沃尔玛与萨玛拉兄弟公司案

判例简介

沃尔玛公司（以下简称沃尔玛）由美国零售业的传奇人物山姆·沃尔顿先生于 1962 年 7 月 2 日在美国阿肯色州成立。截至 2000 年，经过四十余年的发展，沃尔玛已经成为美国最大的私人雇主和世界上最大的连锁零售商。案件发生时沃尔玛在全球十个国家开设了超过 5000 家商场，员工总数 160 多万，分布在美国、墨西哥、波多黎各、加拿大、阿根廷、巴西、中国、韩国、德国和英国等国家。每周光临沃尔玛的顾客近一亿四千万人次，已连续多年成为全球最大的零售企业，其业态分为沃尔玛商店、购物场、山姆会员商店、

---

[1] 此概念对应我国的商业外观概念。我国通过《反不正当竞争法》予以保护，对应该法第 6 条规定的"商品包装装潢等商业标识"，我国最高人民法院司法解释对此进行了扩大解释，将整体商业经营外观纳入保护范围。

社区店四种。

美国商标法不但保护商标名称，而且也保护商标图案和商业表征（Trade Dress）。至于商品设计（product design），则受著作权法和专利法的保护。那么，商品设计是否也受美国商标法的保护呢？答案是肯定的，只不过保护的程度有限而已。2000年美国最高法院对"沃尔玛状告萨玛拉兄弟公司案"的判决，进一步阐明了美国商标法对商品设计的保护力度。

萨玛拉兄弟公司是美国一家儿童服装设计制造商，主打产品是一系列儿童春夏季泡泡纱服装。这批服装从样式到图案均是由萨玛拉兄弟自行设计制作。服装设计突出儿童春夏季服装的特点，简单明快，并装饰以心形、花卉和水果等图案。萨玛拉兄弟为这些图案申请了外观设计专利权，但是并没有按照商标法注册商业表征。这为日后的诉讼埋下了隐患。萨玛拉兄弟公司主要靠遍布美国的连锁超市来销售自己的服装产品。在这些出售萨玛拉兄弟公司产品的超市中，没有全球最大的连锁超市沃尔玛。

沃尔玛的经营方式不同于常规。传统上，生产商制造出产品以后由商店销售，所以制造什么样的产品，主要由生产商来决定。而沃尔玛靠着自己遍布全球的销售系统，可以左右许多企业的生产和销售。沃尔玛经常是先决定自己要卖什么，然后再要求生产商按照其需要进行生产。在儿童服装方面也是如此。1995年，沃尔玛决定增加第二年春夏季儿童服装的花色，便找到一家生产商朱迪–菲律宾公司进行设计生产。

沃尔玛向朱迪–菲律宾公司出示了一些儿童服装设计图案的照片。照片上显示的正是萨玛拉兄弟公司的设计图案。朱迪–菲律宾公司的设计人员照猫画虎，对萨玛拉兄弟公司现有的图案稍加变更之后便为沃尔玛生产儿童服装。沃尔玛和朱迪–菲律宾公司的举动，神不知鬼不觉，完全不为萨玛拉兄弟公司所知。第二年春天，朱迪–菲律宾公司基于萨玛拉兄弟公司的图案所生产的儿童服装摆上了沃尔玛的货架，大受消费者欢迎。沃尔玛当季单在该批儿童服装上就赚了一百多万美金。

沃尔玛以价格低廉著称，在出售朱迪–菲律宾公司设计生产的这批儿童服装时也是以削价方式出售，以低于萨玛拉兄弟公司产品的价格销售。有位消费者在其他超市买了萨玛拉兄弟公司的服装后，看到沃尔玛正以更低的价格出售样式相同的服装，便向萨玛拉兄弟公司抱怨。萨玛拉兄弟公司随即展开调查，发现沃尔玛的确正以极低廉的价格出售与萨玛拉兄弟公司设计图案相同的儿童服装，而这批服装则是由朱迪–菲律宾公司生产。

萨玛拉兄弟公司随即向沃尔玛发出律师函，要求立即停止销售这批涉嫌产品设计侵权的服装，并向联邦法院控告沃尔玛和朱迪–菲律宾公司侵害了其著作权和商业表征。对于侵害著作权的指控，事实和法律都比较清楚，法院容易认证。但是，对于侵害商业表征的指控，双方却展开了旷日持久的较量。本案中的商业表征侵权问题在联邦地区法院和联邦巡回法院间几经反复，最后一直上诉到美国最高法院。

美国最高法院在审理本案时，将问题的焦点集中于商标法在何种情况下应保护没有注册的商业表征。按照美国商标法，商业表征若要受到保护必须符合两个要件：第一，寻求保护的商业表征必须是非功能性的。第二，寻求保护的商业表征不能导致消费者混淆误认。此外，在过去联邦法院的一系列判决中，法院甚至还要求寻求保护的商业表征具有识别性。

对于识别性的要求与美国商标法的有关条文并不完全吻合。美国商标法只在注册商标时要求识别性，在保护未注册的商业表征时，并没有规定识别性的要求。一般而言，商标的识别性是指商标名称与其所代表的产品之间有一种独一无二的联系。一些商标名称本身就是独一无二的，例如，"柯达"胶卷、"万宝路"香烟等。有些商标名称虽然本身并不是独一无二的，但是在消费者中已经建立了第二层意义。例如，"Windows"这个名称并不是独一无二的，但是在电脑软件消费者中"Windows操作系统"已经具有了第二层意义，消费者会把这个名称与微软的"Windows操作系统"联系起来。所以，"Windows"这个名称之于个人电脑操作系统而言也具有了识别性。基于这一法理，美国商标法要求，本身不具有识别性的商标名称，只有在消费者中获得了第二层意义之后，才受到法律的保护。那么，有关商标名称的这一法律，是否适用于商业表征呢？在沃尔玛状告萨玛拉兄弟案中，美国最高法院必须解决这个问题。

在过去的判例中，美国最高法院曾判决，虽然有些商标名称本身就具有识别性，但是某些商标图案本身不可能具有识别性。例如颜色，本身永远不可能具有识别性。如果要寻求保护某种颜色的商标图案，商标所有者必须证明这种颜色在消费者中已经获得了第二层意义，消费者已经在这种颜色与它所代表的商品之间建立了独一无二的联系。

在本案中，美国最高法院认定，商品设计与商标颜色一样，本身不具有识别性。如此一来，商品设计必须在消费者中获得第二层意义后，方能得到法律的保护。在此，最高法院也在商品设计和商品包装之间作出了区别。虽然商品包装和商品设计都可以归入商业表征的范畴，但是在受保护的程度上二者有着重大区别。简言之，商品包装本身可以具有识别性，但是商品设计本身却永远不可能具有识别性。某种商品设计的识别性只能来自于它在消费者中获得的第二层意义。

把这一法理运用到本案中，萨玛拉兄弟公司的儿童服装图案设计，必须在消费者中获得了第二层意义之后，才能受到商标法的保护。如果萨玛拉兄弟公司不能出示有力的证据，证明那些有争议的图案设计已经在消费者中获得了第二层意义，这些图案设计就不受商标法的保护。

显然，美国最高法院的这一判决大大限制了商标法对商品设计的保护。最高法院之所以作出这样的判决，除了商标法的法理因素之外，还有许多政策层面的考虑。首先，一种产品设计如果在没有获得第二层意义的情况下就受到商标法的保护，只会对已经在市场上站稳脚跟的公司有利，却会阻吓那些后来进入市场的竞争者。所以，在商标法上给予商品设计过多的保护，有可能造成商品设计领域的垄断，不利于设计创新和市场竞争。最终受到损害的仍然是消费者。其次，商品设计已经受到著作权法和专利法的充分保护，在遇到商品设计侵权纠纷时，原告应当主要寻求著作权法和专利法的保护。事实上，在本案中，萨玛拉兄弟公司同时指控沃尔玛侵害了其儿童服装图案设计的著作权，而且赢得了著作权的侵权诉讼。之所以再提出商标侵权诉讼，可能主要是为了增加获得赔偿的额度。最高法院的判决表明，法院并不鼓励这种做法。

不过，本案法院的判决并未在法律上为抄袭商品设计打开"方便之门"。它只是限制了商标法保护商品设计的程度和范围。更值得注意的是，这一判例只适用于未经注册的商品设计。一种商品设计按照商标法经过合法注册后，会受到更多的保护。不但如此，一种商品设计即使未按照商标法进行注册，仍然可以按照著作权法取得著作权，或按照专利法申请专利取得专利权，或者双管齐下，同时申请著作权和专利权。经过本案的解释，商品的设计同时在著作权法和专利法之下寻求保护无疑是更周全、更可行及更有效的途径。

本案启示与解析

"第二层意义"是一个法律术语，当一个描述性商标和一个特定的品牌联系在一起的时候就不仅仅是对产品的描述了；具备第二层意义的标记可以直接做主要注册，已具备第二层意义的说明性标记可以争取作为附属注册商标使用。

就商标的保护而言，商标图案和商业表征必须符合三个条件：（1）不能有功能性（nonfunctionality），（2）不能造成消费者混淆误认（likelihood of confusion），（3）必须具有显著性（distinctiveness）。就"显著性"要求而言，又可分为两种情况：一是商标图案或商业包装本身具有显著性；二是若商标图案或商业包装本身不具有显著性，则必须在消费者中获得了"第二层意义"（secondary meaning），并因"第二层意义"而具有了显著性。

例如，微软的 Windows 图案本身作为一种商业表征并没有显著性。但是，电脑软件消费者一见到微软的 Windows 图案就会立即联想到其 Windows 操作系统。这说明 Windows 图案作为商业包装已经在消费者中获得了"第二层意义"，并因"第二层意义"而具有了显著性。人们熟悉的许多商标图案和商业表征均是如此，例如耐克运动产品（Nike）、奔驰汽车（Mercedes-Benz）以及麦当劳（McDonalds）的商标图案等。

引用判决

WAL-MART STORES, INC. v. SAMARA BROTHERS, INC.

OPINION BY SCALIA

In this case, we decide under what circumstances a product's design is distinctive, and therefore protectible, in an action for infringement of unregistered trade dress under § 43 (a) of the Trademark Act of 1946 (Lanham Act), 60 Stat. 441, as amended, 15 U. S. C. § 1125 (a).

I

Respondent Samara Brothers, Inc. ▼, designs and manufactures children's clothing. Its primary product is a line of spring/summer one-piece seersucker outfits decorated with appliques of hearts, flowers, fruits, and the like. A number of chain stores, including JCPenney, sell this line of clothing under contract with Samara.

Petitioner Wal-Mart Stores, Inc. , ▼is one of the nation's best known retailers, selling among other things children's clothing. In 1995, Wal–Mart contracted with one of its suppliers, Judy–Philippine, Inc. , to manufacture a line of children's outfits for sale in the 1996 spring/summer season. Wal–Mart sent Judy–Philippine photographs of a number of garments from Samara's line, on which Judy–Philippine's garments were to be based; Judy–Philippine duly copied, with only minor modifications, 16 of Samara's garments, many of which contained copyrighted elements. In 1996, Wal–Mart briskly sold the so-called knockoffs, generating more than $ 1. 15 million in gross profits.

In June 1996, a buyer for JCPenney called a representative at Samara to complain that she had seen Samara garments on sale at Wal–Mart for a lower price than JCPenney was allowed to charge under its contract with Samara. The Samara representative told the buyer that Samara did not supply its clothing to Wal–Mart. Their suspicions aroused, however, Samara officials launched an investigation, which disclosed that Wal-Mart and several other major retailers——Kmart, Caldor, Hills, and Goody's——were selling the knockoffs of Samara's outfits produced by Judy-Philippine.

After sending cease-and-desist letters, Samara brought this action in the United States District Court for the Southern District of New York against Wal-Mart, Judy-Philippine, Kmart, Caldor, Hills, and Goody's for copyright infringement under federal law, consumer fraud and unfair competition under New York law, and——most relevant for our purposes——infringement of unregistered trade dress under § 43 (a) of the Lanham Act, 15 U. S. C. § 1125 (a) . All of the defendants except Wal-Mart settled before trial.

After a weeklong trial, the jury found in favor of Samara on all of its claims. Wal-Mart then renewed a motion for judgment as a matter of law, claiming, *inter alia*, that there was insufficient evidence to support a conclusion that Samara's clothing designs could be legally protected as distinctive trade dress for purposes of § 43 (a). The District Court denied the motion, 969 F. Supp. 895 (SDNY 1997) , and awarded Samara damages, interest, costs, and fees totaling almost $ 1. 6 million, together with injunctive relief, see App. to Pet. for Cert. 56-58. The Second Circuit affirmed the denial of the motion for judgment as a matter of law, 165 F. 3d 120 (1998) , and we granted certiorari, 528 U. S. 808, 120 S. Ct. 308, 145 L. Ed. 2d 35 (1999) .

II

The Lanham Act provides for the registration of trademarks, which it defines in § 45 to include "any word, name, symbol, or device, or any combination thereof [used or intended to be used] to identify and distinguish [a producer's] goods … from those manufactured or sold by others and to indicate the source of the goods… " 15 U. S. C. § 1127. Registration of a mark under § 2 of the Act, 15 U. S. C. § 1052, enables the owner to sue an infringer under § 32, 15 U. S. C. § 1114; it also entitles the owner to a presumption that its mark is valid, see § 7 (b), 15 U. S. C. § 1057 (b), and ordinarily renders the registered mark incontestable after five years of continuous use, see § 15, 15 U. S. C. § 1065. In addition to protecting registered marks, the Lanham Act, in § 43 (a), gives a producer a cause of action for the use by any person of "any word, term, name, symbol, or device, or any combination thereof … which … is likely to cause confusion … as to the origin, sponsorship, or approval of his or her goods … " 15 U. S. C. § 1125 (a). It is the latter provision that is at issue in this case.

The breadth of the definition of marks registrable under § 2, and of the confusion-producing elements recited as actionable by § 43 (a), has been held to embrace not just word marks, such as "Nike," and symbol marks, such as Nike's "swoosh" symbol, but also "trade dress" ——a category that originally included only the packaging, or "dressing," of a product, but in recent years has been expanded by many courts of appeals to encompass the design of a product. See, e. g. , *Ashley Furniture Industries, Inc.* v. *Sangiacomo N. A. , Ltd.* , 187 F. 3d 363 (CA4 1999) (bedroom furniture); *Knitwaves, Inc.* v. *Lollytogs, Ltd.* , 71 F. 3d 996 (CA2 1995) (sweaters); *Stuart Hall Co. , Inc.* v. *Ampad Corp.* , 51 F. 3d 780 (CA8 1995) (notebooks). These courts have assumed, often without discussion, that trade dress constitutes a "symbol" or "device" for purposes of the relevant sections, and we conclude likewise. "Since human beings might use as a 'symbol' or ' device' almost anything at all that is capable of carrying meaning, this language, read literally, is not restrictive. " *Qualitex Co.* v. *Jacobson Products Co.* , 514 U. S. 159, 162, 131 L. Ed. 2d 248, 115 S. Ct. 1300 (1995) . This reading of § 2 and § 43 (a) is buttressed by a recently added subsection of § 43 (a), § 43 (a) (3), which refers specifically to "civil actions for trade dress infringement under this chapter for trade dress not registered on the principal register. " 15 U. S. C. A. § 1125 (a) (3) (Oct. 1999 Supp.).

The text of § 43 (a) provides little guidance as to the circumstances under which unregistered trade dress may be protected. It does require that a producer show that the allegedly infringing feature is not "functional," see § 43 (a)(3), and is likely to cause confusion with the product for which protection is sought, see § 43 (a)(1)(A), 15 U. S. C.. § 1125 (a)(1)(A). Nothing in § 43 (a) explicitly requires a producer to show that its trade dress is distinctive, but courts have universally imposed that requirement, since without distinctiveness the trade dress would not "cause confusion ... as to the origin, sponsorship, or approval of [the] goods," as the section requires. Distinctiveness is, moreover, an explicit prerequisite for registration of trade dress under § 2, and "the general principles qualifying a mark for registration under § 2 of the Lanham Act are for the most part applicable in determining whether an unregistered mark is entitled to protection under § 43 (a)." *Two Pesos, Inc.* v. *Taco Cabana, Inc.*, 505 U. S. 763, 768, 120 L. Ed. 2d 615, 112 S. Ct. 2753 (1992) (citations omitted).

In evaluating the distinctiveness of a mark under § 2 (and therefore, by analogy, under § 43 (a)), courts have held that a mark can be distinctive in one of two ways. First, a mark is inherently distinctive if "[its] intrinsic nature serves to identify a particular source." *Ibid.* In the context of word marks, courts have applied the now-classic test originally formulated by Judge Friendly, in which word marks that are "arbitrary" ("Camel" cigarettes), "fanciful" ("Kodak" film), or "suggestive" ("Tide" laundry detergent) are held to be inherently distinctive. See *Abercrombie & Fitch Co.* v. *Hunting World, Inc.*, 537 F. 2d 4, 10–11 (CA2 1976). Second, a mark has acquired distinctiveness, even if it is not inherently distinctive, if it has developed secondary meaning, which occurs when, "in the minds of the public, the primary significance of a [mark] is to identify the source of the product rather than the product itself." *Inwood Laboratories, Inc.* v. *Ives Laboratories, Inc.*, 456 U. S. 844, 851, n. 11, 72 L. Ed. 2d 606, 102 S. Ct. 2182 (1982). *

The judicial differentiation between marks that are inherently distinctive and those that have developed secondary meaning has solid foundation in the statute itself. Section 2 requires that registration be granted to any trademark "by which the goods of the applicant may be distinguished from the goods of others" ——subject to various limited exceptions. 15 U. S. C. § 1052. It also provides, again with limited exceptions, that "nothing in this chapter shall prevent the registration of a mark used by the applicant which has become distinctive of the applicant's goods in commerce" ——that is, which is not inherently distinctive but has become so only through secondary meaning. § 2 (f), 15 U. S. C. § 1052 (f). Nothing in § 2, however, demands the conclusion that *every* category of mark necessarily includes some marks "by which the goods of the applicant may be distinguished from the goods of others" *without* secondary meaning——that in every category some marks are inherently distinctive.

Indeed, with respect to at least one category of mark——colors——we have held that no mark can ever be inherently distinctive. See *Qualitex*, 514 U. S. at 162–163. In *Qualitex*, petitioner manufactured and sold green-gold dry-cleaning press pads. After respondent began selling pads of a similar color, petitioner brought suit under § 43 (a), then added a claim under § 32 after obtaining registration for the color of its pads. We held that a color could be protected as a trademark, but only upon a showing of secondary meaning. Reasoning by analogy to the *Abercrombie & Fitch* test developed for word marks, we noted that a product's color is unlike a "fanciful," "arbitrary," or "suggestive" mark, since it does not "almost *automatically* tell a customer that [it] refers to a brand," *ibid.*, and does not "immediately … signal a brand or a product 'source,' " 514 U. S. at 163. However, we noted that, "over time, customers may come to treat a particular color on a product or its packaging … as signifying a brand." 514 U. S. at 162–163. Because a color, like a "descriptive" word mark, could eventually "come to indicate a product's origin," we concluded that it could be protected *upon a showing of secondary meaning. Ibid.*

It seems to us that design, like color, is not inherently distinctive. The attribution of inherent distinctiveness to certain categories of word marks and product packaging derives from the fact that the very purpose of attaching a particular word to a product, or encasing it in a distinctive packaging, is most often to identify the source of the product. Although the words and packaging can serve subsidiary functions——

a suggestive word mark (such as "Tide" for laundry detergent), for instance, may invoke positive connotations in the consumer's mind, and a garish form of packaging (such as Tide's squat, brightly decorated plastic bottles for its liquid laundry detergent) may attract an otherwise indifferent consumer's attention on a crowded store shelf——their predominant function remains source identification. Consumers are therefore predisposed to regard those symbols as indication of the producer, which is why such symbols "almost *automatically* tell a customer that they refer to a brand," 514 U. S. at 162-163, and "immediately ... signal a brand or a product ' source, '" 514 U. S. at 163. And where it is not reasonable to assume consumer predisposition to take an affixed word or packaging as indication of source——where, for example, the affixed word is descriptive of the product ("Tasty" bread) or of a geographic origin ("Georgia" peaches) ——inherent distinctiveness will not be found. That is why the statute generally excludes, from those word marks that can be registered as inherently distinctive, words that are "merely descriptive" of the goods, § 2 (e) (1), 15 U. S. C. § 1052 (e)(1), or "primarily geographically descriptive of them," see § 2 (e)(2), 15 U. S. C. § 1052 (e)(2) . In the case of product design, as in the case of color, we think consumer predisposition to equate the feature with the source does not exist. Consumers are aware of the reality that, almost invariably, even the most unusual of product designs——such as a cocktail shaker shaped like a penguin——is intended not to identify the source, but to render the product itself more useful or more appealing.

The fact that product design almost invariably serves purposes other than source identification not only renders inherent distinctiveness problematic; it also renders application of an inherent-distinctiveness principle more harmful to other consumer interests. Consumers should not be deprived of the benefits of competition with regard to the utilitarian and esthetic purposes that product design ordinarily serves by a rule of law that facilitates plausible threats of suit against new entrants based upon alleged inherent distinctiveness. How easy it is to mount a plausible suit depends, of course, upon the clarity of the test for inherent distinctiveness, and where product design is concerned we have little confidence that a reasonably clear test can be devised. Respondent and the United States as *amicus curiae* urge us to adopt for product design relevant portions of the test formulated by the Court of Customs and Patent Appeals for product packaging in *Seabrook Foods, Inc.* v. *Bar-Well Foods, Ltd.*, <u>568 F. 2d 1342 (1977)</u>. That opinion, in determining the inherent distinctiveness of a product's packaging, considered, among other things, "whether it was a 'common' basic shape or design, whether it was unique or unusual in a particular field, [and] whether it was a mere refinement of a commonly-adopted and well-known form of ornamentation for a particular class of goods viewed by the public as a dress or ornamentation for the goods." <u>*Id*. at 1344</u> (footnotes omitted). Such a test would rarely provide the basis for summary disposition of an anticompetitive strike suit. Indeed, at oral argument, counsel for the United States quite understandably would not give a definitive answer as to whether the test was met in this very case, saying only that "this is a very difficult case for that purpose." Tr. of Oral Arg. 19.

It is true, of course, that the person seeking to exclude new entrants would have to establish the nonfunctionality of the design feature, see § 43 (a)(3), <u>15 U. S. C. A. § 1125 (a)(3)</u> (Oct. 1999 Supp.) ——a showing that may involve consideration of its esthetic appeal, see *Qualitex*, <u>514 U. S. at 170</u>. Competition is deterred, however, not merely by successful suit but by the plausible threat of successful suit, and given the unlikelihood of inherently source-identifying design, the game of allowing suit based upon alleged inherent distinctiveness seems to us not worth the candle. That is especially so since the producer can ordinarily obtain protection for a design that *is* inherently source identifying (if any such exists), but that does not yet have secondary meaning, by securing a design patent or a copyright for the design——as, indeed, respondent did for certain elements of the designs in this case. The availability of these other protections greatly reduces any harm to the producer that might ensue from our conclusion that a product design cannot be protected under § 43 (a) without a showing of secondary meaning.

Respondent contends that our decision in *Two Pesos* forecloses a conclusion that product-design trade dress can never be inherently distinctive. In that case, we held that the trade dress of a chain of Mexican restaurants, which the plaintiff described as "a festive eating atmosphere having interior dining and patio areas decorated with artifacts, bright colors, paintings and murals," 505 U. S. at 765 (internal quotation marks and citation omitted), could be protected under § 43 (a) without a showing of secondary meaning, see 505 U. S. at 776. *Two Pesos* unquestionably establishes the legal principle that trade dress can be inherently distinctive, see, *e. g.*, 505 U. S. at 773, but it does not establish that *product-design* trade dress can be. *Two Pesos* is inapposite to our holding here because the trade dress at issue, the decor of a restaurant, seems to us not to constitute product *design*. It was either product packaging——which, as we have discussed, normally *is* taken by the consumer to indicate origin——or else some *tertium quid* that is akin to product packaging and has no bearing on the present case.

Respondent replies that this manner of distinguishing *Two Pesos* will force courts to draw difficult lines between product - design and product - packaging trade dress. There will indeed be some hard cases at the margin: a classic glass Coca-Cola bottle, for instance, may constitute packaging for those consumers who drink the Coke and then discard the bottle, but may constitute the product itself for those consumers who are bottle collectors, or part of the product itself for those consumers who buy Coke in the classic glass bottle, rather than a can, because they think it more stylish to drink from the former. We believe, however, that the frequency and the difficulty of having to distinguish between product design and product packaging will be much less than the frequency and the difficulty of having to decide when a product design is inherently distinctive. To the extent there are close cases, we believe that courts should err on the side of caution and classify ambiguous trade dress as product design, thereby requiring secondary meaning. The very closeness will suggest the existence of relatively small utility in adopting an inherent - distinctiveness principle, and relatively great consumer benefit in requiring a demonstration of secondary meaning.

* * *

We hold that, in an action for infringement of unregistered trade dress under § 43 (a) of the Lanham Act, a product's design is distinctive, and therefore protectible, only upon a showing of secondary meaning. The judgment of the Second Circuit is reversed, and the case is remanded for further proceedings consistent with this opinion.

It is so ordered.

商业表征的混淆误认

捷威公司状告伴侣产品公司案

判例简介

  成立于 1985 年的捷威公司（Gateway, Inc.）是美国著名的个人电脑制造商，主要生产和销售个人电脑、电脑配件以及电脑相关产品等。1988 年，捷威公司开始在市场上大力宣传捷威电脑品牌，其商标设计独具一格，为黑白分明的奶牛花斑。在此后的各种广告中，捷威公司一直把奶牛和奶牛花斑所代表的乡村风格作为主题，1992 年，捷威公司正式向美国专利商标局申请注册了三维立体奶牛花斑商标，以销售个人电脑及电脑相关产品。

1992 年捷威公司向美国专利商标局申请注册的三维立体奶牛花斑商标

伴侣产品公司（Companion Products, Inc.）是一家以制作绒布动物玩具为主的公司，其商标为"伸缩宠物"（Stretch Pets）。伴侣产品公司生产的伸缩玩具宠物，名副其实，宠物身子是由可伸缩的橡皮绳做成，能够绑到电脑屏幕、机箱或电视上面。伸缩宠物的样式也是五花八门，有北极熊、麋鹿、小狗、企鹅等，也包括黑白花斑的奶牛。其中花斑奶牛的销量最大，伴侣产品公司将其命名为"科迪奶牛"。自1999年起，伴侣产品公司开始销售"科迪奶牛"，共售出七千多个。

从外观看，"科迪奶牛"的花斑图案与捷威公司的奶牛花斑商标十分相似。事实上，两者的类似并不是偶然的。"科迪奶牛"与捷威公司的奶牛花斑的确有一段渊源。当初，伴侣产品公司的总裁看到捷威公司以奶牛和奶牛花斑图案大做广告，便灵机一动，希望能借实力雄厚的捷威公司推广自己的玩具产品。于是，伴侣产品公司的总裁便设计出一款绑在电脑屏幕上的"科迪奶牛"玩具图案，并标以文字说明："献给捷威的创意"。

1999年6月1日，伴侣产品公司的总裁将这幅设计图寄给捷威公司，并附函说明这一创意受捷威奶牛花斑图案的影响。随后，伴侣产品公司的总裁亲自到捷威公司的专售店买了一件捷威公司生产的奶牛玩具，并按照这件玩具设计出第二幅"科迪奶牛"图案，送给捷威公司，希望能够成为捷威公司的长期供应商。

捷威公司拒绝了伴侣产品公司的请求，并且警告伴侣产品公司，黑白颜色的奶牛花斑图案是捷威公司的注册商标，未经捷威公司同意，任何人不得使用。不过，伴侣产品公司没有接受捷威公司的警告，索性独自开工生产"科迪奶牛"绒布玩具，并在自己公司的网站上销售。恰巧，捷威公司有位爱好绒布玩具的员工，在伴侣产品公司的网站上看到"科迪奶牛"玩具，便定购了一个，并向捷威公司举报。

捷威公司接到员工的举报后，立即展开调查。不久，捷威公司的律师向伴侣产品公司发函，指出伴侣产品公司的行为涉嫌侵害捷威公司的商标权，要求伴侣产品公司立即停止生产销售"科迪奶牛"玩具，如果伴侣产品公司不停止生产销售"科迪奶牛"，捷威公司将诉诸法律。不过，像上次一样，伴侣产品公司并没有接受捷威公司的警告。针对捷威公司的侵权指控，伴侣产品公司的律师回应，"科迪奶牛"玩具没有侵害捷威公司的商标权，表示将继续生产、销售"科迪奶牛"。

2001年4月，捷威公司正式向法院起诉伴侣产品公司，指控伴侣产品公司非法使用捷威公司的奶牛花斑商业表征（Trade Dress），侵害了捷威公司的商标权。按照美国商标法和法院的判例，判定商业表征侵权必须符合三项要件。第一，原告必须证明，其商业表征本身具有识别性，或已经因第二层意义（又称客观意义）而获得了识别性。第二，原告必须证明，其商业表征不具有功能性。第三，原告还必须证明，被告模仿原告的商标会造成消费者的混淆误认。

先就第一项要件而言。伴侣产品公司指称，奶牛花斑图案本身不具有识别性，而且捷威公司的奶牛花斑表征并没有在消费者中获得第二层意义，所以，任何人都可以使用这一图案。捷威公司则通过专家证词向法院证明，奶牛花斑图案已经在消费者中获得了第二层意义。专家证词表明，许多消费者一看到奶牛花斑图案会立即将其与捷威电脑联系起来。

就法律上而言，如果消费者已经把一个本身不具有识别性的商业表征与其代表的产品联系起来，说明这个表征已经具有了第二层意义，因而具有了识别性。在专家意见的基础上，法院认定，尽管奶牛花斑本身作为商业表征不具有识别性，但是，消费者已经把奶牛花斑表征与捷威公司的电脑产品联系起来，所以捷威公司的奶牛花斑包装已经在消费者中获得了第二层意义，从而具有了识别性。

再看第二项要件。按照美国商标法，只有非功能性的商业表征才受商标法的保护。所以，原告必须证明自己的商业表征与产品的功能无关，否则便难以赢得商业表征的侵权诉讼。例如，电脑生产商不能用电脑图案或电脑零部件作为商业表征，因为这种图案与电脑的功能密切相关，因而具有功能性，不受商标法保护。

在本案中，伴侣产品公司辩称，捷威电脑的奶牛花斑表征具有功能性，所以不受商标法保护。不过，法院并没有接受伴侣产品公司有关功能性的申辩。法院指出，商标法之所以不保护功能性商标或商业表征，是为了鼓励市场竞争，防止垄断。在商业表征中，功能性的设计既不能按照专利法申请专利，也不能按照著作权法申请著作权，更不能依据商标法注册商标。

法院查明，本案捷威公司的奶牛花斑表征除了辨识捷威公司的品牌之外，没有其他任何功能。奶牛花斑设计既不能提高也不能降低捷威电脑的性能。更重要的是，禁止捷威电脑的竞争对手使用奶牛花斑的商业表征，丝毫不会损害电脑市场的竞争。同时，法院也指出，捷威电脑的奶牛花斑设计也不会将伴侣产品公司在市场竞争中置于不利的地位，因为商标法也不允许其他生产同类玩具的公司使用捷威公司的商业表征。在此基础上，法院认定，捷威公司的奶牛花斑表征不具有功能性。

最后，双方的争论聚焦在伴侣产品公司的"科迪奶牛"是否会导致消费者混淆误认的问题上。法院指出，在个人电脑市场上，捷威电脑已经成为一个知名品牌。捷威公司自成立后已经在世界范围内投入十三亿美金宣传推广其品牌以及奶牛花斑的商业表征。而且，捷威公司自成立后一直在其生产的个人电脑以及电脑相关产品上使用奶牛花斑的表征。经过十余年的努力，电脑消费者已经把黑白奶牛花斑图案与捷威电脑联系起来。

伴侣产品公司参考捷威电脑的奶牛花斑包装，设计出的"科迪奶牛"玩具，不但外形相似，而且实际上已经造成了消费者的混淆误认。考虑到伴侣产品公司生产的"科迪奶牛"玩具售价在二十美金以内，大部分消费者在购买前不会做细致研究，所以更容易将其误认为是捷威公司制造。捷威公司提供的专家证词和消费者抽样调查报告也支持这种结论。

在综合考虑以上因素后，法院认定，伴侣产品公司生产的"科迪奶牛"玩具会造成消费者的混淆误认。捷威公司所提供的证据，也充分地证明了商业表征侵权的三项要件。因此，法院判决，伴侣产品公司制造的"科迪奶牛"侵害了捷威公司的奶牛花斑表征，构成商标侵权。法院责令伴侣产品公司立即停止生产、销售"科迪奶牛"玩具，并赔偿因商标侵权给捷威公司造成的损失。

本案启示与解析

美国商标法不仅保护文字名称和图案商标，而且保护商业表征。按照美国商标法和法院判例，判定商业表征侵权的标准与判定名称或图案商标侵权的标准相同，即必须符合三个条件：第一，原告的商业表征必须具有识别性（Distinctiveness，又译"显著性"）。第二，原告的商业表征不具有功能性（Functionality）。第三，被告模仿原告的商业表征会造成消费者混淆误认（Consumer Confusion）。在捷威公司状告伴侣产品公司案中，原告和被告都把争议的重点放在第一个条件上，即捷威公司的奶牛花斑商业表征是否具有识别性。

就其来源看，识别性可以分为两种：一是商业表征本身就具有识别性。比如说可口可乐瓶装饮料的包装，本身就具有识别性。二是虽然商业表征本身不具有识别性，但是已经因第二层意义而取得了识别性。捷威公司的奶牛花斑商业表征便属于第二种情况。被告伴侣产品公司明确指出，奶牛花斑图案本身并不具有识别性。所以，捷威公司必须证明其奶牛花斑已经在消费者中获得了第二层意义。

在商标侵权攻防战中，原告向法院证明第二层意义的方法主要有两种：一是消费者调查，二是专家作证。首先是消费者抽样调查。如果消费者调查的结果显示，有相当比例的消费者能够把原告的商业表征与原告的产品联系起来，那么这一调查结果就可以有力地证明原告的商业表征已经在消费者中获得了第二层意义。例如，本案中的奶牛花斑表征与捷威电脑。尽管奶牛花斑图案本身不具有识别性，但是已经有相当比例的消费者把奶牛花斑图案与捷威电脑联系起来。法院由此认定，捷威公司的奶牛花斑已经获得了第二层意义，因而具有了识别性。其次，原告还可以经由专家作证的方式向法院证明其商业表征已经获得了第二层意义。虽然消费者抽样调查具有较强的说服力，但一项完备的消费者调查往往需要原告投入大量的人力、物力和时间。而且，调查方法和问卷设计的漏洞经常给被告留下攻击的把柄，使调查的科学性受到法院质疑。在某些极端情况下，法院甚至因此拒绝接受原告的调查结果。与消费者调查相比，专家作证不需要原告投入大量的人力、物力，可为原告节省很多开支。但是，专家作证有时会因为缺少客观性而受到法院质疑。在商标侵权案件中，原告和被告往往是双管齐下，既提供消费者调查结果，也请专家作证。在本案中，捷威公司就采取了这种双管齐下的策略，在法庭上取得了主动的优势。

引用判决

GATEWAY, INC. vs. COMPANION PRODUCTS, INC.

OPINION BY KAREN E. SCHREIER, *UNITED STATES DISTRICT JUDGE*

Defendant, Companion Products, Inc. (CPI), requests modification and clarification of the judgment and a stay of injunction pending its current appeal. Plaintiff, Gateway, Inc. ▾, opposes the motion. Gateway moves to compel CPI to comply with the court's judgment and for sanctions. CPI objects.

BACKGROUND

Gateway is a corporation that sells computers, computer products, computer peripherals, computer accessories, and other electronic products throughout the world. Beginning in 1988, Gateway began using black and white cow spots on their products, packaging, advertising, and promotional materials. In 1992, Gateway registered its trademarks for a stylized black and white cow-spots design and its slogan "Gateway Country." Gateway registered the trademarks in association with computers and computer peripherals.

CPI sells plush stuffed animals called "stretch pets" that wrap around computer monitors, CPUs, or televisions. "StretchPets" is CPI's registered trademark. One of its top selling products is a black and white spotted cow, "Cody Cow," which CPI began selling in 1999. CPI attempted to sell Cody Cow to Gateway, but Gateway rejected the idea. Gateway thereafter sent CPI a cease and desist letter. The letter notified CPI that its Cody Cow infringed on Gateway's trademark and noted that if sales of Cody Cow did not cease, Gateway would file suit. Counsel for CPI informed the company's president, Dennis Byer, that the black and white cow spots did not infringe upon Gateway's trademark. CPI continued to produce Cody Cow.

Gateway filed suit against CPI alleging false designation of origin and unfair competition in violation of §43（a）of the Lanham Act, 15 U. S. C. §1125（a）and the common law of South Dakota; trademark infringement in violation of 15 U. S. C. Ė 1051-1127 and the common law of South Dakota; trademark dilution in violation of 15 U. S. C. §1125（c）; and deceptive trade practices in violation of SDCL 37-24-6（1）and the common law of South Dakota. CPI maintained that its product neither infringed upon nor diluted Gateway's trademark. CPI further argued that the black and white spots were functional and that Gateway's trademark was limited to the spots on a box.

A trial before an advisory jury commenced on February 4, 2003. The jury returned a verdict in favor of CPI on the issues of trademark infringement, trade dress infringement, and dilution. The parties subsequently filed post-trial briefs. The court issued an opinion on August 19, 2003, in which it did not adopt the advisory jury's verdict. The court found in favor of Gateway on the issues of trademark and trade dress infringement and in favor of CPI on the issue of dilution.

CPI now requests clarification of the court's order to "deliver up for destruction all packing, literature, labels, advertising, and other materials of an infringing nature in CPI's possession or control." It argues that the evidence does not show and the court did not find that CPI's boxes and brochures create a likelihood of confusion. CPI also requests a stay of the destruction order pending a decision on its appeal to the Eighth Circuit. Gateway argues that CPI's motion is untimely and does not meet the substantive requirements of either Rule 59（e）or 60（b）. Gateway also maintains that no extraordinary circumstances warrant a stay. Gateway moves for an order compelling CPI to comply with the court's order and for sanctions.

DISCUSSION

1. Motion to Reconsider

The Federal Rules of Civil Procedure do not mention motions to reconsider. The

Eighth Circuit has instructed courts to consider such motions either under Rule 59
(e) or Rule 60 (b). *Sanders v. Clemco Indus.*, 862 F. 2d 161, 168 (8th
Cir. 1988). See also *Schoffstall v. Henderson*, 223 F. 3d 818, 827 (8th Cir. 2000)
(holding that Rule 59 (e) applies to a motion to reconsider); *Broadway v. Norris*,
193 F. 3d 987, 989 (8th Cir. 1999) (analyzing whether Rule 59 (e) or Rule 60
(b) applies to a motion to reconsider). "When the moving party fails to specify the
rule under which it makes a postjudgment motion, that party leaves the characteriza-
tion of the motion to the court's somewhat unenlightened guess." Sanders, 862 F. 2d
at 168.

Rule 59 (e) permits a party to file a motion to alter or amend a judgment
within ten days of that judgment. Fed. R. Civ. P. 59 (e); *Dale & Selby Superette &
Deli v. United States Dep't of Agriculture*, 838 F. Supp. 1346, 1347 (D. Minn.
1993). Motions made after the expiration of ten days are considered under Rule 60
(b). Sanders, 862 F. 2d at 169. The court issued a judgment against CPI on August
19, 2003. CPI requested reconsideration on October 15, 2003. CPI's motion does not
specify the rule under which it was filed. Because it exceeds the ten-day time limit
imposed by Rule 59 (e), the court will consider CPI's motion under Rule 60
(b).

Rule 60 (b) allows a party to seek relief from a final judgment or order if the
party can prove mistake, inadvertence, surprise, excusable neglect, or other reasons. *Wilburn v. Pepsi—Cola Bottling Co. of St. Louis*, 492 F. 2d 1288, 1290 (8th
Cir. 1974). See 6 Charles Alan Wright, Arthur R. Miller, and Mary Kay Kane,
Federal Practice and Procedure § 1489 (2d ed. 1990). "Rule 60 (b) provides for
extraordinary relief which may be granted only upon an adequate showing of exceptional circumstances." *Reyher v. Champion Int'l Corp.*, 975 F. 2d 483, 488 (8th
Cir. 1992). Such motions are disfavored. *Rosebud Sioux Tribe v. A & P Steel*, Inc.,
733 F. 2d 509, 515 (8th Cir. 1984).

A motion to amend a judgment is appropriate "to correct manifest errors of law
or fact or, in some limited situations, to present newly discovered evidence." Dale

& Selby Superette, 838 F. Supp. at 1347. They are not simply "vehicle [s] for ... reargument on the merits. " Broadway, 193 F. 3d at 990. "A motion to reconsider is frivolous if it contains no new evidence or arguments of law explaining why the [judge] should change an original order. " Magnus Elecs. , Inc. v. Masco Corp. of Ind. , 871 F. 2d 626, 629 (7th Cir. 1989) . Failing to present new information not previously considered by the court is "a controlling factor against granting relief. " Sanders, 862 F. 2d at 170.

CPI is entitled to a modification of the judgment under Rule 60 (b) . CPI points to a mistake in the court's judgment that restrains CPI from "doing any other act or thing which dilutes Gateway's cow-spots trademark. " Because CPI prevailed on the issue of dilution, the court erred in restraining any actions that diluted Gateway's trademark. Indeed, the order should restrain CPI from doing any other act or thing which infringes upon Gateway's cow-spots trademark. The court, therefore, will grant CPI's request to modify this portion of the order so that the order now re-strains CPI from "doing any other act or thing which infringes upon Gateway's cow-spots trademark. "

No exceptional circumstances, however, entitle CPI to additional relief from the court's judgment. CPI has neither produced any newly discovered evidence nor ad-vanced new arguments in support of its motion. Indeed, CPI merely raises an issue it previously argued at trial: that because its boxes and brochures are red and promi-nently display the StretchPets trademark, they neither cause consumer confusion nor infringe upon Gateway's trademark. The court has already considered this argument and CPI's supporting evidence and found that CPI's marketing materials and packa-ging also are likely to cause consumer confusion. A district court can deny a motion to reconsider for this reason alone. Broadway, 193 F. 3d at 990.

Indeed, the court's memorandum opinion and order issued on August 19, 2003, considered whether CPI's boxes and labels dispelled the likelihood of consumer con-fusion. The court found that consumer confusion will likely result regardless of CPI's packaging. Accordingly, the judgment includes CPI's boxes, brochures, and in-store displays. The court finds, however, that affixing labels to cover the infringing images of "Cody Cow" complies with the judgment and order. Destruction of this packaging is not necessary as long as the images of "Cody Cow" are covered or deleted. CPI must still provide Gateway a report in writing and under oath settingforth, in detail, how it has complied with the order and prevented any infringing images from reaching the public.

No other alterations of the judgment are warranted. CPI has not pointed to any excusable neglect or misrepresentation. It "failed to state any grounds upon which [it] could justify relief from judgment underRule 60 (b) . " *United States v. Whitford*, 758 F. 2d 329, 331 (8th Cir. 1985) . Accordingly, this court will not further reconsider its order dated August 19, 2003. See id. (motion to reconsider properly denied where party restated its previous arguments and failed to raise any newly discovered issues of material fact not known by the district court at the time of the previous ruling) ; Sanders, 862 F. 2d at 169-70 (district court previously ruled that statute of limitations barred claim; thus motion to reconsider was denied since party raised only issues of law that the court previously rejected).

2. Motion to Stay

Parties seeking a stay pending appeal "must show that (1) they are likely to succeed on the merits, (2) they will suffer irreparable injury unless the stay is granted, (3) no substantial harm will come to other interested parties, and (4) the stay will do no harm to the public interest. " *Arkansas Peace Center v. Arkansas Dept. of Pollution Control*, 992 F. 2d 145, 147 (8th Cir. 1993) .

"The first element goes to the sensible administration of justice: a stay should not ordinarily be granted if the court determines that the injunction will ultimately take effect in any event. " *Reserve Mining Co. v. United States*, 498 F. 2d 1073, 1077 (8th Cir. 1974) . CPI has offered neither argument nor proof to demonstrate that it will likely succeed on the merits. The court previously analyzed these issues in its August opinion and found against CPI. CPI has not raised any novel or complex areas of law. See Arkansas Peace Center, 992 F. 2d at 147 (more likely to succeed on the merits where defendants raised serious and substantial legal issues). Accordingly, this factor weighs against issuing a stay.

Second, CPI has not demonstrated any irreparable harm if the court did not grant the stay. CPI must show that the "injury complained of is of such imminence that there is a clear and present need for equitable relief to prevent irreparable harm." *Packard Elevator v. Interstate Commerce Comm'n*, 782 F. 2d 112, 115 (8th Cir. 1986). Economic loss does not amount to irreparable harm unless the loss threatens the very existence of the party's business. Id. CPI has not specifically alleged how it will suffer irreparable harm if the court does not issue a stay. "Bare allegations of what is likely to occur are of no value since the court must decide whether the harm will *in fact* occur." Id. There is no evidence that CPI is subject to imminent harm that threatens the loss of its business. This factor, therefore, does not favor a stay.

Third, failure to enforce the judgment can potentially harm Gateway. In its August opinion, the court found that CPI's product is likely to cause confusion among consumers. "When a likelihood of confusion exists, plaintiffs' lack of control over the quality of defendants' services constitutes an immediate and irreparable injury, regardless of the actual quality of those services." *Sturgis Area Chamber of Commerce v. Sturgis Rally & Races, Inc.*, 2000 DSD 26, 99 F. Supp. 2d 1090, 1101 (D. S. D. 2000). Thus, this factor dictates against a stay.

Fourth, a stay will harm the public's interest. "Once the likelihood of confusion is shown, it follows that the public interest is damaged if such confusion continues." Id. at 1102 [quoting 5 J. Thomas McCarthy, McCarthy on Trademarks and Unfair Competition, § 30. 52 (4th ed. 1997)]. This court has previously concluded that CPI's product causes confusion among consumers. Accordingly, staying the injunction is detrimental to the public. This factor weighs against granting a stay.

CPI has not presented any evidence nor cited any legal authority to support its request for a stay. It summarily stated that a stay would not harm Gateway, that failing to grant a stay would materially harm CPI, and that there is a likelihood of success on appeal. These conclusions do not justify extraordinary relief in the form of a stay. Furthermore, all four factors dictate against staying the injunction. CPI's request, therefore, is denied.

3. Motion to Comply and Sanctions

Gateway requests an order compelling CPI to comply with the injunction. The judgment orders CPI to deliver up for destruction "all packages, literature, labels, advertising, and other materials of an infringing nature in CPI's possession or control." To the extent that the current order permits CPI to cover or delete the infringing image on its marketing and packaging materials, CPI need not comply with the precise wording of the August 19, 2003, judgment. All other requirements in the judgment remain in effect and CPI is ordered to immediately comply with them. No sanctions against CPI are warranted because the current order of the court clarifies the previous judgment. CPI must now comply with each condition ofthe judgment in light of this order and the court's previous August 19, 2003, order. CPI must also file and serve on Gateway a "report in writing under oath setting forth in detail the manner and form in which CPI has complied with the terms of this injunction."

CONCLUSION

The court will modify the judgment for the reasons previously cited. No other modifications are warranted nor do the circumstances justify a stay of the judgment. CPI is ordered to comply with the judgment. No sanctions will issue against it.

Accordingly, it is hereby

ORDERED that CPI's request for modification of the judgment and clarification of the injunction (Docket 164) is granted in part and denied in part.

Dated December 19, 2003.

著名商标的侵权和淡化

莫斯理与维多利亚的秘密商标侵权案

判例简介

香醇的美酒加水后，味道会大打折扣。著名商标也是同样的道理。如果有不知名的商标模仿著名商标，鱼目混珠，令消费者真假难辨，时日一久，品牌产品在消费者中的信誉定会一落千丈。美国商标法形象地把这种现象称作"淡化"（Dilution）。淡化著名商标是一种与传统商标侵权完全不同的侵害，相对直接侵权而言属于间接损害。商标淡化可分为三种形式：第一，因弱化而造成淡化，弱化是一个逐渐淡化和冲淡的过程，淡化商品与商标之间的唯一联想。由于其他人在其他商品上对该商标的使用会使之变得模糊。第二，因丑化而淡化，这是指将与著名商标相同或近似的标记使用在对该商标的信誉发生损害的商品或服务上的玷污行为。第三，因退化而淡化，这是最严重的一种，即商标彻底丧失了其识别性，不再具有区别功能而成为商品的通用名称。

"维多利亚的秘密"（VICTORIA'S SECRET）是 V 秘密目录公司旗下的著名商标。V 秘密目录公司专门生产和销售"维多利亚的秘密"品牌的女性内衣，在美国设有近八百家连锁店。其店面设计模仿女性的卧室，独具特色。每年V秘密目录公司均投入大量费用维护和宣传"维多利亚的秘密"这个著名商标。仅在1998年，V秘密目录公司就为此投入了5500万美金，并向消费者发送了4亿份产品目录。同年，"维多利亚的秘密"的销售额就超过了15亿美金。

在美国肯塔基州有一个名叫伊丽莎白城的小镇。镇上有一对夫妻，丈夫名叫维克多·莫斯理，妻子名叫凯希·莫斯理。1998年情人节前，莫斯理夫妇在镇上开设了一家店面，将其命名为"维克多的秘密"（VICTOR'S SE-CRET）。开业之际，夫妻两人在当地的一些出版物上刊登了广告，以期把顾客吸引到店里。

伊丽莎白城人口不多，生意有限。但附近有座兵营，驻有大批官兵，是一个不容忽视的消费群体。因此，莫斯理夫妇便在兵营的小报上做了广告："维克多的秘密，情人节前开业大吉，专售性感内衣及成人用品。"正巧，兵营中有一位上校，他的妻子女儿都是"维多利亚的秘密"的顾客。这位上校自然熟悉"维多利亚的秘密"这一商标。看到"维克多的秘密"的广告，他心生疑窦，觉得这家商店使用这样一个名称似乎有损"维多利亚的秘密"的形象和声誉。这位上校路见不平，随即写信给V秘密目录公司，举报了"维克多的秘密"开张的消息。

V秘密目录公司接到举报后，向莫斯理发出律师信，称其使用"维克多的秘密"这一店名销售内衣容易误导消费者，侵害了"维多利亚的秘密"的商标权，淡化了这个著名商标。律师信要求莫斯理立即停止使用"维克多的秘密"这个名称以及类似的名称。莫斯理夫妇既不想放弃"维克多的秘密"这个字号，又不想引来V秘密目录公司的诉讼。

经过一番思量，两人决定将商店名称改成"维克多的小秘密"。不过，这个小小的改动并没有令V秘密目录公司满意。两个月后，"维克多的小秘密"接到V秘密目录公司的诉状。莫斯理夫妇这对名不见经传的小镇商人，一夜之间名声大噪。"维克多的小秘密"也变成一家闻名全国的商店。

V秘密目录公司的起诉书罗列了"维克多的小秘密"的四大罪状，其中包括商标侵权和淡化著名品牌。就商标侵权的指控部分，V秘密目录公司称，

"维克多的小秘密"容易造成消费者混淆,使消费者误以为是"维多利亚的秘密"。但是,V秘密目录公司并没有提供证据证明消费者是否会被或者已经被"维克多的小秘密"所误导。

兵营上校的信,并未说明上校被"维克多的小秘密"所误导,或把"维克多的小秘密"误作"维多利亚的秘密"。相反的,上校的信恰恰说明,他没有被误导,十分清楚"维克多的小秘密"不是"维多利亚的秘密"。同时,莫斯理夫妇也出示证据,证明"维克多的小秘密"主要是销售成人用品,女性内衣只占所销售商品的百分之五左右。在这种情况下,消费者难以被"维克多的小秘密"误导,而将"维克多的小秘密"与"维多利亚的秘密"相混淆。因此,法院拒绝了V秘密目录公司对"维克多的小秘密"商标侵权的指控。

至于淡化著名商标的指控,情况则相当复杂。如果说禁止使用容易造成混淆的商标主要是为了保护消费者不被误导,那么禁止淡化著名商标则主要是为了保护著名商标及其拥有者的商业利益。在美国国会通过《联邦反淡化商标法案》[1]以前,美国法院主要是根据各州法律中相关反淡化著名商标的条款来判案。

1995年7月,美国国会通过了《联邦反淡化商标法案》,以在全国范围内保护著名商标不受损害。与以往各州的反淡化商标法不同,联邦的反淡化商标法提高了认定淡化著名商标的难度。各州的反淡化商标法均将"可能损害"著名商标作为一个重要的考虑因素。而联邦的反淡化商标法却要求"实际损害"。尤其是在被告使用的有争议商标与原告受保护的商标并不完全相同的情况下,原告必须出示证据证明被告的行为已经损害了原告受保护的商标。

在本案中,V秘密目录公司出示兵营上校的信和专家证词作为"维克多的小秘密"淡化著名商标的证据。上校的信表明,他由"维克多的小秘密"广告联想到了"维多利亚的秘密",而且"维克多的小秘密"广告令他感到不快。但是,上校的信并不表明,"维克多的小秘密"使他改变了对"维多利亚的秘密"的正面印象。所以,上校的信不足以证明"维克多的小秘密"已经对V秘密目录公司造成了实际损害。

---

〔1〕 Federal Trademark Dilution Act (FTDA)。

在这种情况下，V 秘密目录公司只能靠专家的证词来证明已经存在"实际损害"。不过，V 秘密目录公司聘请的专家并没有在证词中做到这一点。这位专家提供了大量证据证明"维多利亚的秘密"是一个著名品牌，其价值数以亿美金计。但是，这位专家的意见唯独没有说明"维克多的小秘密"给 V 秘密目录公司造成了多少实际损害，以及如何造成这些损害。

一般而言，在商标侵权和淡化著名商标的诉讼中，原告证明"实际损害"的主要途径包括消费者抽样调查和销售量下降的记录。显然，这两种方式均不太适用于本案。作为小镇上的一家普通商店，"维克多的小秘密"对 V 秘密目录公司在全美国消费群的影响微乎其微，更不会影响 V 秘密目录公司的销售量。而做一项全国性的消费者抽样调查需要 V 秘密目录公司投入大量的资金。也许基于这种考虑，V 秘密目录公司没有提供消费者抽样调查来支持其所称的"实际损害"。在缺少证据的情况下，法院拒绝认定"维克多的小秘密"已经对"维多利亚的秘密"商标造成了实际损害。按照《联邦反淡化商标法案》，如果原告不能证明"实际损害"，淡化著名商标的指控便不能成立。

莫斯理与维多利亚的秘密商标侵权案是近年来美国最高法院审理的为数不多的几个商标侵权和淡化商标案之一。在美国国会通过《联邦反淡化商标法案》8 年后，美国最高法院第一次就这项法案中的"损害条款"作出解释，并要求被告证明已经受到"实际损害"。这无疑提高了"淡化著名商标"诉讼的门槛。可以预见，这一判决在未来数年内将对"淡化著名商标"案件的审理和判决产生深远影响。

本案启示与解析

莫斯理与维多利亚的秘密商标侵权案是一起小商号成功挑战大公司著名商标的判例。在这场双方实力悬殊的商标战中，被告莫斯理沉着应战，策略得当，抓住关键问题集中申辩。首先，在反驳"维多利亚的秘密"商标侵权的指控时，莫斯理把焦点放在消费者的混淆误认上。在商标侵权案中，原告必须证明被告的行为会造成消费者的混淆误认，方能胜诉。莫斯理抓住这一点，对原告提供的证据作出了与原告截然不同的解释，指出兵营上校的信件不但不能证明使消费者混淆误认，相反恰恰说明消费者没有把"维克多的小秘密"误认为"维多利亚的秘密"。被告莫斯理在策略上的高明之处在于，利用原告证据中的矛盾破解原告的指控，并成功地说服了法庭。反观原告 V 秘密目录公司，显然在证据收集和解释方面准备不足，没有成功地回应被告莫斯理的申辩。

其次，在应对原告淡化著名商标的指控时，莫斯理将诉讼的争点集中在"实际损害"上。证明"实际损害"是联邦的反淡化商标法与此前各州的反淡化商标法律最大的不同之处。按照此前各州的反淡化商标法律，原告无须证明"实际损害"，只需证明"可能损害"，法院即可认定被告淡化著名商标的指控成立。但是，联邦的反淡化商标法提高了认定淡化著名商标的门槛。在本案中，原告 V 秘密目录公司显然没有拟定相应的诉讼策略来应对法律上的这一变化。

一般而言，在商标侵权和淡化著名商标的诉讼中，原告证明"实际损害"的主要途径包括消费者调查、产品销售量下降的记录，以及专家证词等。显然，提供消费者调查和产品销量下降的记录两种方式均不太适合本案。作为小镇上的一家普通商店，"维克多的小秘密"对"维多利亚的秘密"在全美国消费群的影响微乎其微，更不会影响 V 秘密目录公司的销售量。而做一项全国性的消费者调查需要 V 秘密目录公司投入大量的资金。也许出于这种考虑，V 秘密目录公司没有提供消费者调查来支持其所称的"实际损害"。在这种情况下，聘请专家作证似乎就成了唯一可行的选择。不过，原告 V 秘密目录公司聘请的专家在法庭上作证时根本没有涉及"实际损害"这一关键问题，可谓是原告在诉讼策略上的重大失误。

引用判决

VICTOR MOSELEY AND CATHY MOSELEY, DBA VICTOR'SLITTLE SECRET, PETITIONERS v. V SECRET CATALOGUE, INC. , ET AL.

OPINION BY STEVENS

In 1995 Congress amended § 43 of the Trademark Act of 1946, 15 U. S. C. § 1125, to provide a remedy for the "dilution of famous marks. " 109 Stat. 985 – 986. That amendment, known as the Federal Trademark Dilution Act (FTDA), describes the factors that determine whether a mark is "distinctive and famous," and defines the term "dilution" as "the lessening of the capacity of a famous mark to identify and distinguish goods or services. " The question we granted certiorari to decide is whether objective proof of actual injury to the economic value of a famous mark (as opposed to a presumption of harm arising from a subjective "likelihood of dilution" standard) is a requisite for relief under the FTDA.

I

Petitioners, Victor and Cathy Moseley, own and operate a retail store named "Victor's Little Secret" in a strip mall in Elizabethtown, Kentucky. They have no employees.

Respondents are affiliated corporations that own the VICTORIA'S SECRET trademark, and operate over 750 Victoria's Secret stores, two of which are in Louisville, Kentucky, a short drive from Elizabethtown. In 1998 they spent over ＄55 million advertising "the VICTORIA'S SECRET brand——one of moderately priced, high quality, attractively designed lingerie sold in a store setting designed to look like a woman's bedroom. " App. 167, 170. They distribute 400 million copies of the Victoria's Secret catalog each year, including 39, 000 in Elizabethtown. In 1998 their sales exceeded $ 1. 5 billion.

In the February 12, 1998, edition of a weekly publication distributed to residents of the military installation at Fort Knox, Kentucky, petitioners advertised the "GRAND OPENING Just in time for Valentine's Day!" of their store "VICTOR'S SECRET" in nearby Elizabethtown. The ad featured "Intimate Lingerie *for every woman*"; "Romantic Lighting"; "Lycra Dresses"; "Pagers"; and "Adult Novelties/Gifts." *Id.*, at 209. An army colonel, who saw the ad and was offended by what he perceived to be an attempt to use a reputable company's trademark to promote the sale of "unwholesome, tawdry merchandise," sent a copy to respondents. *Id.*, at 210. Their counsel then wrote to petitioners stating that their choice of the name "Victor's Secret" for a store selling lingerie was likely to cause confusion with the well-known VICTORIA'S SECRET mark and, in addition, was likely to "dilute the distinctiveness" of the mark. *Id.*, at 190–191. They requested the immediate discontinuance of the use of the name "and any variations thereof." *Ibid.* In response, petitioners changed the name of their store to "Victor's Little Secret." Because that change did not satisfy respondents, they promptly filed this action in Federal District Court.

The complaint contained four separate claims: (1) for trademark infringement alleging that petitioners' use of their trade name was "likely to cause confusion and/or mistake in violation of 15 U. S. C. § 1114 (1)"; (2) for unfair competition alleging misrepresentation in violation of § 1125 (a); (3) for "federal dilution" in violation of the FTDA; and (4) for trademark infringement and unfair competition in violation of the common law of Kentucky. *Id.*, at 15, 20–23. In the dilution count, the complaint alleged that petitioners' conduct was "likely to blur and erode the distinctiveness" and "tarnish the reputation" of the VICTORIA'S SECRET trademark. Ibid.

After discovery the parties filed cross-motions for summary judgment. The record contained uncontradicted affidavits and deposition testimony describing the vast size of respondents' business, the value of the VICTORIA'S SECRET name, and descriptions of the items sold in the respective parties' stores. Respondents sell a "complete line of lingerie" and related items, each of which bears a VICTORIA'S SECRET label or tag. Petitioners sell a wide variety of items, including adult videos, "adult novelties, " and lingerie. Victor Moseley stated in an affidavit that women's lingerie represented only about five per cent of their sales. Id. , at 131. In support of their motion for summary judgment, respondents submitted an affidavit by an expert in marketing who explained "the enormous value" of respondents' mark. *Id.* , at 195 – 205. Neither he, nor any other witness, expressed any opinion concerning the impact, if any, of petitioners' use of the name "Victor's Little Secret" on that value.

Finding that the record contained no evidence of actual confusion between the parties' marks, the District Court concluded that "no likelihood of confusion exists as a matter of law" and entered summary judgment for petitioners on the infringement and unfair competition claims. *V Secret Catalogue, Inc. v. Moseley*, 2000 U. S. Dist. LEXIS 5215, Civ. Action No. 3：98CV – 395 – S (WD Ky. , Feb. 9, 2000), App. to Pet. for Cert. 28a, 37a. With respect to the FTDA claim, however, the court ruled for respondents.

Noting that petitioners did not challenge Victoria Secret's claim that its mark is "famous," the only question it had to decide was whether petitioners' use of their mark diluted the quality of respondents' mark. Reasoning from the premise that dilution "corrodes" a trademark either by " 'blurring its product identification or by damaging positive associations that have attached to it, '" the court first found the two marks to be sufficiently similar to cause dilution, and then found " that Defendants' mark dilutes Plaintiffs' mark because of its tarnishing effect upon the Victoria's Secret mark. " *Id.* , at 38a–39a [quoting *Ameritech, Inc. v. American Info. Technologies Corp.* , 811 F. 2d 960, 965 (CA6 1987)] . It therefore enjoined petitioners "from using the mark ' Victor's Little Secret' on the basis that it causes dilution of the distinctive quality of the Victoria's Secret mark. " App. to Pet. for Cert. 38a – 39a. The court did not, however, find that any " blurring" had occurred. *Ibid.*

The Court of Appeals for the Sixth Circuit affirmed. 259 F. 3d 464 (2001) . In a case decided shortly after the entry of the District Court's judgment in this case, the Sixth Circuit had adopted the standards for determining dilution under the FDTA that were enunciated by the Second Circuit in *Nabisco, Inc.* v. *PF Brands, Inc.* , 191 F. 3d 208 (1999) . See *Kellogg Co.* v. *Exxon Corp.* , 209 F. 3d 562 (CA6 2000) . In order to apply those standards, it was necessary to discuss two issues that the District Court had not specifically addressed——whether respondents' mark is "distinctive," and whether relief could be granted before dilution has actually occurred. With respect to the first issue, the court rejected the argument that VICTORIA'S SECRET could not be distinctive because "secret" is an ordinary word used by hundreds of lingerie concerns. The court concluded that the entire mark was "arbitrary and fanciful" and therefore deserving of a high level of trademark protection. 259 F. 3d at 470. On the second issue, the court relied on a distinction suggested by this sentence in the House Report: "Confusion leads to immediate injury, while dilution is an infection, which if allowed to spread, will inevitably destroy the advertising value of the mark. " H. R. Rep. No. 104-374, p. 1030 (1995). This statement, coupled with the difficulty of proving actual harm, lent support to the court's ultimate conclusion that the evidence in this case sufficiently established "dilution. " 259 F. 3d, at 475-477. In sum, the Court of Appeals held:

"While no consumer is likely to go to the Moseleys' store expecting to find Victoria's Secret's famed Miracle Bra, consumers who hear the name ' Victor's Little Secret' are likely automatically to think of the more famous store and link it to the Moseleys' adult-toy, gag gift, and lingerie shop. This, then, is a classic instance of dilution by tarnishing (associating the Victoria's Secret name with sex toys and lewd coffee mugs) and by blurring (linking the chain with a single, unauthorized establishment). Given this conclusion, it follows that Victoria's Secret would prevail in a dilution analysis, even without an exhaustive consideration of all ten of the *Nabisco* factors. " *Id.* , at 477.

In reaching that conclusion the Court of Appeals expressly rejected the holding

of the Fourth Circuit in *Ringling Bros. – Barnum & Bailey Combined Shows*, *Inc.*
v. *Utah Div. of Travel Development*, 170 F. 3d 449 (1999). In that case, which involved a claim that Utah's use on its license plates of the phrase "greatest *snow* on
earth" was causing dilution of the "greatest *show* on earth," the court had concluded
"that to establish dilution of a famous mark under the federal Act requires proof that
(1) a defendant has made use of a junior mark sufficiently similar to the famous
mark to evoke in a relevant universe of consumers a mental association of the two that
(2) has caused (3) actual economic harm to the famous mark's economic value by
lessening its former selling power as an advertising agent for its goods or services."
Id., at 461 (emphasis added). Because other Circuits have also expressed differing
views about the "actual harm" issue, we granted certiorari to resolve the
conflict. 535 U. S. 985, 152 L. Ed. 2d 463, 122 S. Ct. 1536 (2002).

II

Traditional trademark infringement law is a part of the broader law of unfair
competition, see *Hanover Star Milling Co.* v. *Metcalf*, 240 U. S. 403, 413, 60
L. Ed. 713, 36 S. Ct. 357, 1916 Dec. Comm'r Pat. 265 (1916), that has its sources
in English common law, and was largely codified in the Trademark Act of 1946
(Lanham Act). See B. Pattishall, D. Hilliard, & J. Welch, Trademarks and Unfair
Competition 2 (4th ed. 2000) ("The United States took the [trademark and unfair
competition] law of England as its own"). That law broadly prohibits uses of trademarks, trade names, and trade dress that are likely to cause confusion about the source
of a product or service. See 15 U. S. C. Ë 1114, 1125 (a)(1)(A). Infringement law
protects consumers from being misled by the use of infringing marks and also protects
producers from unfair practices by an "imitating competitor." *Qualitex Co.*
v. *Jacobson Products Co.*, 514 U. S. 159, 163 – 164, 131 L. Ed. 2d 248, 115
S. Ct. 1300 (1995).

Because respondents did not appeal the District Court's adverse judgement on
counts 1, 2, and 4 of their complaint, we decide the case on the assumption that the

Moseleys' use of the name "Victor's Little Secret" neither confused any consumers or potential consumers, nor was likely to do so. Moreover, the disposition of those counts also makes it appropriate to decide the case on the assumption that there was no significant competition between the adversaries in this case. Neither the absence of any likelihood of confusion nor the absence of competition, however, provides a defense to the statutory dilution claim alleged in count 3 of the complaint.

Unlike traditional infringement law, the prohibitions against trademark dilution are not the product of common – law development, and are not motivated by an interest in protecting consumers. The seminal discussion of dilution is found in Frank Schechter's 1927 law review article concluding "that the preservation of the uniqueness of a trademark should constitute the only rational basis for its protection." Rational Basis of Trademark Protection, 40 Harv. L. Rev. 813, 831. Schechter supported his conclusion by referring to a German case protecting the owner of the well–known trademark "Odol" for mouthwash from use on various noncompeting steel products. That case, and indeed the principal focus of the Schechter article, involved an established arbitrary mark that had been "added to rather than withdrawn from the human vocabulary" and an infringement that made use of the identical mark. *Id.* , at 829.

Some 20 years later Massachusetts enacted the first state statute protecting trademarks from dilution. It provided:

"Likelihood of injury to business reputation or of dilution of the distinctive quality of a trade name or trade–mark shall be a ground for injunctive relief in cases of trade–mark infringement or unfair competition notwithstanding the absence of competition between the parties or of confusion as to the source of goods or services." 1947 Mass. Acts, p. 300, ch. 307.

Notably, that statute, unlike the "Odol" case, prohibited both the likelihood of "injury to business reputation" and "dilution." It thus expressly applied to both "tarnishment" and "blurring." At least 25 States passed similar laws in the decades before the FTDA was enacted in 1995. See Restatement (Third) of Unfair

Competition § 25 , Statutory Note (1995).

III

In 1988 , when Congress adopted amendments to the Lanham Act , it gave consideration to an antidilution provision. During the hearings on the 1988 amendments ,
objections to that provision based on a concern that it might have applied to expres-
sion protected by the First Amendment were voiced and the provision was deleted
from the amendments. H. R. Rep. No. 100 – 1028 (1988). The bill, H. R. 1295 ,
104th Cong. , 1st Sess. , that was introduced in the House in 1995 , and ultimately
enacted as the FTDA , included two exceptions designed to avoid those concerns: a
provision allowing "fair use" of a registered mark in comparative advertising or promotion , and the provision that noncommercial use of a mark shall not constitute dilution. See 15 U. S. C. § 1125 (c) (4) .

On July 19 , 1995 , the Subcommittee on Courts and Intellectual Property of the
House Judiciary Committee held a 1–day hearing on H. R. 1295. No opposition to the
bill was voiced at the hearing and , with one minor amendment that extended protection to unregistered as well as registered marks , the subcommittee endorsed the bill
and it passed the House unanimously. The committee's report stated that the "purpose
of H. R. 1295 is to protect famous trademarks from subsequent uses that blur the distinctiveness of the mark or tarnish or disparage it , even in the absence of a likelihood
of confusion. " H. R. Rep. No. 104–374 , p. 1029 (1995). As examples of dilution ,
it stated that "the use of DUPONT shoes , BUICK aspirin , and KODAK pianos would
be actionable under this legislation. " *Id.* , at 1030. In the Senate an identical bill ,
S. 1513 , 104th Cong. , 1st Sess. , was introduced on December 29 , 1995 , and passed on the same day by voice vote without any hearings. In his explanation of the bill ,
Senator Hatch also stated that it was intended "to protect famous trademarks from subsequent uses that blur the distinctiveness of the mark or tarnish or disparage it ," and
referred to the Dupont Shoes , Buick aspirin , and Kodak piano examples , as well as to
the Schechter law review article. 141 Cong. Rec. 38559–38561 (1995).

IV

The VICTORIA'S SECRET mark is unquestionably valuable and petitioners have not challenged the conclusion that it qualifies as a "famous mark" within the meaning of the statute. Moreover, as we understand their submission, petitioners do not contend that the statutory protection is confined to identical uses of famous marks, or that the statute should be construed more narrowly in a case such as this. Even if the legislative history might lend some support to such a contention, it surely is not compelled by the statutory text.

The District Court's decision in this case rested on the conclusion that the name of petitioners' store "tarnished" the reputation of respondents' mark, and the Court of Appeals relied on both "tarnishment" and "blurring" to support its affirmance. Petitioners have not disputed the relevance of tarnishment, Tr. of Oral Arg. 5–7, presumably because that concept was prominent in litigation brought under state antidilution statutes and because it was mentioned in the legislative history. Whether it is actually embraced by the statutory text, however, is another matter. Indeed, the contrast between the state statutes, which expressly refer to both "injury to business reputation" and to "dilution of the distinctive quality of a trade name or trademark," and the federal statute which refers only to the latter, arguably supports a narrower reading of the FTDA. See Klieger, Trademark Dilution: The Whittling Away of the Rational Basis for Trademark Protection, 58 U. Pitt. L. Rev. 789, 812–813, and n. 132 (1997). The contrast between the state statutes and the federal statute, however, sheds light on the precise question that we must decide. For those state statutes, like several provisions in the federal Lanham Act, repeatedly refer to a "likelihood" of harm, rather than to a completed harm. The relevant text of the FTDA, quoted in full in note 1, *supra*, provides that "the owner of a famous mark" is entitled to injunctive relief against another person's commercial use of a mark or trade name if that use "*causes dilution* of the distinctive quality" of the famous mark. 15 U. S. C. § 1125 (c)(1) (emphasis added). This text unambiguously requires a showing of actual dilution, rather than a likelihood of dilution.

This conclusion is fortified by the definition of the term "dilution" itself. That definition provides:

"The term 'dilution' means the lessening of the capacity of a famous mark to identify and distinguish goods or services, regardless of the presence or absence of ——

(1) competition between the owner of the famous mark and other parties, or

(2) likelihood of confusion, mistake, or deception." § 1127.

The contrast between the initial reference to an actual "lessening of the capacity" of the mark, and the later reference to a "likelihood of confusion, mistake, or deception" in the second caveat confirms the conclusion that actual dilution must be established.

Of course, that does not mean that the consequences of dilution, such as an actual loss of sales or profits, must also be proved. To the extent that language in the Fourth Circuit's opinion in the *Ringling Bros.* case suggests otherwise, see 170 F. 3d at 460-465, we disagree. We do agree, however, with that court's conclusion that, at least where the marks at issue are not identical, the mere fact that consumers mentally associate the junior user's mark with a famous mark is not sufficient to establish actionable dilution. As the facts of that case demonstrate, such mental association will not necessarily reduce the capacity of the famous mark to identify the goods of its owner, the statutory requirement for dilution under the FTDA. For even though Utah drivers may be reminded of the circus when they see a license plate referring to the "greatest *snow* on earth," it by no means follows that they will associate "the greatest show on earth" with skiing or snow sports, or associate it less strongly or exclusively with the circus. "Blurring" is not a necessary consequence of mental association. (Nor, for that matter, is "tarnishing.")

The record in this case establishes that an army officer who saw the advertisement of the opening of a store named "Victor's Secret" did make the mental association with "Victoria's Secret," but it also shows that he did not therefore form any different impression of the store that his wife and daughter had patronized. There is a complete absence of evidence of any lessening of the capacity of the VICTORIA'S SECRET mark to identify and distinguish goods or services sold in Victoria's Secret stores or advertised in its catalogs. The officer was offended by the ad, but it did not change his conception of Victoria's Secret. His offense was directed entirely at petitioners, not at respondents. Moreover, the expert retained by respondents had nothing to say about the impact of petitioners' name on the strength of respondents' mark.

Noting that consumer surveys and other means of demonstrating actual dilution are expensive and often unreliable, respondents and their *amici* argue that evidence of an actual "lessening of the capacity of a famous mark to identify and distinguish goods or services," § 1127, may be difficult to obtain. It may well be, however, that direct evidence of dilution such as consumer surveys will not be necessary if actual dilution can reliably be proven through circumstantial evidence——the obvious case is one where the junior and senior marks are identical. Whatever difficulties of proof may be entailed, they are not an acceptable reason for dispensing with proof of an essential element of a statutory violation. The evidence in the present record is not sufficient to support the summary judgment on the dilution count. The judgment is therefore reversed, and the case is remanded for further proceedings consistent with this opinion.

It is so ordered.

CONCUR BY: KENNEDY

As of this date, few courts have reviewed the statute we are considering, the Federal Trademark Dilution Act, 15 U. S. C. § 1125 (c), and I agree with the Court that the evidentiary showing required by the statute can be clarified on remand. The conclusion that the VICTORIA'S SECRET mark is a famous mark has not been challenged throughout the litigation, *ante*, at 6, 13, and seems not to be in question. The remaining issue is what factors are to be considered to establish dilution.

For this inquiry, considerable attention should be given, in my view, to the word "capacity" in the statutory phrase that defines dilution as "the lessening of the capacity of a famous mark to identify and distinguish goods or services. " 15 U. S. C.

§ 1127. When a competing mark is first adopted, there will be circumstances when the case can turn on the probable consequences its commercial use will have for the famous mark. In this respect, the word "capacity" imports into the dilution inquiry both the present and the potential power of the famous mark to identify and distinguish goods, and in some cases the fact that this power will be diminished could suffice to show dilution. Capacity is defined as "the power or ability to hold, receive, or accommodate." Webster's Third New International Dictionary 330 (1961); see also Webster's New International Dictionary 396 (2d ed. 1949) ("Power of receiving, containing, or absorbing"); 2 Oxford English Dictionary 857 (2d ed. 1989) ("Ability to receive or contain; holding power"); American Heritage Dictionary 275 (4th ed. 2000) ("The ability to receive, hold, or absorb"). If a mark will erode or lessen the power of the famous mark to give customers the assurance of quality and the full satisfaction they have in knowing they have purchased goods bearing the famous mark, the elements of dilution may be established.

Diminishment of the famous mark's capacity can be shown by the probable consequences flowing from use or adoption of the competing mark. This analysis is confirmed by the statutory authorization to obtain injunctive relief. 15 U.S.C. § 1125 (c)(2). The essential role of injunctive relief is to "prevent future wrong, although no right has yet been violated." *Swift & Co.* v. *United States*, 276 U.S. 311, 326, 72 L. Ed. 587, 48 S. Ct. 311 (1928). Equity principles encourage those who are injured to assert their rights promptly. A holder of a famous mark threatened with diminishment of the mark's capacity to serve its purpose should not be forced to wait until the damage is done and the distinctiveness of the mark has been eroded.

In this case, the District Court found that petitioners' trademark had tarnished the VICTORIA'S SECRET mark. App. to Pet. for Cert. 38a – 39a. The Court of Appeals affirmed this conclusion and also found dilution by blurring. 259 F. 3d 464, 477 (CA6 2001). The Court's opinion does not foreclose injunctive relief if respondents on remand present sufficient evidence of either blurring or tarnishment.

With these observations, I join the opinion of the Court.

商标指示性使用的正当性

《花花公子》状告泰丽·薇乐丝案

判例简介

美国著名杂志《花花公子》（PLAYBOY）创办于 20 世纪 50 年代初期，创始人是休·海夫纳（Hugh Hefner）。之后，该杂志一度成为美国社会新文化争议的焦点。好莱坞著名影星和美国高层政要等社会各界名流先后成为《花花公子》的封面人物。"汽车、电脑、花花公子"被美国人称之为"美国现代文化的三驾马车。

20 世纪 80 年代初期，本案被告泰丽·薇乐丝（Terri Welles）在美国可谓大名鼎鼎。薇乐丝的出名完全得益于《花花公子》。1981 年，薇乐丝不但成为《花花公子》的封面女郎，而且被《花花公子》杂志评选为当年的"花花伴娘"（Playmate），一夕成名。

薇乐丝离开《花花公子》后，在网络上建立了自己的网站，以联络崇拜者，并拓展生意。崇拜者可以从薇乐丝的网站购买她的照片。就像其他明星的网站一样，薇乐丝的网站也包含一段个人小传，其中自然少不了她当年做《花花公子》封面女郎，并被选为"花花伴娘"的经历。这段经历是薇乐丝模特生涯的闪光点，当然要大书特书。不想，薇乐丝小传中对"花花伴娘"这段经历的描述却引发一场与《花花公子》公司的商标官司。

《花花公子》公司的创始人海夫纳白手起家，经过几十年的苦心经营，

《花花公子》成为美国著名的杂志，"花花公子"这一品牌已家喻户晓。"花花公子"属于《花花公子》公司（Playboy Enterprises, Inc.）的主打品牌，自然属于著名商标，品牌价值不少于几十亿美金。对于一手培植起来的"花花公子"品牌，海夫纳自然爱惜有加，经常不惜重金聘请律师控告侵权的个人和公司。网络科技，一日千里，网络兴起后，《花花公子》公司及时出手，迅速把自己的王国拓展到这个前所未有的新世界。同时，《花花公子》公司也随时警惕网络上的商标侵权现象，一旦发现便立即追究。

薇乐丝网站上的那段小传自然引起了《花花公子》公司的注意。经过一番调查，《花花公子》公司发现，薇乐丝不但在自己的小传和网页广告条中使用《花花公子》和"花花伴娘"两个《花花公子》公司的注册商标，而且还把《花花公子》和"花花伴娘"作为其网站的搜寻关键词。如此一来，网络使用者在搜索引擎中输入"《花花公子》"或"花花伴娘"时，薇乐丝的网站就会和《花花公子》公司的网站一起出现在搜寻结果当中。

《花花公子》公司认为，《花花公子》曾推出过无数封面女郎、数十位"花花伴娘"和数不清的模特。如果她们全都开设自己的网站，借《花花公子》的品牌宣传自己，或用"《花花公子》"作为自己网站的搜索关键词，这无疑会引走一些寻找《花花公子》的网络使用者。有鉴于此，《花花公子》公司决定以商标侵权和淡化著名商标等为由起诉薇乐丝，以期达到"诉"一做百的效果。

薇乐丝被起诉后，立即在自己的网站上发表声明，称其网站与《花花公子》公司无关，并公布了被《花花公子》公司起诉的消息。本案迅速成为各路媒体追踪报导的热点。这自然与原告和被告的知名度有关。一方是鼎鼎大名的《花花公子》，一方是当年的"花花伴娘"。双方交战法院，自然有一番好戏。

不过，从法律的角度而言，这个案件也反映了网络时代商标侵权案中出现的一些新动向。例如，使用他人的商标作为自己网站的搜索关键词算不算商标侵权？用他人的商标作为自己网站的广告链接算不算商标侵权？在此之前，法律对这些问题的规范语焉不详，法院也未就此做过明确的判决。

从诉讼策略上而言，《花花公子》公司作为本案的原告仍然使用商标诉讼中的传统战术，主要是控告对方商标侵权和淡化著名商标，并提供了从薇乐丝网站获得的大量事实来支持自己的指控。表面上看，薇乐丝似乎难以逃脱商标侵权的指控，因为薇乐丝的确在自己的网站上使用了《花花公子》和"花花伴娘"的名称。

但是薇乐丝使用《花花公子》和"花花伴娘"的名称是否会引起消费者的混淆误认，必须经过事实审判才能确定，如此一来，这个案子就极有可能变成一场持久战和消耗战。打持久战和消耗战只会对财大气粗的《花花公子》公司有利，而绝不利于势单力薄的被告。在这种情况下，被告必须以四两拨千斤的方式，出奇制胜，才能化险为夷。

在商标侵权的防守战中，若使用得当，在一定条件下，以"指示性使用"（nominative use）的抗辩理由可以达到四两拨千斤的效果。即使被告一字不差地使用了原告的商标，如果被告的行为被法院认定为属于"指示性使用"，在一定条件下，就不构成商标侵权。换言之，在符合一定条件后，"指示性使用"即是正当地使用别人的商标。

简而言之，所谓"指示性使用"，就是被告用原告的商标来指称原告的产品，而不是来描述被告自己的产品。例如，薇乐丝在自己的网站上说自己曾做过《花花公子》的封面女郎，并被选为1981年的年度"花花伴娘"。毫无疑问，薇乐丝使用了《花花公子》和"花花伴娘"这两个花花公子公司的商标，但是薇乐丝在使用《花花公子》和"花花伴娘"两个商标的时候，并没有用来描述自己的产品，而是用来指称《花花公子》公司的产品。这就是"指示性使用"。

在与《花花公子》公司的诉讼中，薇乐丝的律师便利用了"指示性使用"作为抗辩理由的战术。不过，认定"指示性使用"只是进行"指示性使用"辩护的第一步。若要反守为攻，化险为夷，还必须让"指示性使用"符合三个要件。第一，如果不使用原告的商标就难以简明扼要地辨识其产品；第二，被告使用原告的商标仅限于辨识原告的产品；第三，被告不能以任何方式明示或暗示原告支持或授权使用其商标。只有在符合这三个要件的情况下，"指示性使用"才能实现商标侵权案的完全抗辩。

在《花花公子》告薇乐丝案中，被告薇乐丝的律师便成功地说服法院，薇乐丝对《花花公子》和"花花伴娘"的"指示性使用"符合上述三个要件。就第一个要件而言，除了使用《花花公子》和"花花伴娘"两个商标，薇乐丝没有其他方式可以准确方便地说清她在《花花公子》的工作以及从《花花公子》获得的荣誉。

如果禁止薇乐丝在小传中使用《花花公子》和"花花伴娘"的名称，她就不得不说自己曾做过"海夫纳先生主办的杂志的封面女郎并被该杂志选为1981年最标准的裸体女性"。这毫无必要地增加了公众识别薇乐丝身份的难度。毕竟，大部分知道《花花公子》杂志的人不一定知道海夫纳是何许人也。

除此之外，从现实的角度考虑，如果《花花公子》可以禁止薇乐丝在小传中说自己曾做过《花花公子》的"花花伴娘"，那么芝加哥公牛队就有理由禁止乔丹说自己曾是芝加哥公牛队的主力，国际奥委会就有理由禁止刘易斯说自己是奥运会冠军了。无数人就要被迫拐弯抹角地来描述自己过去的经历和成就，这给人们的交流造成不必要的障碍。法院当然也不希望这种情况发生。

其次，就第二个要件来说，薇乐丝使用《花花公子》的商标只是为了说明自己过去曾经做过《花花公子》的封面女郎并被选为"花花伴娘"。而《花花公子》和"花花伴娘"均是《花花公子》公司的产品。薇乐丝使用《花花公子》的商标只是局限于描述《花花公子》公司的这两个产品，她并没有使用《花花公子》的商标图案或其他文字标志。

最后，薇乐丝也没有以任何方式表示或暗示她的网站得到了《花花公子》公司的赞助或授权。相反，在官司开始后，薇乐丝在自己的网站上及时发表声明，澄清其网站与《花花公子》公司之间不存在任何关系，并将被《花花公子》公司起诉的消息公之于众。

就此而言，薇乐丝对《花花公子》和"花花伴娘"商标的"指示性使用"完全符合法律要求的三个条件，属于正当使用，不构成商标侵权。

法院进一步将以上分析运用到薇乐丝网站使用《花花公子》和"花花伴娘"作为搜索关键词的纠纷上。搜索引擎为网络使用者寻找网上资源提供方便，而网络使用者搜索某一项内容必须输入确切的关键词。薇乐丝做过《花花公子》的封面女郎和1981年度的"花花伴娘"，网络使用者若要在网络上寻找有关薇乐丝的内容自然会输入这两个关键词。

如果薇乐丝不能使用《花花公子》或"花花伴娘"这两个关键词,只会为网络使用者搜索有关内容制造障碍。这种结果不利于信息流通。当然商标法不能保护这种妨碍信息流通的做法。基于这种考虑,法院判定,薇乐丝使用《花花公子》和"花花伴娘"两个名称作为自己网站的搜索关键词,并没有侵犯《花花公子》公司的商标权。

本案启示与解析

《花花公子》状告泰丽·薇乐丝案是法院运用审理商标侵权案件的传统方法成功解决网络商标侵权争议的典型案例。虽然网络时代的商标侵权诉讼出现了许多新问题、新现象,但法院认定侵权的标准却没有发生实质性的改变。同时,本案也显示,尽管原告和被告的侵权争议发生在网络这种新媒体上,在诉讼中出现了一些现有法律尚未涉及的问题,但双方基本上还是运用传统商标战的攻防策略。

从诉讼策略上而言,《花花公子》公司作为本案的原告仍然使用商标战的传统战术,主要控告对方商标侵权和淡化著名商标,并提供了从薇乐丝网站获得的大量事实来支持自己的指控。表面上看,薇乐丝似乎难以逃脱商标侵权的指控,因为薇乐丝的确在自己的网站上使用了《花花公子》和"花花伴娘"的名称。尽管薇乐丝使用《花花公子》和"花花伴娘"的名称是否会引起消费者的混淆误认,必须经过事实审判才能确定,但那样一来,这个案子就极有可能旷日持久。打持久战和消耗战只会对财大气粗的《花花公子》公司有利,而绝不利于势单力薄的被告。在这种情况下,被告必须出奇制胜方能化险为夷。

在商标侵权的防守战中,如若使用得当,在一定条件下,"正当使用"(或称合理使用)的辩护策略就能起到这种四两拨千斤的效果。《花花公子》状告薇乐丝案充分体现了美国商标法中"正当使用"的原则。"正当使用"是商标侵权的一种例外情况。具体讲,在一般情况下,如果被告在未经原告同意的情况下使用了原告的商标，便构成商标侵权。但是，在某些特定情况下，被告未经原告同意即使用了原告的商标也不构成商标侵权。从法律的角度而言，这些特定情况就属于通用法律下的例外。在美国法律中，几乎所有的通用法律都存在例外。"正当使用"就是商标侵权的一种例外。而"指示性使用"则属于"正当使用"的一种。

在本案中，被告薇乐丝就利用了"指示性使用"的例外为自己使用《花花公子》商标的行为进行了成功辩护。对于"正当使用"的内容和要求，案例中已经有较为详尽的描述，在此不再赘言。需要强调的是，"指示性使用"作为商标侵权的一种例外情况，在法律上有着严格的标准。其基本原则是，被告使用原告的商标必须是描述原告的产品，如果被告使用原告的商标描述自己的产品，则无法援用"指示性使用"的例外原则为自己辩护。

引用判决

Playboy Enter Prises Inc. v. Welles

MEMORANDUM

Terri Welles cross-appeals the district court's grant of summary judgment as to her counterclaims against Playboy Enterprises International (PEI) for defamation, intentional infliction of emotional distress, unfair competition, and interference with prospective economic advantage. Michael Mihalko, Stephen Huntington, and Welles appeal the district court's denial of their requests for attorney's fees. We have jurisdiction pursuant to 28 U. S. C. § 1291, and we affirm.

Because the facts are known to the parties, we do not recite them here. We review the district court's grant of summary judgment de novo. Viewing the evidence in the light most favorable to the nonmoving party, we must determine whether there are any genuine issues of material fact and whether the district court correctly applied the relevant substantive law. We may affirm on any ground supported by the record.

As to Welles' claims of defamation, we affirm the district court's grant of summary judgment on the ground that Welles is a limited purpose public figure. The trademark dispute involved in this litigation——the controversy——is a public one. Welles voluntarily placed herself in the center of the public controversy by making various media appearances, by commenting on the controversy in the media and on her website, and by listing articles on her website regarding the metatag issue. Because Welles is a public figure, albeit for the limited purpose of this controversy, the district court correctly required that she demonstrate that a genuine issue of material fact exists regarding PEI's knowledge of the falsity of its statements or its reckless disregard for the truth, and properly held that she did not do so. Accordingly, we affirm.

We also affirm the district court's grant of summary judgment as to Welles' claim for intentional infliction of emotional distress. Although some of PEI's, and particularly Hefner's, conduct towards Welles was reprehensible, it did not rise to the level of extreme and outrageous conduct required for a claim of intentional infliction of emotional distress.

Welles points to nothing in support of her claim for unfair competition, so we affirm the district court's grant of summary judgment on that claim as well. Her claim for intentional interference with prospective economic advantage similarly fails. Wellesrelies on her claims for defamation or unfair competition to show the requisite wrongfulness of the conduct in question. Because those claims are no longer viable, neither is her intentional interference claim.

Finally, we affirm the district court's decision to deny attorney's fees. "Imposition of attorneys' fees is warranted if a plaintiff's case is groundless, unreasonable, vexatious, or pursued in bad faith." The district court did not abuse its discretion when it concluded that fees in this case were unwarranted.

AFFIRMED.

在地理上具有误导性的描述性名称不受保护

日本电讯公司状告美洲日本电讯公司案

判例简介

日本有一位名不见经传的商人，名叫长谷川，以自己的名字在日本注册了"长谷川有限公司"。长谷川在日本多年苦心经营，公司仍然没有多大起色。20 世纪 80 年代，长谷川旅居美国，在日本人聚居的洛杉矶为自己的公司开设了一家子公司，并注册了"日本电讯公司"（Japan Telecom, Inc.）作为这家子公司的名称。

虽然"日本电讯公司"的名称听起来硕大无比，但其业务范围和业务量均十分有限，主要包括销售、安装电话和电脑网络设备。其客户大都是居住在南加利福尼亚州洛杉矶一带的日本人。长谷川的日本电讯公司如其在日本的母公司一样，一直默默无闻地经营了十几年。

在日本有一家大公司，名叫"日本电讯有限公司"（Japan Telecom Company, Ltd.），是日本的第三大电讯公司。20 世纪 90 年代末期，日本电讯有限公司把业务扩展到了美国，并在美国注册成立了一家子公司，名为"美洲日本电讯公司"（Japan Telecom America, Inc）。美洲日本电讯公司主要向客户提供长途电话和数据传输服务。美洲日本电讯公司一成立就立刻引起了长谷川的日本电讯公司的关注。本来两家"日本电讯"公司经营的业务没有重叠，可以井水不犯河水，相安无事。不过，长谷川还是决定先下手为强，遂以商标侵权和不公平竞争为由将美洲日本电讯公司告上法院。

美洲日本电讯公司申请注册的商标

　　一般商标侵权案件大多是大公司告小公司。而这起商标侵权案却是小公司告大公司。日本电讯公司是一个十分响亮的名字，长谷川自然想保住这个商标。而美洲日本电讯公司虽然晚来一步，但也不希望失去"日本电讯"这个响亮的名称。两家"日本电讯"就这样拉开了角逐的序幕。

　　按照美国商标法，面对商标侵权的指控，被告可以提出多种抗辩。例如，被告可以正面反驳原告的指控，出示证据证明有争议的商标和原告的商标之间没有任何相似之处，不至于引起消费者的混淆误认。或者，被告可以采取反守为攻、以退为进的策略，承认自己使用了原告的商标，但是证明自己属于指示性使用，并不构成商标侵权。

　　除此之外，被告还可以采取釜底抽薪之计，证明原告的商标已经变成一个通用名称，不再受到商标法的保护。在日本电讯公司告美洲日本电讯公司案中，上面这些辩护策略似乎都不适用。被告必须另辟蹊径，以谋取制胜之道。

　　美洲日本电讯公司在这起商标侵权案中采取了两种抗辩策略。一是指责原告日本电讯公司的"手不干净"，其"日本电讯"的商标不应受到法律保护。二是辩称"日本电讯"是一个描述性名称，在长谷川的日本电讯公司没有赋予这个名称第二层意义之前，不应受到美国商标法的保护。

　　就第一个抗辩理由而言，也就是被告所称原告"手不干净"的辩护，又称"不洁之手"（unclean hands），系英美法中的理论，亦即在诉讼中权利者必须主张本身的行为无瑕疵，如果权利人本身已有违法行为，则无权主张他人行为的违法性，衡平法院对于以违法行为所获取之不公平竞争优势的权利，不给予支持或不予以执行。按照美国商标法，原告若要向法院寻求保护自己的商标，前提是原告的"手必须干净"。换言之，原告在获得自己的商标时不能有任何作假、误导或欺骗消费者的行为。要成功利用"手不干净"的策略进行抗辩，关键在于证明原告在获得自己的商标时曾有不良意图。

在本案中，如果美洲日本电讯公司能证明日本电讯公司当年在获取"日本电讯"这个商标时有作假、误导或欺骗消费者的不良图谋，那么法院就会认定日本电讯公司的"手不干净"，就不会保护"日本电讯"这个商标。不过，被告要证明原告有"不良图谋"，需要大量证据，不能只凭猜测，更不能空口无凭。

美洲日本电讯公司指称，"日本电讯"本身就属于一个地理上具有误导性的描述性名称。因为日本以生产高品质的电讯产品著称于世，所以"日本电讯"这个名称必然误导消费者联想到日本的电讯产品，而日本电讯公司并不只出售日本的电讯产品。不过，美洲日本电讯公司并没有出示有力的证据支持这种推断。法院显然不愿意在缺少证据的情况下认定"日本电讯"是一个"地理上具有误导性的描述性名称"。

按照法院的分析，要认定一个商标为"地理上具有误导性的描述性名称"，必须同时符合两个要件：一是商标的主要特征必须是一个著名产地；二是消费者有理由相信商标所代表的产品出自这个著名产地，而事实上两者并没有关系。不过，用国家作为商标或公司名称并不必然导致一个商标或名称成为"地理上具有误导性的描述性名称"，因为国家名称除了具有地理意义外，还有文化和社群的意义。

在美国的日本人社区中，有许多公司冠以"日本"的名称，例如"日本餐饮公司""日本园艺公司""日本茶艺公司"等。消费者不太可能误以为这些公司的产品都出自日本。在这种情况下，"日本"这个名称所具有的文化意义和社群意义远远超过其地理意义。基于以上分析，法院拒绝认定日本电讯公司在获取"日本电讯"这个商标时具有作假、误导或欺骗消费者的不良图谋。

既然"手不干净"的抗辩策略没有成功，美洲日本电讯公司便全力集中在第二个抗辩理由，即否认"日本电讯"是一个受法律保护的商标或商业名称。美国商标法按照受保护的程度不同把各种商标分为四大类：第一类是通用名称，完全不受保护，如"Computer"之于电脑产品。第二类是描述性名称，例如"Windows"之于"个人电脑图形界面操作系统"。描述性名称必须在消费者中获得第二层意义后，才受到法律保护。第三类是暗示性名称，例如"Ice"之于薄荷糖。暗示性名称不需要获得第二层意义即受到法律保护。第四类是任意使用或稀奇古怪的名称，比如"Apple"之于电脑，"Kodak"之于胶卷等，这种商标完全受法律保护。

在商标侵权的诉讼战中，如果原告的商标是一个描述性名称，被告经常采取的策略便是攻击原告的商标没有在消费者中获得第二层意义。在本案中，美洲日本电讯公司便采取这种策略，指称"日本电讯"是一个描述性名称，而日本电讯公司并没有赋予这个名称第二层意义，消费者并没有把"日本电讯"与日本电讯公司的产品或服务联系起来。

面对美洲日本电讯公司的反攻，日本电讯公司称"日本电讯"这个名称不是描述性的，而是暗示性的，所以不需要在消费者中获得第二层意义就可得到法律保护。美国法院判断一个商标具有描述性还是暗示性的标准，在于人们是否需要想像力才能把一个商标和其所代表的产品或服务联系在一起。按照这一标准，法院认定"日本电讯"是一个描述性名称，而不是一个暗示性名称。其原因在于，"日本电讯"这个名称一目了然，消费者不需要运用任何想象力就可以把这个名称与其所代表的产品联系起来。

日本电讯公司先失一局，被迫证明"日本电讯"的名称已经在消费者中获得了第二层意义。在确定一个描述性名称或商标是否已经获得第二层意义时，法院要综合考虑几项因素，例如，消费者是否把这个商标与产品的生产商或销售商联系起来，商标所有者是否投入大量广告费用宣传这一商标，是否已经多年使用这个商标生产、销售产品或提供服务，以及商标所有人是否独家使用这一商标等。

日本电讯公司并没有出具强有力的证据证明消费者已经把"日本电讯"与日本电讯公司销售的产品和提供的服务联系起来，也没有证据证明日本电讯公司已经投入大量广告费用宣传"日本电讯"这个商业名称。此外，虽然日本电讯公司已经使用"日本电讯"这一名称长达十余年，但是"日本电讯"的名称也一直被另一家名为"日本电讯有限公司"的公司所使用。基于以上分析，法院认定"日本电讯"这个描述性名称，并没有在消费者中获得第二层意义，所以不应受商标法的保护。

美洲日本电讯公司成功地运用攻击原告商标不受法律保护的策略，反守为攻，化被动为主动，一举摆脱了日本电讯公司的指控。虽然 美洲日本电讯公司进入美国市场的时间比日本电讯公司晚十几年，但却可以合法地在美国市场上使用"日本电讯"的名称和商标。

本案启示与解析

按照商标显著性的强弱，可以将商标分为臆造商标、任意商标、暗示商标和描述性商标。所谓描述性商标（Descriptive Mark），就是商标的内容或含义表述了该商标使用的商品或者该商品的成分、性质、用途、功能、特点、质量、重量、数量或其他的特点。描述性商标可以是词汇，也可以是图形或其他标记。实践中，绝大多数描述性商标由描述性词汇组成。判断某个标识是否属于描述性商标，应当根据相关商品潜在购买者对该标识的理解进行判断，描述性并不意味着某个标识是对所附着商品全方位的描述，只要对产品的用途、大小、颜色、成分、产地、面向的用户等方面作出了明确说明，消费者不用想象力就可以明白其含义，该标识就构成描述性的。大多数企业经营者或者销售人员喜欢使用描述性商标，因为这种商标大大接近于他们宣传与推销该产品的目标。

严格说来，描述性商标由于缺乏任何想象，人们通常不会将其视为商标。与臆造商标、任意商标乃至暗示商标相比，描述性商标的保护程度最低、保护范围最窄。但叙述词经过长期使用，消费者如果实际将其与特定的出处联系在一起，则说明该词客观上起到了区别作用，因此同样可以申请注册受到法律保护。

多数国家的商标法虽然对描述性商标的使用和保护均进行了一定的限制，允许他人合理使用描述性商标的要素，但对合理使用的范围都严格予以控制，认定合理使用的标准也都比较严格。《美国兰哈姆法》第 33 条（b）第（2）项规定，将并非作为商标，而是有关当事人自己商业上的个人名称的使用，或对与该当事人的产地有合法利益关系的任何人的个人名称的使用，或对该当事人的商品或服务，或地理产地有叙述性的名词或图形使用作为合理使用；当然这种使用必须是只用于叙述该当事人的商品或服务的正当的诚实的使用。在我国，描述性的商标不能注册，不能受到法律的保护。当然，如果一个描述性不是很强的商标经过广泛的宣传使用具有了"第二层意义"，也是可以被接受注册的。但要做到这一点，通常需要经过一个比较艰难而又长久的过程，而且具有一定的风险。我国商标法虽然也确立了商标的合理使用制度，但并没有明确合理使用的具体判断标准，以致在司法实践中对合理使用的认定分歧较大。

本案中，日本电讯公司是一个十分响亮的名称，原告长谷川自然知道这个名称所隐含的意义，企图经由诉讼保住这个名称的独家使用权。而美洲日本电讯公司虽然比长谷川晚进入美国市场，但是也不希望失去"日本电讯"的商标权。

不过，日本电讯公司起诉美洲日本电讯公司的时机并不成熟，显然出手过早，在诉讼策略上也多有失误。被告美洲日本电讯公司抓住原告的几点失误，反守为攻，获得了"日本电讯"的商标权。从策略上讲，美洲日本电讯公司的两个辩护均属反守为攻之举。首先美洲日本电讯公司指责原告"手不干净"，运用一个"在地理上具有误导性的描述性名称"（geographically deceptively mis-descriptive name）。

按照美国商标法和法院的相关判例，"在地理上具有误导性的描述性名称"不同于"描述性的地理名称"（geographically descriptive name）。"在地理上具有误导性的描述性名称"不受商标法的保护。比如说，一家美国企业用"SWISS（瑞士）"作为商标销售在美国制造的手表，这就属于使用"在地理上具有误导性的描述性名称"。原因在于，瑞士以制造质量上乘的手表著称于世，如果一家企业用"瑞士"作为商标销售不在瑞士制造的手表，显然会误导消费者。所以，"在地理上具有误导性的描述性商标"不受商标法保护。

不过，在本案中，美洲日本电讯公司并没有说服法院认定长谷川的"日本电讯"是一个"在地理上具有误导性的描述性名称"。显然，美洲日本电讯公司在收集证据方面出现疏漏。如果美洲日本电讯公司能够提供消费者调查结果或聘请专家作证，证明日本的确以制造品质优良的电讯产品著称于世，法院可能会在这个问题上作出不同的裁决。

与"在地理上具有误导性的描述性名称"不同的是单纯的"描述性地理名称"。这种单纯的"描述性地理名称"在地理上不具有误导性，它在消费者中获得了次级意义后就会得到商标法保护。比如说，用"HAWAII（夏威夷）"作为商标销售在美国制造的手表就属于"描述性地理名称"，而不属于"在地理上具有误导性的描述性名称"。原因在于，夏威夷并不以制造高品质的手表著称，消费者不会因为手表上标注"夏威夷"的商标而被误导。

相较于本案，日本电讯公司则属于一个"描述性地理名称"。它必须在获得第二层意义后方可受到商标法的保护。不过，尽管长谷川已经在美国使用日本电讯公司的名称十几年，却没有投入足够的资金来打造这个商标，消费者并没有将日本电讯公司与长谷川公司的产品或服务联系起来。所以，日本电讯公司并没有在美国的消费者中获得次级意义。在这种情况下，长谷川被迫申辩，日本电讯公司是一个"暗示性名称"，而不是一个"描述性地理名称"。按照美国商标法，"暗示性名称"不需要第二层意义即可受到商标法保护。但是，长谷川的此项辩解十分牵强，被法庭驳回，无法避免败诉的结局。

本案的判决结果表明，仅仅使用一个"描述性商标"并不意味着就拥有了独家使用这个商标的权利。描述性商标的所有人必须投入足够的资金来打造这个商标，使之在消费者中获得次级意义。否则，便有可能被别人夺爱。

引用判决

JAPAN TELECOM, INC., v. JAPAN TELECOM AMERICA INC.

OPINION BY Alex Kozinski

Japan Telecom, Inc. ("Japan Telecom") sells and installs telephone and computernetworking equipment in the Los Angeles area. Japan Telecom is a California corporation, and a subsidiary of Hasegawa Company, Ltd. ▼, a small Japanese corporation. After Japan Telecom had been in business for fourteen years, a new kid on the block showed up: Japan Telecom America, Inc. ("Japan Telecom America"). Japan Telecom America is the United States subsidiary of Japan Telecom Company, Ltd. ▾, the third-largest telecommunications company in Japan. While Japan Telecom's business mostly involves the installation of telephone and computer networks, Japan Telecom America sells telecommunications transmission services, including both long-distance telephone and data.

Japan Telecom sued Japan Telecom America in federal court, alleging that Japan Telecom America's use of the "Japan Telecom" name constituted trademark infringement and unfair competition. Later, Japan Telecom sued Japan Telecom America in California state court for unfair competition and trade name infringement on the same theory. Japan Telecom America removed the state suit to federal court, and the district court consolidated the two actions. Japan Telecom's consolidated complaint alleges trade name infringement and unfair competition under the Lanham Act, unfair competition under California law, and "trade name violation under state law".

The district court granted Japan Telecom America's motion for summary judgment on all claims, holding that Japan Telecom had unclean hands. Japan Telecom appeals.

Unclean Hands

"Unclean hands is a defense to a Lanham Act infringement suit." *Fuddruckers, Inc.* v. *Doc's B. R. Others, Inc.*, 826 F. 2d 837, 847 (9th Cir. 1987). Trademark law's unclean hands defense springs from the rationale that "it is essential that the plaintiff should not in his trade mark, or in his advertisements and business, be himself guilty of any false or misleading representation." *Worden* v. *Cal. Fig Syrup Co.*, 187 U. S. 516, 528, 47 L. Ed. 282, 23 S. Ct. 161 (1903). To make out an unclean hands defense, a trademark defendant "must demonstrate that the plaintiff's conduct is inequitable and that the conduct relates to the subject matter of its claims." *Fuddruckers*, 826 F. 2d at 847.

To show that a trademark plaintiff's conduct is inequitable, defendant must show that plaintiff used the trademark to deceive consumers, see *Dollar Sys. , Inc.* v. *Avcar Leasing Sys. , Inc.* , 890 F. 2d 165, 173 (9th Cir. 1989) ("Bad intent is the essence of the defense of unclean hands. ") (citing *Wells Fargo & Co.* v. *Stagecoach Props. , Inc.* , 685 F. 2d 302, 308 (9th Cir. 1982)); *Republic Molding Corp.* v. *B. W. Photo Utils.* , 319 F. 2d 347, 350 (9th Cir. 1963).

The district court held that Japan Telecom had unclean hands solely because "the name by which plaintiff calls itself is deceptive. " Reasoning that the trade name "Japan Telecom, Inc. " suggests a company of Japanese origin, the district court held that Japan Telecom's trade name is "primarily geographically deceptively misdescriptive. " Further, because "Japan is noted for its electronics and telecommunications products," Japan Telecom's name "undoubtedly leads consumers to think of the country. " The district found that this "deception is especially acute" because "plaintiff specifically targets the Japanese American community. " Members of that community, the district court reasoned, are particularly susceptible to false claims of Japanese origin because they "may be interested in the country of origin" more than the rest of the purchasing public. The district court did not find that any consumers had actually been deceived.

The district court erred in finding that Japan Telecom's trade name is primarily geographically deceptively misdescriptive. "Whether a mark is primarily geographically deceptively misdescriptive is a question of fact. " *In re Save Venice New York, Inc.* , 259 F. 3d 1346, 1351 (Fed. Cir. 2001). It may only be resolved on summary judgment if the evidence presented by both sides would permit the trier of fact to come to only one conclusion.

A mark is primarily geographically deceptively misdescriptive if " (1) the mark's primary significance is a generally known geographic location; and (2) consumers would reasonably believe the [marked] goods are connected with the geographic location in the mark, when in fact they are not. " *In re Save Venice New York, Inc.* , 259 F. 3d at 1352.

The parties dispute whether the name "Japan Telecom, Inc." refers to a geographic location. While it is tempting to conclude that "Japan" means "Japan, the country," we cannot examine a trademark or trade name's individual words in isolation. See *Filipino Yellow Pages, Inc.* v. *Asian Journal Publ'ns, Inc.*, 198 F. 3d 1143, 1147-51 (9th Cir. 1999). Using the name of a country in a trade name does not automatically make the trade name geographically descriptive; instead, we must look to whether consumers would reasonably believe that the term is being used geographically. See *In re Save Venice New York, Inc.*, 259 F. 3d at 1352.

The district court erred by ignoring Japan Telecom's evidence that consumers might understand the word "Japan" in its name as referring to a specific ethnic community, rather than the country. Japan Telecom argues that customers seeing its advertising are familiar with a convention of using the word "Japan" in a business' name to indicate that the business caters to Japanese - speaking customers. Japan Telecom offered an affidavit from Chieko Mori, the president of a company that publishes a telephone directory of businesses catering to the "local Japanese community in California." Mori stated that over eighty companies with the word "Japan" in their name——including "Japan Pilot Club," "Japan Landscaping, Inc.," and "Japan Printing Service" ——advertise in Mori's directory, but only a few of those are affiliated with companies in Japan.

Japan Telecom America offered evidence that there is a pattern in the telecommunications industry of using the word "Telecom" after a country's name to signify geographic origin——such as "Deutsche Telecom," "China Telecom," and "British Telecom." Without any evidence of widespread knowledge of this pattern of naming countries, this does not establish that consumers would reasonably believe that Japan Telecom was connected with Japan. At best, it only raises an inference that Japan Telecom's trademark may have confused customers. On summary judgment, the district court must draw all inferences in the non-movant's favor. *Clicks Billiards Inc.* v. *Sixshooters Inc.*, 251 F. 3d 1252, 1257 (9th Cir. 2001). Japan Telecom presented contrary evidence on this point, and therefore created a triable issue of fact.

Japan Telecom America did not meet its burden of showing that customers "would reasonably believe [Japan Telecom's services] are connected with" Japan for yet another reason. *In re Save Venice New York, Inc.*, 259 F. 3d at 1352. Japan Telecom's business is primarily service–related: It installs and maintains telephone and computer networking equipment. Japan Telecom also acts as a sales agent for MCI, a well–known American long distance company. Incident to its services, Japan Telecom sells goods (like telephones and network routers), but there is no evidence that Japan Telecom marks those goods with "Japan Telecom." When services are performed on a customer's site, the customer is unlikely to associate the service with any geographic region other than where the services are performed. Because Japan Telecom can only perform its services in person and on customer premises, it is hard to see how a reasonable customer could conclude that the technician installing his new phone wiring just came off a jet from Tokyo, equipped with the very latest in Japanese wiring know–how.

The district court found that Japan Telecom's use of the word "Japan" played on a popular notion that Japan excels in telecommunications and electronics. But the court did not cite to any evidence that customers have such a favorable impression of Japan's telecommunications industry. Even if there were such evidence, it would hardly follow that the use of the name "Japan Telecom" misled consumers into inferring that Japan Telecom was affiliated with Japan. Our examination of the record reveals at best a disputed issue of fact on this question. We also find no evidence that the consumers Japan Telecom targets would be more likely to hold these views.

Trademark Infringement

To prevail on its infringement claim, Japan Telecom must have a protectable trade name. Trademark law groups terms into four categories: "(1) generic, (2) descriptive, (3) suggestive, and (4) arbitrary or fanciful." *Filipino Yellow Pages,* 198 F. 3d at 1146 (internal quotation marks omitted). Generic terms do not "relate exclusively to the trademark owner's product" because they are common words or phrases that "describe a class of goods rather than an individual product. " *New Kids on the Block* v. *New Am. Publ'g*, *Inc.*, 971 F. 2d 302, 306 (9th Cir. 1992) . Descriptive terms, however, "describe [ ] a person, a place or an attribute of a product. " *Id*. They suffer from the same problem as generic terms: Because they tend to consist of common words that might be the only way to describe a category of goods, we do not grant exclusive property rights in them. *Id*. Nonetheless, a descriptive term can become protectable "provided that it has acquired 'secondary meaning' in the minds of consumers, i. e. , it has become distinctive of the trademark applicant's goods in commerce. " *Filipino Yellow Pages*, 198 F. 3d at 1147 (internal quotation marks o-mitted). Terms that are suggestive, or "arbitrary and fanciful," are protectable with-out a showing of secondary meaning.

Japan Telecom America argues that "Japan Telecom" is descriptive, while Japan Telecom argues that it is suggestive. In deciding who's right, we look at "the i-maginativeness involved in the suggestion, that is, how immediate and direct is the thought process from the mark to the particular product. If the mental leap between the word and the product's attribute is not almost instantaneous, this strongly indicates suggestiveness, not direct descriptiveness. " *Self – Realization Fellowship Church* v. *Ananda Church of Self-Realization*, 59 F. 3d 902, 911 (9th Cir. 1995) (internal quotation marks and citation omitted).

"Japan Telecom" as used by Japan Telecom is descriptive, not suggestive. Japan Telecom's trade name leaves very little to the imagination. Japan Telecom is in the telecommunications business, and its name says so. Consumers who are familiar with the convention of using "Japan" to refer to a business that caters to the Japanese community will immediately understand Japan Telecom's niche. Consumers who don't will still not need to make any mental leap between Japan Telecom's name and what it does.

Because Japan Telecom's trade name is descriptive, it is not protectable unless Japan Telecom shows that the name has acquired secondary meaning. This requires showing that there is "a mental recognition in buyers' and potential buyers' minds that products connected with the [mark] are associated with the same source. " *Self -Realization Fellowship Church*, 59 F. 3d at 911 [quoting*Levi Strauss & Co. v. Blue Bell, Inc.* , 632 F. 2d 817, 820 (9th Cir. 1980)] . Secondary meaning is a question of fact, *see Clicks Billiards*, 251 F. 3d at 1262, so to survive summary judgment Japan Telecom was required to come forward with enough evidence of secondary meaning to establish a genuine dispute of fact. *See* Fed. R. Civ. P. 56 (e) .

In evaluating the sufficiency of evidence of secondary meaning, we look to a number of factors, including " (1) whether actual purchasers of the product bearing the claimed trademark associate the trademark with the producer, (2) the degree and manner of advertising under the claimed trademark, (3) the length and manner of use of the claimed trademark, and (4) whether use of the claimed trademark has been exclusive. " *Comm. for Idaho's High Desert, Inc.* v. *Yost*, 92 F. 3d 814, 822 (9th Cir. 1996) (internal quotation marks omitted). When descriptive marks are especially "weak," we require a "strong showing of strong secondary meaning. " *Filipino Yellow Pages*, 198 F. 3d at 1151.

Here, Japan Telecom hopes to establish secondary meaning through evidence of actual confusion. Japan Telecom's president, Yoshio Hasegawa, stated in a declaration that Japan Telecom received several telephone calls and "many" letters apparently intended for Japan Telecom America. Two of these letters were attached to Hasegawa's declaration: an office supply company invoice, and a mailing from a Japanese business newspaper addressed to "Yuko Yogi, President, Japan Telecom, Incorporated. " (Japan Telecom America says that it has never employed anyonenamed "Yuko Yogi," as president or otherwise.) For its part, Japan Telecom America claims that it has not received any letters or telephone calls intended for Japan Telecom.

This is not enough evidence of actual confusion to establish secondary meaning. We agree with the district court that Hasegawa's affidavit lacks foundation for his statement that Japan Telecom received "many" letters and "several" calls, because

Hasegawa does not state that he personally opens Japan Telecom's mail and answers its phone. The two letters attached to Hasegawa's affidavit are admissible, but they aren't enough. While we have held that seventy-six letters and invoices intended for defendant but sent to plaintiff can be evidence of secondary meaning, see *Am. Scientific Chem., Inc. v. Am. Hosp. Supply Corp.*, 690 F. 2d 791, 793 (9th Cir. 1982), evidence of only two incorrectly addressed letters——one of them from a supplier rather than a buyer and the other possibly not even intended for Japan Telecom America——is not enough to establish that buyers have come to associate the term "Japan Telecom" with a single company. Even if both mailings were intended for Japan Telecom America, such a low volume of misdirected mailings could have been the result of clerical errors rather than a belief that "Japan Telecom" only refers to Japan Telecom.

Japan Telecom attempts to prove actual confusion in another way. It presents six declarations from Japanese-American business owners in Southern California, each containing a more or less identical paragraph: "I have been seeing advertisement of 'Japan Telecom America' recently. First, I was confused with Mr. Hasegawa's company, but soon I figured out that it was a different company. According to my information and belief, however, many people are still confused by the similar names of two companies. [sic] " One of these declarants elaborates by noting that he "was really confused" when, after it took over his former long distance provider, Japan Telecom America began sending him bills for long distance service bearing the words "Japan Telecom." Later he realized that "it was not Mr. Hasegawa's Japan Telecom, Inc. " that was sending him the bills. All of the declarations also contain some version of this paragraph: "I personally know that Japan Telecom, Inc. has been doing telecommunication business in Los Angeles area for many years. When I hear or read the name of Japan Telecom, I could immediately tell that it was the company of Mr. Hasegawa in Los Angeles. "

This is not enough to establish a "mental recognition in buyers' and potential buyers' minds" between Japan Telecom's trade name and a single source. *Self-Realization Fellowship Church*, 59 F. 3d at 911. These declarations all come from business owners who "personally" knew that Japan Telecom had been in business for years. At least one declarant was a former customer. All of the declarants identify the mark " Japan Telecom " not only with plaintiff, but also with its president, "Mr. Hasegawa," whom they know by name. Although all the declarants claim to have the sort of mental recognition that's characteristic of secondary meaning, Japan Telecom has not come forward with evidence that they formed this recognition for any reason other than their personal relationships with Japan Telecom or its president. Consequently, their declarations are not persuasive evidence that a significant number of consumers have formed a similar mental association. 1 Had they formed their mental association with Japan Telecom because of some stimulus that was just as likely to affect members of the buying public as it was likely to affect them (such as advertising), their declarations would have been more persuasive. Every small business with a descriptive name can point to at least a few former customers who remember its name, and every small business owner can point to some acquaintances familiar with what he does for a living. None of that means that the relevant buying public makes the same associations.

Turning to Japan Telecom's other evidence, Japan Telecom notes that it has been using its name since 1984 and has advertised in the annual Japanese Telephone Directory & Guide eleven times. In examining whether a plaintiff's advertising is enough to establish secondary meaning, we look at the advertising's "amount, nature and geographical scope" with an eye towards how likely the advertising is to expose a large number of the relevant consuming public to the use of the symbol as a trademark or trade name. *Am. Scientific Chem. , Inc.* , 690 F. 2d at 793. Here, Japan Telecom has pursued an advertising strategy that is likely to reach only members of the Japanese and Japanese – American business communities in Southern California. Because Japan Telecom's phone directory advertisements appeared in a "yellow pages" section, only individuals who had already decided to look up a phone number for a telephone installation company in the specialized phone directory were likely to see Japan Telecom's name. Even those individuals would have to have gotten as far as

"J" to be exposed to Japan Telecom's entry, because Japan Telecom did not always pay for display advertisements. Giving Japan Telecom the benefit of the doubt, it has at most shown that a tiny subset of relevant buyers has ever seen its ads. Similarly, while Japan Telecom has been using its name since 1984 (and, for most of that time, exclusively), there is no evidence that it has used it in such a way that any more than a small set of buyers has gained any familiarity with it.

This is not enough to establish secondary meaning. To take a descriptive term out of the public domain, a plaintiff must demonstrate that the relevant buying public accords it secondary meaning. Here, because Japan Telecom limits its operations to Southern California, the relevant buying public consists at least of buyers of telephone and network installation services in that region. *See* 2 J. Thomas McCarthy, *McCarthy on Trademarks and Unfair Competition* § 15: 46 (2001). Japan Telecom has not come forward with enough evidence to show that those buyers associate "Japan Telecom" with a single source.

None of Japan Telecom's evidence creates a genuine issue of fact as to secondary meaning. Consequently, its trade name is not protectable. We affirm, on these alternate grounds, the district court's grant of summary judgment to Japan Telecom America on Japan Telecom's Lanham Act claims.

State Law Claims

Japan Telecom also sues for "unfair competition under state law" and "trade name violation under state law. " Japan Telecom's California unfair competition claim fails because its related Lanham Act claims fail. See *Denbicare U. S. A. Inc.* v. *Toys "R" Us, Inc.*, 84 F. 3d 1143, 1152 (9th Cir. 1996) ("Since dismissal of [plaintiff's] Lanham Act claim was proper, dismissal of its § 17200 claim was proper as well. "). Japan Telecom also claims injunctive relief under the California Trade Name Statute, Cal. Bus. & Prof. Code 14401–14418. Ë Japan Telecom argues that it does not need to show secondary meaning in order to prevail under that statute. The only authority Japan Telecom cites for this proposition is *Golden Door*,

Inc. v. *Odisho*, 437 F. Supp. 956 (N. D. Cal. 1977), which holds without analysis that "the California trade name statute does not require plaintiff to prove a secondary meaning or actual confusion. " 437 FS at 967. Japan Telecom claims we adopted this holding in *American Petrofina, Inc. v. Petrofina of Cal. , Inc.* , 596 F. 2d 896, 899 (9th Cir. 1979), but is mistaken. *American Petrofina* cited *Golden Door* for an unrelated proposition, and merely summarized its secondary meaning holding in a parenthetical without adopting it.

We do not find *Golden Door* persuasive. California courts do require plaintiffs suing under the California Trade Name Statute to establish secondary meaning when their trade names are descriptive. See *Cowles Magazines & Broad. , Inc. v. Elysium, Inc.* , 255 Cal. App. 2d 731, 63 Cal. Rptr. 507, 510 (Cal. App. 1967) ("Protection of the use of a tradename composed of one or more words of common usage rests on proof that the name or mark has acquired a meaning other than its primary meaning. "); *Family Record Plan, Inc. v. Mitchell*, 172 Cal. App. 2d 235, 342 P. 2d 10, 15 (Cal. App. 1959) ("While section 14400 ... provides that the acquisition of a trade name is dependent upon its first use, the courts generally apply the common law rule of secondary meaning to trade names ... . "). We are not aware of any California case that holds otherwise. A contrary rule would allow individual corporations to claim, by filing articles of incorporation, the exclusive right to use everyday words in a business name. We doubt that California's legislature intended to give away pieces of the English language, or that it could do so without violating the First Amendment. Because California law requires secondary meaning for descriptive trade names before protecting them, Japan Telecom's claim under the California Trade Name Statute fails.

We therefore affirm the district court's grant of summary judgment for Japan Telecom America on the state law claims.

AFFIRMED.

侵权产品下架回收

尼康公司状告易康公司案

Nikon

判例简介

　　法院认定商标侵权是一个曲折复杂的过程，充满了变数。在认定侵权之后，法院就要决定如何让原告的损失得到公平补偿。这同样是一个充满变数的过程。从法律上讲，商标侵权的补偿不外乎责令被告停止侵权或赔偿已经造成的损失等。其中，在责令被告停止侵害的处分方面，法院一般没有太多置喙的空间，一旦发现被告侵权，最直接的弥补措施就是颁布禁止令（Injunction Order），暂时或永远地禁止被告使用有争议的商标。不过，在决定赔偿金额方面，法院具有极大的裁量权可以决定让被告赔多还是赔少。此外，值得注意的是，除了金钱赔偿之外，法院还可以责令被告收回已经卖出的侵权产品。有时候，这是一种比金钱赔偿更严厉的惩罚。

　　尼康公司（Nikon, Inc.）创建于1917年，原名为"日本光学工业株式会社"。1988年该公司根据旗下畅销的照相机品牌名称，将公司更名为"尼康株式会社"。尼康公司是一家著名的日本照相器材公司，其主打产品为尼康照相机，畅销世界各国，在照相机市场上具有很大的市场占有率。1986年，一位名叫艾罗（Jack Elo）的美国人成立了"易康公司"（Ikon Corp.），专门用"易康"（Ikon）商标销售廉价的自动相机。第二年，艾罗向美国专利商标局申请注册"Ikon"商标被拒绝。原因在于，德国蔡斯公司注册了名为"Zeiss I-

94

kon"的商标，销售高档照相器材。

Nikon

1953 年 2 月 3 日尼康公司注册的美国商标

经过两年交涉，德国蔡斯公司终于和艾罗达成协议[1]，同意艾罗的"Ikon"商标并存，但仅限于使用于销售廉价的傻瓜相机，不得使用于销售单眼相机。在艾罗排除了注册"易康"商标的障碍后，美国专利商标局于 1990 年 5 月 1 日公告"易康"商标申请注册的消息。尼康公司立即提出异议，反对美国专利商标局同意"易康"商标的注册，并向法院控告易康公司侵害了尼康公司的商标权。

Ik&n

1990 年 5 月 1 日美国专利商标局公告的"易康"商标

在商标侵权案件中，决定商标侵权的关键在于被告的商标是否会造成消费者的混淆误认。而法院认定消费者是否会混淆误认需要综合考虑八项因素：第一，法院要看原告商标的知名度。一个商标越是知名，享有保护的力度就越大，范围就越广。第二，法院要看两个商标相似的程度。相似程度越高，引起消费者混淆误认的可能性就越大。第三，原告与被告的产品或服务是否相同或相近。双方的产品或服务越是相近，就越容易造成消费者的混淆误认。第四，法院要看被告使用有争议的商标是否出于恶意。如果法院发现被告故意模仿原告的商标，则容易将天平向原告一方倾斜。第五，法院要看被告的商标是否已经造成了混淆误认。俗话说，事实胜于雄辩，如果原告能让事实

---

[1] 美国商标注册制度中有同意书机制，只要在先商标权人同意让后注册之受阻商标并存，则后注册者亦可取得商标权。

说话，经由消费者抽样调查证明被告的商标已经造成了大量消费者的混淆误认，则胜算大增。第六，法院要看被告的产品或服务的品质如何。品质越是低劣，法院便越容易判定消费者混淆误认。第七，法院要看消费者是否头脑精明。头脑精明的消费者不容易混淆，反之则容易混淆。第八，法院要看原告将来是否会生产被告的产品或提供被告所提供的服务。在这八项因素中，没有任何一项因素是决定性的。法院必须综合考虑这八项因素，来决定被告的商标是否会造成消费者的混淆误认。在本案中，法院在综合考虑了这八项因素之后，发现"易康"照相机会导致消费者混淆误认，错把"易康"当"尼康"。由此判定易康公司侵害了尼康公司的商标权。

在补偿损失方面，尼康公司请求法院判令永远禁止易康公司销售"易康"照相机，并回收所有正在出售的"易康"照相机。易康公司则希望法院能够允许它先卖完现有的存货，以减少损失。否则，易康公司便面临破产的危险。法院拒绝了易康公司的这一要求，颁布了"永久禁止令"，永远禁止易康公司在美国市场上使用"Ikon"商标销售照相机。法院的禁止令立即生效。易康公司或者销毁存货，或者改贴其他商标销售。

既然无法销售存货，易康公司便希望能卖完已经进入市场的"易康"照相机。为了达到这一目的，易康公司提出了一个解决方案，即在正在出售的"易康"照相机上贴上一个标签，说明此货不是"尼康"，以期避免消费者混淆误认。另外，易康公司也强调，收回市场上所有的"易康"照相机，实属不易，要花费大量的人力、物力和财力。在大部分情况下，法院不会要求商标侵权案的被告回收已经进入市场的产品。但是，在特殊情况下，法院偶尔会作出这种决定。

在过去的判例中，法院曾经责令一家寝具用品公司收回所有贴在床垫上的侵权标识。法院作出这种严厉判决的目的，一是为了公平，二是为了惩一儆百，吓阻那些故意侵权者。所以，只有在法院发现被告故意侵权的时候，才有可能责令被告收回市场上的侵权产品。

在本案中，法院在审理"易康"商标是否会造成消费者混淆误认时，已经认定易康公司属于故意侵权，所以，尼康公司要求法院责令易康公司收回已经进入市场的照相机。在尼康公司提供的证据中，法院也注意到，当年艾罗的律师曾经警告过，用"易康"做商标有侵权之嫌，劝告艾罗不要这样做。但是，艾罗一意孤行，最终还是选择了"易康"商标。法院认定，这足以说明艾罗在明知"易康"商标涉嫌侵权的情况下，故意使用这一商标侵害了尼康公司的商标权。

而且，尼康公司指出，易康公司提出的在"易康"照相机上加贴声明标签的做法，并不能保证这些照相机不再侵权。至少，易康公司没有能力监督所有的零售商在销售前不会除去这些标签。法院接受了尼康公司的要求，责令易康公司收回所有正在销售的照相机。

如前所述，责令被告收回侵权产品是一种十分严厉的惩罚。在严厉程度上，也许仅次于责令销毁侵权产品。而只有法院在认定被告故意侵权非常严重的情况下，才会判决销毁侵权产品。

本案启示与解析

收回已经进入市场的侵权产品，既是一种对原告的补偿措施，也是一种对被告极为严厉的惩罚。在一般情况下，法院不会要求商标侵权案的被告，收回已经进入市场的产品。只有在十分特殊的情况下，法院才会作出这种决定。法院作出这种严厉判决的目的，一是为了公平，二是为了惩一儆百，吓阻那些故意侵权者。

在商标侵权争议中，法院在审理被告是否侵害了原告的商标权时，要考虑的一个重要因素就是被告的行为是否出于故意。故意模仿原告的商标，以混淆消费者的视听往往导致法院认定被告故意侵权。而故意侵权则往往意味着，比一般侵权更多的赔偿和更严厉的惩罚。在本案中，尼康公司向法庭提供了大量证据证明易康公司故意侵权。

根据尼康公司的调查，当年艾罗的律师曾经警告过，用"易康"做商标有侵权之嫌，劝告艾罗不要这样做。但是，艾罗一意孤行，最终还是选择了"易康"作为商标。根据尼康公司提供的这类证据，法院认定，艾罗在知道"易康"商标涉嫌侵权的情况下，故意使用这一商标侵犯尼康公司的商标权。

这已经预示了易康公司会遭受格外严厉的惩罚。尼康公司籍此要求法庭，责令易康公司收回已经进入市场的照相机，时机把握得恰到好处。

除了故意侵权的因素之外，法庭拒绝易康公司加贴声明标签继续销售"易康"产品的提议，也是出于现实的考虑。表面上看，这一提议可以避免消费者混淆误认，但是，仔细追究起来并不可行。易康公司没有能力监督所有的零售商，在销售前不会揭去这些声明标签。所以，在"易康"照相机上加贴声明标签的做法，并不能有效地保证这些照相机不会引起消费者的混淆误认。

责令收回侵权产品是一种十分严厉的惩罚。从原告角度讲，为了获得最大可能的赔偿，应当全盘计划，在法院审理有争议商标是否造成消费者混淆误认的阶段，向法庭提交大量证据，证明被告故意侵权，以便顺理成章地要求法院扩大赔偿和惩罚的范围。从被告的角度而言，为了避免遭受过于严厉的惩罚，应该未雨绸缪，在法庭审理有争议商标是否造成消费者混淆误认的阶段，集中力量反驳原告的故意侵权指控，以便在不利的情况下，把损失降到最低。

引用判决

NIKON，INC. v. IKON CORP.

Opinion by TIMBERS，*Circuit Judge*：

This is an appeal from an order entered in the Southern District of New York, Nina Gershon, *Chief Magistrate Judge*, permanently enjoining Ikon Photographic Corp. (IPC) from using its Ikon trademark and recalling all of the company's outstanding products. IPC was found liable for trademark infringement against Nikon, Inc. ▼ (Nikon) under Ë 32 and 43 (a) of the Lanham Act and for trademark dilution under §368－d of the New York General Business Law. On appeal, IPC contends that the magistrate judge improperly deprived it of a jury trial, erred in finding that there was a likelihood of confusion between the marks at issue, misapplied the New York anti-dilution statute, and inappropriately recalled Ikon products.

We reject IPC's claims on appeal. We affirm the district court order in all respects.

I

We summarize only those facts and prior proceedings believed necessary to an understanding of the issues raised on appeal.

In 1986, Jack Elo founded IPC to market inexpensive 35 mm and 110 mm pocket cameras. He claims that he selected the trademark "Ikon" because of the familiarity of the word and the religious connotations associated with it, despite the rare spelling he chose.

Elo was aware of the existence of the trademark name "Zeiss Ikon" (Zeiss), used by a sophisticated photography equipment company, but he claims that he believed the mark was no longer in use. Elo also was aware of the existence of Nikon camera products, but claims he did not foresee a potential for confusion between the two names because he never intended to compete with such a dominant force in the industry. In 1987, IPC began marketing inexpensive "point and shoot" cameras affixed with the Ikon mark and logo.

In 1987, IPC filed an application with the United States Patent and Trademark Office to register the mark and its logo. The application was rejected because of its similarity with the "Zeiss Ikon" mark. In 1989, IPC entered into an agreement with Zeiss in which Zeiss consented to IPC's use of the mark for 110 mm and basic lens shutter cameras, but restricted IPC from using the mark on more complicated single lens reflex (SLR) cameras. The mark was available for registration and published for opposition on May 1, 1990. Nikon commenced the instant action in September 1989, and opposed the registration. The opposition proceeding was stayed pending disposition of the instant action.

In 1990, IPC filed another application to register a mark with a stylized "I" logo. Nikon originally did not oppose the mark. After the mark was registered, Nikon petitioned for its cancellation. That proceeding also was stayed pending the disposition of the instant case.

IPC markets inexpensive cameras which are widely sold through national chain stores and catalogues. Nikon has a reputation for selling more expensive and more complicated SLR cameras, generally through authorized dealers. Since 1983, Nikon has been marketing cheaper and less complicated point and shoot cameras targeted for amateur photographers, and sold in retail stores and through catalogue services. Just before trial, Nikon further bridged the gap between its products and IPC's by introducing an even less expensive 35mm compact camera which would be directly competitive with IPC's cameras. The new Nikon camera is marketed as the "Smiletaker," and is packaged in a yellow graphic box with a smile face logo.

Since 1988, IPC had been marketing a line of point and shoot 110 mm cameras known as its "Smile" line. IPC claims that prior to learning of the Smiletaker camera, it had planned to market a 35 mm "Smile" camera, which it introduced in the fall of 1992. The IPC cameras also are packaged in cardboard boxes, with the word "SMILE" in large letters, but no smile face. The name Ikon appears at the bottom of the box. IPC filed a counterclaim, alleging that Nikon's deliberate adoption of the secondary name "Smiletaker" fosters confusion between Nikon's camera and IPC's. IPC further alleged that Nikon is such a dominant force in the camera market that the confusion would have a severely adverse affect on the Ikon product. IPC sought a preliminary injunction to enjoin Nikon from using the Smiletaker mark. This motion was denied. IPC also made a jury demand for its counterclaim. Nikon moved to strike this demand. The magistrate judge denied Nikon's motion, but severed IPC's counterclaim and scheduled a bench trial on Nikon's claim to be held prior to the jurytrial on IPC's counterclaim.

She held that the IPC mark infringed the Nikon mark. On December 18, 1992, the magistrate judge entered a permanent injunction, effective immediately, enjoining IPC from using the Ikon mark and providing for the recall of all IPC products from the marketplace. The judgment was stayed pending consideration of a motion for an extension of the stay by this Court. On December 29, 1992, a panel of this Court denied the motion but ordered this expedited appeal.

On appeal, IPC contends that (1) the district court erred in finding that there was a likelihood of confusion between the two marks, and therefore there was no infringement; (2) the New York anti-dilution law is inapplicable because the parties to the instant case are competitors and the law should apply only to noncompetitors; (3) the district court erred in severing IPC's counterclaim against Nikon's use of the "Smiletaker" name, precluding it from its right to a jury trial; and (4) the recall of IPC products was inappropriate.

II

On this appeal from a permanent injunction, our function is limited to a review for abuse of discretion. Abuse of discretion can be found if the district court relied upon a clearly erroneous finding of fact or incorrectly applied the law. *Bristol-Myers Squibb Co. v. McNeil-P. P. C. , Inc.* , 973 F. 2d 1033, 1038 (2 Cir. 1992). We must determine therefore whether the court applied the correct standard of law and, if so, whether its determination of the facts was clearly erroneous.

(A) *INFRINGEMENT UNDER Ë 32 AND 43 (a) OF THE LANHAM ACT*

Sections 32 and 43 (a) of the Lanham Act, 15 U. S. C. Ë 1114 & 1125 (1988) prohibit trademark infringement and false designation of origin, respectively. The key issue in these types of trademark cases is whether an appreciable number of consumers are likely to be misled or confused about the source of the product in question. *Lang v. Retirement Living Pub. Co.* , 949 F. 2d 576, 579 - 80 (2 Cir. 1991).

It is well settled that in cases involving a claim under the Lanham Act the trier of fact must consider and balance the factors set forth in *Polaroid Corp. v. Polarad Electronics Corp.* , 287 F. 2d 492, 495 (2 Cir.), *cert. denied*, 368 U. S. 820, 7

L. Ed. 2d 25, 82 S. Ct. 36 (1961) to determine the "likelihood of confusion." The *Polaroid test examines eight factors, including the strength of the senior user's mark, the degree of similarity between the two marks, the proximity of the products, the likelihood that the senior user will bridge the gap between the products, the sophistication of buyers, quality of defendant's product, actual confusion, and the defendant's bad faith in adopting the mark.* Polaroid, supra, 287 F. 2d at 495. This list, however, is not exhaustive, nor is any one factor determinative. Each factor must be balanced with the others to determine the likelihood of confusion. *Lang, supra*, 949 F. 2d at 580.

The court applied the *Polaroid* test in the instant case, thus correctly applying the applicable law for this claim. In reviewing a district court's determination of the *Polaroid* factors, the findings of fact are subject to reversal only if they are clearly erroneous, while the ultimate balancing of the factors is reviewed de novo by our Court. *Bristol-Myers, supra*, 973 F. 2d at 1043. We now turn to the factual findings as to each factor.

(1) *Strength of the Nikon Mark.*

There is no dispute over the strength of the Nikon mark. As such, it deserves broad protection against infringement. *Mobil Oil Corp. v. Pegasus Petroleum Corp.*, 818 F. 2d 254, 258 (2 Cir. 1987).

(2) *Similarity Between the Marks.*

When evaluating the similarity of marks, it is necessary to show that the products are not only similar, but that they also are likely to provoke confusion. *Bristol Myers, supra*, 973 F. 2d at 1046; *Western Publishing Co. v. Rose Art Indus.*, 910 F. 2d 57, 61 (2 Cir. 1990). The court found that, although one of IPC's marks uses a stylized "I" and is not visually very similar to the Nikon mark, the stylized "I" is not used on all of IPC's cameras or packaging. Many advertisements and displays for IPC omit the stylized "I" and the shutter wheel design used on the "o". In several contexts, therefore, the marks are similar.

Further, the court found that the sounds of both marks are extremely similar, differing only by one letter. That letter is easily obscured in statements such as "This is an Ikon," and "This is a Nikon." The court also found that there was similarity in the appearance of the cameras, and the cameras often are displayed outside of their packaging. This latter fact, combined with logos used in advertising, demonstrates that the court did look at the products in their commercial context, despite IPC's assertion that the court looked at the products "divorced from the commercial world." There is sufficient evidence to show that the court's finding was not clearly erroneous.

(3) *Proximity of the Products.*

This factor focuses on whether the products compete. If the products serve the same purposes, fall within the same class, or are used for similar purposes, the likelihood of confusion is greater. *Lang, supra*, 949 F. 2d at 582. While the parties have cameras at opposite ends of the spectrum, there is a substantial overlap of Nikon's low-end cameras with IPC's high-end cameras. These lines produce a substantial percentage of the respective companies' sales. IPC asserts that these products constitute only a small percentage of the products the companies have on the market, but the high percentage of sales does create proximity in the products. Further, the court found that both Nikon and IPC market these products through similar channels of trade and to similar types of customers. These facts all give weight to the court's finding of proximity of the products. That finding is not clearly erroneous.

(4) *Bridging the Gap.*

While this factor turns on the likelihood of whether the senior user will enter the market of the junior user, the court was correct in finding that, if there already is an overlap in the market, the likelihood of confusion is greater. *Hasbro, Inc. v. Lanard Toys, Ltd.*, 858 F. 2d 70, 78 (2 Cir. 1988). Although IPC asserts that Nikon first bridged the gap on the eve of trial with its Smiletaker model, as stated above, the gap actually was bridged in 1983 with Nikon's introduction of its point and shoot line which is marketed for the same consumers as IPC's upper-end line of its cameras. There already is a market overlap, increasing the likelihood of confusion.

(5) *Sophistication of Consumers.*

"The more sophisticated and careful the average consumer of a product is, the less likely it is that similarities in trade dress or trade marks will result in confusion concerning the source or sponsorship of the product. " Bristol–Myers, supra, 973 F. 2d at 1046. *The district court found that, although the purchasers of* Nikon's upper-end line of cameras generally are sophisticated in this area, the purchasers of the lower-end line often are amateur photographers, not unlike the purchasers of IPC cameras. While purchasers of these cameras are not impulsive, less sophisticated consumers could be confused about an affiliation between the products. This finding is not clearly erroneous.

(6) *Quality of Junior User's Product.*

We have taken two approaches about the quality of the junior user's product: (1) an inferior quality product injures the senior user's reputation because people may think they come from the same source; or (2) a product of equal quality promotes confusion that they come from the same source. *Hasbro, supra*, 858 F. 2d at 78. The court here applied both approaches and effectively mooted this factor. For our purposes therefore, it may be helpful to accept IPC's assertion that, unless the junior's product is inferior, the quality factor does not weigh in favor of the senior user. The court found that, while IPC's quality is good for its price, IPC does not have the same quality controls as Nikon does over its products. The court did not err in weighing this factor in favor of Nikon.

(7) *Actual Confusion.*

"Although [evidence of actual confusion] is not necessary to show likelihood of confusion, its lack may under some circumstances be used against a plaintiff. " *Hasbro, supra*, 858 F. 2d at 78. In the instant case, the court found very limited evidence to support a claim of actual confusion. Only a couple of inconsequential isolated incidents of misdelivered mail were cited. Further, Nikon did not undertake a trademark survey to show actual confusion. Thus, the court tipped this factor toward IPC. However, the court found that two incidents of "passing off" ——representing IPC as a division of Nikon at retail stores——mitigated somewhat the lack of other evidence of actual confusion. This finding was not clearly erroneous.

(8) *Bad Faith.*

IPC claims the name Ikon was chosen after Elo saw this spelling of the word in an encyclopedia and thought it would be familiar because of the pictorial religious connotations associated with it. Elo claims that the only problem he thought of was the name "Zeiss Ikon," (although he did not mention this fact at his deposition). Elo's twenty years of experience in the camera business (selling before he began IPC) makes it unlikely that he did not realize there was a significant resemblance between this name and Nikon. There also is evidence that he rejected the advice ofhis counsel to adopt a mark with a word other than Ikon as the dominant part. Elo did not disclose to his counsel his intent to market 35 mm cameras similar to Nikon's. There was sufficient evidence for the court's finding that IPC acted in bad faith.

(9) *Balancing the Factors.*

Although we adhere to a clearly erroneous standard in reviewing the court's determination of the*Polaroid* factors (since they are deemed factual findings), we apply de novo review when balancing the factors. *Bristol—Myers*, *supra*, 973 F. 2d at 1043. Applying the facts found by the court, each factor, with the exception of actual confusion, weighs heavily in favor of Nikon. And there was some evidence of actual confusion. The *Polaroid* factors are an analytical *tool*——not a rigid formula. *Id.* at 1044. No one factor is determinative. We hold that the situation taken as a whole clearly tips in favor of Nikon and supports the finding of a likelihood of confusion and trademark infringement.

(B) *THE NEW YORK ANTI—DILUTION CLAIM*

IPC also was enjoined under the New York General Business Law § 368 – d

(McKinney 1984). At issue is whether this statute was applied properly in this case. There is a split among the district courts in this Circuit as to whether competitors are covered under the statute. Bristol—Myers, *supra*, 973 F. 2d at 1049; *see also* *E. P. Lehmann Co. v. Polk's Modelcraft Hobbies*, 770 F. Supp. 202, 206 (S. D. N. Y. 1991) (citing cases). The language of the statute states that it applies in cases, "notwithstanding the absence of competition between the parties … ." § 368—d. Courts have held that this limits the statute to noncompetitors. They rely on a New York Court of Appeals case which describes the legislative intent as protecting marks from dissimilar products. *Allied Maintenance Corp. v. Allied Mechanical Trades, Inc.*, 42 N. Y. 2d 538, 544, 369 N. E. 2d 1162, 1165, 399 N. Y. S. 2d 628, 632 (1977). This language, however, does not preclude competitive products from being covered; it is not controlling since it is only dictum. As Judge McLaughlin stated in *LeSportsac v. K Mart.*, 617 F. Supp. 316, 319 (E. D. N. Y. 1985), if the "legislature intended to make the absence of competition a prerequisite to § 368—d relief, it could easily have done so."

We hold that this statute is applicable to competitors as well as noncompetitors. Moreover, it is not preempted by the Lanham Act in that they each protect different rights. *Mead Data Cent., Inc. v. Toyota Motor Sales U. S. A*, 702 F. Supp. 1031, 1040 – 41 (S. D. N. Y. 1988), *rev'd on other grounds*, 875 F. 2d 1026 (2 Cir. 1989).

(C) *SEVERANCE OF COUNTERCLAIM*

IPC asserts that its counterclaim against Nikon has been estopped collaterally by the court's action in severing the counterclaim from Nikon's claim and holding the bench trial prior to IPC's jury trial, and that IPC therefore has been deprived of its right to a jury trial on the counterclaim. *Lee Pharmaceuticals v. Mishler*, 526 F. 2d 1115 (2 Cir. 1975); *Heyman v. Kline*, 456 F. 2d 123 (2 Cir.), cert. denied, 409 U. S. 847, 34 L. Ed. 2d 88, 93 S. Ct. 53 (1972). Neither *Lee* nor *Heyman* are applicable in this case. They both involved situations where the district court denied the defendants the right to a jury trial for their counterclaims. In the instant case, the court severed the counterclaim, allowing IPC to have a jury, but in a separate trial.

As for the issue of collateral estoppel, IPC's counterclaim for infringement is based on the alleged confusibility of the Smile camera by IPC and the Smiletaker by Nikon. The counterclaim alleges that "the use of the ' SmileTaker' name and mark by [Nikon] is without permission and authority of [IPC] and constitutes an infringement of [IPC's] mark SMILE... ." Nowhere does the complaint refer to the *Ikon* Smile or the *Nikon* Smiletaker, thus making no connection between the house name and product name. The counterclaim alleged only infringement of the product name.

There is no issue preclusion because of the severance of the counterclaim. IPC should not be denied a jury trial if it continues with its claim. Although IPC claims that it would be necessary for the jury to make a determination about the similarity between the IPC and Nikon marks, as stated above, IPC's action involves different claims from the instant case, alleging likelihood of confusion between "Smile" and "*Smiletaker.*" These issues were not determined in the instant case. The court determined only that the house name Ikon is likely to be confused with Nikon.

IPC, however, argues that a trial of the issue of the likelihood of confusion between "Smile" and "*Smiletaker*" necessarily would involve a determination of the "house" names——Ikon and Nikon. Cases hold that under § 43 (a) of the Lanham Act protecting a trade dress involves looking at the totality of the image of the product, such as its packaging, size, and color combination. *George Basch Co. v. Blue Coral, Inc.*, 968 F. 2d 1532, 1535 (2 Cir.), *cert. denied*, 121 L. Ed. 2d 445, 113 S. Ct. 510 (1992). In the instant case, IPC claims that trial of its counterclaim would involve looking at the house names in connection with the product names to determine the likelihood of confusion. In this case, however, the two names are not connected in the Ikon product and are sufficiently detached. The totality argument therefore is weakened. Moreover, even if it would be necessary to include the house name as part of the totality of the package, its inclusion would be collateral only to the main claim involving the product names.

It was suggested at oral argument that IPC might be better off if its claim against

Nikon were bound by a finding that the names are likely to cause confusion, since it appears that is precisely what IPC will try to prove to the jury. In any event, we hold that IPC will not be prejudiced by collateral estoppel in its claim against Nikon insofar as the issues to be determined in that case are sufficiently different from the instant case. We hold that IPC has not been deprived of its right to a jury trial.

(D) *RECALL OF PRODUCTS*

IPC claims that the recall order was unduly harsh under the circumstances, asserting that Nikon delayed the trial, causing it to last three years. IPC says that Nikon was in no hurry to get IPC products off the market and that a recall is not justified.

We hold that the recall order was appropriate. The district court has broad discretion as to recall orders which are part of permanent injunctions. *Perfect Fit Industries v. Acme Quilting Co.*, 646 *F.*2d 800, 805 (2 *Cir.* 1981), cert. denied, 459 *U.S.* 832, 74 *L. Ed.* 2d 71, 103 *S. Ct.* 73 (1982). As Nikon asserts, IPC was warned by its counsel that the trademarks were similar and that IPC should add to its mark to avoid confusion. IPC also withheld from its counsel its intention to enter the 35 mm market. This is evidence of bad faith on the part of IPC. Moreover, while affixing stickers on the cameras warning customers about Ikon's infringement might be said to be less harsh than a recall, there is no guarantee that retailers would affix the stickers. Further, IPC still could remove the trademark from the cameras and sell them to stores like Job Lot. Although IPC asserts it is a harsh remedy, there is no evidence in the record before us to show that the court abused its discretion in ordering the immediate recall.

III

To summarize:

The district court properly held that IPC violated the Lanham Act and the New York anti-dilution laws, and that its products should be recalled. There should not be issue preclusion on the counterclaim. IPC therefore was not deprived of a jury trial.

Affirmed.

商标使用的属地原则

派森氏公司状告克莱斯曼案

PERSON'S

判例简介

商标使用的效力具有地域性，受到地域或国界的限制。在国际上，商标注册有一个普遍认同的"属地原则"，即先在哪个国家注册，就先受到哪个国家法律的保护。如果该商标是"知名商标"，那么这个商标就会受到国际公约的保护。国际公约同时规定，如果"知名商标"已经存在，而其他公司又申请注册相同商标则构成"侵权"。

所以，在一国使用的商标不一定受到另一国家的保护。市场的全球化并没有完全消除商标使用的地域性，反倒在有些方面加剧了地域性带来的问题。在这种情况下，如果一家公司打算进入外国市场，必须未雨绸缪，做好先期的商标准备工作。最忌讳的是无备而来，临阵磨枪，使一个地域性的名牌商标错失进军国际市场的机会。

"派森氏"（PERSON'S）是派森氏公司（PERSON'S Co., Ltd.）在日本注册的商标。这家日本公司成立于1979年，专门在日本国内销售"派森氏"服装产品。1981年，美国人克莱斯曼（Larry Christman）去日本出差时，偶然发现了派森氏服装的专卖店，并为其商标创意和服装设计所吸引。克莱斯曼购买了几套派森氏服装带回美国，并打算在美国注册"派森氏"商标并销售"派森氏"服装。

克莱斯曼立即聘请熟悉商标法的律师对比进行可行性研究。研究结果表明，的确尚没有人在美国注册过"派森氏"（PERSON'S）商标，美国市场上也尚未发现有日本"派森氏"服装销售。克莱斯曼喜出望外，立即根据他带回美国的日本派森氏服装，依样画葫芦，设计出一系列服装。1982 年 2 月，克莱斯曼与一家美国服装厂签订协议，正式开始生产贴有"派森氏"（PERSON'S）商标的服装。两个月后，克莱斯曼的"派森氏"服装进入市场。至此，世界上便至少有了两家"派森氏"服装，一家在日本，一家在美国。

1983 年 4 月，克莱斯曼正式向美国专利商标局申请注册"PERSON'S"商标销售服装产品。1984 年 9 月，克莱斯曼的申请得到批准。与此同时，日本"派森氏"迅速发展成一个闻名日本的时装品牌，并打算进入美国市场。自1982 年 11 月起，便陆续开始有美国服装商定购日本"派森氏"的产品。在这种情况下，日本派森氏公司正式在美国申请注册"PERSON'S"商标。1985 年 8 月，日本"派森氏"的商标申请得到批准。同年，日本"派森氏"服装在美国市场的销售额便达到 400 万美金。

不久，克莱斯曼便发现日本"派森氏"已经进入美国。几乎同时，日本派森氏公司也发现美国市场上已经有一家"派森氏"服装。两个"派森氏"共存，给消费者造成了混淆。1986 年，日本派森氏公司要求美国专利商标局商标审理与上诉委员会取消克莱斯曼的"派森氏"商标注册，主要理由是引起消费者的混淆误认。克莱斯曼则提出反诉，以第一个在美国市场上使用"派森氏"商标为由，要求商标审理与上诉委员会取消日本派森氏公司的"派森氏"商标注册。

商标审理与上诉委员会经审理判定，尽管日本派森氏公司在日本市场上先于克莱斯曼使用"派森氏"商标，但是克莱斯曼却在美国市场上第一个使用"派森氏"商标，所以克莱斯曼在美国具有优先使用权。因为两家"派森氏"服装在美国市场并存，会造成消费者的混淆误认，所以商标审理与上诉委员会决定取消日本"派森氏"商标的注册。日本派森氏公司不服，便将案件上诉到联邦法院。

在上诉中，双方争执的焦点集中在两个问题上：第一，谁拥有"派森氏"商标在美国市场上的优先使用权？第二，克莱斯曼在美国注册"派森氏"商标是否出于恶意？按照美国商标法，在一个商标注册后5年之内，人们可以对这个商标提出挑战，要求美国专利商标局取消这个商标。如果在法律上理由充分，美国专利商标局有权取消一个商标的注册。在本案中，日本派森氏公司便引用这条法律，要求法院责令美国专利商标局取消克莱斯曼的"派森氏"商标注册。

日本派森氏公司提出的第一个理由是，克莱斯曼不具有"派森氏"商标的优先使用权。美国商标法遵循优先使用原则，即谁先使用一个商标，谁就有权注册这个商标。按照法院的解释，"优先使用"指的是在"商业活动中优先使用"。"商业活动"则是指美国各州间的贸易，美国与国外的贸易以及美国与印第安人的贸易。在本案中，日本派森氏公司坚持，"派森氏"商标在日本市场上开始使用的日期应当作为优先使用的日期。

法院则拒绝了这种说法。法院指出，在日本"派森氏"产品进入美国市场以前，"派森氏"商标在日本市场上的使用对美国商业贸易没有任何影响。所以，法院不能将"派森氏"商标在日本开始使用的日期作为优先使用日期。而是应当把"派森氏"商标在美国市场上开始使用的日期作为优先使用日期。按照这一标准，克莱斯曼早在1982年4月就已经将其"派森氏"服装投入美国市场。而直到1982年11月才有第一批日本"派森氏"服装进入美国市场。由此，法院认定，克莱斯曼在美国市场上拥有"派森氏"商标的优先使用权。

日本派森氏公司所提出的第二个理由是，克莱斯曼在美国注册"派森氏"商标是出于恶意，因为他知道日本已经有一家派森氏服装。法院指出，仅仅是知道日本已经有一个"派森氏"商标，并不必然说明克莱斯曼在美国注册"派森氏"商标是出于恶意。按照法院的解释，要证明克莱斯曼有恶意，日本派森氏公司必须提供证据证明克莱斯曼使用和注册"派森氏"商标会损害日本派森氏公司的商业信誉。

但是在克莱斯曼开始使用"派森氏"商标的时候，日本"派森氏"产品还没有进入美国市场。这意味着，在克莱斯曼开始使用"派森氏"商标的时候，日本派森氏公司在美国市场上尚没有商业信誉可供克莱斯曼损害。而且，因为当时日本派森氏公司的产品还没有进入美国市场，所以克莱斯曼使用"派森氏"商标也不会造成消费者混淆误认。不但如此，法院已经认定克莱斯曼拥有"派森氏"商标的优先使用权,而具有优先使用权的商标持有人不可能在使用和注册这个商标时具有恶意。法院进一步指出,日本派森氏公司指责克莱斯曼出于恶意使用和注册"派森氏"商标,把日本和美国两个市场混为一谈,完全忽略了商标使用的地域性。

按照商标使用的地域性原则,日本派森氏公司要法院认定克莱斯曼有恶意,仅仅证明克莱斯曼知道日本市场上已经有一个"派森氏"商标还不够,还必须证明克莱斯曼知道日本派森氏公司计划进入美国市场。无疑,这大大增加了日本派森氏公司胜诉的难度。不过,法院的这一要求并非没有道理。如果日本派森氏公司有进入美国市场的计划,并及时在美国专利商标局注册"派森氏"商标,克莱斯曼就会知道日本派森氏公司将要进入美国市场。在不知道日本派森氏公司将进入美国市场的情况下,法院没有理由禁止克莱斯曼使用"派森氏"商标。根据以上理由,法院维持了商标审理与上诉委员会的决定,责令美国专利商标局取消日本派森氏公司的"派森氏"商标注册。

不过,本案的判决并不意味着法院给美国商人随意搬用外国名牌商标开了方便之门。在判决书中,法院经由区别不同情况来限制这一判例的适用范围。例如,如果一个外国品牌已经在美国消费者中很有名气,尽管这个品牌的商品还没有直接在美国市场销售,法院也会给予充分保护。相比之下,日本"派森氏"服装在进入美国市场之前,在美国消费者中没有任何知名度。此外,若美国商人使用或注册一个外国名牌商标的目的是拒这个外国名牌于国门之外,法院则会认为这种使用和注册是出于恶意。

本案启示与解析

虽然世界各国商标法内容不尽相同,但都规定对注册商标所有权进行法律保护。过去中国许多企业对商标专用权的意义认识不足,缺乏商标专用权保护意识。有的认为办理商标注册很麻烦,因而不愿到商品进口国去办理注册,有的认为等自己的商品出了名再注册不迟,还有的认为自己的商品还不够畅销,注册不注册一个样。例如用于电视机的"牡丹""PEONY"商标被荷兰销售代理商在荷兰、瑞典、挪威、比利时、卢森堡五国抢注；"红塔山""阿诗玛""云烟""红梅"等香烟商标被菲律宾商人抢注；"丰收"桂花陈酒在法国被抢注；"三角牌""金鸡牌"商标在智利被抢注就是典型的例子。

因此，商标在国外注册不是可有可无的问题。凡是想把自己的产品打入国际市场的企业，都应及早到国外注册商标，以便使自己的商品在销售国不被排挤，销售市场不被他人抢占。

在经济全球化时代，外国企业应充分利用美国商标法以及有关国际公约的规定，及时在美国专利商标局注册商标，并以此作为产品进入美国市场的必要准备。

归纳起来，外国企业在美国注册商标可以采取三种方式。第一种方式是像美国企业一样按照正常的渠道注册。对于许多外国公司来讲，通过这种方式在美国注册商标并不能发挥外国企业的优势。尤其是当外国企业已经在美国之外的国家正在申请注册商标，或已经拥有了合法的注册商标之后，第一种方式不是最佳选择。

外国企业在美国注册商标的第二种方式是，向美国专利商标局申请注册一个已经在国外注册过的合法商标。因为美国商标法并不要求在注册前必须在美国市场上实际使用该商标，所以外国产品在进入美国市场前可以先注册产品的商标，以免出现日本派森氏公司遇到的被动局面。

日本派森氏公司在日本拥有合法的注册商标，而且计划把产品出口到美国市场销售。尽管其产品在美国市场上大受消费者欢迎，但是在美国注册和使用"派森氏"商标时却遇到了重大挫折，导致了难以挽回的损失。客观而言，这种损失是由日本派森氏公司在跨国经营商标战略方面的重大失误造成的。如果日本派森氏公司在日本获得"派森氏"注册商标后，立即在美国专利商标局注册这一商标，便可以有效地避免"派森氏"商标被克莱斯曼抢注，继而获得在美国市场上独家使用"派森氏"商标的权利。

外国企业在美国注册商标的第三种方式是，在美国国外提出商标注册申请后的 6 个月内，在美国申请商标注册，这被称为"国际优先权"。这种方法是在有关专利和商标国际保护的《巴黎公约》中规定的。美国作为《巴黎公约》的成员方，也允许外国企业以这种方式在美国注册商标。这种注册方式的优点在于，美国专利商标局会将外国企业在国外提出商标注册申请时的日期作为优先日期。而且，一旦外国企业的商标注册申请被美国专利商标局批准，其商标将会得到美国商标法的全面保护。对于正在国外申请注册商标的外国公司来讲，以第三种方式在美国同时注册商标可谓是最佳选择。

日本派森氏公司告克莱斯曼案的判例，给所有准备进入或正在进入美国市场的外国企业敲响了警钟。这一判决充分表明了外国企业及时在美国注册商标的必要性。日本派森氏公司因忽视了这一点，而失去了在美国市场上使用"派森氏"商标的机会。这对于一家正在雄心勃勃准备进军美国市场的外国公司来讲，可谓是刻骨铭心的教训。

不过，本案的判决并不意味着，法院会给美国商人随意占用外国名牌商标开绿灯。在判决书中，法院通过区别各种不同的主客观情况，来限制这一判例的适用范围。比如说，如果一个外国品牌已经在美国消费者中很有名气，尽管这个品牌的商品，还没有直接在美国市场销售，法院也会给予充分保护。相比之下，日本"派森氏"产品在进入美国市场之前，在美国消费者中没有任何知名度。再比如说，如果美国商人使用或注册一个外国名牌商标的目的，是拒这个外国名牌于美国国门之外，法院会判定这种使用和注册是出于恶意。

引用判决

PERSON'S CO. , LTD. v. CATHERINE CHRISTMAN, Personal Representative of the Estate of LARRY CHRISTMAN

Opinion by SMITH, *Senior Circuit Judge*.

Person's Co. , Ltd. appeals from the decision of the Patent and Trademark Office Trademark Trial and Appeal Board (Board) which granted summary judgment in favor of Larry Christman and ordered the cancellation of appellant's registration for the mark "PERSON'S" for various apparel items. Appellant Person's Co. seeks cancellation of Christman's registration for the mark "PERSON'S" for wearing apparel on the following grounds: likelihood of confusion based on its prior foreign use, abandonment, and unfair competition within the meaning of the Paris Convention. We affirm the Board's decision.

Background

The facts pertinent to this appeal are as follows: In 1977, Takaya Iwasaki first applied a stylized logo bearing the name "PERSON'S" to clothing in his native Japan. Two years later Iwasaki formed Person's Co., Ltd., a Japanese corporation, to market and distribute the clothing items in retail stores located in Japan.

In 1981, Larry Christman, a U. S. citizen and employee of a sportswear wholesaler, visited a Person's Co. retail store while on a business trip to Japan. Christman purchased several clothing items bearing the "PERSON'S" logo and returned with them to the United States. After consulting with legal counsel and being advised that no one had yet established a claim to the logo in the United States, Christman developed designs for his own "PERSON'S" brand sportswear line based on appellant's products he had purchased in Japan. In February 1982, Christman contracted with a clothing manufacturer to produce clothing articles with the "PERSON'S" logo attached. These clothing items were sold, beginning in April 1982, to sportswear retailers in the northwestern United States. Christman formed Team Concepts, Ltd., a Washington corporation, ▼in May 1983 to continue merchandising his sportswear line, which had expanded to include additional articles such as shoulder bags. All the sportswear marketed by Team Concepts bore either the mark "PERSON'S" or a copy of appellant's globe logo; many of the clothing styles were apparently copied directly from appellant's designs.

In April 1983, Christman filed an application for U. S. trademark registration in an effort to protect the "PERSON'S" mark. Christman believed himself to be the exclusive owner of the right to use and register the mark in the United States and apparently had no knowledge that appellant soon intended to introduce its similar sportswear line under the identical mark in the U. S. market. Christman's registration issued in September 1984 for use on wearing apparel.

In the interim between Christman's first sale and the issuance of his registration, Person's Co., Ltd. became a well known and highly respected force in the Japanese fashion industry. The company, which had previously sold garments under the "PERSON'S" mark only in Japan, began implementing its plan to sell goods under this mark in the United States. According to Mr. Iwasaki, purchases by buyers for re-sale in the United States occurred as early as November 1982. This was some seven months subsequent to Christman's first sales in the United States. Person's Co. filed an application for U. S. trademark registration in the following year, and, in 1985, engaged an export trading company to introduce its goods into the U. S. market. The registration for the mark "PERSON'S" issued in August 1985 for use on luggage, clothing and accessories. After recording U. S. sales near 4 million dollars in 1985, Person's Co. granted California distributor Zip Zone International a license to manu-facture and sell goods under the "PERSON'S" mark in the United States.

In early 1986, appellant's advertising in the U. S. became known to Christman and both parties became aware of confusion in the marketplace. Person's Co. initiated an action to cancel Christman's registration on the following grounds: (1) likelihood of confusion; (2) abandonment; and (3) unfair competition within the meaning of the Paris Convention. Christman counterclaimed and asserted prior use and likelihood of confusion as grounds for cancellation of the Person's Co. registration.

After some discovery, Christman filed a motion with the Board for summary judgment on all counts. In a well reasoned decision, the Board held for Christman on the grounds that Person's use of the mark in Japan could not be used to establish pri-ority against a "good faith" senior user in U. S. commerce. The Board found no evi-dence to suggest that the "PERSON'S" mark had acquired any notoriety in this coun-try at the time of its adoption by Christman. Therefore, appellant had no reputation or goodwill upon which Christman could have intended to trade, rendering the unfair competition provisions of the Paris Convention inapplicable. The Board also found that Christman had not abandoned the mark, although sales of articles bearing the mark were often intermittent. The Board granted summary judgment to Christman and ordered appellant's registration cancelled.

The Board held in its opinion on reconsideration that Christman had not adopted the mark in bad faith despite his appropriation of a mark in use by appellant in a foreign country. The Board adopted the view that copying a mark in use in a foreign country is not in bad faith unless the foreign mark is famous in the United States or the copying is undertaken for the purpose of interfering with the prior user's planned expansion into the United States. Person's Co. appeals and requests that this court direct the Board to enter summary judgment in its favor.

Issues

1. Does knowledge of a mark's use outside U. S. commerce preclude good faith adoption and use of the identical mark in the United States prior to the entry of the foreign user into the domestic market?

2. Did the Board properly grant summary judgment in favor of Christman on the issue of abandonment?

Cancellation

The Board may properly cancel a trademark registration within five years of issue when, e. g. (1) there is a valid ground why the trademark should not continue to be registered and (2) the party petitioning for cancellation has standing. Such cancellation of the marks' registrations may be based upon any ground which could have prevented registration initially. The legal issue in a cancellation proceeding is the right to register a mark, which may be based on either (1) ownership of a foreign registration of the mark in question or (2) use of the mark in United States commerce.

Priority

The first ground asserted for cancellation in the present action is § 2 (d) of the

Lanham Act; each party claims prior use of registered marks which unquestionably are confusingly similar and affixed to similar goods.

Section 1 of the Lanham Act states that "the owner of a trademark *used in commerce* may register his trademark... . " The term "commerce" is defined in Section 45 of the Act as "... . all commerce which may be lawfully regulated by Congress. " No specific Constitutional language gives Congress power to regulate trademarks, so the power of the federal government to provide for trademark registration comes only under its commerce power. The term "used in commerce" in the Lanham Act refers to a sale or transportation of goods bearing the mark in or having an effect on: (1) United States interstate commerce; (2) United States commerce with foreign nations; or (3) United States commerce with the Indian Tribes.

In the present case, appellant Person's Co. relies on its use of the mark in Japan in an attempt to support its claim for priority in the United States. Such foreign use has no effect on U. S. commerce and cannot form the basis for a holding that appellant has priority here. The concept of territoriality is basic to trademark law; trademark rights exist in each country solely according to that country's statutory scheme. Christman was the first to use the mark in United States commerce and the first to obtain a federal registration thereon. Appellant has no basis upon which to claim priority and is the junior user under these facts.

Bad Faith

Appellant vigorously asserts that Christman's adoption and use of the mark in the United States subsequent to Person's Co. 's adoption in Japan is tainted with "bad faith" and that the priority in the United States obtained thereby is insufficient to establish rights superior to those arising from Person's Co. 's prior adoption in a foreign country. Relying on *Woman's World Shops, Inc. v. Lane Bryant, Inc.*, Person's Co. argues that a "remote junior user" of a mark obtains no right superior to the "senior user" if the "junior user" has adopted the mark with knowledge of the "senior user's" prior use. In *Woman's World*, the senior user utilized the mark within a limited geographical area. A junior user from a different geographical area of the United States sought unrestricted federal registration for a nearly identical mark, with the exception to its virtually exclusive rights being those of the known senior user. The Board held that such an appropriation with knowledge failed to satisfy the good faith requirements of the Lanham Act and denied the concurrent use rights sought by the junior user. Person's Co. cites *Woman's World* for the proposition that a junior user's adoption and use of a mark with knowledge of another's prior use constitutes bad faith. It is urged that this principle is equitable in nature and should not be limited to knowledge of use within the territory of the United States.

While the facts of the present case are analogous to those in *Woman's World*, the case is distinguishable in one significant respect. In *Woman's World*, the first use of the mark by both the junior and senior users was in United States commerce. In the case at bar, appellant Person's Co. , while first to adopt the mark, was not the first user in the United States. Christman is the senior user, and we are aware of no case where a senior user has been charged with bad faith. The concept of bad faith adoption applies to remote junior users seeking concurrent use registrations; in such cases, the likelihood of customer confusion in the remote area may be presumed from proof of the junior user's knowledge. In the present case, when Christman initiated use of the mark, Person's Co. had not yet entered U. S. commerce. The Person's Co. had no goodwill in the United States and the "PERSON'S" mark had no reputation here. Appellant's argument ignores the territorial nature of trademark rights.

Appellant next asserts that Christman's knowledge of its prior use of the mark in Japan should preclude his acquisition of superior trademark rights in the United States. The Board found that, at the time of registration, Christman was not aware of appellant's intention to enter the U. S. clothing and accessories market in the future. Christman obtained a trademark search on the "PERSON'S" mark and an opinion of competent counsel that the mark was "available" in the United States. Since Appellant had taken no steps to secure registration of the mark in the United States, Christman was aware of no basis for Person's Co. to assert superior rights to use and registration here. Appellant would have us infer bad faith adoption because of Christman's awareness of its use of the mark in Japan, but an inference of bad faith requires something more than mere knowledge of prior use of a similar mark in a foreign country.

As the Board noted below, Christman's prior use in U. S. commerce cannot be-discounted solely because he was aware of appellant's use of the mark in Japan. While adoption of a mark with knowledge of a prior actual *user* in U. S. commerce may give rise to cognizable equities as between the parties, no such equities may be based upon knowledge of a similar mark's existence or on a problematical intent to use such a similar mark in the future. Knowledge of a foreign use does not preclude good faith a-doption and use in the United States. While there is some case law supporting a finding of bad faith where (1) the foreign mark is famous here or (2) the use is a nominal one made solely to block the prior foreign user's planned expansion into the United States, as the Board correctly found, neither of these circumstances is present in this case.

We agree with the Board's conclusion that Christman's adoption and use of the mark were in good faith. Christman's adoption of the mark occurred at a time when appellant had not yet entered U. S. commerce; therefore, no prior user was in place to give Christman notice of appellant's potential U. S. rights. Christman's conduct in appropriating and using appellant's mark in a market where he believed the Japanese manufacturer did not compete can hardly be considered unscrupulous commercial conduct. Christman adopted the trademark being used by appellant in Japan, but appellant has not identified any aspect of U. S. trademark law violated by such action. Trademark rights under the Lanham Act arise solely out of use of the mark in U. S. commerce or from ownership of a foreign registration thereon; "the law pertaining to registration of trademarks does not regulate all aspects of business morality. " When the law has been crafted with the clarity of crystal, it also has the qualities of a glass slipper: it cannot be shoe-horned onto facts it does not fit, no matter how appealing they might appear.

The Paris Convention

Appellant next claims that Christman's adoption and use of the "PERSON'S" mark in the United States constitutes unfair competition under Articles 6 *bis* and 10 *bis* of the Paris Convention. It is well settled that the Trademark Trial and Appeal Board cannot adjudicate unfair competition issues in a cancellation or opposition proceeding. The Board's function is to determine whether there is a right to secure or to maintain a registration.

Abandonment

Appellant next seeks to cancel Christman's registration of the "PERSON'S" mark on the ground of abandonment, citing (1) the intermittent sales registered by Christman's corporation, Team Concepts, Ltd. , during the years 1983–87; (2) the paucity of orders for replenishment of corporate inventory during the same period; and (3) the lack of significant sales by Team Concepts to commercial outlets. Specifically, appellant argues that the Board erred in failing to draw all permissible inferences from the record in its favor on the abandonment issue.

The burden on the moving party in a summary judgment proceeding under Fed. R. Civ. P. 56 may be discharged by showing that there is an absence of evidence to support the nonmoving party's case. Section 45 of the Lanham Act provides in pertinent part that a mark shall be deemed abandoned "when its use has been discontinued with intent not to resume. Intent not to resume may be inferred from circumstances. " Person's Co. carries the burden of establishing the case for cancellation on grounds of abandonment by a preponderance of the evidence.

Appellant correctly asserts that the critical issue here is whether Christman's actions demonstrate a cessation of commercial use and an intent not to resume such use. Although sales by Christman and his corporation Team Concepts, Ltd. were often intermittent and the inventory of the corporation remained small, such circumstances do not necessarily imply abandonment. There is also no rule of law that the owner of a trademark must reach a particular level of success, measured either by the size of the market or by its own level of sales, to avoid abandoning a mark. After consideration of the record as a whole, the Board found nothing to support appellant's argument that Christman abandoned the mark. We agree with the Board's conclusion that, as a matter of law, the evidence submitted by appellant was insufficient to raise an issue of fact of abandonment of the "PERSON'S" mark.

Conclusion

In *United Drug Co. v. Rectanus Co.*, the Supreme Court of the United States determined that "there is no such thing as property in a trademark except as a right appurtenant to an established business or trade in connection with which the mark is employed. Its function is simply to designate the goods as the product of a particular trader and to protect his goodwill against the sale of another's product as his; and it is not the subject of property except in connection with an existing business." In the present case, appellant failed to secure protection for its mark through use in U. S. commerce; therefore, no established business or product line was in place from which trademark rights could arise. Christman was the first to use the mark in U. S. commerce. This first use was not tainted with bad faith by Christman's mere knowledge of appellant's prior foreign use, so the Board's conclusion on the issue of priority was correct. Appellant also raises no factual dispute which is material to the resolution of the issue of abandonment. Accordingly, the grant of summary judgment was entirely in order, and the Board's decision is affirmed.

AFFIRMED.

淡化著名商标

米德数据公司状告丰田汽车公司案

LEXUS

判例简介

淡化著名商标不仅为美国联邦商标法所禁止，也为美国各州法律所禁止。著名商标的所有者若发现自己的商标被淡化，可同时按照联邦商标法和州法起诉肇事者。不过，在实际商业活动中，商标淡化与正常的商标使用有时候并没有一条绝对明晰的界限。法院在审理商标淡化案时，往往要综合考虑多种因素。

丰田汽车公司（Toyota Motor Corporation）在推出豪华车品牌 LEXUS（中文译为"凌志"，后改译为"雷克萨斯"）时便引发了一起商标淡化诉讼。1987 年以前，日本丰田汽车公司以制造经济型家用轿车闻名于美国汽车市场。在美国站稳脚跟后，丰田汽车公司决定向被欧洲车和美国车统治的豪华汽车市场进军。但由于"丰田"品牌在美国消费者心目中几乎已经成为经济耐用型汽车的别称，所以丰田汽车公司决定为将来的豪华型汽车专门打造一个品牌。

在众多的候选商标中，就有 LEXUS。LEXUS 这一名称朗朗上口，简捷明快，又不失雍容典雅的大家风范，当推豪华车品牌的首选。不过，在选择使用 LEXUS 之前，丰田汽车公司还是费了些思量，因为在美国无数的商标中已经有一个 LEXIS 商标。尽管 LEXUS 是一个生造出来的词，在当时出版的任何英文词典中都查不到，但却可能惹上模仿 LEXIS 商标的嫌疑。为了避免日后引起商标侵权诉讼，丰田汽车公司专门聘请了熟悉商标法的律师进行调查评估。评估的结果表明，使用 LEXUS 商标销售汽车不会与 LEXIS 商标发生任何冲突。依据这个评估结论，丰田汽车公司决定采用 LEXUS 商标。

1987 年 8 月 24 日，丰田汽车公司正式宣布将投产 LEXUS 豪华型轿车。这种豪华轿车的主要市场将瞄准年收入在 5 万美金以上的职业人士。为了打造 LEXUS 商标，丰田汽车公司决定在 1989 年的前 9 个月内投资 1800 万到 2000 万美金的广告费。这一消息引发了一场影响深远的商标大战。丰田汽车公司发布将要投产 LEXUS 豪华轿车的消息不久，就收到 LEXIS 商标的所有者米德数据公司（Mead Data Central, Inc.）的警告信函，称 LEXUS 商标侵害了 LEXIS 商标，要求丰田汽车公司立即停止使用 LEXUS 商标。

在这一要求遭到拒绝后，米德数据公司便依据美国商标法和纽约州法律，起诉丰田汽车公司商标侵权以及淡化著名商标 LEXIS。本案的原告米德数据公司既不生产汽车，也不销售汽车，而是一家法律数据服务公司。自 1972 年起，米德数据公司便开始使用 LEXIS 商标提供电脑化法律数据服务。关于 LEXIS 商标的由来，米德数据公司称，这不是一个现成词汇，而是由米德数据公司的总裁创造出来的新词。据说，米德数据公司总裁创造 LEXIS 一词，也不是完全凭灵感，而是古今结合，引经据典，一直追溯到拉丁文的词源。按照这种解释，LEXIS 一词可以分解成两个部分，其中 LEX 是拉丁文"法律"的意思，"IS"则是"Information System"（讯息系统）的缩写，放在一起就是"法律讯息系统"的意思。

米德数据公司对 LEXIS 商标由来的解释似乎可以自圆其说。但是，法院并没有接受这种说法。法院经由查寻各种权威词典终于找到 LEXIS 的真正词源。法院发现，LEXIS 是个有着悠久历史的古老词汇，在古希腊文和拉丁文中早已经存在，并非米德数据公司总裁的首创。不但如此，在米德数据公司使用 LEXIS 作为商标以前，LEXIS 这个词也已经成为现代英文中的一个普通词汇，至少被收入六十几部现代英文词典中。任何人只要翻开一本英文词典，就会查到这个词。

而且，LEXIS 这个词在拉丁文和英文中的意思都与法律无关，而是"词语"或"词汇"的意思。而且，在美国市场上，不只米德数据公司一家使用LEXIS 作为商标，还有多家公司使用 LEXIS 的名称，比如"LEXIS 有限公司""LEXIS 电脑系统公司""LEXIS 语言讯息服务公司"等。这些取名 LEXIS 的公司不但与米德数据公司没有任何关系，而且在米德数据公司采用 LEXIS 商标以前已经开始使用 LEXIS 的字号。根据以上发现，法院认定，LEXIS 并非米德数据公司总裁所创造的新词，而是一个现代英语中的现成词汇。

在认定 LEXIS 的来源后，米德数据公司与丰田汽车公司争论的焦点便集中在 LEXUS 商标是否淡化了 LEXIS 商标。在本案中，米德数据公司根据纽约州法律提出商标淡化的指控。纽约州商法禁止 淡化著名商标。如前所述，"淡化"在商标法中主要是指，一个不知名品牌模仿一个著名商标，以混淆消费者的视听，导致被模仿的著名商标贬值。例如，一家不知名的饮料公司在商标的文字和设计上模仿可口可乐的商标，使消费者误以为这家公司的饮料是由可口可乐公司生产。这种做法便有"淡化"可口可乐的商标之嫌，也可以说是对可口可乐这一著名商标的"淡化"。

在本案中，LEXUS 商标是否淡化了 LEXIS 商标取决于几项因素。其中，最重要的两项因素是：第一，LEXIS 是否是一个著名商标。第二，LEXUS 是否与 LEXIS 相似到鱼目混珠的程度，足以令消费者混淆误认。

先就第一项因素而言。向法院证明一个商标属于著名商标的最有效方法就是消费者的问卷调查。在消费者中，能够辨识一个商标的人数比例越高，就越能证明一个商标属于著名商标。反之，能够辨识一个商标的消费者比例越低，就越能证明一个商标不属于著名商标。米德数据公司提供的消费者的问卷调查数据显示，有 76%的律师能够辨识 LEXIS 商标，并把 LEXIS 商标与米德数据公司提供的法律数据服务联系起来。法院认为，这一调查结果足以证明，LEXIS 是个著名商标。

再就第二项因素而言。法院会利用以下两个步骤来辨识两个商标是否雷同。第一个步骤，法院先比较两个商标在外观和发音上的差别。例如，LEXUS 与 LEXIS 两个词在拼写方面只有一个字母之差，在发音方面只有一个音节之差。但是，比较 LEXUS 和 LEXIS 两个商标的图案设计，二者所用的字体和徽标却没有任何雷同之处。第二个步骤，法院还要确定两个商标的相似之处是否会导致消费者的混淆误认，错把 LEXUS 豪华轿车当成米德数据公司的 LEXIS 产品。

为了向法院证明，LEXUS 商标不会导致消费者混淆误认，丰田汽车公司做了大量的消费者抽样调查。消费者抽样调查的结果显示，LEXIS 商标的主要市场在律师和会计师中间。76% 的律师和会计师能够把 LEXIS 商标和米德数据公司的数据服务联系起来。但是，只有 1% 的普通消费者能够辨识 LEXIS 商标，并知道 LEXIS 是米德数据公司提供的法律数据服务，而且在这 1% 当中有一半是律师和会计师。

丰田汽车公司提供的调查数据表明，LEXIS 产品的消费者主要是律师和会计师。这个消费群体的特点是受教育程度高，头脑复杂，对商标有着极强的辨别能力。而且，LEXUS 汽车价格昂贵，属于高档消费品，消费者在购买前大多会对品牌做些研究。在这种情况下，消费者不太可能混淆 LEXUS 轿车和 LEXIS 数据。

不但如此，丰田汽车公司在普通消费者中的调查数据也支持这种结论。99% 以上的普通消费者根本不知道有 LEXIS 这一商标，更不知道米德数据公司以 LEXIS 商标提供的法律数据服务。消费者不可能混淆一种自己不知道的品牌。基于以上理由，法院判决丰田汽车公司的 LEXUS 商标没有"淡化"米德数据公司的 LEXIS 商标。多年后的今天，LEXUS 已经成为美国市场上妇孺皆知的豪华汽车品牌，而 LEXIS 仍然是一个只有律师和会计师才知道的专业品牌。

本案启示与解析

在 1995 年 7 月美国国会通过《联邦反淡化商标法案》前，美国并没有全国性的反淡化商标法。美国法院主要是根据各州商法或商标法中相关"反淡化著名商标"的条款来判案。本案即是如此。联邦法院完全依照纽约州商法中，有关禁止淡化著名商标的条款审理本案。从立法目的而言，反淡化法不同于一般的反商标侵权法。如果说禁止使用容易造成混淆的商标，主要是为了保护消费者不被误导，那么禁止淡化著名商标，则主要是为了保护著名商标及其拥有者的商业利益。

由于立法目的上的差别，法院在审理商标侵权案和商标淡化案时的重点也不完全一样。简而言之，在审理一般商标侵权案时，法院着重考虑，被告的行为是否会造成消费者的混淆误认。在审理商标淡化案时，尽管消费者是否会混淆误认是法院要考虑的因素之一，但是法院却要着重考虑，被告的行为是否会给原告造成损害，或已经造成了损害。换言之，如果原告没有证明损害，法庭就无法认定被告的行为构成了淡化著名商标。需要特别指出的是，在证明损害这一点上，联邦反淡化商标法与各州的反淡化商标法存在重大差别。按照各州的反淡化商标法律的规定，原告无须证明"实际损害"，只需证明"可能损害"，法院即可认定被告淡化著名商标的指控成立。但是，于1995年实施的联邦反淡化商标法，则提高了认定淡化著名商标的门槛，要求原告证明被告的行为已经造成实际损害。因此，尽管本案发生在联邦反淡化商标法案实施以前，法院完全按照纽约州商法的"反淡化"条款进行的审理，我们不难想象，即使依据现行的联邦反淡化商标法审理，本案也应会有同样的结果。米德数据公司因无法证明丰田汽车公司的 LEXUS 商标已经对 LEXIS 商标造成了实际损害，而难以胜诉。米德数据公司在无法证明"实际损害"的情况下，便对丰田汽车公司出招兴讼，在商标攻防战中似乎犯了轻敌妄动的错误。

引用判决

MEAD DATA CENTRAL, INC. v. TOYOTA MOTOR SALES, U. S. A. , INC. and TOYOTA MOTOR CORP.

Opinion by VAN GRAAFEILAND, *Circuit Judge*

Toyota Motor Sales, U. S. A. , Inc. and its parent, Toyota Motor Corporation, ▼ appeal from a judgment of the United States District Court for the Southern District of

New York (Edelstein, J.) enjoining them from using LEXUS as the name of their new luxury automobile and the division that manufactures it. The district court held that, under New York's antidilution statute, N. Y. Gen. Bus. Law § 368-d, Toyota's use of LEXUS is likely to dilute the distinctive quality of LEXIS, the mark used by Mead Data Central, Inc. ▼ for its computerized legal research service. 702 F. Supp. 1031 (1988) . On March 8, 1989, we entered an order of reversal, stating that an opinion would follow. This is the opinion.

THE STATUTE

Section 368-d of New York's General Business Law, which has counterparts in at least twenty other states, reads as follows:

Likelihood of injury to business reputation or of dilution of the distinctive quality of a mark or trade name shall be a ground for injunctive relief in cases of infringement of a mark registered or not registered or in cases of unfair competition, notwithstanding the absence of competition between the parties or the absence of confusion as to the source of goods or services.

THE PARTIES AND THEIR MARKS

Mead and Lexis

Mead is a corporation organized under the laws of Delaware with its principal place of business in Miamisburg, Ohio. Since 1972, Mead has provided a computerized legal research service under the trademark LEXIS. Mead introduced evidence that its president in 1972 "came up with the name LEXIS based on Lex which was Latin for law and I S for information systems. " In fact, however, the word "lexis" is centuries old. It is found in the language of ancient Greece, where it had the meaning of "phrase", "word", "speaking" or "diction" . Pinkerton, *Word for Word*, 179 (1982). "Lexis" subsequently appeared in the Latin where it had a substantially similar meaning, *i. e.*, "word", "speech", or "language" . Oxford Latin Dictionary (1983); Lewis and Short, *A Latin Dictionary* (1980); Lewis, *An Ele-*

mentary Latin Dictionary (1979).

Like many other Latin words, "lexis" has been incorporated bodily into the English. It can be found today in at least sixty general dictionaries or other English word books, including Webster's Ninth New Collegiate Dictionary and Webster's New World Dictionary. Moreover, its meaning has not changed significantly from that of its Latin and Greek predecessors; *e. g.*, "Vocabulary, the total set of words in a language" (American Heritage Illustrated Encyclopedic Dictionary); "A vocabulary of a language, a particular subject, occupation, or activity" (Funk & Wagnalls Standard Dictionary). The district court's finding that "to establish that LEXIS is an English word required expert testimony at trial" is clearly erroneous. Anyone with a rudimentary knowledge of English can go to a library or bookstore and find the word in one of the above-mentioned standard dictionaries.

Moreover, the record discloses that numerous other companies had adopted "Lexis" in identifying their business or its product, *e. g.*, Lexis Ltd., Lexis Computer Systems Ltd., Lexis Language and Export Information Service, Lexis Corp., Maxwell Labs Lexis 3. In sum, we reject Mead's argument that LEXIS is a coined mark which originated in the mind of its former president and, as such, is entitled per se to the greater protection that a unique mark such as "Kodak" would receive. See *Esquire, Inc. v. Esquire Slipper Mfg. Co.*, 243 F. 2d 540, 543 (1st Cir. 1957); *Intercontinental Mfg. Co. v. Continental Motors Corp.*, 43 C. C. P. A. 841, 230 F. 2d 621, 623, 109 U. S. P. Q. (BNA) 105 (C. C. P. A. 1956).

Nevertheless, through its extensive sales and advertising in the field of computerized legal research, Mead has made LEXIS a strong mark in that field, and the district court so found. In particular, the district court accepted studies proffered by both parties which revealed that 76 percent of attorneys associated LEXIS with specific attributes of the service provided by Mead. However, among the general adult population, LEXIS is recognized by only one percent of those surveyed, half of this one percent being attorneys or accountants. The district court therefore concluded that LEXIS is strong only within its own market.

As appears in the Addendum to this opinion, the LEXIS mark is printed in block letters with no accompanying logo.

Toyota and Lexus

Toyota Motor Corp. has for many years manufactured automobiles, which it markets in the United States through its subsidiary Toyota Motor Sales, U. S. A. On August 24, 1987 Toyota announced a new line of luxury automobiles to be called LEXUS. The cars will be manufactured by a separate LEXUS division of Toyota, and their marketing pitch will be directed to well-educated professional consumers with annual incomes in excess of $ 50, 000. Toyota had planned to spend $ 18 million to $ 20 million for this purpose during the first nine months of 1989.

Before adopting the completely artificial name LEXUS for its new automobile, Toyota secured expert legal advice to the effect that "there is absolutely no conflict between ' LEXIS ' and ' LEXUS ' " . Accordingly, when Mead subsequently objected to Toyota's use of LEXUS, Toyota rejected Mead's complaints. The district court held correctly that Toyota acted without predatory intent in adopting the LEXUS mark.

The absence of predatory intent by the junior user is a relevant factor in assessing a claim under the antidilution statute, ... since relief under the statute is of equitable origin, ...

Sally Gee, Inc. v. Myra Hogan, Inc. , 699 F. 2d 621, 626 (2d Cir. 1983) (citations omitted).

However, the district court erred in concluding that Toyota's refusal to acknowledge that its use of LEXUS might harm the LEXIS mark, deprived it of the argument that it acted in good faith. If, as we now hold, Toyota's mark did not dilute Mead's, it would be anomalous indeed to hold Toyota guilty of bad faith in proceeding in reliance on its attorney's correct advice to that effect. See *Sweats Fashions, Inc. v. Pannill Knitting Co.* , 833 F. 2d 1560, 1565, 4 U. S. P. Q. 2D (BNA) 1793 (Fed. Cir. 1987); *E. S. Originals Inc. v. Stride Rite Corp.* , 656 F. Supp. 484, 490

(S. D. N. Y. 1987) ; *Inc. Publishing Corp. v. Manhattan Magazine, Inc.,* 616 F. Supp. 370, 394 - 96 (S. D. N. Y. 1985), *aff'd,* 788 F. 2d 3 (2d Cir. 1986); *Procter & Gamble Co. v. Johnson & Johnson, Inc.,* 485 F. Supp. 1185, 1201 - 02 (S. D. N. Y. 1979), *aff'd,* 636 F. 2d 1203 (2d Cir. 1980) . Indeed, even if the attorney's professional advice had been wrong, it does not follow that Toyota's reliance on that advice would have constituted bad faith. *Information Clearing House, Inc. v. Find Magazine,* 492 F. Supp. 147, 161-62 (S. D. N. Y. 1980) .

The LEXUS mark is in stylized, almost script-like lettering and is accompanied by a rakish L logo. *See* Addendum.

THE LAW

The brief legislative history accompanying section 368-d describes the purpose of the statute as preventing "the whittling away of an established trade-mark's selling power and value through *its* unauthorized use by others upon dissimilar products. " 1954 N. Y. Legis. Ann. 49 (emphasis supplied). If we were to interpret literally the italicized word "its", we would limit statutory violations to the unauthorized use of the identical established mark. This is what Frank Schechter, the father of the dilution theory, intended when he wrote *The Rational Basis of Trademark Protection,* 40 Harv. L. Rev. 813 (1927). *See id.* at 830-33; *see also* Shire, *Dilution Versus Deception——Are State Antidilution Laws an Appropriate Alternative to the Law of Infringement,* 77 Trademark Rep. 273-76 (1987) . However, since the use of obvious simulations or markedly similar marks might have the same diluting effect as would an appropriation of the original mark, the concept of exact identity has been broadened to that of substantial similarity. *Community Federal Savings and Loan Ass'n v. Orondorff,* 678 F. 2d 1034 (11th Cir. 1982) (quoting *Pro - phy - lac - tic Brush Co. v. Jordan Marsh Co.,* 165 F. 2d 549, 553 (1st Cir. 1948)); *Dreyfus Fund, Inc. v. Royal Bank of Canada,* 525 F. Supp. 1108, 1124 (S. D. N. Y. 1981); 2 J. McCarthy, *Trademarks and Unfair Competition* § 24: 13 at 215 (2d ed. 1984). Nevertheless, in keeping with the original intent of the statute, the similarity must be substantial before the doctrine of dilution may be applied. See *Alberto - Culver Co. v. Andrea Dumon , Inc.* , 466 F. 2d 705 , 709 (7th Cir. 1972) ; *Consolidated Cosmetics v. Neilson Chemical Co.* , 109 F. Supp. 300 , 310 (E. D. Mich. 1952) ; Ehrlich , *Anti-Dilution Laws Give Plaintiffs Powerful Weapon Against Copiers* , Nat'l L. J. , May 16 , 1983 , at 28.

Indeed , some courts have gone so far as to hold that , although violation of an antidilution statute does not require confusion of product or source , the marks in question must be sufficiently similar that confusion may be created as between the marks themselves. See *Holiday Inns , Inc. v. Holiday Out in America* , 481 F. 2d 445 , 450 (5th Cir. 1973) ; *King Research , Inc. v. Shulton , Inc.* , 324 F. Supp. 631 , 638 (S. D. N. Y. 1971) , *aff'd* , 454 F. 2d 66 (2d Cir. 1972) . We need not go that far. We hold only that the marks must be "very" or "substantially" similar and that , absent such similarity , there can be no viable claim of dilution.

The district court's opinion was divided into two sections. The first section dealt with Toyota's alleged violation of the Lanham Act , and the second dealt with the alleged dilution of Mead's mark under New York's antidilution statute. The district court made several findings on the issue of similarity in its Lanham Act discussion ; it made none in its discussion of section 368-d. Assuming that the district court's finding of lack of physical similarity in the former discussion was intended to carry over into the latter , we would find ourselves in complete accord with it since we would make the same finding. See Addendum ; see also *Blue Bell , Inc. v. Jaymar-Ruby , Inc.* , 497 F. 2d 433 , 435 (2d Cir. 1974) . However , if the district court's statement in its Lanham Act discussion that " in everyday spoken English , LEXUS and LEXIS are virtually identical in pronunciation" was intended to be a finding of fact rather than a statement of opinion , we question both its accuracy and its relevance. The word LEXUS is not yet widely enough known that any definitive statement can be made concerning its pronunciation by the American public. However , the two members of this Court who concur in this opinion use " everyday spoken English" , and we would not pronounce LEXUS as if it were spelled LEXIS. Although our colleague takes issue with us on this point, he does not contend that if LEXUS and LEXIS are pronounced correctly, they will sound the same. We liken LEXUS to such words as "census", "focus" and "locus", and differentiate it from such words as "axis", "aegis" and "iris". If we were to substitute the letter "i" for the letter "u" in "census", we would not pronounce it as we now do. Likewise, if we were to substitute the letter "u" for the letter "i" in "axis", we would not pronounce it as we now do. In short, we agree with the testimony of Toyota's speech expert, who testified:

Of course, anyone can pronounce "lexis" and "lexus" the same, either both with an unstressed I or both with an unstressed U, or schwa——or with some other sound inbetween. But, properly, the distinction between unstressed I and unstressed U, or schwa, is a standard one in English; the distinction is there to be made in ordinary, reasonably careful speech.

In addition, we do not believe that "everyday spoken English" is the proper test to use in deciding the issue of similarity in the instant case. Under the Constitution, there is a " 'commonsense' distinction between speech proposing a commercial transaction, which occurs in an area traditionally subject to government regulation, and other varieties of speech." *Central Hudson Gas & Electric Corp. v. Public Service Comm'n*, 447 U. S. 557, 562, 65 L. Ed. 2d 341, 100 S. Ct. 2343 (1980) (quoting *Ohralik v. Ohio State Bar Ass'n*, 436 U. S. 447, 455 – 56, 56 L. Ed. 2d 444, 98 S. Ct. 1912 (1978)). "The legitimate aim of the anti-dilution statute is to prohibit the unauthorized use of another's trademark in order to market incompatible products or services", and this constitutes a "legitimate regulation of commercial speech." *L. L. Bean, Inc. v. Drake Publishers, Inc.*, 811 F. 2d 26, 32 – 33 (1st Cir.), *cert. denied*, 483 U. S. 1013, 107 S. Ct. 3254, 97 L. Ed. 2d 753 (1987). "Advertising is the primary means by which the connection between a name and a company is established …", *Beneficial Corp. v. Beneficial Capital Corp.*, 529 F. Supp. 445, 448 (S. D. N. Y. 1982), and oral advertising is done primarily on radio and television. When Mead's speech expert was asked whether there were instances in which LEXUS and LEXIS would be pronounced differently, he replied

"Yes, although a deliberate attempt must be made to do so.... They can be pronounced distinctly but they are not when they are used in common parlance, in everyday language or speech. " We take it as a given that television and radio announcers usually are more careful and precise in their diction than is the man on the street. Moreover, it is the rare television commercial that does not contain a visual reference to the mark and product, which in the instant case would be the LEXUS automobile. We conclude that in the field of commercial advertising, which is the field subject to regulation, there is no substantial similarity between Mead's mark and Toyota's.

There are additional factors that militate against a finding of dilution in the instant case. Such a finding must be based on two elements. First, plaintiff's mark must possess a distinctive quality capable of dilution. *Allied Maintenance Corp. v. Allied Mechanical Trades, Inc.*, 42 N. Y. 2d 538, 545, 399 N. Y. S. 2d 628, 369 N. E. 2d 1162 (1977). Second, plaintiff must show a likelihood of dilution, *Sally Gee, Inc. v. Myra Hogan, Inc.*, *supra*, 699 F. 2d at 625. As section 368 – d expressly states, a plaintiff need not show either competition between its product or service and that of the defendant or a likelihood of confusion as to the source of the goods or services. *Allied Maintenance Corp. v. Allied Mechanical Trades, Inc.*, *supra*, 42 N. Y. 2d at 543.

Distinctiveness for dilution purposes often has been equated with the strength of a mark for infringement purposes. *P. F. Cosmetique, S. A. v. Minnetonka, Inc.*, 605 F. Supp. 662, 672 (S. D. N. Y. 1985); *Allied Maintenance Corp. v. Allied Mechanical Trades, Inc.*, *supra*, 42 N. Y. 2d at 545. It also has been defined as uniqueness or as having acquired a secondary meaning. *Allied Maintenance*, *supra*, 42 N. Y. 2d at 545. A trademark has a secondary meaning if it " has become so associated in the mind of the public with that entity [Allied] or its product that it identifies the goods sold by that entity and distinguishes them from goods sold by others. " *Id*. In sum, the statute protects a trademark's " selling power. " *Sally Gee, Inc. v. Myra Hogan, Inc.*, *supra*, 699 F. 2d at 624–25. However, the fact that a mark has selling power in a limited geographical or commercial area does not endow it with a secondary meaning for the public generally. See *Hartman v. Hallmark Cards, Inc.*, 833 F. 2d 117, 121 (8th Cir. 1987); *Truck Equipment Service Co. v. Fruehauf Corp.*, 536 F. 2d 1210, 1219 (8th Cir.), *cert. denied*, 429 U. S. 861, 50 L. Ed. 2d 139, 97 S. Ct. 164, 191 U. S. P. Q. (BNA) 588 (1976) (quoting *Shoppers Fair of Arkansas, Inc. v. Sanders Co.*, 328 F. 2d 496, 499 (8th Cir. 1964)); *Restaurant Lutece, Inc. v. Houbigant, Inc.*, 593 F. Supp. 588, 596 (D. N. J. 1984); *Scott v. Mego International, Inc.*, 519 F. Supp. 1118, 1138 (D. Minn. 1981).

The strength and distinctiveness of LEXIS is limited to the market for its services——attorneys and accountants. Outside the market, LEXIS has very little selling power. Because only one percent of the general population associates LEXIS with the attributes of Mead's service, it cannot be said that LEXIS identifies that service to the general public and distinguishes it from others. Moreover, the bulk of Mead's advertising budget is devoted to reaching attorneys through professional journals.

This Court hasdefined dilution as either the blurring of a mark's product identification or the tarnishment of the affirmative associations a mark has come to convey. *Sally Gee, Inc. v. Myra Hogan, Inc.*, *supra*, 699 F. 2d at 625 (quoting 3A Callman, *The Law of Unfair Competition, Trademarks and Monopolies* § 84. 2 at 954-55). Mead does not claim that Toyota's use of LEXUS would tarnish affirmative associations engendered by LEXIS. The question that remains, therefore, is whether LEXIS is likely to be blurred by LEXUS.

Very little attention has been given to date to the distinction between the confusion necessary for a claim of infringement and the blurring necessary for a claim of dilution. Shire, *supra*, 77 Trademark Rep. at 293. Although the antidilution statute dispenses with the requirements of competition and confusion, it does not follow that every junior use of a similar mark will dilute the senior mark in the manner contemplated by the New York Legislature.

As already stated, the brief legislative history accompanying section 368-d described the purpose of the statute as preventing "the whittling away of an established trademark's selling power and value through its unauthorized use by others upon dissimilar products. " The history disclosed a need for legislation to prevent such "hypothetical anomalies" as "Dupont shoes, Buick aspirin tablets, Schlitz varnish, Kodak pianos, Bulova gowns, and so forth", and cited cases involving similarly famous marks, *e. g.*, *Tiffany & Co. v. Tiffany Productions*, *Inc.*, 147 Misc. 679, 264 N. Y. S. 459 (1932), *aff'd*, 237 A. D. 801, 260 N. Y. S. 821, *aff'd*, 262 N. Y. 482, 188 N. E. 30 (1933); *Philadelphia Storage Battery Co. v. Mindlin*, 163 Misc. 52, 296 N. Y. S. 176 (1937) . 1954 N. Y. Legis. Ann. 49-50.

It is apparent from these references that there must be some mental association between plaintiff's and defendant's marks.

If a reasonable buyer is not at all likely to link the two uses of the trademark in his or her own mind, even subtly or subliminally, then there can be no dilution…. Dilution theory presumes*some kind of mental association* in the reasonable buyer's mind between the two party's [sic] uses of the mark.

2 J. McCarthy, *supra*, § 24. 13 at 213-14.

This mental association may be created where the plaintiff's mark is very famous and therefore has a distinctive quality for a significant percentage of the defendant's market. *Sally Gee*, *Inc. v. Myra Hogan*, *Inc.*, *supra*, 699 F. 2d at 625. However, if a mark circulates only in a limited market, it is unlikely to be associated generally with the mark for a dissimilar product circulating elsewhere. *See*, *e. g.*, *Estee Lauder*, *Inc. v. Cinnabar* 2000 *Haircutters*, *Inc.*, 218 U. S. P. Q. (BNA) 191 (S. D. N. Y.), *aff'd*, 714 F. 2d 112 (2d Cir. 1982); *Markel v. Scovill Mfg. Co.*, 471 F. Supp. 1244 (W. D. N. Y.), *aff'd*, 610 F. 2d 807 (2d Cir. 1979) . As discussed above, such distinctiveness as LEXIS possesses is limited to the narrow market of attorneys and accountants. Moreover, the process which LEXIS represents is widely disparate from the product represented by LEXUS. For the general public, LEXIS has no distinctive quality that LEXUS will dilute.

The possibility that someday LEXUS may become a famous mark in the mind of the general public has little relevance in the instant dilution analysis since it is quite apparent that the general public associates nothing with LEXIS. On the other hand, the recognized sophistication of attorneys, the principal users of the service, has substantial relevance. *See Sally Gee, Inc. v. Myra Hogan, Inc., supra*, 699 F. 2d at 626. Because of this knowledgeable sophistication, it is unlikely that, even in the market where Mead principally operates, there will be any significant amount of blurring between the LEXIS and LEXUS marks.

For all the foregoing reasons, we hold that Toyota did not violate section 368-d. We see no need therefore to discuss Toyota's remaining arguments for reversal.

当文字商标遇上图案商标

美孚石油公司状告飞马石油公司案

判例简介

按照美国商标法的规定，商标可以是一个词语，一个名称，一个符号，一个图案，或其他标识，也可以是这些标识的组合。许多名牌商标既有名称又有符号或图案，例如百事可乐饮料（Pepsi）、丰田汽车（Toyota）、耐克运动鞋（Nike）等。但是，有些著名商标却或者有名称无图案，或者有图案无名称。例如，美孚石油公司（Mobil Oil Corp.）的"飞马"商标，尽管在美国家喻户晓，却只有图案，没有名称。

美孚石油公司的产品上都贴有各种颜色的"飞马"图案商标，却不见任何"飞马"文字。在这种情况下，如果其他公司用"飞马"文字作为商标，是否侵害了美孚石油公司的商标权呢？在1987年美孚石油公司状告飞马石油公司案判决前，这个问题并没有一个明确的答案。

美孚石油公司于 1931 年所使用的 "飞马" 图案商标[1]

美孚石油公司申请注册的 "飞马" 图案商标

美孚石油公司是世界上最大的几家石油公司之一，从 1931 年起就开始使用 "飞马" 图案作为商标。红色的 "飞马" 图案标志在美孚石油公司的加油站和各种产品上随处可见。经过多年经营，"飞马" 图案标志已经成为美孚石油产品的象征，也已经成为世界石油市场上最著名的商标之一。美孚石油公司不仅经营各种石油产品，而且也经营原油贸易。不过，在原油贸易市场上，美孚石油公司并不使用 "飞马" 图案标志。

1981 年，美国一位原油贸易商成立了 "飞马石油公司"（Pegasus Petroleum Corp.），专门从事原油贸易。Pegasus 本是一个希腊词，在希腊神话中是一匹展翅飞翔的马。因此，Pegasus 在英文中作为一个外来词也就有了 "飞马" 的意思。尽管飞马石油公司在原油交易市场上使用 "飞马" 的名称，但是，从来没有使用过任何 "飞马" 图案标志。而且，飞马石油公司的业务仅限于原油交易，而不涉及生产或销售任何石油产品。

---

〔1〕 资料来源 http://www.exxonmobil.com/。

1982 年，美孚石油公司在得知有人使用"飞马"的名称进行原油交易后，对此展开调查，并要求飞马石油公司立即停止使用"飞马"的名称。双方交涉未果，美孚石油公司便向法院提起诉讼，指控飞马石油公司侵害了美孚石油公司的商标权。飞马石油公司则极力申辩称，一个是"飞马"文字，一个是"飞马"标志，两者无相似之处，不会导致消费者的混淆误认，何来侵权之有？不过，两个商标之间的雷同并不是判定消费者是否混淆误认的唯一因素，更不是决定性因素。

在商标侵权诉讼案中，有争议商标的使用是否会引起消费者的混淆误认，是法院判定是否存在侵权的关键。而法院在判断消费者是否会混淆误认时，大多参照著名的"派拉罗"案（Polariod Corp. v. Polarad Elects. Corp.）判例。在"派拉罗"案中，法院总结了判定一个商标是否会导致消费者混淆误认的八项因素。

在本案中，尽管争议双方的商标一个只涉及文字，另一个只涉及图案，法院还是套用了"派拉罗"案的八项因素进行判定。飞马石油公司承认，美孚石油公司的"飞马"标志属于著名商标，理应得到最大限度的保护。但是，飞马石油公司却不同意把"飞马"文字盲目地等同于"飞马"图案，坚持二者毫无相似之处。法院拒绝了飞马石油公司的这一申辩，指出不能单纯从商标的媒介来判定两个商标是否相似，而是要看消费者的反应。消费者在看到"飞马"文字时自然会联想到美孚石油公司的"飞马"标志，反之亦然。所以，"飞马"文字和"飞马"标志在消费者心中会造成雷同的印象。由此，法院认定，尽管两个"飞马"商标，一个是文字，另一个是图案，二者还是构成相似。

飞马石油公司先失两个回合，便希望在"派拉罗"案的第三项因素上有所作为。飞马石油公司指出，它与美孚石油公司只在原油贸易市场上存在竞争，而美孚石油公司从未在原油贸易市场上使用"飞马"标志。双方不在同一个市场上使用"飞马"商标，所以不会造成消费者混淆误认。法院再次拒绝了飞马石油公司的抗辩理由。

法院指出，美孚石油公司不仅经营原油贸易，而且经营各种石油产品，提供各种石油服务，涉足整个石油行业，因此衡量双方的产品是否相近不能仅仅局限于原油贸易市场，而是要看整个石油行业。若把眼光放在整个石油行业中，法院并不排除飞马石油公司的"飞马"名称会造成消费者混淆误认。法院同时强调，不能单纯地看双方的产品或服务是否相近，以及双方是否在同一个市场上竞争，而是必须把这项因素与前两项因素综合起来判断。因为美孚石油公司的"飞马"标志闻名于世，老少皆知，理应享有最大范围的保护，所以法院把衡量第三项因素的范围扩展到整个石油行业，而不仅仅局限于原油贸易市场。

至于第四项因素，法院也作出了不利于飞马石油公司的判定。飞马石油公司承认在使用"飞马"名称前知道美孚石油公司的"飞马"标志，但是不承认自己故意模仿美孚石油公司的"飞马"商标。法院反驳了飞马石油公司的辩词，指出飞马石油公司的创始人曾受过良好的教育，不但了解美孚石油公司的"飞马"商标，而且也知道希腊神话中的飞马形象。在这种情况下，他仍然坚持使用"飞马"文字商标，难逃故意侵权之嫌。按照美国商标法，如果法院发现被告故意侵权，则自动假定被告的侵权会造成消费者混淆误认。

至于第五项因素，法院则依据美孚石油公司提供的消费者抽样调查结果，判定飞马石油公司的"飞马"商标已经在事实上混淆了消费者的视听，令不少消费者把此"飞马"误认为彼"飞马"。

就第六项因素，飞马石油公司辩称，其原油产品与美孚石油公司的原油产品完全相同，品质没有高低之分。虽然法院接受了这种结论，但是却指出飞马石油公司的原油品质高低并不是本案的关键。

就第七项因素而言，法院承认涉足原油贸易市场的都是一些头脑复杂的买主，而且在决定购买大批原油之前都会对卖主做信用调查。在这种情况下，买主不太容易把飞马石油公司误认作美孚石油公司。但是，法院对此指出，问题的关键不在于在交易达成之时买主会不会产生混淆误认，问题在于买主看到"飞马"这一名称时是否会在第一印象上产生混淆误认。按照这一标准，法院判定，即使是原油市场上头脑精明的买主也会在看到"飞马"的第一印象中产生混淆误认。

在判定消费者混淆误认的八项因素中，法院作出七项不利于飞马石油公司的决定。此案的输赢已成定局，法院甚至没有必要再分析第八项因素了。

在此基础上，法院判决飞马石油公司的"飞马"名称侵害了美孚石油公司的"飞马"图案商标。

本案启示与解析

是否会造成消费者"混淆误认"，是法院判定商标侵权的标准。如果被告的商标会造成消费者混淆误认，误把它认作原告的商标，那么法庭就可以确定被告的商标侵权。否则，法院就无法确定被告的商标侵权。应当注意的是，问题的重点在于消费者混淆误认的可能性，而不是被告的商标是否在实际上已经造成了消费者的混淆误认。即使没有证据显示一个商标已经在实际上造成了消费者混淆误认，也不能排除这个商标有可能造成消费者混淆误认。

事实上，根据"派拉罗"案的经典判例，是否在实际上造成了消费者混淆误认，只是法院判定一个商标是否会造成消费者混淆误认的八个因素之一。"派拉罗"判例中列出的八个因素是法院衡量被告商标是否造成消费者混淆误认的标准，俗称"派拉罗"因素。这八个因素包括：一，原告商标的知名度。二，两个商标雷同的程度。三，原告与被告的产品或服务近似的程度。四，被告是否有恶意或故意导致消费者混淆误认。五，被告的商标是否已经在实际上造成了混淆误认。六，被告的产品或服务的品质。七，消费者是否头脑精明。八，原告将来是否会生产被告的产品或提供被告的服务。如今，几乎所有的商标侵权案都会引用"派拉罗"判例，综合考虑这八个因素，以确定被告的商标是否会造成消费者混淆误认。

值得注意的是，一般而言法院不会将八个因素全部逐一进行分析。相反的，法院往往会根据具体案情集中分析这八个因素中的某几个重要因素。所以，法院在运用"派拉罗"因素确定消费者是否会混淆误认时，具有比较大的裁量空间。正因为如此，诉讼各方也不至于因为其中一个或两个因素对自己不利而输掉官司。同样，诉讼各方也不会因为其中一个或两个因素对自己有利而打赢官司。以本案而言，这八个因素并不是每个因素都对原告美孚石油公司有利。但是，综合考虑这八项因素后，法院仍然作出了有利于美孚石油公司的判决。

引用判决

Mobil Oil Corporation, v. Pegasus Petroleum Corporation, Opinion by LUMBARD, *Circuit Judge*:

Mobil Oil Corporation ▼ brought this action in the Southern District charging Pegasus Petroleum Corporation with trademark infringement and unfair competition, 15 U. S. C. § 1114 (1); false designation of origin, 15 U. S. C. § 1125 (a); and trademark dilution, N. Y. Gen. Bus. Law § 368-d. On July 8, 1986, after a three-day bench trial, Judge MacMahon entered judgment for Mobil on each of its claims, dismissed Pegasus Petroleum's counterclaims seeking to cancel Mobil's trademark registration, and enjoined Pegasus Petroleum from using the mark "Pegasus" in connection with the petroleum industry or related businesses. We affirm.

Mobil, one of the world's largest corporations, manufactures and sells a vast array of petroleum products to industrial consumers and to the general public. Since 1931, Mobil has made extensive use of its well known "flying horse" symbol——representing Pegasus, the winged horse of Greek mythology——in connection with its petroleum business. Mobil displays this registered trademark, usually in red, but occasionally in blue, black, white, or outline form, at virtually all its gasoline service stations (usually on an illuminated disk four feet in diameter); in connection with all petroleum products sold at its service stations; in connection with the sale of a variety of its other petroleum products; on its oil tankers, barges, and other vehicles; and on its letterhead. As the district court explained, it is "undisputed that Mobil's extensive use of the flying horse symbol for such a long period of time in connection with all of Mobil's commercial activity has rendered it a very strong mark. Indeed, counsel for [Pegasus Petroleum] could think of few trademarks, if any, that were stronger trademarks in American commerce today."

As part of its petroleum business, Mobil buys and sells crude and refined petroleum products in bulk, an activity known as oil trading, to insure a continuous flow of oil to its refineries, and ultimately to its customers. The oil trading market is tight-knit and sophisticated: It encompasses a select group of professional buyers and brokers, representing approximately 200 oil companies, wholesalers, and oil traders; deals are in the hundreds of thousands, or millions of dollars, and in tens of tons; and, oil traders do not consummate deals with strangers except after a thorough credit check. Mobil does not use its flying horse symbol in connection with its oil trading business.

Pegasus Petroleum, incorporated ▼in 1981, confines its activities to oil trading, and does not sell directly to the general public. Its founder, Gregory Callimanopulos, testified that he selected the name "Pegasus Petroleum" because he wanted a name with both mythical connotations and alliterative qualities. Callimanopulos admitted that he knew of Mobil's flying horse symbol when he picked the name, but claimed that he did not know that the symbol represented Pegasus or that Mobil used the word "Pegasus" in connection with its petroleum business. Shortly after the genesis of Pegasus Petroleum, Ben Pollner, then president of the company, sent a letter to 400-500 people in the oil trading business informing them about Pegasus Petroleum's formation. The letter stated that Pegasus Petroleum was part of the "Callimanopulos group of companies," and used an interlocking double P as a letterhead. Pegasus Petroleum has never used a flying horse symbol and sells no products with the name "Pegasus" on them.

In 1982, Mobil approached Pegasus Petroleum after learning of its use of the mark "Pegasus. " When attempts to reach an agreement failed, Mobil filed the instant suit. The case proceeded to trial before Judge MacMahon, without a jury. After examining the criteria set forth in *Polaroid Corp. v. Polarad Electronics Corp.* , 287 F. 2d 492, 495 (2d Cir.), *cert. denied*, 368 U. S. 820, 131 U. S. P. Q. (BNA) 499, 82 S. Ct. 36, 7 L. Ed. 2d 25 (1961), Judge MacMahon concluded that "there is a sufficient likelihood of confusion between [Mobil's flying horse symbol] and [Pegasus Petroleum's use of the 'Pegasus' mark] to grant [Mobil] relief under the Lanham Act." Judge MacMahon also held for Mobil on its unfair competition, false designation, and antidilution claims; and enjoined Pegasus Petroleum's further use of the mark "Pegasus" in connection with the oil industry. With Mobil's consent, the injunction has been stayed, pending resolution of this appeal.

The Lanham Act prohibits the use of "any reproduction, counterfeit, copy, or colorable imitation of a registered mark" where "such use is likely to cause confusion, or to cause mistake, or to deceive." 15 U. S. C. § 1114 (1)(a). To state a claim under this section, a plaintiff must show a "likelihood that an appreciable number of ordinarily prudent purchasers are likely to be misled, or indeed simply confused, as to the source of the goods in question." *Mushroom Makers, Inc. v. R. G. Barry Corp.*, 580 F. 2d 44, 47 (2d Cir. 1978) (per curiam) (citing cases), *cert. denied*, 439 U. S. 1116, 59 L. Ed. 2d 75, 99 S. Ct. 1022 (1979). A nonexclusive list of eight factors, articulated by Judge Friendly in *Polaroid, supra*, 287 F. 2d at 495, helps guide this inquiry: (1) the strength of the plaintiff's mark: (2) the degree of similarity between the two marks; (3) the competitive proximity of the products or services; (4) the existence of actual confusion; (5) the likelihood that the plaintiff will "bridge the gap" between the two markets; (6) the defendant's good faith in adopting its mark; (7) the quality of the defendant's product; and (8) the sophistication of the purchasers. We agree with both the district court's determination of each of the *Polaroid* factors and its balancing of those factors to arrive at its conclusion that Pegasus Petroleum infringed upon Mobil's senior mark——the flying horse. Pegasus Petroleum does not dispute the district court's conclusion that the strength of Mobil's flying horse mark is "without question, and perhaps without equal." As an arbitrary mark——there is nothing suggestive of the petroleum business in the flying horse symbol——Mobil's symbol deserves "the most protection the Lanham Act can provide." *Lois Sportswear, U. S. A. , Inc. v. Levi Strauss & Co.*, 799 F. 2d 867, 871 (2d Cir. 1986). On the other hand, Pegasus Petroleum vigorously attacks the district court's finding of similarity between the two marks. Pegasus Petroleum argues that the district court erred by blindly equating the word "Pegasus" with its pictorial representation——Mobil's flying horse. While we agree that words and their pictorial representations should not be equated as a matter of law, a district court may make such a determination as a factual matter. See, e. g. , *Beer Nuts, Inc. v. King Nut Co.* , 477 F. 2d 326, 329 (6th Cir.) ("It is well settled that words and their pictorial representation are treated the same in determining the likelihood of confusion between two marks. "), *cert. denied*, 414 U. S. 858, 38 L. Ed. 2d 108, 94 S. Ct. 66, 179 U. S. P. Q. (BNA) 322 (1973); *Izod, Ltd. v. Zip Hosiery Co.* , 56 C. C. P. A. 812, 405 F. 2d 575, 577, 160 U. S. P. Q. (BNA) 202 (1969) ("Members of the purchasing public viewing appellant's pictorial representation of a feline animal as applied to men's and women's outer shirts and appellee's literal designation TIGER HEAD for men's work socks might well and reasonably conclude that the respective goods of the parties emanated from the same source. "): *Instrumentalist Co. v. Marine Corps League*, 509 F. Supp. 323, 328 (N. D. Ill. 1981) ("the fact that defendants' certificate most prominently displays a picture of Sousa (rather than a literal transcription of his name) does not preclude a finding of infringement"). *See generally* 2 J. McCarthy, *Trademarks and Unfair Competition*, § 23: 8 at 68 & n. 10 (2d ed. 1984) (citing cases). Judge MacMahon made such a determination here.

We find that the similarity of the mark exists in the strong probability that prospective purchasers of defendant's product will equate or translate Mobil's symbol for "Pegasus" and vice versa.

We find that the word "Pegasus" evokes the symbol of the flying red horse and that the flying horse is associated in the mind with Mobil. In other words, the symbol of the flying horse and its name "Pegasus" are synonymous. That conclusion finds support in common sense as well as the record.

The third *Polaroid* factor addresses the competitive proximity between the two marks. Pegasus Petroleum points out that while Judge MacMahon correctly found that Mobil and Pegasus Petroleum both compete in the oil trading business, Mobil does not use its flying horse trademark in that field. However, "direct competition between the products is not a prerequisite to relief.... Confusion, or the likelihood of confusion, not competition, is the real test of trademark infringement." *Continental Motors Corp. v. Continental Aviation Corp.*, 375 F. 2d 857, 861, 153 U. S. P. Q. (BNA) 313 (5th Cir. 1967) (citations omitted). Both Mobil and Pegasus Petroleum use their marks in the petroleum industry. See, *e. g.*, *AMF Inc. v. Sleekcraft Boats*, 599 F. 2d 341, 350 (9th Cir. 1979) (competitive proximity may be found where goods are similar in use and function); *Syntex Laboratories, Inc. v. Norwich Pharmacal Co.*, 437 F. 2d 566 (2d Cir. 1971) (same).

Moreover, competitive proximity must be measured with reference to the first two *Polaroid* factors: The unparalleled strength of Mobil's mark demands that it be given broad protection against infringers. See, *e. g.*, *James Burrough Ltd. v. Sign of Beefeater, Inc.*, 540 F. 2d 266, 276 (7th Cir. 1976) ("A mark that is strong because of its fame or its uniqueness, is more likely to be remembered and more likely to be associated in the public mind with a greater breadth of products or services than is a mark that is weak...."); *R. J. Reynolds Tobacco Co. v. R. Seelig & Hille*, 201 U. S. P. Q. (BNA) 856, 860 (T. M. T. A. B. 1978) ("the law today rewards a famous or well known mark with a larger cloak of protection than in the case of a lesser known mark because of the tendency of the consuming public to associate a relatively unknown mark with one to which they have long been exposed if the [relatively unknown] mark bears any resemblance thereto"). Mobil's ubiquitous presence throughout the petroleum industry further increases the likelihood that a consumer will confuse Pegasus Petroleum with Mobil. See *Armco, Inc. v. Armco Burglar Alarm Co.*, 693 F. 2d 1155, 1161 (5th Cir. 1982) ("Diversification makes it more likely that a potential customer would associate the non-diversified company's services with the diversified company, even though the two companies do not actually compete."). Finally, the great similarity between the two marks——the district court concluded that they were "synonymous" ——entitles Mobil's mark to protection over a broader range of related products. *Cf. Squirtco v. Seven-Up Co.*,

147

美国商标法判例研究

628 F. 2d 1086, 1091 (8th Cir. 1980) (closely related products require less similarity to support a finding of trademark infringement). We agree with the district court's finding of competitive proximity.

Our evaluation of the first three *Polaroid* factors, perhaps the most significant in determining the likelihood of confusion, see *Vitarroz v. Borden, Inc. , 644 F. 2d 960, 966 (2d Cir. 1981)*, strongly supports the district court's conclusion that such a likelihood exists. The district court's finding under the fourth *Polaroid* factor that Pegasus Petroleum did not innocently select its potentially confusing mark reinforces this conclusion: Intentional copying gives rise to a presumption of a likelihood of confusion. *Perfect Fit Industries v. Acme Quilting Co. , 618 F. 2d 950, 954 (2d Cir. 1980)* (citing cases). The district court discredited Gregory Callimanopulos's testimony that "he did not intentionally choose the tradename 'Pegasus' with either the symbol of Mobil's flying horse or Mobil's wordmark in mind. " The court explained:

Mr. Callimanopulos is obviously an educated, sophisticated man who, from his prior shipping business, was familiar with the flying horse and from his own background and education and awareness of Greek mythology could not have escaped the conclusion that the use of the word 'Pegasus' would infringe the tradename and symbol of the plaintiff.

In response, Pegasus Petroleum first contends that this finding is clearly erroneous given the objective evidence before the court, specifically pointing to its letter to the trade of June, 1982, which stated that it was a member of the Callimanopulos group of companies. While this correspondence was one piece of evidence for the district court to consider, it falls far short of establishing, by itself, Pegasus Petroleum's good faith. Pegasus Petroleum also notes that "actual and constructive notice of another company's prior registration of the mark ... [is] not*necessarily* indicative of bad faith, because the presumption of an exclusive right to use a registered mark extends only so far as the goods or services noted in the registration certificate. " *McGregor-Doniger, Inc. v. Drizzle, Inc. , 599 F. 2d 1126, 1137 (2d Cir. 1979)* (emphasis added). However, actual or constructive knowledge *may* signal bad faith. Indeed,

148

"in this circuit and others, numerous decisions have recognized that the second comer has a duty to so name and dress his product as to avoid all likelihood of consumers confusing it with the product of the first comer. " *Harold F. Ritchie Inc. v. Chesebrough–Pond's, Inc.* , 281 F. 2d 755, 758 (2d Cir. 1960) (footnote omitted); *see generally* 2 J. McCarthy, *supra*, § 23: 33 at 148 ("Where we can perceive freedom of choice with full knowledge of a senior user's mark, we can readily read into defendant's choice of a confusingly similar mark the intent to get a free ride upon the reputation of a well–known mark. "). We believe the record clearly substantiates Judge MacMahon's inference of bad faith.

The existence of some evidence of actual confusion, the fifth*Polaroid* factor, further buttresses the finding of a likelihood of confusion. See, *e. g.* , *World Carpets, Inc. v. Dick Littrell's New World Carpets*, 438 F. 2d 482, 489 (5th Cir. 1971) ("While … it is not necessary to show actual confusion … there can be no more positive or substantial proof of the likelihood of confusion than proof of actual confusion. "). Both Mobil and Pegasus Petroleum offered surveys of consumers and of members of the oil trading industry as evidence relating to the existence of actual confusion between the two marks. The district court properly admitted these surveys into evidence, despite claims of statistical imperfections by both sides, as those criticisms affected the weight accorded to the evidence rather than its admissibility. See, *e. g.* , *Grotrian, Helfferich, Schulz, Th. Steinweg Nachf. v. Steinway & Sons*, 523 F. 2d 1331, 1341 (2d Cir. 1975) . After reviewing these surveys, Judge MacMahon concluded that there was "evidence of actual confusion. " His decision was not clearly erroneous. *Id.*

Pegasus Petroleum argues that the absence of misdirected mail and telephone calls between the parties, and the fact that Pegasus Petroleum must post a letter of credit as security during its oil trading deals while Mobil need not, prove that no actual confusion between the two firms existed. This argument misunderstands the district court's opinion. Judge MacMahon found a likelihood of confusion not in the fact that a third party would do business with Pegasus Petroleum believing it related to Mobil, but rather in the likelihood that Pegasus Petroleum would gain crucial credibility during the initial phases of a deal. For example, an oil trader might listen to a cold phone call from Pegasus Petroleum——an admittedly oft used procedure in the oil trading business——when otherwise he might not, because of the possibility that Pegasus Petroleum is related to Mobil. The absence of misdirected phone calls and the difference in the letter of credit requirements are other matters.

Pegasus Petroleum never rebutted the inference of a likelihood of confusion. The district court did not examine the sixth *Polaroid* factor——whether Mobil would "bridge the gap" by expanding its use of the flying horse symbol into the oil trading market (Mobil presently competes, but does not use its flying horse trademark, in the oil trading field). Nevertheless, "sufficient likelihood of confusion may be established although likelihood of bridging the gap is not demonstrated." *McGregor – Doniger, supra*, 599 F. 2d at 1136. The absence of an intent to bridge the gap does not negate a finding of a likelihood of confusion in the market as presently constituted. See *Scarves by Vera, Inc. v. Todo Imports Ltd.*, 544 F. 2d 1167, 1174 (2d Cir. 1976). The Lanham Act extends trademark protection to related goods in order to guard against numerous evils in addition to restraints on the possible expansion of the senior user's market, including consumer confusion, tarnishment of the senior user's reputation, and unjust enrichment of the infringer. 2 J. McCarthy, *supra*, § 24: 5 at 177–81.

The seventh *Polaroid* factor suggests that the court examine the quality of Pegasus Petroleum's product. The district court made no findings on this issue. Pegasus Petroleum argues that its product——oil——does not differ from that sold by Mobil. However, a senior user may sue to protect his reputation even where the infringer's goods are of top quality. See, *e. g.*, *Wesley – Jessen Div. of Schering Corp. v. Bausch & Lomb Inc.*, 698 F. 2d 862, 867 (7th Cir. 1983) ("Even if the infringer's goods are of high quality, the victim has the right to insist that its reputation not be imperiled by another's actions."); *James Burrough, Ltd. v. Ferrara*, 6 Misc. 2d 692, 694, 165 N. Y. S. 2d 825, 826 (Sup. Ct. 1957) ("plaintiff is not required to put its reputation in defendant's hands, no matter how capable those hands may be"); 2 J. McCarthy, *supra*, § 24: 5 at 176−77 ("If the other user sometime in the future engaged in false advertising, or cheated customs, or employed a rude salesperson, or simply sold some shoddy merchandise, the first user of the mark would suffer because buyers would link them together through the medium of the similar marks. ").

We finally turn to the eighth *Polaroid* factor, the sophistication of purchasers. The district court concluded that, "even though defendant's business is transacted in large quantities only with sophisticated oil traders, there is still and nevertheless a likelihood of confusion. " We agree. As explained above, the district court's concerns focused upon the probability that potential purchasers would be misled into an initial interest in Pegasus Petroleum. Such initial confusion works a sufficient trademark injury. *Steinway & Sons*, *supra*, 523 F. 2d at 1342. The district court's concerns had a sufficient basis in fact despite the sophistication of the oil trading market: Pegasus Petroleum admits that it solicits business through telephone calls to potential customers. Pegasus Petroleum also acknowledges that "trust, in the oil industry, is of paramount importance. " Finally, Mobil's Oil Trading Department executive, Thomas Cory, testified that he did not undertake an investigation of a new company before initially dealing with it. Such an investigation was undertaken only prior to the culmination of a deal.

For the foregoing reasons, we agree with the district court's finding that Pegasus Petroleum infringed on Mobil's registered flying horse trademark and therefore affirm its judgment. Mobil's "unfair competition claim is governed by essentially the same considerations as its infringement claim. " *Steinway & Sons*, *supra*, 523 F. 2d at 1342 n. 21. Therefore, we also affirm the district court on Mobil's unfair competition claim. As the judgment finds full support in the district court's findings on Mobil's first two claims, we need not consider Mobil's other two claims——false designation of origin, and trademark dilution under New York law.

Affirmed.

商标的真正使用

宝洁公司状告强生公司案

Sure

判例简介

宝洁公司（Procter & Gamble Company）和强生公司（Johnson & Johnson, Inc.）均是美国排名前三十位的超大企业。宝洁公司成立于 1837 年，现在世界各地雇有 10 万多名员工，生产近 300 多种产品，年销售额高达 500 亿美金。强生公司成立于 1886 年，现在世界上 50 多个国家设有分公司，产品行销世界各国，销售额与宝洁公司不相上下。在宝洁公司和强生公司生产的众多产品中都包括了个人卫生保健用品，如除臭剂、卫生棉、漱口水等。

在美国个人卫生保健用品市场上，宝洁、强生两大公司的几个品牌竞争激烈，新产品层出不穷。虽然各个公司采取的品牌战略不同，但新产品的推出必然伴随着商标问题。有时候，公司采用"旧瓶装新酒"的办法，在新产品上贴着旧商标。这样做的好处是，消费者已经认同了已有的商标，所以公司不用冒太大风险启用一种新商标。有时候，公司则采用"新瓶装新酒"的办法，为新产品打造一个新商标。这样做自然名正言顺，但是，也有一定风险，消费者不一定认同一个新品牌。为了减少这种不被消费者认同的风险，各大公司的消费者研究部门都会先做研究，调查消费者对一个新商标的反应。宝洁公司和强生公司也不例外。只不过，与强生公司相比，宝洁公司的商标战略更加虎视眈眈、咄咄逼人。

20 世纪 70 年代，宝洁公司和强生公司展开了激烈的商标诉讼战。双方的诉讼缘起于两个商标 Sure 和 Assure。1964 年，宝洁公司准备注册 Sure 这个商标，用以生产销售腋下除臭剂和妇女卫生棉。谁知，这个商标早已被另一家生产除臭剂的公司注册。宝洁公司为此打了四年官司，才从那家公司购得 Sure 这个商标，并于 1968 年正式在美国专利商标局申请注册。

SURE

宝洁公司于 1968 年 6 月 11 日注册的商标

正在宝洁公司购得 Sure 这个商标之际，半路又杀出个程咬金。原来，还有一家公司拥有一个名为 Assure 的商标，与 Sure 十分相近。无奈，宝洁公司又出资购得 Assure 商标，准备用来生产、销售漱口水和洗发水。1972 年，宝洁公司正式将 Sure 这一品牌的除臭剂推入市场，大获成功，一跃而成美国市场上销量最大的腋下除臭剂。1974 年，宝洁公司终于将第一批妇女卫生棉投入市场。但是，宝洁公司并没有用 Sure 商标，而是用了 Rely 商标。

按照美国商标法，一个商标在注册之后并不就此一劳永逸。注册之后，还需要维护。而维护的关键是必须在商品交易中使用这个商标。如果一个商标在注册之后连续三年没有在商品交易中使用，就不再受法律保护。这就是美国商标法中的使用原则。使用原则主要是为了防止抢注商标，造成商标资源浪费或不公平竞争。

美国商标法中的使用原则令一些希望储存商标资源的大公司伤透脑筋，纷纷想出各种应对之策。宝洁公司为此专门建立了一个名为"次要品牌"的计划，专门维护那些已经注册却还没有正式在市场中使用的商标。宝洁公司在注册了 Sure 商标生产妇女卫生棉和 Assure 商标生产漱口水以后，并没有将这两个品牌的产品正式投入市场。于是，Sure 牌卫生棉和 Assure 牌漱口水便进入了"次要品牌"计划，成为被维护的商标。当然，Sure 牌的腋下除臭剂仍然是宝洁公司的主打品牌，因为已经正式投放市场，所以不需要"次要品牌"计划来专门维护。

1977年，强生公司研制出一种新型防漏卫生棉。在将这种卫生棉投入市场前，强生公司决定专门为其打造一个新商标。强生公司先后挑选了一些商标名称，但是对消费者抽样调查的结果都不令人满意。最后，强生公司的目光集中到 Assure 这个商标上。消费者抽样调查的结果显示，这一商标可望获得消费者认同。与此同时，强生公司又开发出一种新型妇女用卫生棉，并决定以 Sure & Natural 的商标将其投入市场。

在使用 Assure 和 Sure & Natural 两个商标前，强生公司的律师发现，宝洁公司已经分别在1968年和1970年注册了 Sure 和 Assure 两个商标。强生公司立即在全国市场展开调查，发现宝洁公司在1968年注册 Sure 商标以后，用其销售腋下除臭剂，而没有发现宝洁公司用这一商标销售妇女卫生棉或卫生护垫。而且，强生公司发现宝洁公司只在1970年注册了 Assure 这个商标，但是并没有发现宝洁公司用这个商标销售任何产品。

ASSURE

1970年宝洁公司经转让取得 Assure 文字商标

根据这份调查的结果，强生公司的律师建议，强生公司可以注册使用 Assure 这个商标生产妇女卫生棉。原因在于，宝洁公司虽然注册了 Sure 商标生产卫生棉和 Assure 商标生产漱口水，但是从来没有在市场上用 Sure 销售卫生棉，或用 Assure 销售任何产品。这意味着，商标法已经不再保护宝洁公司使用 Sure 商标销售卫生棉或使用 Assure 销售任何产品的权利。

在律师的建议下，强生公司便开始将新型卫生棉和新型卫生护垫两种产品投放市场，并投入巨资宣传 Assure 和 Sure & Natural 两个商标。这一行为的结果必然会导致宝洁公司的诉讼。果然，宝洁公司以商标侵权等为由向法院起诉强生公司，要求强生公司立即停止使用这两个有争议的商标。

面对宝洁公司的指控，强生公司显然是有备而战。俗话说，进攻是最佳的防御。在商标战中也不例外。商标战中的被告并不一定完全处于守势，被动挨打。在一定条件下，被告完全可以采取主动进攻的策略，转攻为守。在宝洁公司告强生公司的商标侵权案中，强生公司便采取了主动攻击的策略。

具体而言，强生公司在辩护中直接攻击宝洁公司的"次要品牌"项目，称这个项目并不符合商标法规定的商标要在"商品交易中使用"的要求，没有有效地维护 Sure 和 Assure 两个商标。按照商标法，商标在注册之后必须在商品交易中连续使用。如果一个商标连续三年不在商品交易中使用，这个商标就进入了公共领域，任何其他人或公司都可以使用。强生公司称，宝洁公司在注册了 Sure 商标生产卫生棉和 Assure 商标生产漱口水后，超过三年没有在商品交易中使用，所以这两个商标已经进入了公共领域。任何人可以用 Sure 商标来生产卫生棉，用 Assure 商标来生产漱口水或其他产品。

宝洁公司则申诉，在注册了 Sure 和 Assure 两个商标后，宝洁公司一直在通过"次要品牌"计划使用这两个商标。按照宝洁公司"次要品牌"计划的规定，宝洁公司在每个次要品牌下每年要向市场投入五十件产品。宝洁公司的具体做法是，在自己的产品或买来的其他产品上贴上宝洁公司次要品牌的商标，然后将这些产品销往美国至少十个州。法院发现，宝洁公司的"次要品牌"计划共包括 127 个商标，涉及 180 种产品。这些品牌足以供宝洁公司挑选使用五十年。

在本案中，宝洁公司按照"次要品牌"计划的规定，每年都会在五十件卫生棉产品上贴上 Sure 的商标，并将这些产品销往至少十个州。从 1964 年宝洁公司开始使用 Sure 这个商标起到这起诉讼开始的十二年间，宝洁公司 Sure 牌卫生棉的累计销售额只有 874.70 美元。而且，宝洁公司早已将自己的卫生棉产品投放市场，但是并没有标示 Sure 这个商标进行销售。同样，宝洁公司从 1970 年开始拥有 Assure 商标，每年在五十件漱口水和洗发水产品上贴上 Assure 的商标，并将这些产品销往十个州。迄至诉讼开始，宝洁公司 Assure 牌漱口水和洗发水的累积销售额只有 491.30 美元。

法院指出，美国商标法规定商标在注册后必须在商品交易中连续使用。这意味着，商标所有者必须诚心诚意地在商品交易中使用这个商标，而不只是出于维护商标的目的象征性地使用。法院发现，宝洁公司每年销售五十件 Sure 牌的卫生棉以及 Assure 牌的漱口水和洗发水不符合在商品交易中连续使用这两个商标的条件。因此，法院宣判，美国商标法不再保护宝洁公司使用

Sure 这个商标生产卫生棉，或使用 Assure 这个商标生产任何产品。

本案启示与解析

人们可能听说过企业囤积原料、囤积产品等情况，但是大概没有听说过企业囤积商标的事情。而本案所涉及的正是一个企业囤积商标的问题。宝洁公司利用"次要品牌"计划囤积商标的做法是否可取，暂且不论，这种做法至少有力地说明了商标是一种资源、一种财富。商标有时甚至会左右一件产品的销路。这意味着，在其他因素相同或相似的情况下，商标会决定一件产品的市场竞争力。正因为看到了商标在推广产品方面的重要性，宝洁公司才专门设立了以囤积商标为目标的"次要品牌"计划，不惜重金购买囤积商标，以备将来之用。

显然，宝洁公司的"次要品牌"计划是依照美国商标法中"使用原则"的要求设计的，可谓上有政策，下有对策。按照使用原则，如果一个商标在注册后的连续三年内，没有在商业中使用，这个商标就进入了公共领域，商标权人就不再拥有这个商标的所有权和独家使用权。所以，商标拥有者在注册商标后，必须在商业中连续使用，才能保住这个商标的所有权。

表面上看，宝洁公司的"次要品牌"计划似乎符合"使用原则"的要求，因为宝洁公司每年都会在五十件产品上使用囤积的商标，销往美国各地。但是，这种做法显然有悖于美国商标法中使用原则的立法目的。美国商标法之所以要求商标注册后必须在商业中连续使用，一个重要目的就在于避免抢注商标，以造成商标资源的浪费。强生公司正是抓住宝洁公司"次级品牌"计划的弱点，成功地虎口夺宝，如愿获得了自己钟情的两个商标。

在与宝洁公司的商标争夺战中，强生公司可谓有备而来，而且在战略上技高一筹。首先，在决定使用 Sure 和 Assure & Natural 两个商标前，强生公司做了大量的研究和调查，对宝洁公司在市场上使用 Sure 和 Assure 两个商标的情况了如指掌。其次，面对宝洁公司的指控，强生公司有备而战，制定了适当的应战策略。

俗话说，进攻是最好的防御。在商标战中，也是如此。在一定条件下，被告完全可以采取主动进攻的策略，以攻为守。在本案中，面对宝洁公司的起诉，强生公司便采取了主动攻击的策略。具体而言，强生公司在辩护中直接攻击宝洁公司的"次要品牌"计划，称这个计划并不符合美国商标法规定的商标要在"商业中使用"的要求，没有有效地维护 Sure 和 Assure 两个商标。事实证明，强生公司的这一策略达到了预期目的，成功地说服了法院作出对其有利的判决。

引用判决

The PROCTER & GAMBLE COMPANY, v.
JOHNSON & JOHNSON INCORPORATED
and Personal Products Company

Opinion by SUPPLEMENTAL FINDINGS

Upon submission of forms of judgment for entry, P&G contends that PPC's application for the cancellation of P&G's Assure marks for mouthwash and shampoo should be denied because PPC has failed to demonstrate that it is damaged by the continued registration of those marks. P&G contends that such proof of damage is required by the terms of § 14 of the Lanham Act, 15 U. S. C. § 1064. See *Fuller Products Co. v. Fuller Brush Co.*, 299 F. 2d 772 (7th Cir. 1962); *D. M. & Antique Import Corp. v. Royal Saxe Corp.*, 311 F. Supp. 1261, 1269 (S. D. N. Y. 1970).

PPC responds that the provisions of § 14 are only applicable when the petitioner initiates an action seeking cancellation. It argues that where cancellation is sought defensively, the provisions of § 37, 15 U. S. C. § 1119, establish the court's power to order cancellation irrespective of proof of damage. See *Abercrombie & Fitch Co. v. Hunting World, Inc.*, 537 F. 2d 4 (2d Cir. 1972).

Assuming, but not deciding that P&G is correct in its statutory interpretation, I find that PPC has demonstrated such damage as may be required by the terms of § 14. P&G brought this action in part on behalf of its Assure marks seeking to enjoin PPC's use of Assure for tampons. When PPC was forced to defend this action, it sustained damage and was put in fear of further damage sufficient to justify its plea for cancellation.

If, while P&G's action was pending, PPC had brought a cancellation proceeding in the Patent Office directed at the Assure marks, I have no doubt that the fact of P&G's attack on PPC's Assure mark would have provided the showing of harm necessary to satisfy the damage requirement of § 14. This is no less so because PPC chose to assert the plea by answer and counterclaim rather than by a separate cancellation proceeding in the patent office. At the time these demands were asserted by PPC it was clear that P&G's demand for an injunction presented a real possibility of damage to PPC. PPC cannot have lost such standing by prevailing in the lawsuit. P&G, having required PPC to defend a lawsuit brought on behalf of P&G's Assure marks, cannot reasonably be heard to deny that its Assure marks are damaging to PPC. Damage has already been inflicted.

Moreover, P&G's action suggests the possibility of still further harm to PPC's right to register, freely use, and expand its use of its Assure mark if registration of P&G's marks is continued.

Accordingly the judgment will provide for cancellation of P&G's Assure marks. So ordered.

广告不实与禁止令

可口可乐公司状告纯品康纳公司案

*It's the only leading brand not made
with concentrate and water.*

判例简介

当今社会，广告已经成为人们生活中不可或缺的一部分。从街头广告牌到电视广告、网络广告、邮寄广告，广告可谓无孔不入。在美国，电视对人们生活的影响远远超过其他媒体。大量电视节目通过各种有线和无线电视网进入千家万户，也为企业提供了商机。电视对人们生活有着如此重大的影响，自然就成为企业商标战的必争之地。电视广告随之成为企业树立和维护商标品牌必不可少的渠道。

美国国会于1914年通过《联邦贸易委员会法》，并据此建立了联邦贸易委员会（Federal Trade Commission，FTC）。主要职责是制定广告管理规章并负责监督实施，调查处理消费者对广告的控告，召开听证会，处理虚假不实不公平的广告等。FTC将不法商业广告予以规格化，其形式共包含下列内容：不实及欺诈性广告、不正当广告、吹嘘广告、诱饵广告、虚假不实的推荐或证言广告、保证广告、电视模型试验广告、香烟广告和信用消费广告等内容。FTC给不实广告所作的定义是：任何具有误解、省略，或其他可能误导大批理性消费者使其受到伤害的广告。无须任何证据证明消费者实际受到欺骗。

广告表现可以是明确的或暗含的，关键在于广告是否传达了虚假印象——即使文字上无可挑剔。

依照 FTC 的原则，有些广告虽然不具有欺骗性，但也会被认定为不正当。不正当广告意味着对消费者的"不正当的伤害"或"对公共规则（例如其他政府法令）的违背"。换句话说，不正当广告的产生是由于缺乏"完整的信息"或广告的其他一些外部特性。例如，事先未经证实的声明，利用弱势群体（如老人、儿童）的声明，以及消费者因广告主隐瞒了产品或广告中提及的竞争对手产品的重要信息而无法作出真正的选择，上述行为均属不正当行为。

电视广告宣传的品牌和产品五花八门，但招数都十分接近，不外乎老王卖瓜，自卖自夸。不过，即使夸耀自己的产品，也必须在公平交易的原则下为之，如果损害了其他企业的利益，便可能因违反商标法被告上法院。可口可乐公司状告纯品康纳公司一案，便是一起因一则 30 秒钟的电视广告所引起的商标侵权案件。

纯品康纳公司和可口可乐公司是美国市场上两大橙汁饮料生产商。可口可乐公司的主打橙汁品牌是"时刻伴侣"（Minute Maid），纯品康纳公司的主打橙汁品牌则是"金装"（Premium Pack）。这两种橙汁产品口味接近，价格相当，在同一市场上相互竞争。为了占领更大的市场占有率，两家竞争对手想尽办法，除了产品创新和提高品质外，也在广告方面投入大笔资金。无疑，电视广告是两家公司广告战的重头戏。

1983 年 2 月，纯品康纳公司发起广告攻势，重金礼聘在美国家喻户晓的奥运十项全能冠军布鲁斯·杰纳（Bruce Jenner），拍摄了一段 30 秒钟的电视广告，在各大电视台同时播出。在这段广告节目中，杰纳手握一个柳橙，同时口中念着："这是经低温杀菌的纯橙汁，由新鲜柳橙榨出。"然后，杰纳一边把挤压出的橙汁倒入纯品康纳公司的"金装"包装盒中，一边交口称赞："这是唯一不是浓缩和加水淡化的名牌橙汁。"

纯品康纳公司的这则广告一播出，就引起了可口可乐公司的注意。可口可乐公司立即要求法院禁播这则广告，理由是这则广告包含虚假内容，违反了美国商标法。美国商标法禁止公司运用虚假广告宣传产品。如果一个公司因竞争对手的虚假广告而受到损害，可以依据美国商标法向联邦法院申请禁止令（Injunction Order）。

不过，由于禁止令往往会对被告造成重大影响，法庭在颁布禁止令时十分谨慎，要求原告必须证明已经符合了三项要件：第一，原告必须证明，如果被告的行为不被立即禁止，就会给原告造成无法挽回的损害（Irreparable Harm）。第二，原告必须证明，经过法庭审判，原告很有胜诉的可能（Likelihood of Success）。第三，原告必须证明，除了禁止令之外，在法律上没有其他补偿途径。

这三项要件之中，第一项要件的难度最大。许多商标侵权案的原告因为无法证明第一项要件，而不能如愿地从法院获得禁止令。那么，在本案中，可口可乐公司如何才能有效地证明，如果纯品康纳公司的这则广告不被禁止播出，就会给可口可乐公司带来无法挽回的损害呢？按照法院的解释，如果原告可以证明自己产品的销量有所下降，即使下降原因不明，也可以符合证明"无法挽回的损害"这一条件。但是，可口可乐公司并没有向法院提供销量下降的证据。

不过，销量下降的证据并非必要证据。在证明"无法挽回的损害"时，法院并不要求原告提供确凿无疑的证据。法院只是要求原告为自己的说法提供合理的事实基础。在本案中，既然可口可乐公司称，如果纯品康纳公司这则有争议的广告不被禁止播出，就会给可口可乐公司带来无法挽回的损害，那么，可口可乐公司就必须摆出事实，证明自己这种说法是有根据的。在涉及申请禁止令的商标战中，原告经常通过问卷调查的方式来提供这种根据。

在本案中，可口可乐公司就采用了问卷调查的方式，来证明纯品康纳公司的广告将会给可口可乐公司造成无法挽回的损害。为了保证调查的可信度，可口可乐公司雇用了两家问卷调查公司，同时在消费者中展开问卷调查。调查集中在，消费者是否会被纯品康纳公司的广告所误导。如果一名消费者在看了纯品康纳公司的电视广告后，认为纯品康纳公司的橙汁是直接从橙子中榨出来的，没有经过加热或冷却处理，而其他品牌（包括可口可乐）的橙汁，都是浓缩和加水淡化的果汁，那么，这位消费者无疑会受到纯品康纳公司电视广告的误导，自然会觉得纯品康纳公司的"金装"橙汁优于可口可乐公司的"时刻伴侣"橙汁。这样一来，受到误导的消费者便不再购买可口可乐公司的"时刻伴侣"橙汁，导致销量下降，给可口可乐公司造成无法挽回的损害。

在本案中，两家调查公司的问卷调查结果显示，的确有一些消费者在看了纯品康纳公司的广告后，认为纯品康纳公司的"金装"橙汁直接由橙子榨出，而可口可乐公司的"时刻伴侣"橙汁则是用浓缩和加水淡化出来的果汁。法院认为，这两份调查结果已经足以证明，如果不禁播纯品康纳公司的这则广告，将会给可口可乐公司造成无法挽回的损害。

在符合了第一个条件之后，可口可乐公司还必须证明，在将来的审判中自己很可能胜诉。在本案中，可口可乐公司指控纯品康纳公司制作播出虚假的电视广告。所以，在未来的审判中，可口可乐公司关键是要证明，纯品康纳公司的这则广告内容虚假。如果能证明这一点，可口可乐公司便有极大的可能胜诉。美国法院把内容不实的广告分为两种：一种是表面内容虚假（literally false）；另一种是广告隐含着虚假内容，会误导消费者。

在本案中，纯品康纳公司的广告通过画面和配音向观众演示，"金装"橙汁是由柳橙直接榨汁包装而成。而事实上，纯品康纳公司的"金装"橙汁在包装之前，先加热再冷却。另外，纯品康纳公司的这则广告称"经低温杀菌的纯橙汁，由新鲜柳橙榨出"，这也与事实不符。"金装"橙汁在包装前均经过巴氏高温杀菌，根本不是"由新鲜柳橙榨出"。法院发现，纯品康纳公司的这则电视广告，至少在这两点上表面内容虚假，误导消费者。

区分表面内容虚假的广告与隐含着虚假内容的广告，将对案件的审理产生重大影响。按照法院的解释，如果一则广告表面上内容并不虚假，而是隐含着虚假的内容，那么原告若想胜诉，就必须证明消费者在事实上已经被这则广告所误导。如果一则广告表面上内容虚假，那么原告就不需要证明，消费者事实上已经被误导。法院只凭这则表面内容虚假的广告，就可判定原告能够胜诉。在本案中，法院认定纯品康纳公司的电视广告表面内容虚假，可口可乐公司不必再提出证据，证明消费者事实上已经被这则广告误导。基于以上理由，法庭批准了可口可乐公司的请求，颁布了禁止令，暂时禁止播放纯品康纳公司的这则电视广告，以等待正式审判的结果。

本案启示与解析

世界上多数国家的商标法都规定商标获得注册后，商标权人负有连续使用的义务。因为注册商标长期搁置不用，将造成社会资源的浪费，不但发挥不了商标应有的功能和作用，而且还会影响到他人的注册或使用。我国商标法规定，注册商标连续 3 年不使用的，由国家工商总局责令限期改正或者撤销其注册商标。很显然，申请撤销制度的设置，不但可以弥补商标管理机关监管力度的不足，而且也可以给予利害关系人相应的救济途径。

一般说来，主管部门很难掌握某个商标是否在使用。在实践中，提出撤销申请的一般都是与该注册商标具有利害关系的人，撤销对方的商标已经成为一种商务战略手段被广泛运用。在美国，竞争者或者其他具有"相关利益"的人可以根据美国商标法起诉广告发布者；根据这个法令起诉同行的案例有很多，多数起诉者不在乎赔偿金，主要是为了让法庭下令对方立即停止虚假广告的发布。

美国法院的禁止令分为两种：第一种是暂时禁止令（Preliminary Injunction），第二种是永久禁止令（Permanent Injunction）。这两种禁止令各有利弊。简而言之，临时禁止令的优点是申请过程短、效率高、速度快，不需要等到法庭对案件作出正式审判；其缺点是有时间期限。永久禁止令的优点是没有时间期限，缺点是申请过程漫长，效率较低，往往要等到法庭对案件作出正式审判。在可口可乐公司状告纯品康纳公司案中，可口可乐公司便是向法庭申请暂时禁止令，要求法庭在正式审判前禁止继续播放这则有争议的广告。

值得注意的是，法庭在颁布暂时禁止令时，案件尚未开始审判，涉案双方谁输谁赢尚未可知。同时，被告的行为将会给原告带来何种后果，也并不十分明朗。在这种情况下，法院要求原告向法庭证明的是一种将来一旦进入审判阶段，原告将会胜诉的可能性，以及被告的行为会给原告造成无可挽回的损失的可能性。显然，这种可能性越大，原告从法院获得暂时禁止令的希望就越大。

一般而言，原告是在情况十分急迫的情况下，才向法庭申请暂时禁止令的。虽然情况紧急，但是原告仍然必须充分准备法庭的听证，向法庭提出必要的证据，以确保法庭作出对自己有利的判决。在本案中，可口可乐公司向法庭出示了消费者问卷调查结果，充分证明了被纯品康纳公司广告误导的消费者的消费倾向，会从可口可乐公司的"时刻伴侣"橙汁转至纯品康纳公司的"金装"橙汁，从而导致可口可乐公司的"时刻伴侣"橙汁销量下降。所以，纯品康纳公司的广告会给可口可乐公司造成无法挽回的损失。如果法庭不禁播纯品康纳公司的广告，这种可能性就会实现。无疑地，暂时禁止令是在紧迫情况下，法院强行中断被告侵权行为的一种应急措施。如果原告运用得当，暂时禁止令可及时有效地保护原告的商标权益，把因被告的不法行为所造成的损失降低到最低程度。

引用判决

The COCA-COLA COMPANY, v.
TROPICANA PRODUCTS, INC.

Opinion by CARDAMONE, *Circuit Judge*

A proverb current even in the days of ancient Rome was "seeing is believing." Today, a great deal of what people see flashes before them on their TV sets. This case involves a 30-second television commercial with simultaneous audio and video components. We have no doubt that the byword of Rome is as valid now as it was then. And, if seeing something on TV has a tendency to persuade a viewer to believe, how much greater is the impact on a viewer's credulity when he both sees and hears a message at the same time?

In mid-February of 1982 defendant Tropicana Products, Inc. ▼ (Tropicana) began airing a new television commercial for its Premium Pack orange juice. The commercial shows the renowned American Olympic athlete Bruce Jenner squeezing an orange while saying "It's pure, pasteurized juice as it comes from the orange," and then shows Jenner pouring the fresh – squeezed juice into a Tropicana carton while the audio states "It's the only leading brand not made with concentrate and water."

Soon after the advertisement began running, plaintiff Coca – Cola Company ▼ (Coke, Coca–Cola▼), maker of Minute Maid orange juice, brought suit in the United States District Court for the Southern District of New York, 538 F. Supp. 1091, against Tropicana for false advertising in violation of section 43 (a) of the Lanham Act. The statute provides that anyone who uses a false description or representation in connection with goods placed in commerce "shall be liable to a civil action by [anyone] .... who believes that he is or is likely to be damaged by the use of .... such false description or representation." 15 U. S. C. § 1125 (a) (1976) . Coke claimed the commercial is false because it incorrectly represents that Premium Pack contains unprocessed, fresh – squeezed juice when in fact the juice is pasteurized (heated to about 200 degrees Fahrenheit) and sometimes frozen prior to packaging. The court below denied plaintiff's motion for a preliminary injunction to enjoin further broadcast of the advertisement pending the outcome of this litigation. In our view preliminary injunctive relief is appropriate.

I

Scope of Review

A party seeking issuance of a preliminary injunction in this Circuit must always show that it is likely to suffer possible irreparable harm if the requested relief is not granted. In addition, it must demonstrate either (1) a likelihood of success on the merits of its case or (2) sufficiently serious questions going to the merits to make them a fair ground for litigation and a balance of hardships tipping decidedly in its favor. *Sperry International Trade, Inc. v. Government of Israel*, 670 F. 2d 8, 11 (2d Cir. 1982); *Jackson Dairy, Inc. v. H. P. Hood & Sons, Inc.*, 596 F. 2d 70, 72 (2d Cir. 1979) (per curiam); *Caulfield v. Board of Education*, 583 F. 2d 605, 610 (2d Cir. 1978); *see Mulligan, Preliminary Injunction in the Second Circuit*, 43 Brooklyn

L. Rev. 831 (1977).

The grant or refusal to grant interlocutory injunctive relief rests in the sound discretion of the district court judge. Upon appeal, the order granting or denying a preliminary injunction will not be disturbed unless it results from an abuse of judicial discretion, *see Doran v. Salem Inn*, *Inc.*, 422 U. S. 922, 931 – 32, 45 L. Ed. 2d 648, 95 S. Ct. 2561 (1975), or is contrary to some rule of equity, *Meccano*, *Ltd. v. John Wanamaker*, *New York*, 253 U. S. 136, 141, 64 L. Ed. 822, 40 S. Ct. 463 (1920).

As so often is the case, the rule is easily stated; its precise meaning is more elusive. In reviewing the action of a trial court, an appellate court is not limited to reversing only when the lower court's action exceeds any reasonable bounds and to rubber – stamping with the imprimatur of an affirmance when it does not. *Omega Importing Corp. v. Petri—Kine Camera Co.*, 451 F. 2d 1190, 1197 (2d Cir. 1971) (Friendly, C. J.). Congress, in enacting 28 U. S. C. § 1292 (a) (1) to give appellate courts jurisdiction over interlocutory injunctions, surely did not envision that appellate review should be limited to a choice between the monster Scylla and the abyss of Charybdis. *See Omega Importing*, 451 F. 2d at 1197; *Carroll v. American Federation*, 295 F. 2d 484, 488 (2d Cir. 1961). The scope of review over the exercise of a trial court's discretion is broader, lying between——not relegated to—— these two extremes. Thus, as Learned Hand defined it, abuse of discretion "means no more than that we will not intervene, so long as we think that the [discretion exercised] is within permissible limits," *Barnett v. Equitable Trust Co. of New York*, 34 F. 2d 916, 920 (2d Cir. 1929), *modified and aff'd sub nom. United States v. Equitable Trust Co. of New York*, 283 U. S. 738, 75 L. Ed. 1379, 51 S. Ct. 639 (1930).

An abuse of discretion may consist of an error of law, an error of fact, or an error in the substance or form of the trial court's order. For example, the trial judge may have an erroneous view of the law which controls the pending suit——a statute, standard or line of cases may be misapprehended——or the judge may have misapplied the rules governing the issuance of injunctive relief. The Supreme Court has viewed an error of law as an abuse of a trial court's discretion. *See United States v. Corrick*, 298 U. S. 435, 438, 80 L. Ed. 1263, 56 S. Ct. 829 (1936) . Our Court has reasoned that where a trial court's denial of an injunction is based "in substantial measure upon conclusions of law which can and should be reviewed because of their basic nature" in the pending litigation, the order may be reversed and the case remanded in light of the appropriate legal principles. *Ring v. Spina*, 148 F. 2d 647, 650 (2d Cir. 1945) , *cert. denied*, 335 U. S. 813, 93 L. Ed. 368, 69 S. Ct. 30 (1948) .

Beginning decades ago, we have not hesitated to reverse an order denying a preliminary injunction where the district court reached an erroneous conclusion on the facts before it, *see Schey v. Turi*, 294 F. 679, 680 (2d Cir. 1923) ; *Palmer v. Superior Manufacturing Co.*, 210 F. 452, 453 (2d Cir. 1913) ; or, as stated now under Rule 52 (a) of the Federal Rules of Civil Procedure, where the findings of fact are clearly erroneous, *see Unicon Management Corp. v. Koppers Co., Inc.*, 366 F. 2d 199, 203 (2d Cir. 1966) . Further, an abuse of discretion may be found in the form that the order itself takes, e. g. , an injunction may be too broad or too long in duration, or several injunctions may issue where one will do, *see Donovan v. Bierwirth*, 680 F. 2d 263, 276–77 (2d Cir. 1982) .

These various errors of law, fact, substance and form, singly or in combination, may affect the relief granted at the trial level. Upon review, if an error is found which did not actually form the basis for the determination whether the injunction issued or not, no abuse of discretion will have occurred because such an error will be deemed harmless. However, when the error, whatever its nature, is the *predicate* for the trial court's order, an appellate court must reverse because in such case the order would plainly result from an improvident exercise of the trial court's discretion.

An appellate court discharges its statutory obligation to review when it independently examines the relevant factors considered by the trial court in reaching its conclusion. *See In re Josephson*, 218 F. 2d 174, 182 (1st Cir. 1954) . The appellate court presupposes that the trial judge understood and applied the applicable law and took into account all the circumstances of the case. Reversal is warranted only upon a firm conviction that such presupposition was, in a given case, misplaced. A trial court's discretion should not be disturbed where a question as to its validity is perched precariously, as though on a swaying aerial catwalk, subject to doubt and uncertainty.

We believe that the outlined scope of review and the authorities cited suffice for us to reverse in the instant case where the trial court, by a misapplication of the irreparable injury standard (discussed at II, *infra*), concluded that Coca-Cola ▾had failed to show an essential requirement for injunctive relief. This error of law constitutes an abuse of discretion which mandates reversal. In addition, we conclude that the trial court's finding of no facial falseness in defendant's TV commercial (discussed at III, *infra*) was an error of fact.

II

Irreparable Injury

Perhaps the most difficult element to demonstrate when seeking an injunction against false advertising is the likelihood that one will suffer irreparable harm if the injunction does not issue. It is virtually impossible to prove that so much of one's sales will be lost or that one's goodwill will be damaged as a direct result of a competitor's advertisement. Too many market variables enter into the advertising – sales equation. Because of these impediments, a Lanham Act plaintiff who can prove actual lost sales may obtain an injunction even if most of his sales decline is attributable to factors other than a competitor's false advertising. *Johnson & Johnson v. Carter-Wallace, Inc.*, 631 F. 2d 186, 191 (2d Cir. 1980). In fact, he need not even point to an actual loss or diversion of sales. *Id.* at 190-191.

The Lanham Act plaintiff must, however, offer something more than a mere subjective belief that he is likely to be injured as a result of the false advertising, *Id.* at 189; he must submit proof which provides a reasonable basis for that belief, *Vidal Sassoon, Inc. v. Bristol-Myers Co.*, 661 F. 2d 272, 278 (2d Cir. 1981). The likelihood of injury and causation will not be presumed, but must be demonstrated in some manner. *Johnson & Johnson*, 631 F. 2d at 190.

Two recent decisions of this Court have examined the type of proof necessary to satisfy this requirement. Relying on the fact that the products involved were in head-to-head competition, the Court in both cases directed the issuance of a preliminary injunction under the Lanham Act. *Vidal Sassoon*, 661 F. 2d at 227; *Johnson & Johnson*, 631 F. 2d at 189–91. In both decisions the Court reasoned that sales of the plaintiffs' products would probably be harmed if the competing products' advertising tended to mislead consumers in the manner alleged. Market studies were used as evidence that some consumers were in fact misled by the advertising in issue. Thus, the market studies supplied the causative link between the advertising and the plaintiffs' potential lost sales, and thereby indicated a likelihood of injury.

Applying the same reasoning to the instant case, if consumers are misled by Tropicana's commercial, Coca – Cola ▾ probably would suffer irreparable injury. Tropicana and Coca–Cola ▾ are the leading national competitors for the chilled (ready-to-serve) orange juice market. If Tropicana's advertisement misleads consumers into believing that Premium Pack is a more desirable product because it contains only fresh-squeezed, unprocessed juice, then it is likely that Coke will lose a portion of the chilled juice market and thus suffer irreparable injury.

Evidence in the record supports the conclusion that consumers are likely to be misled in this manner. A consumer reaction survey conducted by ASI Market Research, Inc. and a Burke test, measuring recall of the commercial after it was aired on television, were admitted into evidence, though neither one was considered by the district court in reference to irreparable injury. The trial court examined the ASI survey regarding the issue of likelihood of success on the merits, and found that it contained various flaws which made it difficult to determine for certain whether a large number of consumers were misled. We do not disagree with those findings. We note, moreover, that despite these flaws the district court ruled that there were at least a small number of *clearly* deceived ASI interviewees. Our examination of the Burke test results leads to the same conclusion, i. e. , that a not insubstantial number of consumers were clearly misled by the defendant's ad. Together these tests provide sufficient evidence of a risk of irreparable harm because they demonstrate that a significant number of consumers would be likely to be misled. The trial court should have considered these studies on the issue of irreparable injury. If it had, we think that it would surely have concluded, as did this Court in *Vidal Sassoon* and *Johnson & Johnson*, that the commercial will mislead consumers and, as a consequence, shift their purchases from plaintiff's product to defendant's. Coke, therefore, demonstrated that it is likely to suffer irreparable injury.

III

Likelihood of Success on the Merits

Once the initial requisite showing of irreparable harm has been made, the party seeking a preliminary injunction must satisfy either of the two alternatives regarding the merits of his case. We find that Coca-Cola ▾satisfies the more stringent first alternative because it is likely to succeed on the merits of its false advertising action.

Coke is entitled to relief under the Lanham Act if Tropicana has used a false description or representation in its Jenner commercial. *See* 15 U. S. C. § 1125 (a). When a merchandising statement or representation is literally or explicitly false, the court may grant relief without reference to the advertisement's impact on the buying public. *American Home Products Corp. v. Johnson & Johnson*, 577 F. 2d 160, 165 (2d Cir. 1978) ; *American Brands, Inc. v. R. J. Reynolds Tobacco Co.* , 413 F. Supp 1352, 1356 (S. D. N. Y. 1976) . When the challenged advertisement is implicitly rather than explicitly false, its tendency to violate the Lanham Act by misleading, confusing or deceiving should be tested by public reaction. *American Home Products*, 577 F. 2d at 165.

In viewing defendant's 30-second commercial at oral argument, we concluded that the trial court's finding that this ad was not facially false is an error of fact. Since the trial judge's finding on this issue was based solely on the inference it drew from reviewing documentary evidence, consisting of the commercial, we are in as good a position as it was to draw an appropriate inference. *See San Filippo v. United Brotherhood of Carpenters & Joiners*, 525 F. 2d 508, 511 (2d Cir. 1975) . We find, therefore, that the squeezing-pouring sequence in the Jenner commercial is false on its face. The visual component of the ad makes an explicit representation that Premium Pack is produced by squeezing oranges and pouring the freshly-squeezed juice directly into the carton. This is not a true representation of how the product is prepared. Premium Pack juice is heated and sometimes frozen prior to packaging. Additionally, the simultaneous audio component of the ad states that Premium Pack is "pasteurized juice as it comes from the orange." This statement is blatantly false——pasteurized juice does not come from oranges. Pasteurization entails heating the juice to approximately 200 degrees Fahrenheit to kill certain natural enzymes and microorganisms which cause spoilage. Moreover, even if the addition of the word "pasteurized" somehow made sense and effectively qualified the visual image, Tropicana's commercial nevertheless represented that the juice is only squeezed, heated and packaged when in fact it may actually also be frozen.

Hence, Coke is likely to succeed in arguing that Tropicana's ad is false and that it is entitled to relief under the Lanham Act. The purpose of the Act is to insure truthfulness in advertising and to eliminate misrepresentations with reference to the inherent quality or characteristic of another's product, *Vidal Sassoon*, 661 F. 2d at 278. The claim that Tropicana's Premium Pack contains only fresh-squeezed, unprocessed juice is clearly a misrepresentation as to that product's inherent quality or characteristic. Since the plaintiff has satisfied the first preliminary injunction alternative, we need not decide whether the balance of hardships tips in its favor.

Because Tropicana has made a false representation in its advertising and Coke is likely to suffer irreparable harm as a result, we reverse the district court's denial of plaintiff's application and remand this case for issuance of a preliminary injunction preventing broadcast of the squeezing-pouring sequence in the Jenner commercial.

混淆误认与商标转让

坎普状告大黄蜂水产公司案

判例简介

  路易·坎普（Louis E. Kemp）生于水产世家，祖上即以做水产生意为生。1985 年，路易·坎普继承祖业，成立了坎普水产公司（Kemp Foods, Inc.），专门生产销售人造蟹肉。人造蟹肉的主要原料是一种鱼浆。坎普水产公司开张两年后，被路易·坎普以 400 万美元的价格卖给奥斯卡水产公司（Oscar Mayer Foods Corporation）。

  按照双方的协议，路易·坎普将其公司使用的所有商标全都转让给奥斯卡水产公司。这些商标包括 "KEMP" "KEMP'S" 以及 "KEMP'S & Design"。路易·坎普同意，未经奥斯卡水产公司允许，他无权再使用这些商标以及类似的商标。同时，双方的协议也包含一项保留条款，约定路易·坎普可保留使用这些商标销售某些产品的权利。不过，路易·坎普在行使这项权利时，必须事先征得奥斯卡水产公司的同意。

  该协议签订半年后，奥斯卡水产公司进一步要求路易·坎普同意奥斯卡水产公司使用 "LOUIS KEMP" 的商标销售鱼浆。双方就此展开了谈判。奥斯卡水产公司本想独家使用 "LOUIS KEMP" 商标，要求路易·坎普彻底放弃使

172

用这个商标的权利。路易·坎普则希望自己能保留使用"LOUIS KEMP"这个商标销售某些产品的权利。最终，没有一方完全达到自己的目的。

按照双方签订的补充协议，路易·坎普授权奥斯卡水产公司使用并注册"LOUIS KEMP"商标用以销售鱼浆。路易·坎普则保留使用包含"KEMP"字样的商标销售某些产品的权利。这一模棱两可的协议为日后的商标争议埋下了伏笔。

数年之后，奥斯卡水产公司的生意几经转让，最后到了大黄蜂水产公司（Bumble Bee Seafoods, Inc.）手中。而经过这段时期的经营，"LOUIS KEMP"渐渐成为一个著名的鱼浆商标。至 1995 年 10 月止，包括大黄蜂水产公司在内的几家公司累计投入近五千万美元用以宣传"LOUIS KEMP"商标。

LOUIS KEMP

大黄蜂水产公司申请注册的文字商标（1859815）

大黄蜂水产公司申请注册的商标（1859816）

大黄蜂水产公司申请注册的商标（1859817）

大黄蜂水产公司申请注册的商标（1879931）

最后商标权人 TRIDENT SEAFOODS CORPORATION 在网络上公开使用的商标

皇天不负苦心人，"LOUIS KEMP"终于成为美国鱼浆市场上的最大品牌，年销售量高达2000万磅，在美国市场上拥有55%的市场占有率。根据过去的几个转让协议，大黄蜂水产公司拥有"KEMP""LOUIS KEMP"等路易·坎普当初转让给奥斯卡水产公司的商标。

1995年，路易·坎普看到自己的名字成为美国第一大鱼浆商标，决定要与大黄蜂水产公司分一杯羹。当然，路易·坎普知道依照当初与奥斯卡水产公司的协议，自己已经把使用"LOUIS KEMP"商标生产销售鱼浆的权利转让出去了。所以，按照协议，路易·坎普不能再用该商标生产鱼浆，即使是使用该商标生产销售其他水产品，也有违反协议之嫌。

在这种情况下，路易·坎普决定用"LOUIS KEMP"这个商标生产糙米[1]食品。为了确定这样做不至于引起与大黄蜂水产公司的商标权纠纷，路易·坎普便请律师出具法律意见。律师的法律意见书建议，路易·坎普可以使用自己的名字"LOUIS KEMP"作为商标，但是不能生产或销售任何包含鱼浆的产品，也不能在商标外观上与使用在鱼浆上的"LOUIS KEMP"商标有任何雷同。路易·坎普按照律师的法律意见书行事，找人设计了与鱼浆的"LOUIS KEMP"风格不同的"LOUIS KEMP"商标。

一切妥当后，路易·坎普便为自己的"LOUIS KEMP"糙米食品寻找生产商，因为他自己的公司并没有生产能力。但是，要找一家愿意生产"LOUIS KEMP"糙米产品的生产商并不容易。许多有生产能力的公司知道"LOUIS KEMP"是著名的水产品商标，都不愿日后惹上商标纠纷。经路易·坎普极力游说，称"LOUIS KEMP"已经是一个水产品的驰名品牌，如果用这个品牌生

---

〔1〕 一般在国外所称的"wild rice"系指"糙米"。

产糙米食品，既能借这个品牌促销，又不违反商标法，何乐而不为？在路易·坎普的大力游说下，终于有一家公司（Quality Finer Foods）愿意做他的生产商。不过，为了控制潜在的商标争议将会造成的损失，这家公司坚持，一旦发生商标争议，将有权立即终止与路易·坎普的生产销售协议。

1995 年 10 月，路易·坎普开始在市场上使用"LOUIS KEMP"的商标宣传糙米食品。同时，路易·坎普也向美国专利商标局申请注册"LOUIS KEMP"商标销售糙米食品。美国专利商标局拒绝了他的申请，理由是这一商标会与大黄蜂水产公司的"LOUIS KEMP"商标混淆。

值得注意的是，在正式使用"LOUIS KEMP"商标销售糙米食品之前，路易·坎普并没有按照当初与奥斯卡水产公司签订的协议事先获得"LOUIS KEMP"商标所有者的同意。时隔不久，路易·坎普便接到大黄蜂水产公司的律师函，要求他立即停止使用"LOUIS KEMP"商标。路易·坎普拒绝了这一要求，称当初他与奥斯卡水产公司签订的补充协议授予他使用"LOUIS KEMP"商标生产销售非鱼浆产品的权利。路易·坎普继而求助于法院，要求法院就他使用"LOUIS KEMP"商标的权利作出一项确认判决（Declaratory Judgment）。

本案中的商标争议主要涉及两大问题。一是路易·坎普使用的"LOUIS KEMP"商标是否会与大黄蜂水产公司的鱼浆"LOUIS KEMP"商标造成混淆。二是当初路易·坎普与奥斯卡水产公司所签订的授权协议是否授予路易·坎普使用"LOUIS KEMP"商标销售非鱼浆产品的权利。只要法院就这两个问题中的一个作出有利于路易·坎普的判决，路易·坎普就可以继续使用"LOUIS KEMP"商标销售糙米食品。

第一个问题涉及商标法。美国法院在商标侵权案件中判断混淆误认问题时需考虑以下几项因素[1]：（1）受保护商标的知名度。（2）受保护商标与有争议商标的相似性。（3）两种产品竞争的程度。（4）被指控侵权一方是否

---

[1] 本案的审判法院为第八巡回上诉法院，该院关于混淆误认的判断因素包括：（1）the strength of the owner's mark；（2）the similarity of the owner's mark and the alleged infringer's mark；（3）the degree to which the products compete with each other；（4）the alleged infringer's intent to pass off its goods as those of the trademark owner；（5）incidents of actual confusion；and（6）the type of product, its costs and conditions of purchase.

有意造成消费者混淆误认。（5）事实上是否已经造成混淆误认。（6）产品的种类、价格等因素。其中，没有一项因素具有决定性，法院在判决时要综合考虑这六项因素。

在法庭上，尽管路易·坎普承认"LOUIS KEMP"是一个著名商标，却坚持综合考虑六项因素后的结果是对自己有利的。不过，法院并没有接受路易·坎普的辩解。法院强调，判断两个商标的相似性不能与某种产品的消费群体的特点分开。糙米食品和鱼浆食品都不属于贵重产品，消费者在购买前一般不会对这两种产品的商标进行细致研究，两个商标之间的任何雷同都容易造成消费者混淆误认。

而且，路易·坎普已经承认，"LOUIS KEMP"是一个著名商标，越是知名商标，所享有的保护力度就越大，所要求的相似程度就越低。由此，法院认定，尽管路易·坎普设计的"LOUIS KEMP"商标在风格和颜色上都与大黄蜂水产公司的"LOUIS KEMP"商标不同，但是这些细微的差别并不足以让法院认定两个商标不具有相似性。

法院进一步认定，路易·坎普想借"LOUIS KEMP"这个知名商标促销自己的糙米食品，事实上说明他有意使消费者混淆其糙米食品的来源。同时，大黄蜂水产公司请路易·坎普的前销售员出庭作证。根据证词显示，许多消费者在购买"LOUIS KEMP"的糙米产品时先询问这种产品是否与"LOUIS KEMP"鱼浆出自一家公司。法院认定，这足以说明，路易·坎普的"LOUIS KEMP"产品已经在事实上造成了消费者的混淆误认。法院在综合考虑了六项因素后，判决路易·坎普的"LOUIS KEMP"糙米食品商标会造成与大黄蜂水产公司的"LOUIS KEMP"鱼浆商标的混淆误认。

路易·坎普先失一局，只好在当初与奥斯卡水产公司签订的协议和补充协议上做文章，坚持当初的协议已经授权路易·坎普使用"LOUIS KEMP"生产非鱼浆产品的权利。法院对此并没有深究，而是简明扼要地指出，当初路易·坎普签订的商标授权协议的确有类似的授权。不过，这一授权却附带着一个重要条件，即路易·坎普在使用"LOUIS KEMP"商标时，必须首先征得奥斯卡水产公司的同意。

大黄蜂水产公司经由转让协议获得了奥斯卡水产公司对"LOUIS KEMP"

商标的所有权利。路易·坎普在使用"LOUIS KEMP"商标时，必须依据当初与奥斯卡水产公司达成的协议，应先征得大黄蜂水产公司的同意。在没有征得大黄蜂水产公司同意的情况下，路易·坎普使用"LOUIS KEMP"商标，不仅侵害了大黄蜂水产公司的商标权，而且违反了与奥斯卡水产公司的协议。在这场商标战中，路易·坎普两局皆输，走投无路，只得宣布破产。

本案启示与解析

我国《商标法》规定，注册商标所有人在法律允许的范围内，将其注册商标转移给他人所有；或企业因合并、分离或兼并应当办理转让注册商标的手续。转让注册商标的，商标转让人对其在同一种商品或类似商品上注册的相同或近似的商标，必须一并转让，转让后的商标所有人不再是原注册人。

注册商标的转让形式有合同转让和继承转让。合同转让是指转让人和受让人之间通过签订转让合同的方式转让注册商标；继承转让是指依法登记的个体工商户死亡或丧失行为能力，由法定继承人继受其注册商标。转让注册商标经核准后，予以公告。受让人自公告之日起享有商标专用权。

商标转让是商标法与合同法的交叉地带，也是一个经常出现纠纷的领域。根据我国商标法的有关规定，转让注册商标时，应注意以下事项：

（1）转让注册商标，转让人和受让人应当签订转让协议，并共同向商标局提出申请；

（2）转让人如果在同种或者类似的商品上注册了几个相同或近似的商标，转让时应一并转让，不能单独转让其中某一个；

（3）转让人应将注册商标的专用权全部转让，不允许将注册商标指定保护的商品进行部分转让；

（4）转让人转让用于药品、卷烟、报刊的注册商标，受让人应提交有关部门批准经营的有效证明文件；

（5）转让正在许可他人使用的注册商标，转让人须征得被许可人的同意，方可将商标转让给第三方。

商标转让合同的关键在于严谨、清晰、细致，尽量避免模棱两可的语言。商标转让合同必须对转让商标的名称、图案设计、转让范围、转让时间，以及转让人保留的权利等作出具体规定。尤其是在以自己姓名做商标的情况下，转让人更应当慎重行事。否则，转让人有可能彻底失去用自己姓名作为商标的权利。

本案中，商标让与人路易·坎普便为一纸模棱两可的转让协议付出了沉重的代价，丧失了用自己姓名做商标的权利。路易·坎普在与奥斯卡水产公司签订的转让协议中几乎完全放弃了"KEMP""KEMP'S"以及"KEMP'S & Design"三个商标的所有权和使用权。按照这一协议，奥斯卡水产公司可以自行决定使用这三个商标，而路易·坎普在使用这三个商标时，甚至与这三个商标类似的商标时都必须首先征得奥斯卡水产公司的同意。显然，这一协议完全有利于奥斯卡水产公司，将路易·坎普置于十分被动的地位。不过，这份协定并没有完全限制路易·坎普使用自己的姓名做商标的权利。这可以说是路易·坎普在不利境地中唯一有利的地方。可惜的是，在补充协议中，路易·坎普把这唯一的主动权也拱手送给了奥斯卡水产公司，彻底把自己置于处处被动的境地。

与路易·坎普相比，奥斯卡水产公司在商标转让方面不但具有前瞻眼光，而且手段高明，出手及时，成为这起商标转让纠纷的大赢家。如上所述，与路易·坎普的第一份转让协议已经使奥斯卡水产公司掌握了使用"KEMP""KEMP'S"以及"KEMP'S & Design"三个商标的主动权。但是，这份协议仍然为日后路易·坎普使用这几个商标留了余地，因为路易·坎普仍然可以用自己的姓名销售非鱼浆产品。在这种情况下，奥斯卡水产公司主动出击，与路易·坎普签订补充协议，获得了路易·坎普姓名的商标权，填补了第一份协议中的漏洞。这份转让协议和补充协议不但授予了奥斯卡水产公司对"LOUIS KEMP"商标的所有权，而且成为大黄蜂水产公司在日后处理与路易·坎普的商标纠纷取得优势的重要依据。

本案给我们的另一个重要启示是，商标侵权纠纷在许多方面不同于一般的民事侵权。商标权属于知识产权（Intellectual Property），一个商标越知名，受到法律保护的程度就越高。所以，在涉及著名商标的侵权纠纷中，原告和被告并不完全处于同等地位。法院的天平往往会向著名商标所有者倾斜。在这种情况下，如果发生涉及著名商标的侵权纠纷，就必须制定可行的攻防策略，以避免陷入不利的境地。

引用判决

Louis E. Kemp, Superior Seafoods, Inc. , and Quality Finer Foods, Inc. , v. Bumble Bee Seafoods, Inc.

Opinion by MELLOY, *Circuit Judge.*

Defendant-Appellant Bumble Bee Seafoods, Inc. ▼ ("Bumble Bee") appeals the district court's adverse rulings following a bench trial on the trademark issues of likelihood of confusion and dilution. Because we find that confusion was likely, we reverse and remand for entry of judgment in favor of Bumble Bee.

I. Background

Plaintiff-Appellee Louis E. Kemp ("Mr. Kemp") is from a family that had been engaged in the wholesale and retail seafood business since 1930. In 1985, Mr. Kemp started Kemp Foods, Inc. , which made and sold artificial crab products containing surimi, a low-fat, processed fish product. In 1987, Mr. Kemp sold the seafood business to Oscar Mayer Foods Corporation ▼ for $ 4 million pursuant to a Stock Acquisition Agreement. Under the Agreement, Mr. Kemp transferred all trademarks used in his business, including KEMP, KEMP'S and KEMP'S & Design to Oscar Mayer. He further agreed not to use these marks "or any variation thereof" on any products, except as permitted under the Agreement. Under the Agreement, Mr. Kemp retained the right to "market, sell or otherwise distribute [certain listed products] bearing a composite trademark consisting of the word KEMP or KEMP's and preceded by one or more additional words, the selection of which shall be approved in advance in writing by [Oscar Mayer] . "

About six months after signing the Agreement, an Oscar Mayer executive asked Mr. Kemp for permission to use the name LOUIS KEMP to market surimi products. Oscar Mayer previously had achieved success with two – word or full – name marks (e. g. Oscar Mayer, Louis Rich). Mr. Kemp agreed and entered negotiations with Oscar Mayer to amend the Agreement. Ultimately, the amended Agreement did not contain all of Oscar Mayer's desired terms, namely, express permission to use the term LOUIS KEMP on all products and exclusion of Mr. Kemp from using the term LOUIS KEMP on any food products. Similarly, the amended Agreement did not contain Mr. Kemp's desired term, namely, the express reservation of a broad right to use the term LOUIS KEMP on products other than surimi.

Under the amended Agreement, Mr. Kemp granted Oscar Mayer the right to use and register the marks LOUIS KEMP and LOUIS KEMP SEAFOOD CO (the "LOUIS KEMP marks") for surimi – based products and other seafood accessory products within the natural zone of expansion. The amended Agreement also included a revised reservation of rights for Mr. Kemp that provided:

It is agreed that [Mr. Kemp], or any entity in which [he] has an interest, may utilize a composite trademark consisting of the word KEMP or KEMP's and preceded or followed by one or more additional words the selection of which shall be approved in advance in writing by [Oscar Mayer] in connection with the marketing, selling, or distribution of [certain listed products].

In 1992, Oscar Mayer sold the surimi business to Tyson Foods, Inc., who in turn sold the business to Bumble Bee. Con Agra Foods subsequently acquired Bumble Bee. Before October 1995, Bumble Bee and its predecessors spent over $ 49 million to promote and advertise the LOUIS KEMP marks. By October 1995, the LOUIS KEMP marks had achieved a brand awareness of 47%, Bumble Bee's Louis Kemp Seafood Company held a 77% share of the market for retail pre–packaged seafood and LOUIS KEMP was the number one surimi seafood brand with a 55% market share. It is undisputed that Bumble Bee owns numerous registered trademarks for KEMP, including the term KEMP without restriction as to font, trade dress or form, and more narrow registrations for the term KEMP along with certain design elements. In addition, Bumble Bee owns registration numbers 1, 859, 815 and 1, 859, 816 (for the mark LOUIS KEMP) and 1, 859, 817 and 1, 879, 931 (for the mark LOUIS KEMP SEAFOOD COMPANY).

In April and May 1995, Mr. Kemp wrote to Jeno F. Paulucci of Luigino's, Inc. , a prospective business partner, to propose the formation of a new company "to develop and sell a line of precooked wild rice products. " Mr. Kemp noted his intention to take advantage of the goodwill associated with the LOUIS KEMP marks (goodwill that Bumble Bee, Tyson, and Oscar Mayer had invested $ 49 million to develop) when he stated:

Non-fish products can use the 'Louis Kemp' brand name which has national recognition with over $ 50 million spent on advertising, 20 million lbs of 'Louis Kemp' product sold annually with a 67% market share of the prepackaged retail market in its category. [April 1995 letter] We could use the "Louis Kemp" brand name where we can and want to, to take advantage of the considerable equity it possesses and or any and all other brands the company can utilize, now and in the future to develop any other specialty food items that would meet the company's goal for growth and success. [May 1995 letter]

While Mr. Kemp expressly stated that he desired to "take advantage of the considerable equity" that the "Louis Kemp" brand name possessed, and while he may have believed that he was entitled to do so under the contract, he also recognized the risk attendant to this appropriation of goodwill. He sought and obtained an opinion letter from counsel in which counsel advised that he could use his name, "Louis Kemp" for precooked wild rice products. In counsel's opinion, these products were sufficiently different from fish products to avoid confusion. Counsel did advise against using the term "Louis Kemp Seafood Company," using type font or script similar to that used by [then] Tyson, and using the marks on products that contained surimi.

Mr. Kemp and his newly formed company, Quality Finer Foods entered a "Custom Packing and Sales Agreement" with Luigino's, Inc. Under the Sales Agreement,

Mr. Kemp granted Luigino's the right to cancel the agreement "if any meaningful action (in the sole discretion of Luigino's attorney) is threatened or commenced against Quality Finer Foods or its owner, Louis Kemp, for trade mark infringement, violation and the like. " Apparently, Mr. Paulucci, his attorney, or others at Luigino's also recognized the risk attendant to using the trademark LOUIS KEMP.

In October 1995, Mr. Kemp began commercial use of the mark LOUIS KEMP on wild rice, chicken and wild rice soup, and wild rice with stir fry vegetables. Mr. Kemp did not seek Bumble Bee's approval, as per the amended Agreement, for use of the two-word mark on wild rice products. Mr. Kemp's use was accompanied by trade dress that differed from Bumble Bee's trade dress and did not include the words "Seafood Co. " In particular, Bumble Bee displayed its LOUIS KEMP SEAFOOD CO. ▾mark against a blue background and Mr. Kemp displayed the LOUIS KEMP mark against a white and red striped background, using a different font. Mr. Kemp juxtaposed the mark with a scene of lakes and wild rice while Bumble Bee's mark appeared on see-through packages that permitted potential consumers to view the surimi product. Mr. Kemp sought registration of the trademark LOUIS KEMP as applied to precooked wild rice products. The Patent and Trademark Office rejected Mr. Kemp's application based on a finding that Mr. Kemp's mark was confusingly similar to Bumble Bee's mark.

On March 13, 1996, Tyson, then owner of the LOUIS KEMP marks, sent Mr. Kemp a cease and desist letter. Tyson alleged infringement and likelihood of confusion. On March 21, 1996, Mr. Kemp responded by explaining that he believed the amended Agreement permitted his use of the trademark LOUIS KEMP on nonsurimi products. Mr. Kemp then filed this suit to seek a declaratory judgment regarding a contractual right to use the trademark LOUIS KEMP. Mr. Kemp also brought tortious interference and unfair competition claims against Tyson and Bumble Bee. Tyson and Bumble Bee filed trademark infringement and dilution counterclaims against Mr. Kemp based on federal and Minnesota law. In 1998, Mr. Kemp stopped selling wild rice products under the LOUIS KEMP mark.

Over the next few years, litigation proceeded on many fronts, including state and bankruptcy courts in California, as well as the United States District Court in Minnesota. On May 21, 2001, upon stipulation of the parties, the district court below entered an Order Granting Consent Judgment which held that the only remaining issues were the issues of trademark infringement and dilution as set forth in Tyson and Bumble Bee's counterclaims.

The district court then held a bench trial to resolve the outstanding issues of whether Mr. Kemp's use of the LOUIS KEMP mark infringed or diluted Bumble Bee's trademark rights. The evidence included the trial testimony of Mr. Kemp's former salesman for the wild rice products, Patrick Melby. Mr. Melby claimed that actual confusion existed among brokers. In fact, Mr. Melby testified that these professional buyers "always" asked if there was a connection between the wild rice and surimi companies and that they "always" had to have it explained to them that the two products came from different companies. This evidence was undisputed. The district court, however, discounted this evidence and stated, "The Court does not extract from his testimony the inference or conclusion that confusion among brokers was rampant."

Tyson and Bumble Bee submitted a customer survey that purported to show confusion among relevant consumers. The district court discounted the survey as infirm. The district court noted that the pool of survey participants did not accurately reflect the target market and that problems with the format of the surveyor's questions called into doubt the validity of the survey's results.

Mr. Kemp testified that during the many years that he sold seafood products under the KEMP trademarks, another firm sold dairy products under an identical KEMP trademark with no reports of actual consumer confusion. An executive from Con Agra (the company that owned Bumble Bee) testified that he was not aware of any reports of actual confusion between the LOUIS KEMP seafood products and the third party's dairy products. Also, the evidence showed that Mr. Kemp promoted the sale of his wild rice products as side dishes for fish, and Bumble Bee promoted its surimi products for use with rice.

Finally, during trial, Mr. Kemp again made clear his intention to take advantage of the goodwill and brand equity that Bumble Bee and its predecessors had built in the trademark LOUIS KEMP:

Q. Well, isn't it a fact that you used the mark LOUIS KEMP on your wild rice products solely to take advantage of the huge investment that Oscar Mayer and Tyson invested in the brand?

A. Absolutely true and that's because the agreement I made with them and they made with me.

The district court applied the six factor test from *Squirtco v. Seven-Up Co.*, 628 F. 2d 1086, 1091 (8th Cir. 1980) (listing the following as factors to consider in assessing the likelihood of confusion: (1) the strength of the owner's mark; (2) the similarity of the owner's mark and the alleged infringer's mark; (3) the degree to which the products compete with each other; (4) the alleged infringer's intent to "pass off" its goods as those of the trademark owner; (5) incidents of actual confusion; and (6) the type of product, its costs and conditions of purchase (the "Squirtco factors"). The district court noted Mr. Kemp's concession that the first and sixth factors weighed in favor of finding a likelihood of confusion. The district court then analyzed the remaining four factors. In doing so, the district court conducted a side-by-side comparison of the parties' respective products' trade dress; discounted similarities in the marks due to differences in the trade dress; noted the absence of competition between the products; found that Mr. Kemp did not intend consumers to associate his products with Bumble Bee's products; found no evidence of actual confusion; and, ultimately, found that there was neither a likelihood of confusion nor actual dilution. As a result, the district court granted judgment in favor of Mr. Kemp.

II. Analysis – Likelihood of Confusion

We review application of the Squirtco factors and the ultimate determination of a likelihood of confusion for clear error. *Children's Factory, Inc. v. Benee's Toys, Inc.*,

160 F. 3d 489, 493（8th Cir. 1998）; *Conagra, Inc. v. George A. Hormel, & Co.*, 990 F. 2d 368, 370-71（8th Cir. 1993）. Reversal under the clear error standard is appropriate in this case because, after reviewing the record, we are "left with the definite and firm conviction that a mistake has been committed." *Anderson v. City of Bessemer City*, 470 U. S. 564, 573, 84 L. Ed. 2d 518, 105 S. Ct. 1504（1985）[quoting United States v. *United States Gypsum Co.*, 333 U. S. 364, 395, 92 L. Ed. 746, 68 S. Ct. 525（1948）].

Mr. Kemp argues that minor differences in trade dress, as previously described, establish that the marks are dissimilar. He argues further that he did not have an intent to misappropriate the goodwill consumers associate with Bumble Bee's mark and that his receipt of advice from counsel proves this fact. He also argues that the underlying products were not in competition with one another and that there was no evidence of actual confusion. Although he concedes that the first factor（the strength of the mark）and the sixth factor（the type of product, its costs, and conditions of purchase）support a finding that confusion is likely, he argues that, on balance, the Squirtco factors support the conclusion that no confusion is likely.

The factors from Squirtco guide our analysis, but the ultimate determination of whether confusion is likely is not to be mechanically determined through rigid application of the factors. Under Squirtco, no one factor controls, and because the inquiry is inherently case-specific, different factors may be entitled to more weight in different cases. Squirtco, 628 F. 2d at 1091（"Resolution of this issue does not hinge on a single factor but requires a consideration of numerous factors to determine whether under all the circumstances there is a likelihood of confusion."）. Further, the factors are not entirely separable. For example, it is inappropriate to conduct a side-by-side comparison of the elements of two products' trade dress, as urged by Mr. Kemp, without reference to the senior mark's strength or the market conditions under which likely consumers would see the marks. See, e. g., *Wynn Oil Co. v. Thomas*, 839 F. 2d 1183, 1187（6th Cir. 1988）（"It is axiomatic in trademark law that 'side-by-side' comparison is not the test."）[quoting Levi

Strauss & Co. v. Blue Bell, Inc. , 632 F. 2d 817, 822 (9th Cir. 1980)] . Rather, our comparison of the similarity between marks and products must occur in a context that recognizes how consumers encounter the products and how carefully consumers are likely to scrutinize the marks. See *Homeowner's Group*, Inc. v. Home Marketing Specialists, Inc. , 931 F. 2d 1100, 1109 (6th Cir. 1991) ("Instead, the marks must be viewed in their entirety and in context. [A] court must determine, in the light of what occurs in the marketplace, whether the mark will be confusing to the public when singly presented. ") (internal quotations omitted).

Applying the factors in this manner, Mr. Kemp's concession that Bumble Bee's mark is strong means that there must be greater degree of dissimilarity between the senior mark and the offending mark. Compare *General Mills, Inc. v. Kellogg Co. *, 824 F. 2d 622, 626 (8th Cir. 1987) ("Determining that a mark is weak means that consumer confusion has been found unlikely because the mark's components are so widely used that the public can easily distinguish slight differences in the marks, even if the goods are related. ") with Squirtco, 628 F. 2d at 1091 ("A strong and distinctive trademark is entitled to greater protection than a weak or commonplace one. "). Also, a greater level of dissimilarity is required because the products in this case are not priced or sold in a manner that suggests a high level of consumer sophistication or deliberation in the identification of product source. See *First National Bank, in Sioux Falls v. First National Bank, South Dakota*, 153 F. 3d 885, 889–90 (8th Cir. 1998) ("Consumers tend to exercise a relatively high degree of care in selecting banking services. As a result, customers are more likely to notice what, in other contexts, may be relatively minor differences in names. "); *Astra Pharm. Prods. , Inc. v. Beckman Instruments, Inc. *, 718 F. 2d 1201, 1206 (1st Cir. 1983) ("There is always less likelihood of confusion where goods are expensive and purchased after careful consideration. "); *Electronic Design & Sales, Inc. v. Elec. Data Sys. Corp. *, 954 F. 2d 713, 718 (Fed. Cir. 1992) ("Purchaser [ ] … sophistication is important and often dispositive because 'sophisticated consumers may be expected to exercise greater care. '") (third bracket in original) [quoting

Pignons S. A. de Mecanique de Precision v. Polaroid Corp., 657 F. 2d 482, 489 (1st. Cir. 1981)〕; Squirtco, 628 F. 2d at 1091 (" 'The kind of product, its cost and the conditions of purchase are important factors in considering whether the degree of care exercised by the purchaser can eliminate the likelihood of confusion which would otherwise exist. '")〔quoting *Grotrian, Helfferich, Schulz, Th. Steinweg Nachf. v. Steinway & Sons*, 523 F. 2d 1331, 1342 (2d. Cir. 1975)〕.

As to the second Squirtco factor, then, we reject Mr. Kemp's argument that slight differences in trade dress such as type font, text color, and package art make confusion unlikely. Bumble Bee's mark and Mr. Kemp's mark share a dominant feature——the phrase Louis Kemp. Viewed in reference to the facts that Bumble Bee's mark is strong and likely consumers are not expected to exercisegreat scrutiny in the purchase of low-price, supermarket items, we must conclude that the second Squirtco factor, similarity of the marks, does not strongly support Mr. Kemp's position. Turning to the third factor, the degree of competition, we note that the two products, wild rice products and surimi-based products, were not in direct competition. A showing of direct competition, however, is not required, and the factor, "degree of competition" requires a broader examination of the products' relationship in the market. See 15 U. S. C. § 1125 (a)(1)(A) (providing for protection against confusion regarding " origin, sponsorship, or approval"); Mutual of Omaha Ins. Co. v. Novak, 836 F. 2d 397, 399 (8th Cir. 1987) (stating that "it is error to assume that trademark law protects against use of a mark only on directly competitive products" and that where "there was little or no direct competition … infringement still could be found … for confusion, not competition, is the touchstone of trademark infringement. "); Squirtco, 628 F. 2d at 1091 ("Competitive proximity is one factor to be considered, even though infringement may be found in the absence of direct competition. "). Where products are wholly unrelated, this factor weighs against a finding that confusion is likely. Where products are related, however, it is reasonable for consumers to think that the products come from the same source, and confusion, therefore, is more likely. *Anheuser-Busch, Inc. v. Balducci Publ'ns*, 28 F. 3d 769,

774 (8th Cir. 1994) (noting that protection extends "against use of [plaintiff's] mark on any product or service which would reasonably be thought by the buying public to come from the same source, or thought to be affiliated with, connected with, or sponsored by, the trademark owner") (quoting J. Thomas McCarthy, Trademarks and Unfair Competition § 24. 03 (3d. 1992)).

Here, the record clearly reflects a connection between the two products. Mr. Kemp advocated the marketing of his rice products with fish and Bumble Bee promoted its surimi product for use with rice. Mr. Kemp's products were intended as side dishes, likely to be served with meat, fish, or poultry. Because direct competition is not the only aspect of this inquiry (although a showing of direct competition may increase the likelihood of confusion), proper application of this factor requires exploration of the likelihood that consumers would draw a connection between the two products and be confused as to the identities of their respective sources. Here, the products were similarly marketed, similarly priced, and intended for use as compliments to one another. Accordingly, this factor weighs in favor of a finding that confusion was likely.

Turning to the fourth factor, the alleged infringer's intent to pass off his goods as those of the trademark owner, we believe the evidence supports only one permissible view of Mr. Kemp's admission, namely, his desire to cause consumers to associate his brand with that of Bumble Bee. The evidence of this clear intention to appropriate for his own benefit the considerable equity, i. e. , the trademark goodwill, of the LOUIS KEMP brand name was undisputed. Further, this intention did not change over time. Rather, Mr. Kemp noted his intent in his solicitation letters to Mr. Paulucci and again testified at trial that his subsequent, actual use of the name was designed to take advantage of the investment Oscar Mayer and Tyson had made in the mark.

Rarely will a junior user admit such an intention. Mr. Kemp apparently did so in this case because he believed contract rights entitled him to use the trademark LOUIS KEMP. His subjective opinions regarding his contract rights, however, in no way diminish the effect of his statement. He openly admitted his intention to market his products to take advantage of the considerable equity of the Oscar Mayer and Tyson investments. The only way to take advantage of this brand equity is to cause consumers to mistakenly believe there is, at a minimum, an association between the sources of the products.

No party contemplated, much less used, a composite term that contained the words "LOUIS KEMP" to market surimi-based seafood products——or any other food products——prior to Oscar Mayer's request that precipitated renegotiation of the Agreement. Accordingly, no party enjoyed trademark rights related to the phrase "LOUIS KEMP" before Oscar Mayer invested and developed its mark in association with its surimi business. There are no claims before the court related to state law rights of publicity nor claims that Mr. Kemp enjoyed celebrity status that would merit protection of his personal name under such laws. Accordingly, when Mr. Kemp referred to "the considerable equity" of the LOUIS KEMP brand name, the only equity to which he could have been referring was the equity built by Bumble Bee's predecessors.

We cannot discount this intent based on the fact that Mr. Kemp believed the contract entitled him to play on the goodwill of Bumble Bee's marks. As noted, the contract conditioned Mr. Kemp's right to use a related mark upon Oscar Mayer's prior approval, which Mr. Kemp did not seek. Further, we cannot discount this intent based on the fact that Mr. Kemp received advice of counsel and slightly modified his presentation of his LOUIS KEMP mark. Discounting a showing of intent based on minor changes in presentation is inappropriate because:

Few businesspeople are foolhardy enough to be so blatant in their attempt to increase profits. To find trademark infringement only by exact identity and not where the junior user makes some slight modification would be in effect to reward the cunning infringer and punish only the bumbling one.

J. Thomas McCarthy, Trademarks and Unfair Competition § 23. 20 (4th ed. 2002) (citations and internal quotations omitted). Clearly, Mr. Kemp attempted to minimize his legal risk. His desire to minimize his legal risk, however, cannot be equated with a diminution of his desire to "take advantage of the considerable equity" of Bumble Bee's trademark.

It is importantto note that intent as a Squirtco factor is relevant not because trademark infringement requires intent, bad faith, or any other*mens rea*. Instead, this Squirtco factor is relevant because it demonstrates *the junior user's true opinion* as to the dispositive issue, namely, whether confusion is likely. Accordingly, it is irrelevant that he may have believed contract rights excused his use. He adopted the mark LOUIS KEMP specifically to take advantage of the "considerable equity" Bumble Bee and its predecessors had built in the mark. He admitted this regarding his prospective intentions in his letter to solicit Mr. Paulucci as a partner, and he admitted this under examination regarding his intentions surrounding his actual use. We believe this evidence permits only one possible conclusion, namely, that Mr. Kemp believed consumers would associate his products with those of the senior user. Accordingly, this factor weighs very strongly in favor of finding that confusion was likely.

Finally, turning to the fifth factor, incidents of actual confusion, we cannot say that the district court committed clear error in discounting the survey. The district court acted well within its broad fact finding authority when it chose to discount the surveyevidence. We believe, however, that the undisputed testimony of Mr. Kemp's salesman for the wild rice products, Patrick Melby, that actual confusion existed among sophisticated professional buyers, supports a finding of actual confusion. Such buyers are individuals who make their living purchasing food products like those of Bumble Bee and Mr. Kemp, and they may be presumed to exercise a high standard of care. See, e. g. , *Ford Motor Co. v. Summit Motor Prods.* , Inc. , 930 F. 2d 277, 293 (3d. Cir. 1991) ("Professional buyers, or consumers of very expensive goods, will be held to a higher standard of care. ") ; *Oreck Corp. v. U. S. Floor Sys.* , Inc. , 803 F. 2d 166, 173−74 (5th Cir. 1986) (finding that buyers for professional and institutional purposes were likely to be informed, deliberative buyers not easily confused as to product source). As such, when even professional buyers are confused, it serves as strong evidence that the average consumer, who exercises less scruti-ny, is likely to be confused. See *Checkpoint Sys. v. Check Point Software Techs.*, *Inc.*, 269 F. 3d 270, 285 (3d. Cir. 2001) ("Professionals or commercial buyers fa-miliar with the field … are sophisticated enough not to be confused by trademarks that are closely similar. That is, it is assumed that such professional buyers are less likely to be confused than the ordinary consumer.") (quoting J. Thomas McCarthy, Trademarks and Unfair Competition, § 23: 101 (4th ed. 2000)); see also; Perini Corp. v. Perini Constr., Inc., 915 F. 2d 121, 128 (4th Cir. 1990) ("In a market with extremely sophisticated buyers, the likelihood of consumer con-fusion cannot be presumed on the basis of the similarity in trade name alone.").

The district court, as the fact－finder in this case, was entitled to discount Mr. Melby's testimony. We do not believe, however, that the district court's opinion contains a finding that Mr. Melby was non－credible. The district court merely found that Mr. Melby's testimony failed to demonstrate that instances of confusion were "rampant." Accordingly, the record contains undisputed testimony that there were instances of actual confusion, even if those instances were not "rampant." When, as here, it is shown by an alleged infringer's own salesman that even sophisticated pro-fessional buyers experienced actual confusion, such evidence supports a finding that confusion is likely.

In summary, a balancing of the Squirtco factors support a finding that consumer confusion was likely and Mr. Kemp's use was infringement. Having found infringement due to a likelihood of confusion, and there being no remedies for dilution separate from the available remedies for infringement, we need not address the issue of dilution. The judgment of the district court is reversed and this case is remanded for determination of an appropriate remedy.

商标转让与优先使用原则

克拉克公司状告哈特兰公司案

HEARTLAND

判例简介

美国的商标注册实行"优先使用"（Prior use）的原则，即商标的最先使用者受法律的保护。美国法律规定必须先有贸易和商标的实际使用，才能获得商标的法律保护。虽然美国引入了注册制度，但优先使用原则仍然是申请注册的先决条件。1988 年，美国商标法作出修改，允许申请人基于"意图使用"而申请商标，对优先使用原则有所松动。但事实上，1988 年修正案所规定的基于"意图使用"的注册申请，仍然带有浓厚的"使用"色彩，申请人只有在 36 个月内真实使用后，并且美国专利商标局提交真实使用的证明才有可能获得商标注册。

"哈特兰"（Heartland）并非一个著名商标，却引发了一场牵涉三家美国公司的商标大战。美国商标法遵循优先使用原则，即谁先使用某个商标谁就拥有商标权。这本来不属于一个复杂问题。但是，现代社会的商业交往日益复杂，商标转让已经成为现代商业活动的重要组成部分，商标转让有时候会使优先使用问题变得复杂。

本案被告哈特兰公司自 1985 年 7 月起开始使用"哈特兰"商标销售衬衫、T 恤、裤子等服饰产品。本案原告克拉克公司（Clark & Freeman Corp.）晚来一步，从 1986 年 4 月才开始使用"哈特兰"商标销售男鞋、男靴。本来两个公司的产品种类不同，不在同一个市场上竞争，可以井水不犯河水，但相安无事几年后，克拉克公司不满于只生产销售男鞋、男靴的现状，决定开始用"哈特兰"商标生产销售其他服饰产品。此举等于将有两家"哈特兰"品牌在服饰市场上竞争。克拉克公司的市场扩张必然打破与哈特兰公司相安无事的局面。服装市场也不会容许两个"哈特兰"商标并存。为了把"哈特兰"服装挤出市场，克拉克公司向法院要求禁止哈特兰公司使用"哈特兰"商标销售服装。表面上看，克拉克公司的要求没有道理，因为它晚于哈特兰公司使用"哈特兰"商标，按照美国商标法的优先使用原则，"哈特兰"商标应当归哈特兰公司所有，而不应归克拉克公司所有。

不过，几年前克拉克公司签订的一个商标转让协议令"哈特兰"商标的优先使用日期变得复杂起来。1986年7月，克拉克公司向美国专利商标局申请注册"哈特兰"商标。当年11月，美国专利商标局接受了克拉克公司的申请，并将"哈特兰"商标公开刊登在美国专利商标局的公报上。公报出刊后，其他公司或个人可以对上面刊登的商标提出异议。如果异议理由充分，美国专利商标局可以根据异议理由拒绝注册这个商标。

克拉克公司的"哈特兰"商标刚刚刊登9天，就遭到了挑战。而且，挑战"哈特兰"商标的正是大名鼎鼎的席尔斯公司（Sears, Roebuck & Co.）。席尔斯公司称，自己从1983年起就开始使用"哈特兰"商标生产女鞋，所以拥有"哈特兰"商标的优先使用权。席尔斯公司继而要求美国专利商标局拒绝克拉克公司注册"哈特兰"商标的要求，否则将诉诸法院。

克拉克公司不愿失去注册"哈特兰"商标的机会，便主动与席尔斯公司讲和，化干戈为玉帛。经过谈判，席尔斯公司同意以15000美元的价格将"哈特兰"商标转让给克拉克公司。转让协议生效后，席尔斯公司立即停止使用"哈特兰"商标生产销售产品。双方的商标转让协议为克拉克公司注册"哈特兰"商标扫清了障碍。1987年7月，美国专利商标局正式批准了克拉克公司注册"哈特兰"商标。

因为克拉克公司晚于哈特兰公司使用"哈特兰"商标，所以在与哈特兰公司的商标纠纷中，克拉克公司与席尔斯公司签订的转让协议就成为关键。如果席尔斯公司经由这个协议把"哈特兰"商标的优先使用权转让给了克拉克公司，那么，在与哈特兰公司的商标纠纷中，克拉克公司便拥有"哈特兰"商标的优先使用权。否则，哈特兰公司便拥有"哈特兰"商标的优先使用权。

按照美国商标法，转让商标与转让商标的优先使用权是两回事。如果商标转让属于"一般性转让"[1]，则不包括转让商标优先使用权。在本案中，哈特兰公司便坚持，当初席尔斯公司将"哈特兰"商标转让给克拉克公司，属于"一般性转让"，没有转让"哈特兰"商标的优先使用权。所以，克拉克公司与席尔斯公司签订的转让协议并不影响哈特兰公司对"哈特兰"商标的优先使用权。

一般而言，法院在确定商标转让是否属于"一般性转让"时，主要看商标在转让时是否将商标与其所代表的产品一起转让。例如，可口可乐公司把"可口可乐"商标转让给另一家公司生产皮鞋，这就属于"一般性转让"。因为"可口可乐"是一个碳酸饮料商标，如果转让后生产与碳酸饮料无关的产品，便属于"一般性转让"，这种转让便不包括优先使用权。相反，如果可口可乐公司将"可口可乐"商标转让给另一家公司生产碳酸饮料，这就不属于"一般性转让"，这种转让就包括优先使用权。

区别是否是"一般性转让"的目的是保证一个商标与其代表的商业信誉被一起转让。一个商标的商业信誉是与这个商标代表的具体产品分不开的。例如，"可口可乐"这个商标的商业信誉，是与这个商标所代表的饮料分不开的。如果一个公司用转让的"可口可乐"商标销售电脑，就必须靠自己建立"可口可乐"商标电脑的商业信誉，而不能靠"可口可乐"饮料的商业信誉。

在本案中，对于克拉克公司来讲，争取优先使用权的唯一途径就是避免被法院认定席尔斯公司转让的"哈特兰"商标属于"一般性转让"。克拉克公司提出两大理由证明"哈特兰"商标的转让不属于"一般性转让"。第一个理由是，在转让协议生效后，席尔斯公司立即停止了使用"哈特兰"商标。第二个理由是，"哈特兰"商标转让后代表的产品与转让前代表的产品极其类似。法院首先拒绝了克拉克公司的第一个理由，认定席尔斯公司是否在转让后停止使用"哈特兰"商标与"一般性转让"的问题无关。

---

[1] "assigned in gross" 本文译为"一般性转让"。

　　然后，法院详细地分析了克拉克公司提出的第二个理由。在本案中，法院要确定席尔斯公司将"哈特兰"商标转让给克拉克公司是否属于"一般性转让"，就必须先确认"哈特兰"商标是否与其所代表的产品一起被转让给了克拉克公司。在转让之前，席尔斯公司用"哈特兰"商标销售女鞋，克拉克公司获得转让的"哈特兰"商标后，用其销售男鞋和服装。显然，转让前后的两种产品有所不同。

　　不过，按照法院的解释，转让前后的两种产品可以不同，但是两者必须"实质相似"（Substantial Similarity）。但是，对于如何才算"实质相似"，法院却没有泾渭分明的界线。法院主要根据两种产品是否具有大体相同的市场和消费群体进行判断。如果市场和消费群相近，那么消费者就会了解这个商标在转让前所代表的产品，就能分辨这个商标所代表的产品的商业信誉。

　　在本案中，转让前的"哈特兰"是一个女鞋商标，转让后成为一个男鞋和服装的商标。虽然女鞋和男鞋都属于鞋类，市场和消费群体却大不相同。衣服则属于与鞋类不同的产品。男鞋和服装的消费者似乎不太可能了解"哈特兰"这个女鞋商标的商业信誉。由此，法院认定，席尔斯公司将"哈特兰"商标转让给克拉克公司，属于"一般性转让"，没有转让"哈特兰"商标的优先使用权。因此，克拉克公司必须自己建立"哈特兰"商标的优先使用权。但是，在克拉克公司使用"哈特兰"商标之前，哈特兰公司已经率先使用了这一商标，按照美国商标法的优先使用原则，哈特兰公司拥有"哈特兰"商标的优先使用权。基于这种理由，法院拒绝了克拉克公司的要求，允许哈特兰公司继续使用"哈特兰"商标销售服装。

本案启示与解析

　　与许多国家的商标法不同，美国商标法遵循优先使用原则。简单地讲，在符合其他条件的情况下，谁先使用了某个商标生产销售产品，谁就拥有该商标。显然，在商标争夺战中，优先使用原则使得确定"优先使用日期"尤为重要。与中国商标的构成要素相比，美国商标法允许注册的商标的构成要素要宽泛得多，这就意味着美国商标法保护的范围更广。

本案的关键问题，不在于克拉克公司何时开始使用"哈特兰"商标，而在于席尔斯公司在转让"哈特兰"商标时，是否也将这一商标的优先使用日期一并转让给克拉克公司。因为克拉克公司实际上晚于哈特兰公司使用"哈特兰"商标，所以克拉克公司必须向法庭证明，席尔斯公司已经把"哈特兰"商标的优先使用权转让给克拉克公司。否则，克拉克公司就只好把从席尔斯公司重金买来的这个商标，拱手让给哈特兰公司。

美国商标法中有关"一般性转让"的规定使得"优先使用日期"问题变得复杂起来。在一般性转让中，商标转让者只转让商标，而不转让商标所代表的产品或服务。换言之，一般性转让所转让的只是商标本身，而没有转让商标所代表的商业信誉。本案中，席尔斯公司在将"哈特兰"商标转让给克拉克公司前用这个商标销售女鞋。所以，"哈特兰"商标在转让前的商业信誉在女鞋上。转让后，克拉克公司用"哈特兰"商标销售男鞋和服装。一个在女鞋产品上建立起商业信誉的商标，不一定在男鞋和服装产品上也有同样的信誉。既然如此，法院便要求克拉克公司在获得"哈特兰"商标销售男鞋和服装产品后，必须重新建立"哈特兰"商标的商业信誉。

事实上，法院的判决阐明的"一般性转让"中断了一个商标的"优先使用日期"。转让后的"优先使用日期"，必须从获得商标的企业实际开始使用这个商标的时间重新起算。换言之，一般性转让并不包括转让"优先使用日期"。之所以如此，一方面是为了更有效地保护消费者的利益，另一方面也是为了平衡商业竞争对手的利益。首先，商标法的主要立法目的就是保护消费者的利益，尽可能避免消费者对不同企业的产品混淆误认。如果一个企业通过转让获得某个商标，生产与这个商标已经在消费者中享有信誉的产品不同的产品，那么它必须重新建立这个商标的商业信誉，以免误导消费者。其次，法院不允许一个企业通过商标转让的方式，把已经在消费者中建立起商标的商业信誉的竞争对手挤出市场。那样做有悖于公平竞争的原则，也可能造成大公司滥用商标商誉，恶意挤压小公司，最终影响消费者权益。

美国的商标注册制度对于中国有一定的借鉴意义，当然这种认识需要一定的时间。法治的进程一定是经济发展进程的客观需要，中国的社会经济发展状况决定了中国的商标制度还有很长的路要走。

引用判决

CLARK & FREEMAN CORP. and HEARTLAND SHOE COMPANY, INC. v. THE HEARTLAND COMPANY LTD. and STEVEN KLINE

Opinion by JOHN S. MARTIN, JR., *District Judge*

This case involves the competing claims of two companies to the exclusive right to use the name "Heartland" in connection with their business operations. Defendants have been using the name since July of 1985 in connection with their sales of shirts, sweaters, trousers and jackets. Plaintiffs first commenced using the name "Heartland" on April 26, 1986 in connection with the sale of men's shoes and boots.

Had each of the parties continued with their original operations, plaintiffs selling men's shoes and boots and defendants selling shirts, trousers and jackets, there would have been little need for either to seek the intervention of the Court. While some evidence of confusion was introduced at trial, such confusion was limited and not sufficient to justify interfering with the parties' continued operating in their separate lines of merchandise. Recently, however, plaintiffs have decided that they wish to launch a clothing line under the "Heartland" name and, thus, this lawsuit.

Although plaintiffs began using the name "Heartland" after defendants, plaintiffs claim priority because in 1987 they obtained an assignment of the "Heartland" name from Sears, Roebuck & Co. which had used the name since 1983 in connection with the sale of women's boots. Plaintiffs filed an application to register the "Heartland" mark with the U. S. Patent and Trademark Office on July 3, 1986. On November 25, 1986, the application was allowed and published in the official Gazette. Nine days later on December 4, 1986, Sears notified plaintiffs of their prior use of the "Heartland" name and threatened to bring opposition proceedings. Ultimately, Sears agreed to settle the matter by assigning the "Heartland" name to plaintiffs in exchange for $ 15, 000. The settlement was affected on April 6, 1987, and, on July 28, 1987, plaintiffs' mark was registered by the U. S. Patent and Trademark Office.

Since plaintiffs' own use of the name "Heartland" did not commence until after defendants' use of that trademark, plaintiffs can prevail in this action only if they have succeeded to the priority rights in the trademark "Heartland" which were enjoyed by Sears. Defendants contend, however, that the assignment of the trademark from Sears to plaintiffs was an assignment in gross and, therefore, plaintiffs may not tack on the period of Sears' prior use to defeat defendants' claim of priority.

Generally, an assignment of a trademark and its accompanying goodwill will entitle the assignee to "step into the shoes" of the assignor, gaining whatever priority the assignor might have had in the mark. *Money Store v. Harriscorp Fin. , Inc. , 689 F. 2d 666* (7th Cir. 1982); *G's Bottoms Up Social Club v. F. P. M. Industries, Inc. , 574 F. Supp. 1490, 220 U. S. P. Q. 874, 879* (S. D. N. Y. 1983); 1 McCarthy, *Trademarks and Unfair Competition* 805 (2d ed. 1984); *accord* 15 U. S. C. § 1060. However, where a trademark has been assigned "in gross," i. e. without the accompanying goodwill, then the assignment is invalid, *Haymaker Sports, Inc. v. Turian*, 581 F. 2d 257 (C. C. P. A. 1978), and the "assignee" must instead rely upon his or her own use to establish priority. *Merry Hull & Co. v. Hi-Line Co. , 243 F. Supp. 45* (S. D. N. Y. 1965); *see* McCarthy, *supra*, at 807.

Marshak v. Green, 746 F. 2d 927 (2d Cir. 1984), discusses the rationale behind the assignment in gross rule: "Use of the mark by the assignee in connection with a different goodwill and different product would result in a fraud on the purchasing public who reasonably assume that the mark signifies the same thing, whether used by one person or another. " *Id.* at 929; *see Money Store*; *Pepsico, Inc. v. Grapette Co. , 416 F. 2d 285, 289* (8th Cir. 1969) .

Plaintiffs claim that the assignment is valid for two reasons: (1) Because Sears immediately ceased manufacture and marketing of its "Heartland" boots, there was an *ipso facto* transfer of goodwill to plaintiffs; (2) Because plaintiffs were applying the trademark to "substantially similar" goods, they had acquired the goodwill as well as the mark.

Plaintiffs' first argument can be easily dismissed. Plaintiffs cite no case establishing the proposition that forbearance by the assignor operates to transfer goodwill *ipso facto*. See *Greenlon, Inc. of Cincinnati v. Greenlawn, Inc.*, 542 F. Supp. 890, 895 (S. D. Ohio 1982) (discussing cases where assignor *continued* use in order to establish converse proposition); *Hy-Cross Hatchery, Inc. v. Osborne*, 303 F. 2d 947, 950 (C. C. P. A. 1962) (using forbearance only as one element in transfer of goodwill determination). Indeed, if forbearance alone were sufficient, then discussion of "consumer deception" would be irrelevant, since an assignee could use the mark for any product desired as long as the assignor halted operations. Goodwill is not such a mechanistic concept.

Plaintiffs' second contention presents a closer question. It is well established that "courts have upheld such assignments if they find that the assignee is producing a product or performing a service substantially similar to that of the assignor and that the customers would not be deceived or harmed." *Marshak*, 746 F. 2d at 930; see *Defiance Button Mach. Co. v. C & C Metal Prod.*, 759 F. 2d 1053 (2d Cir.), *cert. denied*, 474 U. S. 844, 106 S. Ct. 131, 88 L. Ed. 2d 108 (1985) (same); *Stetson v. Howard D. Wolf & Assoc.*, 1991 WESTLAW 149753 (S. D. N. Y.), *aff'd*, 955 F. 2d 847 (2d Cir. 1992) (same). This is the case even if no physical or tangible assets have been transferred. *Defiance Button*, 759 F. 2d at 1059; *Hy-Cross Hatchery*, 303 F. 2d at 950. The key question is whether plaintiffs produced a product "substantially similar" to that of Sears such that "the customers would not be deceived or harmed."

For these purposes, it is not dispositive that plaintiffs' footwear is of high quality. It is not merely the quality of the product, but its similarity to that produced by the assignor that determines whether goodwill has been transferred. A trademark may be validly transferred without the simultaneous transfer of any tangible assets, as long as the recipient continues to produce goods of the same quality *and nature* previously associated with the mark." *Defiance Button*, 759 F. 2d at 1059 (emphasis added). Plaintiffs' argument that customers cannot be harmed or deceived either because their shoes are of such high quality or because they are available for inspection prior to purchase misses the mark; by that rationale, plaintiffs could have produced the finest quality jet engines under the mark "Heartland" and claimed to have acquired Sears' goodwill in ladies boots. Substantial similarity demands more than quality.

Case law on "substantial similarity" is only moderately instructive, since the facts of each case are distinct and dispositive. *Cf. Pepsico, Inc. v. Grapette Co.*, 416 F. 2d 285 (8th Cir. 1969) ("A case by case treatment of the problem as specific facts present themselves is desirable"). Many cases have involved products that were virtually identical, thus easily satisfying the "substantial similarity" test. *See, e. g.*, *Marshak*, 689 F. 2d at 678 (service mark; money lending services); *Glamorene Prods. Corp. v. Procter & Gamble Co.*, 538 F. 2d 894, 895 (C. C. P. A. 1976) (dry cleaning detergent); *Hy−Cross Hatchery*, 303 F. 2d at 950 (breeding chicks); *Bambu Sales*, 683 F. Supp. at 905−06 (cigarette paper).

Some courts have found "substantial similarity" even though the products differed in some respects. In *Main Street Outfitters v. Federated Dep't Stores*, 730 F. Supp. 289 (D. Minn. 1989), "substantial similarity" was found to establish a goodwill transfer where the assignor had sold "all−weather coats and women's coats" and the assignee was using the mark on "various items of clothing including jackets, rain wear and various items of apparel." *Id.* at 290. The court found dispositive that "[assignee] conducted a business of selling apparel, especially women's apparel, as had its assignor. The goods sold by [assignee] had substantially the same characteristics, that is: apparel, as those of the assignor." *Id.* at 292.

In *Mulhens & Kropff v. Ferd Muelhens, Inc.*, 38 F. 2d 287, 293 (D. N. Y. 1929), the district court found assignor's and assignee's colognes to be "substantially similar" even though the assignor retained the secret formula to its cologne. But the court of appeals reversed, stating that "a majority of the court believe that assignment of the recipe is essential to give the assignee the exclusive right to a mark which denotes a product manufactured thereunder. " 43 F. 2d 937, 939 (2d Cir.), *cert. denied*, 282 U. S. 881, 51 S. Ct. 84 (1930) .

In *Warner – Lambert Pharm. Co. v. General Foods Corp.* , 164 U. S. P. Q. 532 (T. T. A. B. 1970), the court found that assignor's mineral–vitamin pharmaceutical was not similar enough to assignee's anti–caries (tooth decay preventative) preparation in chewable tablet and capsule form to establish a transfer of goodwill.

Even minor differences can be enough to threaten customer deception. In the oft –cited *Pepsico, Inc. v. Grapette Co.* , 416 F. 2d 285 (8th Cir. 1969), the court found that assignor's cola–flavored syrup and assignee's pepper–flavored syrup were sufficiently different to prevent a transfer of goodwill, and thus invalidate the assignment: " [The assignee] 's intended use of the mark is one simply to describe its new pepper beverage. The evidence is clear that [the assignee] did not intend to adopt or exploit any 'goodwill' from the [trademark] and [the assignor] 's long association and use of it with a cola syrup. " *Id.* at 289–90.

The facts of record in this case support a finding of assignment in gross here. Sears sold only women's pixie boots under the mark "Heartland," while plaintiffs immediately applied it only to men's shoes, then later to men's hiking boots. The markets for the two goods are substantially distinct; it is unlikely that men buying plaintiffs' "Heartland" shoes would be considering a reputation for footwear generally that Sears built by selling women's boots. That plaintiffs was using the "Heartland" mark before the assignment is also relevant, in that it tends to show that plaintiffs sought only to gain the ability to use the name "Heartland" rather than the goodwill associated with it. *Cf. Pepsico.* This is further supported by the fact that plaintiffs did not attempt to obtain the assignment from Sears until after Sears threatened to bring opposition proceedings to prevent plaintiffs from registering the "Heartland" trademark.

Since the assignment from Sears was an assignment in gross, defendants have shown priority in the use of the name "Heartland" and, therefore, plaintiffs may not enjoin defendants from using the "Heartland" name for the sale of its current line of products.

Assuming *arguendo* that the assignment from Sears was not an assignment in gross, injunctive relief would not be appropriate. Even where a party has a valid trademark and there is some likelihood of confusion, the issuance of an injunction barring use of the junior user's mark is not mandatory. As the Second Circuit observed in *Jim Beam Brands Co. v. Beamish & Crawford*, *Ltd.* , 937 F. 2d 729, 737 (2d Cir. 1991), *cert. denied*, 117 L. Ed. 2d 415, 112 S. Ct. 1169 (1992):

the court may, after "equitably balancing the conflicting interest of the parties involved", *McGregor-Doniger*, *Inc. v. Drizzle*, *Inc.* , 599 F. 2d at 1140, determine that no injunctive relief would be appropriate

See also *Vitarroz Corp. v. Borden*, *Inc.* , 644 F. 2d 960, 969 (2d Cir. 1981) .

I find that defendants adopted the use of the "Heartland" name in good faith. There is no evidence that when defendants began using the "Heartland" mark in 1985 they had any knowledge of the prior use of that mark by Sears. Plaintiffs argue that defendants did not act in good faith because defendants were aware in 1986 that the "Heartland" name had been registered as a trademark for carpets and t-shirts. While these facts may explain the reluctance of the defendants to attempt to register their name at that time, there is no evidence that defendants thought that any of the other known uses of the "Heartland" name would preclude them from using it for shirts, sweaters, trousers and jackets.

In order for the registered trademark owner, such as plaintiffs, to obtain an injunction to bar a junior user's use of a trademark on a different product, the owner must show the "likelihood that the prior owner would bridge the gap" *Polaroid Corp. v. Polarad Electronics Corp.* , 287 F. 2d 492, 495 (2d Cir.), *cert. denied*, 368 U. S. 820, 82 S. Ct. 36, 7 L. Ed. 2d 25 (1961) . As of the time plaintiffs commenced this action in 1992, they had not bridged the gap by distributing clothing similar to that on which defendants' mark appeared. Rather it was because they were planning to go into this area that they brought this action.

When defendants commenced using "Heartland" in 1985, plaintiffs, through their predecessor Sears, were using the name only in women's boots. At that time, there was no real likelihood that plaintiffs would bridge the gap by applying the "Heartland" label to the types of products defendants were selling. See *Mushroom Makers, Inc. v. R. G. Barry Corp.* , 580 F. 2d 44, 49 (2d Cir. 1978) (per curiam), cert. denied, 439 U. S. 1116, 99 S. Ct. 1022, 59 L. Ed. 2d 75 (1979) . Since then, defendants, acting in good faith, have built up substantial goodwill in the name "Heartland" as applied to clothing. It would be inequitable to allow plaintiffs to exploit defendants' substantial goodwill at this late date, simply because they are the senior user. As Judge Learned Hand stated in discussing expansion into related markets: "The owner's rights in such appendant markets are easily lost; they must be asserted early, lest they be made the means of reaping a harvest which others have sown. " *Dwinell − Wright Co. v. White House Milk Co.* , 132 F. 2d 822 (2d Cir. 1943); *see also* McCarthy, *supra*, at Ë 24: 5, 31: 7. "Merely winning the race to the trademark office door does not entitle a senior user to relief in equity. " *Mushroom Makers, Inc.* , 580 F. 2d at 49.

While the above disposes of the plaintiffs' claims, defendants have made a cross−claim for an order cancelling plaintiffs' trademark registration or requiring the issuance of a registration to defendants for its clothing products. 15 U. S. C. § 1119. The Court finds that cancellation of plaintiffs' trademark would be inequitable, but that defendants are entitled to have the Patent and Trademark Office accept their application for registration as to clothing.

Although defendants' determination not to seek trademark registration in 1985 did not amount to bad faith, that delay does make it appropriate for the Court to conclude that defendants' request for equitable relief is barred by the doctrine of laches. *Construction Technology, Inc. v. Lockformer Co.* , 704 F. Supp. 1212 (S. D. N. Y. 1989); *Simon Says Enters. , Inc. v. Schaefer*, 214 U. S. P. Q. 436 (S. D. N. Y. 1986); *Haviland & Co. v. Johann Haviland China Corp.* , 269 F. Supp. 928, 937 (S. D. N. Y. 1967) . Accordingly, the

Court will not order cancellation of plaintiffs' trademark registration.

However, because the Court finds that plaintiffs and defendants can continue in their respective businesses without substantial likelihood of confusion, defendants shall be permitted to proceed with application for registration of the "Heartland" mark for clothing, plaintiffs' registration notwithstanding. *See Massa v. Jiffy Prods. Co.*, 240 F. 2d 702 (9th Cir.), *cert. denied*, 353 U. S. 947, 77 S. Ct. 825, 1 L. Ed. 2d 856 (1957); *In re Fortex Ind., Inc.*, 18 U. S. P. Q. 1224 (Comm'r PTO 1991).

For the foregoing reasons, plaintiffs' and defendants' applications for injunctions are denied, and the complaint and counterclaims are dismissed, except as to the request for an order allowing defendants' application for registration to proceed.

Defendant, The Heartland Company, Ltd., shall have the right to register on the Principal Register of the U. S. Patent and Trademark Office the trademarks (a) "The Heartland Company Ltd." and (b) "The Heartland Company Ltd." and mailing frank design, as applied to clothing products not including shoes; the Commissioner of Patents and Trademarks is ordered to grant said defendant such registrations, subject to publication for opposition and all other required procedures, except that plaintiffs' registration No. 1, 449, 814 shall be no bar to registration.

SO ORDERED.

Dated: January 6, 1993

JOHN S. MARTIN, JR., U. S. D. J.

商标侵权与言论自由

旧金山艺术及体育运动公司状告美国奥林匹克委员会案

判例简介

协调商标权与言论自由之间的冲突是一件相当困难的事情，美国在 1988 年提交审议联邦商标淡化法时，就因为该法在一定程度上剥夺和限制了言论自由而没有被通过。在 1995 年再次审议该法案时，法案提议者一直强调该法不会禁止或威胁那些不属于商业活动的滑稽模仿、讽刺、评论等非商业性表达。

在商标侵权的众多辩护策略中，有一项名为"第一修正案辩护"。这项辩护的原理在于，美国宪法第一修正案保护言论自由，商标作为一种"言论"，理应受到宪法第一修正案的保护。因为宪法是凌驾于一切法律和权利之上的根本大法，所以，如果一种言论受宪法第一修正案的保护，也就不存在商标侵权问题了。不过，在商标侵权案中，被告运用宪法第一修正案进行辩护必须十分慎重。美国宪法第一修正案虽然保护言论自由，但是对于"商业言论"（Commercial Speech）保护的力度却十分有限。而大部分商标侵权案中有争议的商标言论都可以归入"商业言论"的范畴。

旧金山艺术及体育运动公司状告美国奥林匹克委员会案是此类案件中的一宗典型判例。美国最高法院如何界定"商业言论",如何处理商标侵权与言论自由的关系,以及如何平衡宪法保障的言论自由权与商标拥有者的财产权,从本案中可见一斑。

本案起因于一家名为"旧金山艺术及体育运动公司"的同性恋运动组织。当初,这家组织曾经向加州政府申请注册"金门奥林匹克协会",被加州政府拒绝。原因在于,美国商标法中特别规定不得注册带有"奥林匹克"字样的公司名称。无奈,这家组织只得改名注册为"旧金山艺术及体育运动公司"。该公司于 1981 年成立后,便展开宣传活动,筹备于 1982 年 8 月在旧金山举办"同性恋奥林匹克运动会"。该公司向公众散发了大量印有"同性恋奥林匹克运动会"字样的宣传品。同时,该公司的信纸上也印有"同性恋奥林匹克运动会"的抬头。

筹办中的"同性恋奥林匹克运动会"历时 9 天,从开幕前后的活动,比赛项目安排,奖项设置均模仿世界奥林匹克运动会。其中,将有 2000 人参加"同性恋奥林匹克火炬"传递活动,从纽约开始到旧金山为止。为了筹款,旧金山艺术及体育运动公司制作了大量印有"同性恋奥林匹克运动会"的运动衫、徽章等纪念品,并向公众出售。

正当旧金山艺术及体育运动公司如火如荼地筹备"同性恋奥林匹克运动会"时,却收到美国奥林匹克委员会的警告信函。美国奥林匹克委员会依据《美国业余运动法案》要求旧金山艺术及体育运动公司立即停止使用"奥林匹克"的名称。

根据《美国业余运动法案》,美国奥林匹克委员会有权禁止他人在某些商业或宣传活动中使用"奥林匹克"的名称或标志。1981 年 12 月,美国奥林匹克委员会便引用《美国业余运动法案》向旧金山艺术及体育运动公司发函,要求其立即停止使用"奥林匹克"的名称。旧金山艺术及体育运动公司答应了美国奥林匹克委员会的要求,用"同性恋体育运动会"代替了"同性恋奥林匹克运动会"。不过,一个月后,旧金山艺术及体育运动公司又恢复使用"同性恋奥林匹克运动会"的名义进行宣传。

1982 年 8 月，就在"同性恋奥林匹克运动会"即将开幕的前夕，美国奥林匹克委员会将旧金山艺术及体育运动公司告上法院，要求法院禁止被告使用"奥林匹克"的名称。在联邦地区法院作出有利于美国奥林匹克委员会的判决之后，旧金山艺术及体育运动公司一直把案件上诉到美国最高法院。

这起诉讼本质上是涉及围绕"奥林匹克"名称的商标纠纷，但是，又不同于一般的商标纠纷。《美国业余运动法案》给予"奥林匹克"比一般商标更多的保护。具体而言，在涉及"奥林匹克"的商标侵权案中，美国奥林匹克委员会不用证明被告使用"奥林匹克"的名称会造成消费者混淆误认，被告也不能依据商标法为自己辩护。这大大降低了美国奥林匹克委员会证明商标侵权的难度。

显然，旧金山艺术及体育运动公司必须先攻克《美国业余运动法案》为"奥林匹克"设置的保护层，才有希望引用商标法为自己的行为辩护。为了达到这一目的，旧金山艺术及体育运动公司便依据宪法第一修正案和商标法提出了两个没有侵权的理由。第一，旧金山艺术及体育运动公司称，"奥林匹克"是一个通用名称，不受商标法的保护，人人可以使用。《美国业余运动法案》禁止人们使用一个不受商标法保护的名称，损害了人们的言论自由，违反了宪法第一修正案。所以，《美国业余运动法案》对"奥林匹克"名称的保护无效。第二，旧金山艺术及体育运动公司称，宪法第一修正案也要求，美国奥林匹克委员会必须证明被告使用"奥林匹克"的名称会造成消费者混淆误认，才能判定商标侵权。《美国业余运动法案》使美国奥林匹克委员会无须证明消费者混淆误认，就可判定被告使用"奥林匹克"的名称侵权，这损害了人们的言论自由，所以《美国业余运动法案》违反了宪法第一修正案。

美国最高法院一一反驳了旧金山艺术及体育运动公司的两项抗辩理由。首先，美国最高法院指出，"奥林匹克"不是一个通用名称。自从 1896 年现代奥林匹克运动开始以来，"奥林匹克"这一名称已经获得了商标法上所讲的"第二层意义"。人们已经把"奥林匹克"这一名称与现代奥林匹克运动联系起来。所以，作为一个商标名称，"奥林匹克"已经因"第二层意义"而获得了识别性。在这种情况下，国会有权制定《美国业余运动法案》，授予美国奥林匹克委员会独家使用"奥林匹克"名称的权利。这项法案既不违反美国商标法,也没有因为不当地限制人们的言论自由而违反宪法第一修正案。

其次,美国最高法院也支持《美国业余运动法案》授予美国奥林匹克委员会在商业、体育和演出活动中独家使用"奥林匹克"名称的权利。美国最高法院重申,尽管宪法第一修正案保护言论自由,但是"商业言论"只享有有限的保护。在本案中,旧金山艺术及体育运动公司使用"奥林匹克"名称,便属于"商业言论"。值得注意的是,美国法院在十分宽泛的意义上定义了"商业言论",几乎将所有涉及商业活动的言论都归入"商业言论"。

按照法院的解释,旧金山艺术及体育运动公司为了筹款,向公众销售印有"奥林匹克"名称的运动衫、徽章等纪念品,这完全属于商业活动。在这些商业活动中使用"奥林匹克"名称,便属于"商业言论",只受到宪法第一修正案的有限保护。因此,旧金山艺术及体育运动公司难以要求法院以宪法第一修正案保护政治言论的标准来保护其"商业言论"。而按照宪法第一修正案保护"商业言论"的标准,《美国业余运动法案》关于美国奥林匹克委员会无须证明被告使用"奥林匹克"名称会造成消费者混淆误认就可判定商标侵权的规定,并没有违反宪法第一修正案。

在抗辩理由中,旧金山艺术及体育运动公司也指出,《美国业余运动法案》不仅授权美国奥林匹克委员会在商业活动中独家使用"奥林匹克"名称,而且也不允许他人在与体育和演出有关的活动中使用"奥林匹克"名称。针对这一条款,旧金山艺术及体育运动公司称,即使禁止他人在商业活动中使用"奥林匹克"名称没有违反宪法第一修正案,禁止他人在体育和演出中使用"奥林匹克"名称也违反了宪法第一修正案。所以,法院不能禁止旧金山艺术及体育运动公司举办"同性恋奥林匹克运动会",因为这场运动会只涉及体育竞技和表演。

就此,美国最高法院指出,"奥林匹克"这一商标的价值是由现代奥林匹克运动创造的。在美国,"奥林匹克"这一商标属于美国奥林匹克委员会。美国奥林匹克委员会投入了大量的人力物力打造和维护这一著名商标。因为"奥林匹克"这一商标是在体育运动和表演中创立的,所以它在与体育运动和表演有关的活动中享有充分的保护。旧金山艺术及体育运动公司不能以"言论自由"的名义摘取美国奥林匹克委员会培养的果实。所以,宪法第一修正案不保护旧金山艺术及体育运动公司的做法。因此，美国最高法院维持了联邦地区法院和联邦巡回法院的判决，永远禁止旧金山艺术及体育运动公司在商业、体育和表演活动中使用"奥林匹克"的名称。

本案启示与解析

我国一贯注重保护奥林匹克标志的知识产权。早在 2001 年，北京市高级人民法院在"中国奥林匹克委员会诉汕头市金味食品工业有限公司侵犯奥林匹克五环标志专用权案"中，根据我国相关法律和《奥林匹克宪章》《中国奥林匹克委员会章程》的规定，判决金味食品公司未经中国奥林匹克委员会的许可使用奥林匹克五环标志的行为构成侵权。我国取得 2008 年奥运会承办权后，更是通过专门的法规《奥林匹克标志保护条例》大大加强了对奥林匹克标志的法律保护。"北京一线飞天商贸有限公司侵权奥林匹克知识产权案"就是很典型的案例。北京一线飞天商贸有限公司于 2005 年 12 月开始，在未取得奥组委授权的情况下，在其经营地点的大门上张贴了带有奥运会吉祥物"福娃"图案的广告张贴画，涉嫌侵犯了奥林匹克标志专有权。北京市工商局海淀分局依据《奥林匹克标志保护条例》之规定，责令北京一线飞天商贸有限公司立即停止侵权行为，并罚款 1 万元。很显然，我国对这些案件的处理多以"行政执法保护"为中心。在缺乏相关国内典型案例作为研究对象的情况下，分析国外的奥林匹克标志的司法保护经验具有一定的理论和现实意义。

在美国，奥林匹克标志的权利人是美国奥林匹克委员会。美国国会在 1978 年通过《美国业余运动法案》授予美国奥林匹克委员会奥林匹克标志、商标、口号等的商业应用的权利。"奥林匹克"不但是一个运动会的名称和运动组织的名称，而且还是一个著名商标，受到世界各国商标法的保护。"奥林匹克"在美国不仅受商标法保护，而且受《美国业余运动法案》的保护。事实上，《美国业余运动法案》给予"奥林匹克"商标比普通商标更多的保护。比如说，在一般的商标侵权案中，商标法要求原告必须证明被告的行为会造成消费者混淆误认，法院方可认定被告侵权。但是，根据《美国业余运动法案》，美国奥林匹克委员会无需证明被告使用"奥林匹克"美国商标会造成消费者混淆误认，法院就可以判定被告侵权。因此可以说，在《业余运动法案》的保护下，"奥林匹克"是美国商标领域的"特殊公民"，美国奥林匹克委员会绝对垄断了"奥林匹克"商标的所有权和使用权。

正是因为《美国业余运动法案》给予"奥林匹克"商标更多的保护，所以被告在辩护时，必须先破除《美国业余运动法案》这一保护层。在美国的法律制度下，如果被告无法依照具体的法律成功辩护，则可以用宪法挑战现有法律，指出现有法律违反宪法之处。如果法院发现具体法律违反宪法中的某一条款，则会宣判这一法律无效。在本案中，旧金山艺术及体育运动公司试图说服法院判决《美国业余运动法案》违反宪法第一修正案的言论自由条款。在《美国业余运动法案》对旧金山艺术及体育运动公司十分不利的情况下，这一辩护策略不能说不正确。问题出在"第一修正案辩护"是否适用于本案。

在宪法第一修正案的言论自由辩护中，美国最高法院区分了"政治言论"与"商业言论"。一般来说，政治言论享有充分的宪法第一修正案保护。但是，商业言论却只享有非常有限的宪法第一修正案保护。所以，商业言论寻求宪法第一修正案保护成功的案例并不多。在本案中，当法院将被告旧金山艺术及体育运动公司使用"奥林匹克"名称的行为归入"商业言论"时，事实上已经等于宣布旧金山艺术及体育运动公司的行为不受宪法第一修正案的保护。这意味着，被告无法借助宪法第一修正案破除"奥林匹克"商标的特殊保护层。至此，旧金山艺术及体育运动公司再无回天之术，本案的胜负已成定局。

可以看出，美国法院在此案中实际上降低了判定奥林匹克标志侵权的门槛，从而提高了保护力度。如何认定"使用不会使人联想到赞助从而引起混淆"在一定程度上依赖于法官的自由裁量。作为奥运会主办国，这种自由裁量背后的政策考虑往往是加强对奥林匹克标志的法律保护。我国《奥林匹克标志保护条例》并没有明确奥林匹克标志侵权的具体判定标准，奥林匹克标志应该比照著名商标进行保护，并且保护强度可以强于著名商标。

引用判决

SAN FRANCISCO ARTS & ATHLETICS, INC. , ET AL. v. UNITED STATES OLYMPIC COMMITTEE ET AL.

Opinion by JUSTICE POWELL

In this case, we consider the scope and constitutionality of a provision of the Amateur Sports Act of 1978, 36 U. S. C. Ë 371 – 396, that authorizes the United States Olympic Committee to prohibit certain commercial and promotional uses of the word "Olympic. "

I

Petitioner San Francisco Arts & Athletics, Inc. (SFAA) is a nonprofit California corporation. The SFAA originally sought to incorporate under the name "Golden Gate Olympic Association," but was told by the California Department of Corporations that the word "Olympic" could not appear in a corporate title. App. 95. After its incorporation in 1981, the SFAA nevertheless began to promote the "Gay Olympic Games," using those words on its letterheads and mailings and in local newspapers. *Ibid.* The games were to be a 9–day event to begin in August 1982, in San Francisco, California. The SFAA expected athletes from hundreds of cities in this country and from cities all over the world. *Id.* , at 402. The Games were to open with a ceremony "which will rival the traditional Olympic Games. " *Id.* , at 354. See *id.* , at 402, 406, 425. A relay of over 2, 000 runners would carry a torch from New York City across the country to Kezar Stadium in San Francisco. *Id.* , at 98, 355, 357, 432. The final runner would enter the stadium with the "Gay Olympic Torch" and light the "Gay Olympic Flame. " *Id.* , at 357. The ceremony would continue with the athletes marching in uniform into the stadium behind their respective city flags. *Id.* , at 354, 357, 402, 404, 414. Competition was to occur in 18 different contests, with the winners receiving gold, silver, and bronze medals. *Id.* , at 354–

355, 359, 407, 410. To cover the cost of the planned Games, the SFAA sold T-shirts, buttons, bumper stickers, and other merchandise bearing the title "Gay Olympic Games." *Id.*, at 67, 94, 107, 113-114, 167, 360, 362, 427-428.

Section 110 of the Amateur Sports Act (Act), 92 Stat. 3048, 36 U. S. C. § 380, grants respondent United States Olympic Committee (USOC) the right to prohibit certain commercial and promotional uses of the word "Olympic" and various Olympic symbols. In late December 1981, the executive director of the USOC wrote to the SFAA, informing it of the existence of the Amateur Sports Act, and requesting that the SFAA immediately terminate use of the word "Olympic" in its description of the planned Games. The SFAA at first agreed to substitute the word "Athletic" for the word "Olympic," but, one month later, resumed use of the term. The USOC became aware that the SFAA was still advertising its Games as "Olympic" through a newspaper article in May 1982. In August, the USOC brought suit in the Federal District Court for the Northern District of California to enjoin the SFAA's use of the word "Olympic." The District Court granted a temporary restraining order and then a preliminary injunction. The Court of Appeals for the Ninth Circuit affirmed. After further proceedings, the District Court granted the USOC summary judgment and a permanent injunction.

The Court of Appeals affirmed the judgment of the District Court. 781 F. 2d 733 (1986) . It found that the Act granted the USOC exclusive use of the word "Olympic" without requiring the USOC to prove that the unauthorized use was confusing and without regard to the defenses available to an entity sued for a trademark violation under the Lanham Act, 60 Stat. 427, as amended, 15 U. S. C. § 1051 *et seq.* It did not reach the SFAA's contention that the USOC enforced its rights in a discriminatory manner, because the court found that the USOC is not a state actor bound by the constraints of the Constitution. The court also found that the USOC's "property righ [t] [in the word 'Olympic' and its associated symbols and slogans] can be protected without violating the First Amendment. " 781 F. 2d, at 737. The court denied the SFAA's petition for rehearing en banc. Three judges dissented, finding that the panel's interpretation of the Act raised serious First Amendment issues. 789 F. 2d 1319, 1326 (1986) .

We granted certiorari, 479 U. S. 913 (1986), to review the issues of statutory and constitutional interpretation decided by the Court of Appeals. We now affirm.

II

The SFAA contends that the Court of Appeals erred in interpreting the Act as granting the USOC anything more than a normal trademark in the word "Olympic" . The "starting point in every case involving construction of a statute is the language itself. " *Kelly* v. *Robinson*, 479 U. S. 36, 43 (1986) [quoting *Blue Chip Stamps* v. *Manor Drug Stores*, 421 U. S. 723, 756 (1975) (POWELL, J. , concurring)] Section 110 of the Act provides:

"Without the consent of the [USOC] , any person who uses for the purpose of trade, to induce the sale of any goods or services, or to promote any theatrical exhibition, athletic performance, or competition——

" (4) the words 'Olympic', 'Olympiad', 'Citius Altius Fortius' , or any combination or simulation thereof tending to cause confusion, to cause mistake, to deceive, or to falsely suggest a connection with the [USOC] or any Olympic activity;

"shall be subject to suit in a civil action by the [USOC] for the remedies provided in the [Lanham] Act. " 36 U. S. C. § 380 (a) .

The SFAA argues that the clause "tending to cause confusion" is properly read to apply to the word "Olympic. " But because there is no comma after "thereof," the more natural reading of the section is that "tending to cause confusion" modifies only "any combination or simulation thereof. " Nevertheless, we do not regard this language as conclusive. We therefore examine the legislative history of this section.

Before Congress passed § 110 of the Act, unauthorized use of the word "Olympic" was punishable criminally. The relevant statute, in force since 1950, did not require the use to be confusing. Instead, it made it a crime for:

"*any person* ... other than [the USOC] ... for the purpose of trade, theatrical exhibition, athletic performance, and competition or as an advertisement to induce the sale of any article whatsoever or attendance at any theatrical exhibition, athletic performance, and competition or for any business or charitable purpose *to use … the words ' Olympic ', ' Olympiad ', or ' Citius Altius Fortius' or any combination of these words.* " 64 Stat. 901, as amended, 36 U. S. C. § 379 (1976 ed.) (emphasis added).

The House Judiciary Committee drafted the language of § 110 that was ultimately adopted. The Committee explained that the previous "criminal penalty has been found to be unworkable as it requires the proof of a criminal intent. " H. R. Rep. No. 95– 1627, p. 15 (1978) (House Report). The changes from the criminal statute "were made in response to a letter from the Patent and Trademark Office of the Department of Commerce, " *ibid.* , that the Committee appended to the end of its Report. This letter explained:

"Section 110 (a)(4) makes actionable not only use of the words ' Olympic', ' Olympiad', ' Citius Altius Fortius', and any combination thereof, but also any simulation or confusingly similar derivation thereof tending to cause confusion, to cause mistake, to deceive, or to falsely suggest a connection with the [USOC] or any Olympic activity… .

"Section 110 *carries forward some prohibitions from the existing statute enacted in* 1950 *and adds some new prohibitions*, *e. g. words described in section* (*a*) (4) *tending to cause confusion*, to cause mistake, or to deceive with respect to the [USOC] or any Olympic activity. " *Id.* , at 38 (emphasis added).

This legislative history demonstrates that Congress intended to provide the USOC with exclusive control of the use of the word "Olympic" without regard to whether an unauthorized use of the word tends to cause confusion.

The SFAA further argues that the reference in § 110 to Lanham Act *remedies* should be read as incorporating the traditional trademark *defenses* as well. See 15 U. S. C. § 1115 (b) . This argument ignores the clear language of the section. Also, this shorthand reference to remedies replaced an earlier draft's specific list of remedies typically available for trademark infringement, *e. g.*, injunctive relief, recovery of profits, damages, costs, and attorney's fees. See Lanham Act Ë 34, 35, 15 U. S. C. Ë 1116, 1117. This list contained no reference to trademark defenses. 124 Cong. Rec. 12865, 12866 (1978) (proposed § 110 (c)). Moreover, the USOC already held a trademark in the word "Olympic." App. 378–382. Under the SFAA's interpretation, the Act would be largely superfluous. In sum, the language and legislative history of § 110 indicate clearly that Congress intended to grant the USOC exclusive use of the word "Olympic" without regard to whether use of the word tends to cause confusion, and that § 110 does not incorporate defenses available under the Lanham Act.

III

This Court has recognized that "national protection of trademarks is desirable … because trademarks foster competition and the maintenance of quality by securing to the producer the benefits of good reputation. " *Park 'N Fly*, *Inc.* v. *Dollar Park and Fly*, *Inc.*, 469 U. S. 189, 198 (1985). In the Lanham Act, 15 U. S. C. § 1051 *et seq.*, Congress established a system for protecting such trademarks. Section 45 of the Lanham Act defines a trademark as "any word, name, symbol, or device or any combination thereof adopted and used by a manufacturer or merchant to identify and distinguish his goods, including a unique product, from those manufactured or sold by others." 15 U. S. C. § 1127 (1982 ed., Supp. III). Under § 32 of the Lanham Act, the owner of a trademark is protected from unauthorized uses that are "likely to cause confusion, or to cause mistake, or to deceive." § 1114 (1)(a). Section 33 of the Lanham Act grants several statutory defenses to an alleged trademark infringer. § 1115.

The protection granted to the USOC's use of the Olympic words and symbols differs from the normal trademark protection in two respects: the USOC need not prove that a contested use is likely to cause confusion, and an unauthorized user of the word does not have available the normal statutory defenses. The SFAA argues, in effect, that the differences between the Lanham Act and § 110 are of constitutional dimension. First, the SFAA contends that the word "Olympic" is a generic word that could not gain trademark protection under the Lanham Act. The SFAA argues that this prohibition is constitutionally required and thus that the First Amendment prohibits Congress from granting a trademark in the word "Olympic." Second, the SFAA argues that the First Amendment prohibits Congress from granting exclusive use of a word absent a requirement that the authorized user prove that an unauthorized use is likely to cause confusion. We address these contentions in turn.

A

This Court has recognized that words are not always fungible, and that the suppression of particular words "run [s] a substantial risk of suppressing ideas in the process." *Cohen* v. *California*, 403 U. S. 15, 26 (1971) . The SFAA argues that this principle prohibits Congress from granting the USOC exclusive control of uses of the word "Olympic," a word that the SFAA views as generic. Yet this recognition always has been balanced against the principle that when a word acquires value "as the result of organization and the expenditure of labor, skill, and money" by an entity, that entity constitutionally may obtain a limited property right in the word. *International News Service* v. *Associated Press*, 248 U. S. 215, 239 (1918). See *Trade-Mark Cases*, 100 U. S. 82, 92 (1879) .

There is no need in this case to decide whether Congress ever could grant a private entity exclusive use of a generic word. Congress reasonably could conclude that the commercial and promotional value of the word "Olympic" was the product of the USOC's "own talents and energy, the end result of much time, effort, and expense." *Zacchini* v. *Scripps – Howard Broadcasting Co.* , 433 U. S. 562, 575 (1977) . The USOC, together with respondent International Olympic Committee (IOC), have used the word "Olympic" at least since 1896, when the modern Olympic Games began. App. 348. Baron Pierre de Coubertin of France, acting pursuant to a government commission, then proposed the revival of the ancient Olympic Games to promote international understanding. D. Chester, The Olympic Games Handbook 13

(1975). De Coubertin sought to identify the "spirit" of the ancient Olympic Games that had been corrupted by the influence of money and politics. See M. Finley & H. Pleket, The Olympic Games: The First Thousand Years 4 (1976). De Coubertin thus formed the IOC, that has established elaborate rules and procedures for the conduct of the modern Olympics. See Olympic Charter, Rules 26-69 (1985). In addition, these ruls direct every national committee to protect the use of the Olympic flag, symbol, flame, and motto from unauthorized use. *Id*. , Bye-laws to Rules 6 and 53. Under the IOC Charter, the USOC is the national olympic committee for the United States with the sole authority to represent the United States at the Olympic Games. Pursuant to this authority, the USOC has used the Olympic words and symbols extensively in this country to fulfill its object under the Olympic Charter of "ensur [ing] the development and safeguarding of the Olympic Movement and sport. " *Id*. , Rule 24.

The history of the origins and associations of the word "Olympic" demonstrates the meritlessness of the SFAA's contention that Congress simply plucked a generic word out of the English vocabulary and granted its exclusive use to the USOC. Congress reasonably could find that since 1896, the word "Olympic" has acquired what in trademark law is known as a secondary meaning——it "has become distinctive of [the USOC's] goods in commerce. " Lanham Act, § 2 (f), <u>15 U. S. C. § 1052 (f)</u> . See *Park 'N Fly*, *Inc*. v. <u>*Dollar Park and Fly*, *Inc*. , 469 U. S. , at 194</u>. The right to adopt and use such a word "to distinguish the goods or property [of] the person whose mark it is, to the exclusion of use by all other persons, has been long recognized. " *Trade - Mark Cases*, *supra*, at 92. Because Congress reasonably could conclude that the USOC has distinguished the word "Olympic" through its own efforts, Congress' decision to grant the USOC a limited property right in the word "Olympic" falls within the scope of trademark law protections, and thus certainly within constitutional bounds.

B

Congress also acted reasonably when it concluded that the USOC should not be required to prove that an unauthorized use of the word "Olympic" is likely to confuse the public. To the extent that § 110 applies to uses "for the purpose of trade [or] to induce the sale of any goods or services," 36 U. S. C. § 380 (a), its application is to commercial speech. Commercial speech "receives a limited form of First Amendment protection. " *Posadas de Puerto Rico Assoc.* v. *Tourism Company of Puerto Rico*, 478 U. S. 328, 340 (1986); *Central Hudson Gas & Electric Corp.* v. *Public Service Comm'n of New York*, 447 U. S. 557, 562–563 (1980). Section 110 also allows the USOC to prohibit the use of "Olympic" for promotion of theatrical and athletic e-vents. Although many of these promotional uses will be commercial speech, some uses may go beyond the "strictly business" context. See *Friedman* v. *Rogers*, 440 U. S. 1, 11 (1979). In this case, the SFAA claims that its use of the word "Olympic" was intended to convey a political statement about the status of homosexuals in society. Thus, the SFAA claims that in this case § 110 suppresses political speech.

By prohibiting the use of one word for particular purposes, neither Congress nor the USOC has prohibited the SFAA from conveying its message. The SFAA held its athletic event in its planned format under the names "Gay Games I" and "Gay Games II" in 1982 and 1986, respectively. See n. 2, *supra*. Nor is it clear that § 110 restricts purely expressive uses of the word "Olympic. " Section 110 restricts only the manner in which the SFAA may convey its message. The restrictions on expressive speech properly are characterized as incidental to the primary congressional purpose of encouraging and rewarding the USOC's activities. The appropriate inquiry is thus whether the incidental restrictions on First Amendment freedoms are greater than necessary to further a substantial governmental interest. *United States* v. *O'Brien*, 391 U. S. 367, 377 (1968).

One reason for Congress to grant the USOC exclusive control of the word "Olympic," as with other trademarks, is to ensure that the USOC receives the benefit of its own efforts so that the USOC will have an incentive to continue to produce a "quality product," that, in turn, benefits the public. See 1 J. McCarthy, Trademarks and Unfair Competition § 2: 1, pp. 44–47 (1984). But in the special circumstance of the USOC, Congress has a broader public interest in promoting, through the activities of the USOC, the participation of amateur athletes from the United States in "the great four-yearly sport festival, the Olympic Games." Olympic Charter, Rule 1 (1985). The USOC's goal under the Olympic Charter, Rule 24 (B), is to further the Olympic movement, that has as its aims: "to promote the development of those physical and moral qualities which are the basis of sport"; "to educate young people through sport in a spirit of better understanding between each other and of friendship, thereby helping to build a better and more peaceful world"; and "to spread the Olympic principles throughout the world, thereby creating international goodwill." *Id*., Rule 1. See also *id*., Rule 11 (aims of the IOC). Congress' interests in promoting the USOC's activities include these purposes as well as those specifically enumerated in the USOC's charter. Section 110 directly advances these governmental interests by supplying the USOC with the means to raise money to support the Olympics and encourages the USOC's activities by ensuring that it will receive the benefits of its efforts.

The restrictions of § 110 are not broader than Congress reasonably could have determined to be necessary to further these interests. Section 110 primarily applies to all uses of the word "Olympic" to induce the sale of goods or services. Although the Lanham Act protects only against confusing uses, Congress' judgment respecting a certain word is not so limited. Congress reasonably could conclude that most commercial uses of the Olympic words and symbols are likely to be confusing. It also could determine that unauthorized uses, even if not confusing, nevertheless may harm the USOC by lessening the distinctiveness and thus the commercial value of the marks. See Schechter, The Rational Basis of Trademark Protection, 40 Harv. L. Rev. 813, 825 (1927) (one injury to a trademark owner may be "the gradual whittling away or dispersion of the identity and hold upon the public mind of the mark or name" by nonconfusing uses).

In this case, the SFAA sought to sell T-shirts, buttons, bumper stickers, and other items, all emblazoned with the title "Gay Olympic Games." The possibility for confusion as to sponsorship is obvious. Moreover, it is clear that the SFAA sought to exploit the "commercial magnetism," see *Mishawaka Rubber & Woolen Mfg. Co.* v. *S. S. Kresge Co.*, 316 U. S. 203, 205 (1942), of the word given value by the USOC. There is no question that this unauthorized use could undercut the USOC's efforts to use, and sell the right to use, the word in the future, since much of the word's value comes from its limited use. Such an adverse effect on the USOC's activities is directly contrary to Congress' interest. Even though this protection may exceed the traditional rights of a trademark owner in certain circumstances, the application of the Act to this commercial speech is not broader than necessary to protect the legitimate congressional interest and therefore does not violate the First Amendment.

Section 110 also extends to promotional uses of the word "Olympic," even if the promotion is not to induce the sale of goods. Under § 110, the USOC may prohibit purely promotional uses of the word only when the promotion relates to an athletic or theatrical event. The USOC created the value of the word by using it in connection with an athletic event. Congress reasonably could find that use of the word by other entities to promote an athletic event would directly impinge on the USOC's legitimate right of exclusive use. The SFAA's proposed use of the word is an excellent example. The "Gay Olympic Games" were to take place over a 9-day period and were to be held in different locations around the world. They were to include a torch relay, a parade with uniformed athletes of both sexes divided by city, an "Olympic anthem" and "Olympic Committee," and the award of gold, silver, and bronze medals, and were advertised under a logo of three overlapping rings. All of these features directly parallel the modern-day Olympics, not the Olympic Games that occurred in ancient Greece. The image the SFAA sought to invoke was exactly the image carefully cultivated by the USOC. The SFAA's expressive use of the word cannot be divorced from the value the USOC's efforts have given to it. The mere fact that the SFAA claims an expressive, as opposed to a purely commercial, purpose does not give it a First Amendment right to "appropriat [e] to itself the harvest of those who have sown. " *International News Service* v. *Associated Press*, 248 U. S. , at 239-240. The USOC's right to prohibit use of the word "Olympic" in the promotion of athletic events is at the core of its legitimate property right.

IV

The SFAA argues that even if the exclusive use granted by § 110 does not violate the First Amendment, the USOC's enforcement of that right is discriminatory in violation of the Fifth Amendment. The fundamental inquiry is whether the USOC is a governmental actor to whom the prohibitions of the Constitution apply. The USOC is a "private corporatio [n] established under Federal law. " 36 U. S. C. § 1101 (46). In the Act, Congress granted the USOC a corporate charter, § 371, imposed certain requirements on the USOC, and provided for some USOC funding through exclusive use of the Olympic words and symbols, § 380, and through direct grants.

The fact that Congress granted it a corporate charter does not render the USOC a Government agent. All corporations act under charters granted by a government, usually by a State. They do not thereby lose their essentially private character. Even extensive regulation by the government does not transform the actions of the regulated entity into those of the government. See *Jackson* v. *Metropolitan Edison Co.* , 419 U. S. 345 (1974) . Nor is the fact that Congress has granted the USOC exclusive use of the word "Olympic" dispositive. All enforceable rights in trademarks are created by some governmental act, usually pursuant to a statute or the common law. The actions of the trademark owners nevertheless remain private. Moreover, the intent on the part of Congress to help the USOC obtain funding does not change the analysis. The Government may subsidize private entities without assuming constitutional responsibility for their actions. *Blum* v. *Yaretsky*, 457 U. S. 991, 1011 (1982); *Rendell-Baker* v. *Kohn*, 457 U. S. 830, 840 (1982) .

This Court also has found action to be governmental action when the challenged entity performs functions that have been " 'traditionally the *exclusive* prerogative' " of the Federal Government. *Id.* , at 842 (quoting *Jackson* v. *Metropolitan Edison*

Co., *supra*, at 353; quoted in *Blum* v. *Yaretsky*, *supra*, at 1011) (emphasis added by the *Rendell—Baker* Court). Certainly the activities performed by the USOC serve a national interest, as its objects and purposes of incorporation indicate. See n. 17, *supra*. The fact "that a private entity performs a function which serves the public does not make its acts [governmental] action." *Rendell — Baker* v. *Kohn*, *supra*, at 842. The Amateur Sports Act was enacted "to correct the disorganization and the serious factional disputes that seemed to plague amateur sports in the United States." House Report, at 8. See *Oldfield* v. *Athletic Congress*, 779 F. 2d 505 (CA9 1985) (citing S. Rep. No. 95 – 770, pp. 2 – 3 (1978)). The Act merely authorized the USOC to coordinate activities that always have been performed by private entities. Neither the conduct nor the coordination of amateur sports has been a traditional governmental function.

Most fundamentally, this Court has held that a government "normally can be held responsible for a private decision only when it has exercised coercive power or has provided such significant encouragement, either overt or covert, that the choice must in law be deemed to be that of the [government]." *Blum* v. *Yaretsky*, *supra*, at 1004; *Rendell—Baker* v. *Kohn*, *supra*, at 840. See *Flagg Bros.*, *Inc.* v. *Brooks*, 436 U. S. 149, 166 (1978); *Jackson* v. *Metropolitan Edison Co.*, *supra*, at 357; *Moose Lodge No.* 107 v. *Irvis*, 407 U. S. 163, 173 (1972); *Adickes* v. *S. H. Kress & Co.*, 398 U. S. 144, 170 (1970). The USOC's choice of how to enforce its exclusive right to use the word "Olympic" simply is not a governmental decision. There is no evidence that the Federal Government coerced or encouraged the USOC in the exercise of its right. At most, the Federal Government, by failing to supervise the USOC's use of its rights, can be said to exercise "mere approval of or acquiescence in the initiatives" of the USOC. *Blum* v. *Yaretsky*, 457 U. S., at 1004 – 1005. This is not enough to make the USOC's actions those of the Government. *Ibid.* See *Flagg Bros.*, *Inc.* v. *Brooks*, *supra*, at 164 – 165; *Jackson* v. *Metropolitan Edison Co.*, *supra*, at 357. 29Because the USOC is not a governmental actor, the SFAA's claim that the USOC has enforced its rights in a discriminatory manner must fail.

V

Accordingly, we affirm the judgment of the Court of Appeals for the Ninth Circuit.

It is so ordered.

附　录

美国兰哈姆（商标）法[1]

目　录

---

〔1〕　资料来源于国家工商行政管理总局商标局中国商标网。

诉委员会

1068. 专利商标局局长在抵触、异议以及并存使用注册或撤销程序中的职权

1069. 在双方当事人参加的程序中衡平法原则的应用

1070. 不服审查员的决定向商标审判和上诉委员会提出上诉

1071. 向法院上诉

    （a）有权上诉的人；美国联邦巡回上诉法院；民事诉讼的放弃；另一方当事人对民事诉讼的选择权；程序

    （b）民事诉讼；权利人；法院的管辖权；专利商标局局长的地位；程序

1072. 注册作为所有权要求的推定通知

Ⅱ. 辅注册簿

1091. 辅注册簿

    （a）可注册的商标

    （b）申请和注册的程序

    （c）商标的性质

1092. 公告；不能被提异议；撤销

1093. 在主注册簿和辅注册簿上注册商标的注册证不同

1094. 本法可适用于在辅注册簿上注册的规定

1095. 不排除在主注册簿上注册

1096. 在辅注册簿上的注册不能用来阻止进口

Ⅲ. 一般条款

1111. 注册的标注；在商标上展示；在侵权诉讼中追索权益和赔偿

1112. 商品和服务的分类；多类注册

1113. 费用

    （a）申请；服务；材料

    （b）放弃；印第安产品

（1）基础申请

（2）基础注册

（3）缔约方

（4）登记日期

（5）有真诚的意图在商业中使用商标的声明

（6）延伸保护

（7）国际注册的所有人

（8）国际申请

（9）国际局

（10）国际注册簿

（11）国际注册

（12）国际注册日期

（13）马德里议定书

（14）驳回通知书

（15）缔约方的主管局

（16）原属局

（17）异议期限

1141a. 基于在美国的申请和注册的国际申请

（a）一般条款

（b）有资格的所有人

1141b. 国际申请的证明

（a）证明程序

（b）传送

1141c. 基础申请和基础注册的限制、放弃、撤销和到期

1141d. 在国际注册之后的延伸保护请求

1141e. 基于马德里议定书将国际注册的保护延伸至美国

1141f. 提交请求将国际注册的保护延伸至美国的效力

1141g. 请求延伸保护至美国的优先权

1141h. 延伸保护请求的审查和异议；驳回通知

1141i. 延伸保护的效力

1141j. 在美国的延伸保护对作为其基础的国际注册的依附性

1141k. 宣誓书和费用

1141l. 延伸保护的转让

1141m. 不容置疑性

1141n. 延伸保护的权利

Ⅰ. 主注册簿

1051 注册申请；证明

（a）已使用商标的申请

（1）通过缴纳规定的费用，按照专利商标局局长规定的格式向专利商标局递交一份申请和一份已宣誓之声明，按专利商标局局长要求的份数提交该商标的使用图样或复制品，将该商标使用于商业的所有人可申请在依本法建立的主注册簿上注册其商标。

（2）申请书应写明申请人的住址和国籍，申请人第一次使用该商标的日期，申请人在商业上第一次使用该商标的日期，使用该商标的有关商品和商标图样。

（3）申请人应对其声明宣誓，指明：

（A）宣誓人确信其本人或其所代表的法人确系申请注册商标的所有人；

（B）就宣誓人所知，申请所陈述的事实是准确的；

（C）该商标确系正在商业中使用，并且；

（D）就宣誓人所知，在商业中他人无权在其商品或与其相关联的商品上使用与该商标相同或相似的商标，以致引起混淆、误认或欺骗。除非是提出并存使用要求的申请，申请人应：

（ⅰ）声明专用权要求的例外情况，并且；

（ⅱ）就宣誓人所知，指明

（I）他人并存使用的情况，

（II）并存使用的或有关联的商品及并存使用的区域，

（III）使用的时间范围，

（IV）申请人拟注册的商品和区域。

（4）申请人应遵守专利商标局局长所规定的规章条例。专利商标局局长应制定规章，规定申请及获得申请日的要求。

（b）有真诚的意图使用商标的申请

（1）有真诚的意图在商业上使用商标的人，在表明其诚意的情况下，通过缴纳规定的费用，按照专利商标局局长规定的格式向专利商标局递交一份申请和一份已宣誓之声明，可申请在依本法建立的主注册簿上注册其商标。

（2）申请书应写明申请人的住址和国籍，以及申请人有真诚的意图使用该商标的有关商品，并提供该商标的图样。

（3）申请人应对其声明宣誓，指明：

（A）宣誓人确信其本人或其所代表的法人有权在商业中使用该商标；

（B）申请人有真诚的意图在商业中使用该商标；

（C）就宣誓人所知，申请所陈述的事实是准确的；

（D）就宣誓人所知，在商业中他人无权在其商品或与其相关联的商品上使用与该商标相同或相似的商标，以致引起混淆、误认或欺骗。

除按照本法第1126条提交的申请外，在申请人满足本条下述（c）（d）款的规定前，商标不应予以注册。

（4）申请人应遵守专利商标局局长所规定的规章条例。专利商标局局长应制定规章，规定申请及获得申请日的要求。

（c）为达到（a）款的要求，根据（b）款进行的申请修改

已在商业中使用该商标的申请人，在依照本条（b）款提交的申请被审查的期间，可以随时修改其申请书，使之符合本条（a）款的规定，从而要求依照本法的目的获得使用的权益。

（d）已在商业中使用该商标的已宣誓之声明

（1）自依照本法第1063条（b）（2）款向本条（b）款规定的申请人发出其商标的准许通知书之日起6个月内，该申请人应向专利商标局提交一份已

宣誓之声明，说明该商标已在商业中使用、申请人第一次在商业中使用该商标的日期、该准许通知书中所指定的在商业中使用该商标的或与该商标相关的商品或服务，同时提交专利商标局局长所要求的一定份数的在商业中使用的商标的图样或复制品，并缴纳规定的费用。该使用声明经审查接受后，该商标即在专利商标局获得注册，按照该使用声明中所列该商标有权注册的商品或服务颁发注册证，并在专利商标局的官方公告中发布注册通知。上述审查包括本法第 1052 条（a）至（e）款所列因素的审查。注册通知中应列明该商标注册的商品或服务。

（2）在上述（1）段规定的 6 个月期限届满前，若申请人提出书面请求，专利商标局局长可将上述（1）段规定的提交使用声明的期限延长 6 个月。除上述规定的延长期外，若申请人的理由充分，专利商标局局长还可根据申请人在前一次的延期届满前提出的书面请求，对上述（1）段规定的提交使用声明的期限再次延长，但累计不得超过 24 个月。任何基于本段所提交的延期请求应附有一份已宣誓之声明，表明申请人有真诚的意图继续在商业中使用该商标，并列出准许通知书中载明的该申请人有真诚的意图继续在商业中使用其商标的或与其商标有关的商品或服务。任何基于本段所提之延期请求应缴纳规定的费用。专利商标局局长应发布条例确定构成本段所述"理由充分"的指导原则。

（3）专利商标局局长应当通知申请人其所提交的使用声明是否被接受，若该使用声明被驳回，则应通知申请人驳回的理由。申请人可修改其使用声明。

（4）如果申请人没有在（1）段规定的期限内提交已宣誓之使用声明，也没有按（2）段规定如期提交延期请求，则该申请将被视为放弃，除非专利商标局局长同意此回复的耽搁并非故意，在此情况下，提交声明的日期可以延长，但此期限不能超过（1）和（2）段中规定的提交使用声明的期限。

（e）为送达传票和通知指定某居民

若申请人在美国无住所，应向美国专利商标局提交一份文件，指明一名美国居民的姓名和住所，以便在涉及该商标的相关程序中向其送达传票或通知。所述传票或通知将按最后提交的文件中指明的地址交付或邮递送达给该指定的人。如果按文件中的地址不能找到被指定人，或注册人没有向美国专利商标局提交文件指定一名美国居民的姓名和地址，以便在涉及该商标的相关程序中向其送达传票或通知，则所述传票或通知将送达专利商标局局长。

1052. 可在主注册簿上注册的商标；并存注册

根据商标的性质，凡能将申请人的商品区别于他人商品的商标，不应驳回其在主注册簿上的注册，除非该商标：

（a）包含不道德、欺骗或诽谤性内容；或含有对生者或死者、机构、信仰或国家象征有贬损或引起错误联想的内容，或包含使之蒙受鄙视或破坏其名誉的内容；或包含一个地理标志，当其用于葡萄酒或烈性酒或与其相关时，它与一个并非该商品原产地的地名相同，而且在世界贸易组织协定（见第19篇3501条第（9）款）在美国生效之日一年以后，申请人才第一次使用于葡萄酒或烈性酒上。

（b）包含美国或其州、市或外国的旗帜、盾形纹章或其他徽章，以及对上述的模仿。

（c）包含与特定在世人物相同的姓名、肖像或签名，经其本人书面同意的除外，或者，在已故美国总统的遗孀尚健在时，包含已故美国总统的姓名、签字或肖像，经其遗孀书面同意的除外。

（d）包含与已在专利商标局注册的商标，或他人在美国在先使用且尚未放弃的商标或商号相似的商标，以致其使用在申请人的商品上或与之相关时易于造成混淆或误认或欺骗；除非专利商标局局长认为在使用方式、使用地域、使用商品的条件和限制下，两人以上对相同或近似商标的连续使用不会造成混淆、误认或欺骗，这些人将获得并存注册，假如在下列日期之前他们在商业中的并存合法使用已使他们有权使用该商标：

（1）待审的申请或依本法核准的注册中最早的申请日；

（2）对依1881年3月3日或1905年2月20日的法案核准并至1947年7月5日仍有效的注册，1947年7月5日；或

（3）对依1905年2月20日的法案提交的申请并于1947年7月5日后注册，1947年7月5日。

如果待审申请或已注册的商标所有人同意授予申请人并存注册，则无须要求其在该待审申请或已注册的商标申请日之前已经使用。如果有管辖权的法院终审决定两人以上均有权在商业中使用相同或近似的商标，专利商标局局长将准予并存注册。在准予并存注册时，专利商标局局长应规定各商标的所有人使用其商标的方式、地域或商品的条件和限制。

（e）构成商标的要素：

（1）在用于申请人的商品上或与之相关时，仅是对这些商品的描述或欺骗性的错误描述；

（2）在用于申请人的商品上或与之相关时，主要是对这些商品的地理描述，依照本法第 1054 条的规定可作为原产地标记注册的除外；

（3）在用于申请人的商品上或与之相关时，主要是对这些商品地理方面欺骗性的错误描述；

（4）主要仅是一个姓氏；

（5）包含的内容，作为一个整体，具有功能性。

（f）除本条（a）、（b）、（c）、（d）、（e）（3）和（e）（5）款明确排除的以外，如果申请人已在商业中使用的商标，在其商品上获得了显著性，本章中的其他规定都不能阻碍其注册。专利商标局局长将接受在提出显著性要求之日前五年申请人在商业上实质性独占并连续使用该商标的证明作为该商标用于申请人的商品上或与之相关时的已具有显著性的表面成立之证据。如果申请人的商标使用在其商品上或与其相关时，主要是对这些商品地理方面欺骗性的错误描述，但该商标于 1993 年 12 月 8 日之前已在商业上使用，并在申请人的商品上已具有显著性时，本章中的其他规定都不能阻碍其注册。

根据本法第 1125 条（c）款规定，当一个商标的使用将导致淡化时，该商标的注册将按照本法第 1063 条规定的程序予以驳回。根据本法第 1125 条（c）款规定，当一个商标注册后，其使用将导致淡化时，该商标的注册将按照第 1064 条或第 1092 条规定的程序予以撤销。

1053. 服务商标可予注册

根据可适用的关于商标注册的规定，服务商标应以与商标相同的方式注册，并具有相同的效力，且在注册后，有权享有本法为商标提供的保护。本条有关申请和程序的规定应尽可能与有关商标注册的规定一致。

1054. 集体商标和证明商标可予注册

根据可适用的关于商标注册的规定，集体商标和证明商标，包括原产地标记，应根据本法以与商标相同的方式注册，并具有相同的效力，且在注册后，有权享有本法为商标提供的保护。注册人应为对申请注册商标的使用有合法控制权的个人、国家、州、市等，即使注册人不拥有一个工业或商业企业。但将证明商标用于虚假地表示该商标的所有人或使用人在其制造或销售的商品或提供的服务上使用该商标或与之相关的情况除外。本条有关申请和程序的规定应尽可能与有关商标注册的规定一致。

1055. 关联公司的使用将影响有效性和注册

如果一个已注册的商标或一个申请注册的商标已由或将由关联公司合法地使用，只要这种使用的方式并没有欺骗公众，那么这种使用则有利于注册人或注册申请人的利益，并且不应影响商标的有效性或其注册。如果商标被某人首先使用，但在其商品或服务的性质和质量方面，是由该商标的注册人或注册申请人控制的，那么这种首先使用则有利于注册人或注册申请人的利益。

1056. 不能注册内容的声明放弃

（a）强制的和主动的放弃

专利商标局局长可要求申请人放弃商标不能注册的组成部分。申请人可以主动放弃申请注册商标的某一组成部分。

（b）权利的损害

该放弃，包括依照本法第 1057 条（e）款进行的放弃，不应损害或影响申请人或注册人对被放弃部分的已有的或以后产生的权利，若被放弃的部分已成为或将要成为区别其商品或服务的显著部分时，也不应损害或影响其在另一申请中的注册权利。

1057. 注册证

（a）颁发和格式

商标注册证，将以美利坚合众国的名义颁发给在主注册簿上注册的商标，并由专利商标局盖章，由专利商标局局长签字或载有其签名，并在专利商标局记录存档。注册证上应有商标的图样，并指明该商标是依据本法在主注册簿上注册，列明该商标初次使用的日期、在商业上初次使用的日期、指定使用的商品或服务、注册号和注册日期、有效期限、专利商标局收到该商标注册申请的日期，以及对该注册可能附加的条件和限制。

（b）注册证作为表面成立之证据

依照本法设立的主注册簿上商标的注册证，应是注册商标有效性和商标注册的表面成立之证据，也是注册人商标所有权的表面成立之证据，同时是注册人在商业活动中根据注册证上列明的条件和限制在注册证指定的商品或服务项目上使用该注册商标的专用权的表面成立之证据。

（c）商标的注册申请作为其推定使用

依据本法关于在主注册簿上注册商标的规定，一个商标的注册申请应构成对该商标的推定使用，授予其在注册的商品或服务上全国有效的优先权，以对抗其他人，但对具有下列情况的人除外，即，他的商标尚未被放弃，并在申请提交前

（1）已经使用该商标；

（2）已经提交了一个商标注册申请，正等待审查或已经核准注册；或者

（3）已经提交了一份外国商标注册申请，并以此获得优先权，并根据本法第 1126 条（d）款及时地提交了商标注册申请，正等待审查或已经核准注册。

（d）向受让人颁发注册证

商标注册证可以颁发给申请人的受让人，但该转让必须先在专利商标局登记。办理转让时，在所有人提交请求，提供合理理由并缴纳规定的费用后，专利商标局局长应向受让人颁发其名下所述商标新的注册证，期限为原注册期限未届满部分。

（e）注册人的放弃、撤销或修改

经注册人申请，专利商标局局长可准许放弃注册而予以撤销，并在撤销时应在专利商标局的存档记录中作适当的记载。经注册人申请和缴纳规定的费用后，专利商标局局长基于合理的理由可准许对任何注册进行修改或放弃商标的一部分，但是该修改或放弃不得在实质上改变该商标的性质。应在专利商标局的存档记录中及注册证上作适当记载，如果注册证已遗失或毁坏，应在经认证的副本上作适当记载。

（f）以专利商标局存档记录复印件为证据

专利商标局有关商标的存档记录、簿册、文件或图样的复印件，以及注册副本，经专利商标局盖章认证和专利商标局局长认证或专利商标局局长正式指定的局内工作人员以专利商标局局长的名义认证后，在任何情况下作为证据具有与原件同等的效力；并且任何人经申请并缴纳规定的费用后，均可得到这种复印件。

（g）专利商标局错误的更正

当专利商标局的责任而导致的注册的实质性错误在专利商标局的存档记录中清楚地显示出来时，专利商标局将免费颁发证明书，说明这一事实和错误的性质，并作记录，在每一份注册证的印刷文本后附上一份该证明书的印刷文本，并且此后该更正的注册如同原先以正确形式注册具有同样的效力，或者专利商标局局长也可自行决定免费颁发一个新注册证。依据专利商标局的规章颁发的所有更正证明书及其所依附的注册如同法律特别授权颁发的证明书具有同等的效力。

（h）申请人错误的更正

当有显示表明注册中的错误，是由申请人无意中的失误导致，专利商标局局长有权颁发更正证明书，或者由专利商标局局长自行决定，在申请人缴纳规定的费用后，向其颁发一个新的注册证，但更正的内容不能导致该商标的重新公告。

1058. 有效期

（a）一般情况

每一注册的有效期为 10 年，但是商标在其应适用的下列期限届满之时没有达到本条（b）款的规定，专利商标局局长应当撤销该注册：

（1）根据本法规定注册的商标，注册之日起 6 年届满时；

（2）根据本法 1062 条（C）款的规定公告的注册，依该条款公告之日起 6 年届满时；

（3）所有的注册，在注册之日起每个连续的 10 年届满时。

（b）连续使用宣誓书

在本条（a）款列出的适用期限届满前一年内，注册的所有人应缴纳规定的费用，并向专利商标局提交：

（1）一份宣誓书，列明在注册中指定的该商标在商业中使用的或与之相关的商品或服务，并按照专利商标局局长的要求附上一定数量能表明该商标当前使用情况的图样或复制品；或者

（2）一份宣誓书，列明在注册中指定的该商标未在商业中使用的或与之相关的商品或服务，并提供能够解释未使用的特殊情况，并非有任何放弃该商标的意图。

（c）递交的宽展期；不规范

（1）注册商标的所有人可以在本条（a）款规定的适用期限届满后的六个月宽展期内递交本条规定的材料。递交材料的同时应缴纳专利商标局局长规定的额外费用。

（2）如果依照本条规定递交的材料存在不规范，该不规范可以在法定的期限后，及不规范通知规定的期限内予以改正。递交材料的同时应缴纳专利商标局局长规定的额外费用。

（d）宣誓书要求的通知

本条规定的宣誓书要求的特殊通知，应附在每一个注册证后面及本法第 1062 条（c）款规定的公告通知中。

（e）宣誓书的接受或驳回通知

专利商标局局长应通知按照本条规定提交了宣誓书的所有人，商标专员是否接受了其宣誓书，如果驳回，说明驳回的理由。

（f）为送达传票和通知指定某居民

若注册人在美国无住所，应向美国专利商标局提交一份文件，指明一名美国居民的姓名和住所，以便在涉及该商标的相关程序中向其送达传票或通知。所述传票或通知将按最后提交的文件中指明的地址交付或邮递送达给该指定的人。如果按文件中的地址不能找到被指定人，或注册人没有向美国专利商标局提交文件指定一名美国居民的姓名和地址，以便在涉及该商标的相关程序中向其送达传票或通知，则所述传票或通知将送达专利商标局局长。

1059. 注册的续展

（a）续展的期限；续展的时间

根据第 1058 条的规定，在缴纳规定的费用及按专利商标局局长规定的形式递交书面申请后，每个商标自注册之日起的每个连续 10 年届满时可续展 10 年。该申请可在商标注册或续展的每个连续 10 年届满前一年内的任何时候提出，也可以在每个连续 10 年届满后的 6 个月宽展期内提出，但须缴纳规定的费用和额外的费用。如果根据本条提出的申请存在不规范，该不规范可在收到不规范通知后规定的期限内补正，但需缴纳规定的额外费用。

（b）续展的驳回通知

如果专利商标局局长驳回了注册续展申请，应通知注册人商标专员的驳回决定及驳回的理由。

（c）为送达传票和通知指定某居民

若注册人在美国无住所，应向美国专利商标局提交一份文件，指明一名美国居民的姓名和住所，以便在涉及该商标的相关程序中向其送达传票或通知。所述传票或通知将按最后提交的文件中指明的地址交付或邮递送达给该指定的人。如果按文件中的地址不能找到被指定人，或注册人没有向美国专利商标局提交文件指定一名美国居民的姓名和地址，以便在涉及该商标的相关程序中向其送达传票或通知，则所述传票或通知将送达专利商标局局长。

1060. 转让

（a）（1）一件已经注册或已经申请注册的商标可以连同使用该商标的商业信誉，或与该商标的使用相关并由该商标所象征的部分商誉一并转让。然而，在依据本法第 1051 条（c）款提交修改申请并达到本法第 1051 条（a）款的规定之前，或在依据本法第 1051 条（d）款提交已宣誓之声明前，依据本法第 1501 条（b）款提交的商标注册申请不得转让，除非转让给该申请人企业的继承人，或企业与该商标相关部分的继承人，条件是该企业仍在营业和存在。

（2）在本条规定的转让中不必包括在商业中与其他商标的使用相关并由其他商标象征的商业信誉，也不必包括在商业中与该企业经营名称或风格的使用相关并由它们象征的商业信誉。

（3）转让应以书面形式正式签署。承认书可作为转让生效的表面成立之证据；当规定的转让信息在美国专利商标局登记后，该记录可作为转让生效的表面成立之证据。

（4）一项转让对以等价有偿的方式购买该商标并且不知晓前述转让的后续购买者无效，除非在转让后或后续购买前 3 个月内已在美国专利商标局登记了规定的转让信息。

（5）美国专利商标局应按专利商标局局长规定的形式保存一份转让信息的记录。

（b）若受让人在美国无住所，应向美国专利商标局提交一份文件，指明一名美国居民的姓名和住所，以便在涉及该商标的相关程序中向其送达传票或通知。所述传票或通知将按最后提交的文件中指明的地址交付或邮递送达给该指定的人。如果按文件中的地址不能找到被指定人，或受让人没有向美国专利商标局提交文件指定一名美国居民的姓名和地址，以便在涉及该商标的相关程序中向其送达传票或通知，则所述传票或通知将送达专利商标局局长。

1061. 承认书和证明书的签署

本法规定的承认书和证明书可在美国境内向法律规定有权主持宣誓的人

当面作出，或者，在国外，向美国外交或领事馆官员当面作出，或向有权在某外国主持宣誓的官员当面作出。该官员的权力应由美国外交官员或领事馆官员出具证明证实，或者由外国指定的官员加签证实。根据条约或公约，该加签与在美国境内指定官员作出的加签具有同等的效力，并且如果加签符合作出地政府或国家的法律，该官员的权力有效。

1062. 公告

（a）审查和公告

在提交注册申请并缴纳规定的费用后，专利商标局局长应当将该申请交给主管商标注册的审查员进行审查，并且，如果经审查认为该申请人有权注册，或者根据本法第 1051 条（d）款接受使用声明后有权注册，专利商标局局长应当将该商标在美国专利商标局的官方公告中予以公告。但是，如果申请人主张并存使用，或者按本法第 1066 条的规定，申请处于干预程序，如果该商标可以注册，应依照这些程序对当事人的权利的裁定而决定是否予以公告

（b）注册的驳回；申请的修改；放弃

如果审查员认为申请人无权注册，应向申请人提出建议并说明原因。申请人应在 6 个月期限内答复或修改其申请，然后该申请将被重新审查。这一程序可重复直至

（1）审查员最终驳回该商标的注册，或者

（2）该申请人未能在 6 个月的期限内答复，或修改或上诉，

在这种情况下，该申请应被视为已放弃，除非专利商标局局长同意此回复的耽搁并非故意，在这种情况下，该期限可以延长。

（c）依据修改前的法案注册的商标重新公告

依照 1881 年 3 月 3 日或 1905 年 2 月 20 日的法案注册商标的注册人，可于注册有效期届满前任何时候，在缴纳规定的费用后，向专利商标局局长提交一份宣誓书，列明在注册中指定的该商标在商业中使用的商品，并主张该商标享有本法的权益。专利商标局局长应当在官方公告中发布带有该商标图样的通知，并通知注册人该公告和本法第 1058 条（b）款规定的使用或无使

用宣誓书的要求。按本款规定公告的商标不适用本法第 1063 条的规定。

1063. 注册的异议

（a）任何人确信一个商标在主注册簿上的注册会使其受到损害，包括依据本法第 1125 条（c）款产生的淡化结果，可在缴纳了规定的费用后，于该申请注册的商标按本法第 1062 条（a）款规定公告后 30 天内向专利商标局提出异议，并说明理由。基于异议人在 30 天期限届满前的书面请求，提出异议的时间可以延长 30 天，并且在延长的期限届满前，专利商标局局长基于异议人的请求和合理的理由，可准予再次延长期限。专利商标局局长应将每次异议期限的延长通知申请人。异议可按照专利商标局局长规定的条件进行修改。

（b）除非异议理由成立，否则

（1）根据本法第 1051 条（a）款或第 1126 条规定提出申请有权在主注册簿上注册的商标，应在专利商标局注册，颁发注册证，并在专利商标局的官方公告中发布注册通知；或者

（2）对根据本法第 1051 条（b）款申请注册的申请人发出准许通知书。

1064. 注册的撤销

任何人确信在依照本法建立的主注册簿上注册的商标，或依据 1881 年 3 月 3 日的法案，或 1905 年 2 月 20 日的法案注册的商标已经对其造成损害或将要造成损害，包括依据第 1125 条（c）款产生的淡化结果，可在申明其所依据的理由并缴纳规定的费用后，在下列规定的时间提出撤销该商标注册请求：

（1）依照本法注册的商标，注册之日起 5 年内；

（2）依照 1881 年 3 月 3 日的法案或 1905 年 2 月 20 日的法案注册的商标，按本法第 1062 条（c）款规定公告之日起 5 年内；

（3）任何时候，如果注册商标成为指定的商品或服务或其一部分的通用名称，或具有功能性，或已被放弃，或其注册是以欺骗性手段获得，或违反本法第 1054 条或第 1052 条（a）、（b）或（c）款有关注册商标的规定，或违反修改前的法案有关注册商标类似的禁止性规定，或者在注册人使用注册商标时，或在他人经注册人允许使用商标时，虚假地表示了该注册商标使用

或与其相关的商品或服务的产源。如果该注册商标并不是其注册的全部商品或服务的通用名称，可以申请只撤销部分商品或服务的注册。不能仅因为商标被用作某一独特产品或服务的名称或用来识别某一独特产品或服务，而被视为商品或服务的通用名称。注册商标对相关公众的主要意义而不是购买者的动机，是作为决定注册商标是否属于其使用或相关商品或服务项目的通用名称的检验标准。

（4）任何时候，如果商标依据 1881 年 3 月 3 日的法案或 1905 年 2 月 20 日的法案注册，且未按本法第 1062 条（C）款规定公告。

（5）任何时候，如果证明商标的注册人

（A）对该商标的使用不予控制，或不能合法地行使控制，或

（B）从事该证明商标指定商品或服务的生产或销售，或

（C）允许以证明以外的目的使用证明商标，或

（D）歧视性的拒绝为某人达到该证明商标标准或条件的商品或服务提供证明或继续证明：

如果联邦贸易委员会将基于本条第（3）和（5）款规定的理由申请撤销在依本法建立的主注册簿上注册的商标，可免交规定的费用。第（5）款中的任何规定都不能阻止注册人在广告或促销中使用证明商标以提高证明程序或符合注册人证明标准商品或服务的认知度。只要注册人自己没有生产、制造或销售其证明商标指定证明的商品或服务，这种对证明商标的使用不能成为依据第（5）款撤销的理由。

1065. 在某些条件下使用商标的不容置疑的权利

除了根据本法第 1064 条第（3）和（5）款规定可随时提出撤销申请的理由外，并且，除了在主注册簿上注册商标的使用在某种程度上侵犯了，另一个通过商标或企业名称在该注册商标依本法注册之日前的连续使用而依任何州或地区的法律获得的有效权利外，如果自注册之日起该注册商标在其指定的商品或服务或其相关方面已连续使用 5 年，并且仍在商业中使用，则该注册人对该注册商标在商业中的使用权不容置疑，只要：

（1）没有不利于注册人对该商标在上述商品或服务上所有权主张的终局

决定，或不利于注册人在上述商品或服务上注册该商标或在注册簿上保持该商标在上述商品或服务上权利的终局决定；

（2）在专利商标局或法院没有涉及上述权利的程序还未审查和最终处理；

（3）在任一5年期限届满后一年内向专利商标局局长提交一份宣誓书，列明该商标在注册中指定的已连续使用了5年，并且仍继续在商业中使用或与之相关的商品或服务，及本条（1）和（2）款所列事项；以及

（4）一商标若系其注册的商品或服务或其一部分的通用名称，则不可获得不容置疑的权利。

依照本条上述规定的条件，依本法注册商标不容置疑的权利也应适用于依据1881年3月3日的法案或1905年2月20日的法案注册的商标，但需在根据本法第1062条（c）款的规定公告该商标之日起的任何一个连续5年期满后一年内向专利商标局局长提交一份宣誓书。

专利商标局局长应当通知按上述规定提交宣誓书的注册人受理事项。

1066. 抵触；专利商标局局长声明

如果申请注册的商标与他人在先注册的商标相似，或者与他人在先申请的商标相同，当其使用在申请人的商品或服务上或与之相关时可能造成混淆、误认或欺骗时，专利商标局局长可基于有特殊情况的请求，宣布抵触的存在。对一个申请注册的商标和一个使用权已经不容置疑的注册商标之间不应宣布抵触。

1067. 抵触、异议，以及并存使用注册或撤销的程序；通知；商标审判及上诉委员会

（a）在每一抵触案件，异议案件，合法并存使用人的注册申请，或撤销商标注册的申请中，专利商标局局长应通知各方当事人，并指定一个商标审判及上诉委员会来决定各方对注册的相关权利。

（b）商标审判及上诉委员会应当包括专利商标局局长、专利专员、商标专员以及专利商标局局长指定的商标行政审查官。

1068. 专利商标局局长在抵触、异议，以及并存使用注册或撤销的程序中的职权

在这些程序中，如果有关当事人的权利得以确立，专利商标局局长可驳回被异议商标的注册，可全部或部分地撤销注册，可通过对指定商品或服务的限定而修改申请或注册，还可以在注册簿上限制或更正注册商标的注册，驳回任何或所有抵触商标的注册，也可核准有资格的权利人的商标注册；如果在基于并存使用的商标注册案件中，专利商标局局长应根据本法第 1052 条（d）款的规定决定并确定条件和限制。然而，如果基于本法第 1051 条（b）款的申请人没有在依照本法第 1057 条（c）款确立推定使用前取得优势，在其商标获得注册前，终局决定将不会有利于该申请人。

1069. 在双方当事人参加的程序中衡平法原则的应用

在一切当事人双方参加的程序中，延误、不得反悔和默认等衡平法原则，在可适用的情况下可以考虑应用。

1070. 不服审查员的决定向商标审判及上诉委员会提出上诉

对主管商标注册的审查员作出的任何终局决定不服的，可向商标审判及上诉委员会提出上诉，并缴纳规定的费用。

1071. 向法院上诉

（a）有权上诉的人；美国联邦巡回上诉法院；民事诉讼的放弃；另一方当事人对民事诉讼的选择权；程序

（1）商标注册申请人、抵触程序的当事人、异议程序的当事人、作为合法并存使用者申请注册的当事人、撤销程序的当事人、已按本法第 1058 条的规定提交了宣誓书的注册人，或者续展注册的申请人，如果对专利商标局局长或商标审判及上诉委员会的决定不服，可向美国联邦巡回上诉法院提出上诉，从而放弃其根据本条（b）款规定继续的权利；如果在上诉人按照本款第（2）段规定提交上诉通知书后的 20 天内，除专利商标局局长外的程序另一方当事人向专利商标局局长递交通知，选择按本条（b）款规定办理所有后续的

程序，该上诉将被驳回。对此，上诉人应在随后的 30 天内按照本条（b）款规定提起民事诉讼，否则被上诉的决定将适用于该案的后续程序。

（2）上诉人向美国联邦巡回上诉法院提出上诉的同时，应于被上诉决定作出之日后专利商标局局长规定的期限内，向专利商标局局长提交一份有关上诉的书面通知，且该期限在任何情况下不得少于决定之日后 60 天。

（3）专利商标局局长应将经认证的专利商标局档案文件清单转交美国联邦巡回上诉法院。在上诉审理期间，法院可以要求专利商标局局长提交有关文件的原件或经认证的复印件。在单方当事人参与的案件中，专利商标局局长应向法院递交一份关于专利商标局决定理由的简短说明，涉及上诉中的所有问题。法院在审理上诉案件以前，应将审理的时间和地点通知专利商标局局长和上诉的各方当事人。

（4）美国联邦巡回上诉法院应根据专利商标局的档案记录重新审查被上诉的决定。法院应根据其作出的决定，向专利商标局局长发布命令和意见。这些命令和意见应记录于专利商标局的档案，并适用于该案件后续的程序。然而，如果基于本法第 1051 条（b）款的申请人没有在依照本法第 1057 条（c）款确立推定使用前取得优势，在其商标获得注册前，终局决定将不会有利于该申请人。

（b）民事诉讼；权利人；法院的管辖权；专利商标局局长的地位；程序

（1）如果依据本条（a）款有权向美国联邦巡回上诉法院提起上诉的人对专利商标局局长或商标审判及上诉委员会的决定不服，可以在自决定作出之日起专利商标局局长指定的或本条（a）款规定的不少于 60 天的期限内，采取民事诉讼补救措施，除非对该决定的上诉已提交美国联邦巡回上诉法院。法院可根据该案的事实情况判定申请人是否有资格获得有关申请的注册，或一项注册是否应被撤销，或程序中需解决的其他问题。这类判决应授权专利商标局局长依照法律规定采取必要的行动。然而，如果基于本法第 1051 条（b）款的申请人没有在依照本法第 1057 条（c）款确立推定使用前取得优势，在其商标获得注册前，终局决定将不会有利于该申请人。

（2）专利商标局局长不得成为本款规定的当事人双方参加程序的一方当事人，但是受理申诉法院的工作人员应通知专利商标局局长有关申诉，并且专利商标局局长有权介入该诉讼。

（3）在单方当事人参与的案件中，起诉书的副本应送达专利商标局局长，并且无论终局决定是否有利于起诉人，该程序的所有费用均由起诉人支付，除非法院认定费用不合理。在依以下规定提出的诉讼中，经任何一方当事人请求，并满足法院规定的期限和条件，如成本、费用和对证人的进一步审问等，专利商标局的档案记录应在不影响任何一方当事人进一步取证权利的情况下得到承认。专利商标局的档案记录中的证言和证物，一经承认，应与诉讼中取得和产生的证据具有同等的效力。

（4）如有另一方当事人，则这类诉讼中可对在决定被申诉时专利商标局的档案中所记载的有利害关系的当事人提出，但任何有利害关系的当事人都可成为诉讼的一方当事人。如果各方当事人住所地所在的多个地区不在同一个州内，或者一方当事人的住所地在外国，则美国联邦哥伦比亚特区地区法院享有管辖权，并且可将当事人的传票送达当事人住所地的司法官。住所地在外国的当事人的传票可通过公告方式送达或按法院指定的方式送达。

1072. 注册作为所有权要求的推定通知

商标在依本法建立的主注册簿上的注册，或者依照 1881 年 3 月 3 日法案或 1905 年 2 月 20 日法案的注册，应为注册人所有权主张的推定通知。

Ⅱ. 辅注册簿

1091. 辅注册簿

（a）可注册的商标

除主注册簿外，专利商标局局长应按 1920 年 3 月 19 日《关于使 1910 年 8 月 20 日在阿根廷共和国布宜诺斯艾利斯制定和签署的保护商标和商号及其他目的公约的某些条款生效的法案》第 1 条（b）款的规定建立一本注册簿的附录，称为辅注册簿。所有在商业中由其所有人在商品和服务上使用或与之相关时能够区分申请人的商品或服务，且不能在依本法建立的主注册簿上注册的商标（依据本法第 1052 条（a）、（b）、（c）、（d）和（e）(3) 款的规定被宣布不能注册的商标除外），在缴纳规定的费用并达到其可适用本法第 1051 条（a）和（e）款的规定后，可在辅注册簿上注册。如果依据本法第 1052 条（e)(3) 款被宣布不能注册的商标能区分申请人的商品或服务，且不能依据本法在主注册簿上注册，则本条的规定不能阻止其在辅注册簿上的注册，条件是该商标在 1993 年 12 月 8 日以前，已经在商业中由其所有人在商品和服务上或其相关方面合法使用。

（b）申请和注册的程序

提交在辅注册簿上注册商标的申请并缴纳规定的费用后，专利商标局局长应将该申请转交负责商标注册的审查员进行审查。如果经审查显示该申请人有权获得注册，则应核准注册。如果发现该申请人无权获得注册，则应当适用第 1062 条（b）款的规定。

（c）商标的性质

拟在辅注册簿上注册的标志，可由任何商标、符号、标签、包装、商品外形、名称、文字、标语、词组、姓氏、地理名称、数字、图形，或任何整体上不具有功能性的内容，或任何上述要素的组合，但这些标志必须能区别申请人的商品或服务。

1092. 公告；不能被提异议；撤销

辅注册簿上的商标将不会以异议为目的公告也不能被提异议，但在其注册后应当在专利商标局的官方公告中予以公告。任何人认为一个商标在辅注册簿上的注册已经损害了其利益或将会损害其利益，包括本法第 1125 条（c）款规定的淡化结果，可以在任何时候请求专利商标局局长撤销该注册，并缴纳规定的费用，提交请求书申明理由。专利商标局局长应将上述申请提交商标审判及上诉委员会。该委员会应将上述申请通知注册人。如果经该委员会审查后发现该注册人无权获得注册，或者该商标已被放弃，该注册应由专利商标局局长撤销。然而，如果基于本法第 1051 条（b）款的申请人没有在依照本法第 1057 条（c）款确立推定使用前取得优势，在其商标获得注册前，终局决定将不会有利于该申请人。

1093. 在主注册簿和辅注册簿上注册商标的注册证不同

在辅注册簿上注册商标的注册证与颁发给主注册簿上注册商标的注册证有显著的不同。

1094. 本法可适用于辅注册簿上注册的规定

本法适用于主注册簿上的申请和注册的规定，在可能的情况下，也适用于辅注册簿上的申请和注册，但辅注册簿上的申请和注册不能适用本法第1051 条（b）款、第 1052 条（e）款、第 1052 条（f）款、第 1057 条（b）款、第 1057（c）款、第 1062 条（a）款、第 1063 条至第 1068 条、第 1072条、第 1115 条和第 1124 条的规定，也不能因此获益。

1095. 不排除在主注册簿上注册

辅注册簿上的商标注册，或依据 1920 年 3 月 19 日法案的注册，不能排除该注册人在依本法建立的主注册簿上的注册。商标在辅注册簿上的注册不构成对其不具备显著性的认可。

1096. 在辅注册簿上的注册不能用以阻止进口

辅注册簿上的商标注册，或依据 1920 年 3 月 19 日法案的注册，不得向财政部备案或用以阻止进口。

III. 一般条款

1111. 注册标注；在商标上展示；在侵权诉讼中追索权益和赔偿

尽管有本法第 1072 条的规定，在专利商标局注册商标的注册人可在其商标上标注"已在美国专利商标局注册"的文字或 R 加一个圈，即®，以显示其商标已获注册；注册人如未作如上注册标注，在其依本法提起的侵权诉讼中，将不能依据本法的规定获得权益或损害赔偿，除非被告已事实上知道了该注册。

1112. 商品和服务的分类；多类注册

专利商标局局长可建立商品和服务的分类，以便于专利商标局的管理，但不得限制或扩大申请人或注册人的权利。申请人可以就其在商业中正在使用或有真诚的意图使用的或与之相关的任何或所有商品或服务，申请商标注册。倘若专利商标局局长以条例的形式准许在多个类别的商品或服务提交商标注册申请，申请人所应缴纳的费用相当于每一类单独申请的费用总和，而且对于该商标，专利商标局局长可仅颁发一个注册证。

1113. 费用

（a）申请；服务；材料

专利商标局局长应确定商标或其他标记注册申请和处理的费用，以及专利商标局提供与商标和其他标志相关的所有服务和材料的费用。根据劳动部长确定的消费品物价指数，专利商标局局长可每年对依据本款制定的费用进行调整，以总体上反映过去 12 个月期间的物价波动。少于 1% 的变化可以忽略。依据本条制定的费用应在联邦公报和专利商标局官方公告中发布至少 30 天后才能生效。

（b）放弃；印第安产品

应政府部门机构或其官员的临时请求，专利商标局局长可放弃对商标或其他标记相关服务或材料的收费。对于印第安工艺美术委员会用于表示印第安产品或个别印第安部落和团体产品的纯正和品质的政府商标，免收注册的任何费用。

1114. 救济；侵权；印刷商和出版商非故意侵权

（1）未经注册人同意，任何人

（a）将一注册商标的复制品、伪造品、仿冒品或欺骗性的仿制品在商业中运用于商品或服务的销售、许诺销售、分销或推广中，可能引起混淆，误

认或欺骗；或

（b）复制、伪造、仿冒或欺骗性仿制一注册商标，并将复制、伪造、仿冒或欺骗性仿制的商标在商业中应用于商品或服务的销售、许诺销售、分销或推广所使用或相关的标签、标识、印刷品、包装、包装纸、容器或广告上，可能引起混淆，误认或者欺骗的，应当在注册人为获得以下规定的救济而提起的民事起诉中承担责任。根据本款规定，除非这种行为是在明知会引起混淆、误认或欺骗的情况下采取的，否则注册人无权追索收益或损害赔偿。

本款所用"任何人"一词包括美利坚合众国及其所有机构和部门、所有以美国的名义并获得美国授权及同意的个人、企业和其他人，任何州、州的部门、任何履行其职责的州和州的部门的官员或职员。美利坚合众国及其所有机构和部门、所有以美国的名义并获得美国授权及同意的个人、企业、公司和其他人，任何州、州的部门、任何履行其职责的州和州的部门的官员或职员应和任何非政府实体一样，在同样的方式和程度上遵守本法的规定。

（2）尽管有本法的任何其他规定，依照本法给予被侵权人或依本法第1125条（a）款或（d）款提起诉讼的起诉人的救济应限制如下：

（A）如果侵权者或违法者仅是替他人印刷商标或违法品，并确认其为非故意侵权者或违法者，被侵权人或依照本法第1125条（a）款提起诉讼的起诉人，仅有权禁止这类侵权者或违法者今后的印刷。

（B）如果被起诉的侵权或违法行为包含在报纸、杂志、其他类似期刊或美国法典第8编第2510条（12）款规定的电子通讯的付费广告内容中或是其一部分，则被侵权人或依照本法第1125条（a）款提起诉讼的起诉人针对这类报纸、杂志、其他类似期刊或电子通讯的出版者或发行者的救济，应仅限于禁止其在今后发行的报纸、杂志、其他类似期刊或在传送的电子通讯中展示这些广告内容。本款的限制只适用于非故意侵权者和违法者。

（C）如果制止在某期期刊或电子通讯中的侵权或违法内容的散布会延误该期刊按时投递或电子通讯的按时传送，并且这种延误是由于该期刊出版发行的方法或电子通讯传送的方法是按照良好商业的惯常做法进行的，而并非由于采取了回避本条的任何方法或措施，也并非阻止或延迟发布有关这类侵权内容或违法内容的强制令或制止令，则被侵权人或依照本法第1125条（a）

款提起诉讼的起诉人将不能得到强制性救济。

（D）（ⅰ）（Ⅰ）实施第（ⅱ）款规定的影响一个域名行为的域名注册员、域名注册处或其他域名注册管理机构，不应为该行为向任何人承担金钱救济，或强制性救济（除第（Ⅱ）款的规定之外），不论域名是否最终被认定为侵犯或淡化了某一商标。

（Ⅱ）第（Ⅰ）款所述之域名注册员、域名注册处或其他域名注册管理机构，应承担强制性救济，如果该域名注册员、域名注册处或其他域名注册管理机构：

（aa）未能及时地向受理域名处分权诉讼的法院提交足以确立法院对域名注册和使用的控制和管理的文件；

（bb）在诉讼审查过程中转让、中止或以其他方式修改了域名，依据法院命令的情况除外；

（cc）故意不遵守该法院的命令。

（ⅱ）本条（ⅰ）（Ⅰ）款所述之行为是指：

（Ⅰ）遵守本法第1125（d）条规定的法院命令而采取的；或

（Ⅱ）域名注册员、域名注册处或其他域名注册管理机构为禁止注册与他人商标相同、混淆性相似或淡化他人商标的域名而执行的合理政策中。

针对一域名的驳回注册、取消注册、转让、临时禁用或永久撤销。

（ⅲ）若无显示表明域名注册员、域名注册处或其他域名注册管理机构具有从域名的注册或维持中牟利之恶意，域名注册员、域名注册处或其他域名注册管理机构不应为域名的注册或维持造成的本条规定的损失承担赔偿责任。

（ⅳ）如果域名注册员、域名注册处或其他域名注册管理机构采取第（ⅱ）款所述之行为，是以为域名与某一商标相同或混淆性相似，或淡化了某商标，或根据他人虚报的材料认为域名与某一商标相同或混淆性相似，或淡化了某商标，则使其产生错误想法和虚报材料的人应对损失承担赔偿责任，包括域名注册人因此行为而产生的诉讼费和律师费。法院也可给予域名注册人强制性救济，包括重新激活域名或将域名转让给域名注册人。

（ⅴ）依据第（ⅱ）（Ⅱ）款所述之政策，域名被中止、禁用或转让之后，域名注册人可在向商标所有人发出通知之后，提起民事诉讼，以确认该注册人根据本章对域名的注册及使用并不违法。法院也可给予域名注册人强制性救济，包括重新激活域名或将域名转让给域名注册人。

（E）本段所使用的：

（i）"违法者"一词是指违反本法第 1125 条（a）款的人；以及

（ii）"违法内容"一词是指本法第 1125 条（a）款规定的违法涉及的内容。

1115. 在主注册簿上的注册作为商标专用权的证据；辩护

（a）证据价值；辩护

由诉讼一方当事人拥有的依据 1881 年 3 月 3 日的法案颁发的注册，或依据 1905 年 2 月 20 日的法案颁发的注册，或在依据本法建立的主注册簿上的商标注册，可以作为证据使用，并且是该注册商标和商标注册有效性的表面成立之证据，是注册人对该商标所有权有效性的表面成立之证据，也是该注册人在商业中按注册的条件和限制在指定的商品或服务上或其相关方面使用该注册商标专用权有效性的表面成立之证据，但不得阻碍他人证实法律上或衡平法上的辩护理由或缺陷的存在，包括（b）款所列明的，如果该商标未注册，就会被认定的项目。

（b）不容置疑性；辩护

根据本法第 1065 条的规定，注册商标的使用权已不容置疑的情况下，该注册应成为注册商标和商标注册有效性的确凿证据，注册人对该商标的所有权有效性的确凿证据，以及其在商业中使用注册商标的专用权有效性的确凿证据。依照注册或宣誓书或续展申请中规定的条件与限制，这种确凿证据应与依据本法第 1065 条规定提交的宣誓书中列明的商品和服务上使用商标的专用权有关，或者如果在续展中指定的商品或服务数目较少，与依据本法第 1059 条规定提交的续展申请书中列明的商品和服务上或其相关方面使用商标的专用权有关。这种注册商标使用权的确凿证据应服从于本法第 1114 条规定的侵权证据，并应服从于下列辩护或缺陷：

（1）该商标的注册或不容置疑的使用权是以欺骗方式取得的；或

（2）该商标已被注册人放弃；或

（3）该注册商标正由注册人或注册人的共同利益人使用，或经注册人或

注册人的共同利益人同意而使用，导致了对使用该商标或与其相关的商品或服务的来源的误认；或

（4）被指控为侵权的名称、术语或图形的使用，并非是作为商标的使用，而是对当事人自己商业的个人名称的使用，或者对当事人共同利益人的个人名称的使用，或者对具有描述性且公正善意地描述了当事人的商品或服务或其来源的术语或图形的使用；或

（5）由一方当事人使用的被指控为侵权的商标是在不知道注册人在先使用的情况下采用的，并且在下列日期之前，一直被当事人或其共同利益人连续使用：

（A）根据本法第 1057 条（c）款的规定确立商标推定使用的日期；

（B）如果注册申请是在 1988 年商标法修正案生效日期之前提交的，则为依据本章的商标注册日；或者

（C）按照本法第 1062 条（c）款规定的注册商标公告日

但条件是这种辩护或缺陷仅适用于在先连续使用得到证实的区域；或

（6）其使用被指控为侵权的商标是在注册人的注册商标依本法注册之前注册和使用的或依本法第 1062 条（c）款公告之前注册和使用的，而且并未放弃，但条件是这种辩护或缺陷仅适用于注册人的商标在注册或公告之前已使用的区域；或

（7）商标的使用已经或正在违反美国的反托拉斯法；或

（8）商标具有功能性；或

（9）衡平法的原则，包括延误、不得反悔和默认，可以适用。

1116. 强制性救济

（a）管辖；送达

对依本法产生的民事诉讼有管辖权的法院应有权按照衡平法原则和法院认为合理的条件颁布强制令，以防止对专利商标局注册商标的注册人权利的侵犯或本法第 1125 条（a）、（c）或（d）款规定的侵权。这种强制令可以包括一项对被告的指示，告知被告在强制令送达后 30 天内，或者法院指定的延长期内，向法院提交并向原告送达一份经宣誓的书面报告详细说明被告履行

强制令的方法和形式。由美国地区法院经审理颁发的强制令，在通知被告后，送达美国境内可以找到的该强制令所针对的其他当事人，并产生效力，且由颁发强制令的法院，或由其他对被告具有管辖权的美国地区法院，通过惩罚藐视程序或其他程序执行。

（b）法院文件证明文本的转发

根据本法的规定，上述法院应对强制令的执行具有管辖权，正如同执行该强制令的法院颁布的强制令一样。法院的工作人员或颁发强制令的法官应按受理强制令执行申请法院的要求，立即将其本院存档的颁发强制令的全部文件的证明文本转交给上述法院。

（c）通知专利商标局局长

法院的工作人员有责任在依据本法注册商标的行动、诉讼或程序提起后一个月内书面通知专利商标局局长，根据其所知按顺序列明诉讼当事人的姓名和地址，该行动、诉讼或程序所涉及注册的指定号码。如果随后通过修改、答辩或请求，有其他注册包括到了该行动、诉讼或程序中，法院的工作人员应将上述情况通知专利商标局局长，并且于作出判决或提出上诉后一个月内，法院工作人员应将上述情况通知专利商标局局长，专利商标局局长有责任在接到所述通知后立即将同样内容批注在所述注册的文件封套上，并将该内容作为该文件封套的一部分。

（d）由使用仿冒商标引起的民事诉讼

（1）（A）在基于本法第1114条（1）（a）款或美国法典第36篇第220506条产生的民事诉讼中，对于在销售、许诺销售、商品和服务的分销中的使用仿冒商标的侵权，法院可基于单方当事人的申请，依照本款规定颁发本条（a）款规定的命令，扣押侵权涉及的商品和仿冒商标，制造此类商标的工具，以及与侵权有关的制造者、销售或物品收据的文件记录。

（B）本款所称的"仿冒商标"是指：

（i）对在美国专利商标局的主注册簿上注册，使用在销售、许诺销售或分销的商品或服务上，并正在使用的商标的伪造品，无论救济所针对的人是否知道这一商标已经注册；或者

（ii）与根据美国法典第36篇第220506条的规定可得到本法救济的标示

完全相同或实质上不能区分的欺骗性标示；

但是，该名词不包括商标或标示的使用权人授权的生产商或制造商在其生产制造的商品或服务上或其相关方面使用的商标或标示。

（2）依照本款的规定，法院不应受理这种申请，除非申请人已在合理的情况下将申请的通知告知了发布该命令的司法管辖区的美国检察官。检察官可参与因这一申请而引起的程序，如果这些程序可能影响一项对美国犯罪的证据。如果法院认定在潜在诉讼中的公众利益有此需要，可以驳回该申请。

（3）本款规定的命令申请应当：

（A）提交陈述事实的宣誓书和经证实的申诉，充分支持颁布命令所需要事实调查结果和法律结论；以及

（B）包含须在命令中列明的本款第（5）段要求的其他信息。

（4）法院不应批准这种申请，除非：

（A）根据本款规定获得命令的人提交了由法院决定的保证金，足够支付任何人因本款规定的错误扣押或错误的扣押企图遭受的损失；以及

（B）法院发现具体的事实清楚地显示：

（i）除单方面扣押命令外的其他命令不足以达到本法第1114条的目的；

（ii）申请人没有公布其请求的扣押；

（iii）申请人有可能成功的证明扣押命令所针对的人在销售、许诺销售或分销的商品或服务上使用了仿冒商标；

（iv）如果不颁发扣押令，将会立刻发生不可挽回的损害；

（v）将要被扣押的物品可在申请书指明的地点找到；

（vi）驳回申请对申请人的损害超过批准申请给被颁发扣押令的人合法利益的损害；以及

（vii）如果申请人通知被颁发扣押令的人，被颁发扣押令的人或与之协同行动的人会销毁、转移、隐藏这些物品或以其他办法使法院难以找到这些物品。

（5）本款规定的命令应列明：

（A）颁发命令所需要的事实调查结果和法律结论；

（B）对将被扣押物品的详细描述和对将被扣押物品每一所在地点的描述；

（C）扣押实施的期限，自命令颁发之日起不超过七天；

（D）依照本款需提交的保证金金额；

（E）依照本款第（10）项规定的审理日期。

（6）法院应采取适当措施，保护本款规定的命令所针对的人，不受原告或由原告指使的人对此项命令和依据此项命令的扣押的宣传影响。

（7）依照本款扣押的材料应由法院保管。法院应就被扣押的记录颁布适当的保护令以防止申请人发现。该保护令应规定适当的程序以保证所述记录中所包含机密信息不会不适当的向申请人公开。

（8）本款规定的命令，连同证明文件，应予密封，直至该命令针对的人有机会对该命令进行辩驳，但该命令针对的人在扣押后应当接触此项命令及证明文件的除外。

（9）法院应命令，本款规定命令的副本应由联邦法律执行官（如美国司法官，或美国海关、特工机关、联邦调查局或邮局的官员或代理人）送达，或由州或地方的法律执行官送达。这些法律执行官应于送达后依照命令执行扣押。法院应当在适当的时候颁发命令，保护被告在扣押过程中不会因商业秘密或其他机密信息的公开而遭受不当的损害，包括在适当的时候颁发命令，限制申请人（或申请人的代理人或职员）接触这些秘密或信息。

（10）（A）法院应按扣押命令中规定的日期开庭审理，除非各方当事人都放弃。开庭审理日期不得早于命令颁发之后 10 天，也不得晚于命令颁发之后 15 天，除非此项命令的申请人基于充分理由提出另一日期，或者除非此项命令针对的当事人同意改到另一日期审理。在开庭审理时，获得命令的当事人应有举证义务，证明用以支持该命令所必需的事实调查结果和法律结论的事实仍然有效。如果该当事人未能履行举证义务，该扣押命令应予解除或适当的修改。

（B）在本段所规定的审理中，为了防止审理目的受挫，法院可依照民事诉讼规则作出命令，变更提交证据的期限。

（11）由于本款规定的错误扣押而遭受损害的人有理由对该扣押命令的申请人起诉，并有权获得适当的救济，包括收益损失、材料成本、商誉损失以及在恶意请求扣押时的惩罚性损害赔偿，并且，除非法院发现情有可原的情况，还可取得合理的律师费。法院可酌情决定，按照美国法典第 26 篇第 6621 条（a）（2）款确定的年利率，给予本段规定的救济补偿预判决利息，从索赔人列明本段规定的请求之诉状送达之日起至给予补偿之日止，或者适用法院认为适当的较短时间。

1117. 对被侵犯权利的补偿

（a）收益、损害和诉讼费；律师费

对在专利商标局注册的商标的注册人权利的侵犯，或者依照本法第 1125 条（a）款或（d）款规定的侵权，或者依照本法第 1125 条（c）款规定的故意侵权，在依照本法提出的民事诉讼中确认后，原告有权，根据本法第 1111 条和第 1114 条的规定和衡平法原则，获得以下补偿：

（1）被告的收益，

（2）原告遭受的损害，

（3）诉讼的成本。法院应对这些收益和损害予以评估或在其指示下进行评估。在评估收益时，原告只需证实被告的销售额；被告必须证实其所主张的成本或扣除额的所有因素。在评估损害时，法院可根据案情，作出高于实际损害额的判决，但不超过该数额的三倍。如果法院认为基于收益的补偿数额不足或过多，法院可根据案情酌情作出法院认为公正数额的判决。在上述任何情况下的数额均属补偿，并非处罚。在特殊的案件中，法院可判给胜诉方合理的律师费。

（b）使用仿冒商标的三倍损害赔偿

除非法院认为情有可原，在依照本条（a）款对损害进行评估时，如遇任何违反本法第 1114 条（1）（a）款或美国法典第 36 篇第 220506 条规定，明知一商标或标示为仿冒商标（本法第 1116 条（d）款所定义的）而故意在销售、许诺销售或分销的商品或服务上使用这种商标或标示的情况，法院应作出该收益或损害金额（选其中数额较大者）三倍的裁决，并包括合理的律师费。在这种情况下，法院可酌情决定，按照美国法典第 26 篇第 6621 条（a）（2）款确定的年利率，判给该金额预判决利息，从索赔人列明获得该判决请求之诉状送达之日起至此项判决作出之日止，或者适用法院认为适当的较短时间。

（c）使用仿冒商标的法定损害赔偿

在销售、许诺销售或分销的商品或服务上使用仿冒商标（本法第 1116 条
（d）款所定义的）案件中，在初审法院作出最终判决之前的任何时候，原告
可以放弃（a）款规定的实际损害和收益的补偿，而选择判给对这类在销售、
许诺销售或分销的商品或服务上使用仿冒商标的法定损害赔偿，其金额为：

（1）法院认为公正的数额，对用于每类销售、许诺销售或分销的商品或
服务上的每一仿冒商标，不少于 500 美元或不超过 10 万美元；或

（2）如果法院认为对仿冒商标的使用系故意，法院认为公正的数额，对
用于每类销售、许诺销售或分销的商品或服务上的每一仿冒商标，不超过 100
万美元。

（d）本法第 1125 条（d）(1) 款规定侵权的法定损害赔偿

在本法第 1125 条（d）(1) 款规定侵权案件中，在初审法院作出最终判决
之前的任何时候，原告可以放弃实际损害和收益的补偿，而选择判给法院认
为公正数额的法定损害赔偿，每个域名不少于 1000 美元或不超过 10 万美元。

1118. 销毁侵权物品

在依照本法产生的对在专利商标局注册的商标的注册人权利的侵犯，或
者依照本法第 1125 条（a）款规定的侵权，或者依照本法第 1125 条（c）款
规定的故意侵权进行确认的诉讼中，法院可以颁布命令，将被告所持有的带
有该注册商标的所有标签、标识、印刷品、包装、包装纸、容器或广告上交
并销毁，或者在依照本法第 1125 条（a）款规定的侵权或者依照本法第 1125
条（c）款规定的故意侵权案件中，将侵权涉及的文字、术语、名称、符号、
图形或其组合、标示、描述或表述，或者其复制品、伪造品、仿冒品或欺骗
性的仿制品，以及所有印版、铸模、字模和其他复制工具，全部上交并销毁。
依照本条规定寻求获得对本法第 1116 条（d）款规定的扣押物品进行销毁命
令的当事人，应提前 10 天通知发布该命令的司法管辖区的美国检察官（除非
有充分理由显示预先通知的时间可较短一些），并且如果该项销毁可能影响到
一项对美国犯罪的证据，该美国检察官可以请求对该项销毁进行审理或者参
加其他关于该项销毁进行的审理。

1119. 法院对注册的权力

在涉及注册商标的诉讼中，法院可以确定注册的权利，命令撤销整个或部分商标的注册，恢复已撤销的注册，以及对注册簿上诉讼当事人的注册进行其他修改。法院应将经证明的裁定或命令送达专利商标局局长；专利商标局局长应在专利商标局的档案上作相应的记录；裁定和命令受法院控制。

1120. 虚假或欺骗性注册的民事责任

任何以口头或书面的虚假或欺骗性声明或表述，或其他虚假手段，在专利商标局取得商标注册的人，在受害人提出的民事诉讼中，对其因此遭受的损害承担责任。

1121. 联邦法院的管辖权；州和地方要求改变注册商标或以不同的 形式展示；禁止

（a）对于所有依本法提起的诉讼，无论争议数额的大小或各方当事人的公民权利有无差异，美国联邦地区法院和属地法院享有原始管辖权，美国联邦上诉法院（除美国联邦巡回上诉法院外）享有上诉管辖权。

（b）美国的州或其他管辖区，或政治分区或其机构，不得要求改变注册商标，或要求将可与注册商标联合或结合的附加商标、服务商标、商号名称或公司名称，以不同于在美国专利商标局颁发的注册证中所展示的该注册商标所预期的附加商标、服务商标、商号名称或公司名称的显示方式在商标中显示出来。

1122. 美国，各州，及其机关和官员的责任

（a）美国放弃国家豁免权

美国及其所有部门和机构，以及所有代表美国和获得美国授权和同意的个人、企业和其他人，在被任何人，包括任何政府或非政府实体，向联邦法院或州法院提出本法规定的侵权诉讼中，不享有豁免权。

（b）州放弃豁免权

任何州、州的部门或任何履行其职务的州或州的部门的官员或职员，根据美国宪法第11次修正案或其他任何国家豁免权原则，在被任何人，包括任何政府或非政府实体，向联邦法院提出本法规定的侵权诉讼中，不享有豁免权。

（c）救济

在本条（a）款或（b）款所述的侵权诉讼中，对于侵权所提供的救济（包括法律救济和衡平法救济），在程度上，与针对除美国或其任何部门和机构，或任何代表美国和获得美国授权和同意的个人、企业和其他人，或任何州、州的机关或任何履行其职务的州或州的机关的官员或雇员以外任何人的侵权诉讼中所提供的救济相同。此类救济包括本法第1116条规定的强制性救济，本法第1117条规定的实际损害、收益、诉讼费和律师费，本法第1118条规定的销毁侵权物品，本法第1114条、第1119条、第1120条、第1124条和第1125条规定的救济和本法规定的其他救济。

1123. 专利商标局进行程序处理的规章条例

专利商标局局长应制定不与法律相抵触的规章条例，用于专利商标局依照本法进行程序处理。

1124. 禁止进口带有侵权商标或名称的商品

除美国法典第19篇第1526条（d）款的规定外，进口商品，如果复制或模仿了国内制造者、生产商或商人的名称，或者按照条约、公约或法律享有与美国公民类似特权的外国生产商或商人的名称，或复制或模仿了根据本法规定注册的商标，或带有诱导公众相信该物品系美国制造，或非该物品实际产地的其他国家或地区制造的名称或商标，将被美国海关禁止入境；并且，为了协助海关官员执行此强制令，国内生产商和商人，以及根据美国和其他国家之间的条约、公约、声明或协议的规定有权在商标和商业名称方面享有与美国公民同样法律特权的外国生产商和商人，可以请求将其名称、住址和其商品生产地区的名称以及根据本法规定颁发的商标注册证副本，按照财政部长制定的规章在财政部基于此目的建立的登记簿上登记，并可向财政部提

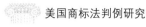

供其名称、其商品生产地区的名称，或其注册商标的复制品，财政部长随即会将这些材料的一份或多份复印件转交给海关的每个收税员或其他主管官员。

1125. 禁止虚假的原产地标示、虚假的描述和淡化

（a）民事诉讼

（1）任何人在商业中，在商品或服务上或与之相关方面，或在商品的容器上，使用任何文字、术语、名称、符号或图形，或其组合，或任何虚假的原产地标记，对事实的虚假或误导性描述，或对事实的虚假或误导性表述，

（A）可能引起对该人与他人的附属、联合或结合关系的混淆、误认或欺骗，或者对其商品或服务或商业活动来源于他人、由他人赞助或认可的混淆、误认或欺骗，或者

（B）在商业广告或推广中，错误标示了他或她或他人的商品或服务或商业活动的性质、特征、质量或原产地，

在任何人认为这种行为已经或可能使其蒙受损害而提起的民事诉讼中，该人应承担责任。

（2）本款所用"任何人"一词包括任何州、州的机关或任何履行其职务的州或州的机关的雇员。任何州、州的机关、官员或雇员，应和任何非政府实体一样，以同样的方式和在同样的程度上受本法约束。

（3）依据本法的规定，对没有在主注册簿上注册的商业外观侵权的民事诉讼中，主张商业外观保护的人有责任证明需要被保护的内容不具有功能。

（b）进口

任何带有违反本条规定商标或标签的商品不得进口到美国或准许从美国海关入境。依照本条被海关拒绝入境商品的所有人、进口人或收货人，可依照海关税收法通过抗议或上诉获得追索权，或者依照本法在涉及商品被拒绝入境或被扣押的情况下得到救济。

（c）知名商标淡化的救济

（1）如果他人在商业中对商标或商号的商业性使用是在该商标取得知名之后，而且导致了该知名商标显著性的淡化，知名商标的所有人有权依照衡平法的原则和法院认为合理的条件，获得对该使用的强制令，以及本款规定

的其他救济。在判断一个商标是否显著和知名时，法院可以考虑但不限于下列因素：

（A）该商标固有的和经使用取得的显著性程度；

（B）该商标在相关商品或服务上持续使用的时间和程度；

（C）该商标广告宣传的持续时间和程度；

（D）该商标被使用的商业区域的地理范围；

（E）使用该商标的商品或服务的商业渠道；

（F）该商标在商标所有人和强制令所针对的人的商业区域和商业渠道内的知名度；

（G）第三方对相同或相似商标使用的性质和程度；以及

（H）该商标是否已依据1881年3月3日的法案，或1905年2月20日的法案注册，或已在主注册簿上注册。

（2）在依据本款提出的诉讼中，知名商标的所有人仅有权获得本法第1116条规定的强制性救济，除非强制令所针对的人故意利用其声誉进行商业活动或故意导致该知名商标被谈化。如果这种故意被证实，则知名商标所有人还有权依照法院的自由裁量权和衡平法原则享有本法第1117条（a）款和第1118条所列明的救济。

（3）任何人对依据1881年3月3日法案或1905年2月20日法案的有效注册，或主注册簿上的有效注册的所有权，可完全阻止他人依据普通法或一个州的法规针对该所有权人提出的有关该商标的诉讼，即防止商标、标签或广告形式的显著性被淡化的诉讼。

（4）下列情况不可依照本条规定起诉：

（A）为识别知名商标所有人的竞争商品或服务，由他人在比较商业广告或推广中对该知名商标的公平使用。

（B）对商标的非商业性使用。

（C）所有形式的新闻报道和新闻评论。

（d）域名抢注的防范

（1）（A）不考虑当事人的商品或服务，应当在由商标（包括根据本条作为商标保护的人名）所有人提起的民事诉讼中承担责任的人，应当

（i）有从该商标（包括根据本条作为商标保护的人名）获利的恶意；并且

（ii）注册、买卖或使用了一个域名

（I）在该域名注册时该商标具有显著性的情况下，与该商标完全相同或混淆性相似；

（II）在该域名注册时该知名商标已经知名的情况下，与该商标完全相同或混淆性相似或淡化了该商标；或

（III）是基于美国法典第18编第706条，或第36编第220506条的理由而受保护的商标、文字或名称。

（B）（i）在判断某人是否具有（A）段所述之"恶意"时，法院可考虑但不限于下列因素：

（I）该域名中所包含的该人的商标或其他知识产权，如果存在这种情况；

（II）该域名中所包含的该人的法律名称或其他通常用于识别该人的名称的程度；

（III）与商品或服务的善意提供相关的，该人对于该域名在先使用，如果存在这种情况；

（IV）在该域名下可访问的网站中，该人对于商标善意的非商业性使用或公平使用；

（V）为了牟取商业收益，或通过对网站来源、主办者、附属机构或批准关系制造混淆的可能，进而污蔑或贬低商标，该人故意将消费者由商标所有人在线网址转移至该域名下可访问的网站，可能损害商标所代表的商誉；

（VI）该人为营利目的提出向商标所有人或任何第三方转让、销售或以其他方式出让该域名，却没有在商品或服务的善意提供中使用该域名或没有使用该域名的意图，或该人先前的行为显示了这种行为模式；

（VII）该人在申请域名注册时提供了关键的误导性虚假联系信息，该人故意不保持正确的联系信息，或该人先前的行为显示了这种行为模式；

（VIII）不考虑当事人的商品或服务，该人注册或获得了大量域名，并且知道这些域名与他人所有的、在域名注册时具有显著性的商标完全相同或混淆性近似，或对他人所有的、在域名注册时已知名的知名商标构成了淡化；

以及

（IX）该人的域名注册中所包含的商标在本条第（c）（1）款规定的含义内，是否显著或知名的程度。

（ii）如果法院确认该人相信并有合理的理由相信其对域名的使用是公平的使用或者其他合法的使用，在该案件中不应认定存在（A）段所描述的"恶意"。

（C）在根据本段提起的涉及域名注册、交易或使用的民事诉讼中，法院可命令没收或撤销该域名，或将该域名转让给商标的所有人。

（D）只有域名的注册人或该注册人授权的被许可人才应对（A）段规定的域名使用承担责任。

（E）本段所使用的"交易"一词，包括但不限于销售、购买、出借、质押、许可、货币交换和其他对价转让或对价交换的交易。

（2）（A）商标所有人可以在域名注册员，域名注册处或其他域名注册或转让机构所在地的司法管辖区，对域名提起对物民事诉讼，如果：

（i）该域名侵犯了在专利商标局注册的或依本条第（a）款或第（c）款受保护的商标所有人的权利，并且

（ii）法院查明该所有人——

（I）无法在依第（1）段提起的民事诉讼中对本应作为被告的人取得对人管辖；或者

（II）在经过以下审慎调查后仍无法找到依第（1）段提起的民事诉讼中本应作为被告的人：

（aa）按域名注册人向注册处提供的邮政地址和电子邮件地址，向注册人发出含有所指控的侵权行为和依本段规定进行后续程序意图的通知；并且

（bb）在起诉后，依据法院立即作出的指示，公布诉讼通知。

（B）第（A）（ii）款规定的行为应构成送达程序。

（C）在本段规定对物诉讼中，一域名所在地的司法管辖区应当是：

（i）域名注册员，域名注册处或其他域名注册或转让机构的所在地；或

（ii）足以确立对注册权的处分和域名的使用进行控制及管理的文件被提交保管的法院。

（D）（i） 本段规定的对物诉讼的救济措施应仅限于没收或撤销该域名，或将该域名转让给商标的所有人的法院命令。在收到商标所有人依本段规定向美国联邦地区法院提交的已盖章起诉书的书面通知后，域名注册员，域名注册处或其他域名管理机构应：

（I）迅速将足以确立对注册权的处分和域名的使用进行控制及管理的文件提交于法院保管；并且

（II）除非根据法院命令，在诉讼审理过程中不得转让、中止或以其他方式修改域名。

（ii） 除非有恶意或严重漠视（包括故意不遵守法院的命令）的情形，域名注册员，域名注册处或其他域名管理机构不应对依本段作出的强制性救济或金钱救济承担责任。

（3）根据第（1）段提起的民事诉讼与根据第（2）段提起的对物诉讼及上述任一种诉讼所提供的救济，应是对其他可适用的民事诉讼或救济的补充。

（4）依据第（2）段确立的对物管辖，应是对其他既有管辖的补充，无论对物或是对人。

1126. 国际公约

（a） 由国际局传送来商标的注册簿

专利商标局局长应保存一份由国际局传送来的全部商标的注册簿。该国际局是依据美国已经加入或可能加入的保护工业产权、商标、商号和商业名称以及反不正当竞争公约成立的。在缴纳公约规定的费用和本法规定的费用后，专利商标局局长可将传送来的商标在该注册簿上登记。注册簿上应显示商标或商号或商业名称的图样；注册人的名称、国籍和地址；该商标首次注册的注册号、注册日期和地点，包括该商标注册的申请日、核准日和有效期；原属国注册中该商标所申请的商品或服务清单，以及关于该商标的其他必要的数据。此注册簿应为依据 1920 年 3 月 19 日的法案第 1 条（a）款建立的注册簿的附录。

（b） 原属国为公约或条约成员国的公民可享受本条规定的权益。

如果原属国和美国均为有关商标、商号或商业名称，或反不正当竞争公约或条约的成员国，或原属国依法给予了美国公民对等权利，则在满足公约、条约或对等法律有关条款生效的必要条件下，除本法授予商标所有人的其他权利外，原属国的公民还享受本条规定的权益。

（c）在原属国的在先注册；原属国的定义

本条（b）款所述申请人的商标在其原属国注册之前，在美国不能核准注册，除非申请人声明已经在商业中使用了该商标。

为了达到本条的目的，申请人的原属国应是申请人设有真实有效的工商营业场所的国家，或者如果他没有工商营业场所，应是申请人有住所的国家，或者如果申请人在本条（b）款所述的国家无住所，则应是指其拥有国籍的国家。

（d）优先权

本条（b）款所述申请人依照本法第 1051 条、第 1053 条、第 1054 条或第 1091 条或本条（e）款提交商标注册申请以前，已在本条（b）款所述国家正式提交了同一商标的注册申请，则该商标注册申请应与其申请在该外国首次提交的同一天在美国提交同样的申请享有同样的效力，条件是：

（1）该商标在美国的申请是在该外国首次申请之日起六个月内提交的；

（2）该申请尽可能符合本法的要求，包括申请人有真诚的意图在商业中使用该商标的声明；

（3）第三方在该商标的外国首次申请提交日期前获得的权利决不应该受到依本款提交申请获得的注册的影响；

（4）依照本条获准注册的所有人无权依据本款的规定对其商标在美国注册之日前发生的行为起诉，除非其注册是基于在商业中的使用取得的。

按照类似的方式及相同的条件和要求，本条规定的权利可基于在同一外国提交的后续定期申请，而不是外国的首次申请，只要在该后续申请之前提交的外国申请已经撤回、放弃或另行处理，并尚未被公开供公众查阅，也未遗留任何未解决的权利，并且没有也不会作为主张优先权的根据。

（e）在主注册簿或辅注册簿上的注册；外国注册证副本

已由外国申请人在其原属国正式注册的商标，如果符合条件，可在主注册簿上注册，否则应按本法规定在辅注册簿上注册。该申请人应在专利商标局局长规定的期限内，提交其原属国注册的真实副本、复印件、证明或经证明的复印件。申请书必须表明申请人有在商业中使用该商标的真诚意图，但不要求在注册前已经在商业中使用。

（f）国内注册独立于外国注册

本条（b）款所述申请人依本条（c）、（d）和（e）款的商标注册应独立于原属国的注册，并且该注册在美国的期限、效力或转让应按本法的规定进行。

（g）外国公民的商号或商业名称不经注册即受保护

本条（b）款所述之人的商号或商业名称，无论它们是否构成商标的一部分，无须申请或注册即受保护。

（h）保护外国公民不受到不公平的竞争

本条（b）款指定的享受本法权益并受本法规定约束的人，应有权获得有效保护从而不受到不公平的竞争，并且本法为商标侵权提供的救济在合适的范围内可适用于抑制不正当竞争行为。

（i）美国公民和居民有权享受本条的权益。

美国公民或居民应享有依据本条给予本条（b）款所述之人同样的权益。

1127. 解释和定义；本章目的

除非内容显示明显相反，对本法的解释中：

美国，包括和包含在其管辖和控制下的所有领土。

"商业"一词是指可由国会依法调控的所有商业。

"主注册簿"一词是指依据本法第1051～1072条规定建立的注册簿；"辅注册簿"一词是指依据本法1091～1096条规定建立的注册簿。

"人"一词和其他指代申请人或依本法规定享有权益或特权或负有责任的人的任何词语或术语，包括法人和自然人。"法人"一词包括可以在法院起诉和被诉的企业、协会、社团或其他组织。

"人"一词还包括美国或其任何部门和机构，或任何代表美国和获得美国授权和同意的个人及企业。美国或其任何部门和机构，或任何代表美国和获得美国授权和同意的个人、企业，应与任何非政府实体一样，在同样的方式和程度上遵守本法的规定。

"人"一词还包括任何州、州的部门、任何履行其职责的州和州的部门的官员或职员。任何州、州的部门、官员或职员，应与任何非政府实体一样，在同样的方式上和程度上遵守本法的规定。

"申请人"和"注册人"包括该申请人和注册人的法律代表、被继承人、继承人和受让人。

"专利商标局局长"一词是指商务部负责知识产权事务的副部长和美国专利商标局的局长。

"相关公司"一词是指对一个商标的使用，在该商标的使用或与之相关的商品或服务的性质和质量上，受控于商标所有人的人。

"商号"和"商业名称"是指一个人用以识别其企业或职业的任何名称。

"商品商标"一词包括任何文字、名称、符号或图形，或其组合，

（1）由一个人使用，或

（2）一个人有真诚意图在商业中使用，并申请在依本法建立的主注册簿上注册，

用以在他人生产或销售的商品中，识别和区分其商品，包括一个独特的产品，以及用来表明商品来源，即使该来源并不知名。

"服务商标"一词是指任何文字、名称、符号或图形，或其组合，

（1）由一个人使用，或

（2）一个人有真诚意图在商业中使用，并申请在依本法建立的主注册簿上注册，

用以在他人提供的服务中，识别和区分其服务，包括一个独特的服务，以及用来表明服务来源，即使该来源并不知名。无线电广播或电视节目的标题、人物名和其他显著特征，可作为服务商标进行注册，尽管它们，或这些节目，可能宣传了赞助人的商品。

"证明商标"一词是指任何文字、名称、符号或图形，或其组合，

（1）由除其所有人外的他人使用，或

（2）其所有人有真诚的意图允许除该所有人外的其他人在商业中使用，并申请在依本法建立的主注册簿上注册，

用以证明该他人商品或服务的地区或其他来源、材料、生产方式、质量、精度或其他特征，或证明该商品或服务上的工作或劳动是由一个协会或其他组织的会员提供的。

"集体商标"一词是指一个商品商标或服务商标

（1）由一个合作社、协会或其他集体组织或团体的成员使用，或

（2）该合作社、协会或其他集体组织或团体有真诚的意图在商业中使用，并申请在依本法建立的主注册簿上注册，

并且包括表明一个社团、协会或其他团体会员资格的商标。

"商标"一词包括任何商品商标、服务商标、集体商标或证明商标。

"在商业中使用"一词是指在日常商业活动中对一个商标的真诚使用，而不仅仅是为保留一个商标的权利。依本法的目的：

（1）一个商标应被视为在商业中使用于商品，当

（A）商标以任何形式展示在商品上或其容器上，或与之相关的展示品上，或粘贴在商品上的标牌或标签上，或者，如果由于商品的性质不能这样展示，则展示在与商品或其销售相关的文件上，以及

（B）商品在商业中销售和运输时，以及

（2）一个商标应被视为在商业中使用于服务，当商标在服务的销售或广告中使用或展示时，而且服务是在商业中提供的，或者服务是在一个以上的州或在美国和外国提供的，并且服务提供者从事着与该服务相关的商业。

发生下列任一情况下，商标应被视为"放弃"：

（1）商标的使用停止时有不再重新使用的意图。不再重新使用的意图可根据情况推断出来。连续三年不使用应为放弃的表面成立之证据。一个商标的"使用"是指在日常商业活动中对该商标的真诚使用，而不仅仅是为保留一个商标的权利。

（2）由于商标所有人的任何行为，包括不作为和作为，导致商标成为其使用的商品或服务或与之相关的商品或服务的通用名称或者导致其失去其他作为商标的显著性。购买者动机不得作为判断本款所述放弃的检验标准。

"淡化"一词是指降低知名商标识别和区别商品或服务方面的能力，无论是否存在：

（1）知名商标所有人和其他当事人之间的竞争，或者

（2）混淆、误认或欺骗的可能性。

"欺骗性的仿制品"一词包括任何与注册商标非常相似，有可能引起混淆或误认或欺骗的商标。

"注册商标"一词是指依照本法或依照 1881 年 3 月 3 日的法案，或 1905 年 2 月 20 日的法案，或 1920 年 3 月 19 日的法案，在美国专利商标局注册的商标。"在专利商标局注册的商标"即指注册商标。

"1881 年 3 月 3 日的法案""1905 年 2 月 20 日的法案"或"1920 年 3 月 19 日的法案"是指历次修改的商标法。

"仿冒商标"即与注册商标相同或实质上不能区分的冒牌商标。

"域名"一词是指由域名注册员、域名处或其他域名注册管理机构注册或转让的作为互联网电子地址一部分的字母代号。

"互联网"一词具有美国法典第 47 篇第 230 条（f）(1) 款所定义的含义。

单数形式的词语也适用于复数的情况，反之亦然。

本法的目的是通过使在商业中对商标的欺骗性和误导性的使用可诉，而在国会的控制下调控商业；保护在商业中使用的注册商标不受州或地区立法的干预；保护从事商业的人不受不正当的竞争；防止因使用注册商标的复制品、伪造品、仿冒品或欺骗性的仿制品而造成商业中的欺诈和欺骗；通过美国和外国签订的关于商标、商号和不公平竞争的条约和公约的规定提供权利和救济。

1128. 国家知识产权执法协调委员会

（a）设立

现设立国家知识产权执法协调委员会（本条简称为"委员会"）。该委员会由下列成员组成：

（1）商务部负责知识产权的副部长和美国专利商标局的局长，他将担任委员会的联合主席。

（2）负责刑事局的助理总检察长，他将担任委员会的联合主席。

（3）负责经济及农业事务的副国务卿。

（4）美国贸易副代表（大使）。

（5）海关总监。

（6）商务部负责国际贸易的副部长。

（b）职责

依据（a）款设立的委员会应在联邦和国外机构之间协调国内和国际知识产权法律的执行。

（c）所需的商议

有关版权及相邻权利和问题的法律执行问题，委员会应与版权局局长商议。

（d）不可减损。

本条的规定不得减损美国法典第 19 编第 2171 条规定的国务卿的职责和美国贸易代表的职责，也不得减损版权局局长的职责和作用，或以其他的方式改变与版权问题相关的现存权力机关。

（e）报告

委员会应每年向总统、参议院和众议院的拨款委员会和司法委员会报告其协调活动。

（f）资金

尽管有美国法典第 31 编第 1346 条的规定和本法第 610 条的规定，依照本法或其他法案在 2000 财政年度及此后提供的资金，应当包括国家知识产权执法协调委员的部门间资金。

1129. 域名抢注中对个人的保护

（1）一般规定

（A）民事责任

任何人注册的域名，如果包含另一个在世者的姓名，或包含一个与该在世者姓名实质性和混淆性相似的姓名，而未经该在世者同意，并且该注册人有通过向该在世者或任何第三方出售域名换取经济收益而从该姓名中获取利益的明确意图，则该注册人应在由该在世者提起的民事诉讼中承担责任。

（B）例外规定

若某人以善意注册的域名包含有另一个在世者的姓名，或包含一个与该在世者姓名实质性和混淆性相似的姓名，但该姓名在根据美国法典第 17 编受到著作权保护的作品中使用、附属于该作品或与其有关联，包括美国法典第17编第101条所定义的雇佣作品，并且如果该域名注册人是作品的版权所有人或被许可人，在合法利用作品的过程中试图出售该域名的人，并且该注册没有被注册人与拥有该姓名的人之间的合同所禁止，则根据本段的规定该注册人不应承担责任。本段规定的例外仅适用于根据第（1）段提起的民事诉讼，并且不能以任何方式限制由1946年商标法案（美国法典第15篇第1051条及随后的条款）或其他联邦或州法律提供的保护。

（2）救济

在根据第（1）段提起的民事诉讼中，法院可提供强制性救济，包括没收或撤销域名或将域名转让给原告。法院也可酌情决定，判决胜诉方获偿诉讼费和律师费。

（3）定义

在本款中，"域名"一词具有1946年商标法案第45条（美国法典第15篇第1127条）所定义的含义。

（4）生效日期

本款适用于1999年11月29日以后注册的域名。

IV 马德里议定书

1141. 定义

在本章中：

（1）基础申请

"基础申请"指已向缔约方主管局提交并构成该商标国际注册申请基础的商标注册申请。

（2）基础注册

"基础注册"指已由缔约方主管局核准并构成该商标国际注册申请基础的商标注册。

（3）缔约方

"缔约方"指作为马德里议定书成员的任何国家或政府间组织。

（4）登记日期

"登记日期"指国际注册核准之后的延伸保护请求在国际注册簿上登记的日期。

（5）有真诚的意图在商业中使用商标的声明

"有真诚的意图在商业中使用商标的声明"指寻求商标保护延伸至美国的国际注册商标的申请人或所有人签署的声明，内容包括：

（A）申请人或所有人有真诚的意图在商业中使用该商标；

（B）声明人确信其本人或其所代表的企业或协会有权在商业中使用该商标；

（C）就声明人所知，无其他个人、企业或协会有权在商业中在该个人、企业、公司或协会的商品上或与其商品相关方面使用与该商标相同或相似的商标，以致引起混淆、误认或欺骗。

（6）延伸保护

"延伸保护"指根据马德里议定书，基于国际注册所有人的请求，一项国际注册产生的保护延伸至美国。

（7）国际注册的所有人

"所有人"指以其名义在国际注册簿登记国际注册的自然人或法人。

（8）国际申请

"国际申请"指依马德里议定书，提交的国际注册申请。

（9）国际局

"国际局"指世界知识产权组织国际局。

（10）国际注册簿

"国际注册簿"指由国际局保存的关于国际注册数据的正式汇编，该数据系议定书或其实施细则要求登记或允许登记的。

（11）国际注册

"国际注册"指依马德里议定书进行的商标注册。

（12）国际注册日期

"国际注册日期"指国际局给国际注册指定的日期。

（13）马德里议定书

"马德里议定书"指于 1989 年 6 月 27 日在西班牙马德里通过的《商标国际注册马德里协定有关议定书》。

（14）驳回通知书

"驳回通知书"指美国专利商标局向国际局发出的声明一项延伸保护不能被核准的通知。

（15）缔约方的主管局

"缔约方的主管局"指：

（A）缔约方负责商标注册的主管局或政府组织；或

（B）被国际局认可的几个缔约方负责商标注册的共同局和政府组织。

（16）原属局

"原属局"指一项基础申请提交的或被核准的缔约方的主管局。

（17）异议期限

"异议期限"指允许向美国专利商标局提出异议的时间，包括本法第 1063 条所允许的延长期限。

1141a. 基于在美国的申请和注册的国际申请

（a）一般条款

一项在美国专利商标局待处理的基础申请的所有人，或一项已被美国专利商标局核准的基础注册的所有人，可以按照专利商标局局长规定的方式向美国专利商标局提交一项国际申请的书面申请，并缴纳专利商标局局长规定的费用。

（b）合格的所有人

根据（a）项的规定，一个合格的所有人

（1）应是美国的国民；

（2）应在美国有住所；或

（3）应在美国设有真实有效的工业或商业营业所。

1141b. 国际申请证明

（a）证明程序

在一项国际注册的申请提交和缴费之后，专利商标局局长应审查该国际申请，以证明该国际申请所包含的信息与基础申请或基础注册所包含的信息一致。

（b）传送

在国际申请经审查和证明之后，专利商标局局长应将该国际申请传送给国际局。

1141c. 基础申请和基础注册的限制、放弃、撤销和到期

有关基于本法第1141b条传送给国际局的国际申请，当其基础申请或基础注册在国际注册所列的部分或全部商品或服务上被限制、放弃、撤销和到期时，专利商标局局长应在以下期限内通知国际局

（1）国际注册日后的5年内；或

（2）国际注册日后的5年后，如果该基础申请或基础注册的限制、放弃或撤销是由一个5年期限内开始的诉讼产生的。

1141d. 在国际注册之后的延伸保护请求

以在美国专利商标局申请的基础申请或被美国专利商标局核准的基础注册为基础的国际注册的所有人，可以通过下列方式请求其国际注册的延伸保护——

（1）直接向国际局提出该请求；或

（2）按照专利商标局局长规定的方式请求美国专利商标局向国际局传送该请求，并缴纳专利商标局局长规定的传送费用。

1141e. 基于马德里议定书将国际注册的保护延伸至美国

（a）一般而言。根据第1141h条的规定，一项国际注册的所有人有权将该国际注册的保护延伸至美国，达到使马德里议定书的相关条款生效的程度。

（b）如果美国是原属局。如果美国专利商标局是一个商标申请或注册的原属局，任何基于该申请或注册的国际注册，不能用来在美国获得马德里议定书的权益。

1141f. 提交请求将国际注册的保护延伸至美国的效力

（a）对延伸保护请求的要求

由国际局传送给美国专利商标局的一项将国际注册的保护延伸至美国的请求，如果在国际局收到该请求时附上了该国际注册的申请人或所有人有真诚的意图在商业中使用该商标的声明，则应视为在美国的合格申请。

（b）合格申请的效力

除非根据本法第 1141h 的规定延伸保护被驳回，根据（a）项提出的合格的延伸保护请求，应构成该商标在下列日期中最早的日期时的推定使用，享有本法第 1057（C）条规定的权利：

（1）如果是在国际申请中提出延伸保护请求，则为国际注册日期；

（2）如果是在国际注册日期后提出的延伸保护请求，则为该延伸保护请求登记的日期；

（3）根据本法第 1141g 条提出的优先权日期；

1141g. 请求延伸保护至美国的优先权

请求延伸保护至美国的国际注册所有人有权根据《保护工业产权巴黎公约》第 4 条含义范围内的优先权主张优先权日期，若

（1）延伸保护请求包含了优先权的主张；同时

（2）国际注册日期或请求延伸保护至美国的登记日期在第一次定期国家申请（《保护工业产权巴黎公约》第 4（A）(3）条）或后续申请（《保护工业产权巴黎公约》第 4（C)(4）条）之日后 6 个月内。

1141h. 延伸保护请求的审查和异议；驳回通知

（a）审查和异议

（1）符合本法第 1141f（a）条规定的延伸保护请求应作为在依据本法建立的主注册簿上注册的申请一样被审查，并且如果经审查认为该申请人有权依据本法第 1141 条及其后条款的规定受到延伸保护，专利商标局局长应在美国专利商标局的官方公告中公告该商标。

（2）依据（c）项的规定，可根据本法第 1063 条的规定对本法第 1141 条及其后条款中的延伸保护请求提出异议。

（3）延伸保护不能以该商标没有在商业中使用为理由驳回。

（4）不能在主注册簿上注册的领土延伸商标应当予以驳回。

（b）驳回通知

如果依据（a）项的规定，一项延伸保护请求被驳回，专利商标局局长应在（依据（c）款规定）驳回通知中声明该延伸保护不能被核准及其被驳回所基于的所有理由。

（c）通知国际局

（1）在国际局将一份延伸保护请求通知专利商标局之日起的 18 个月内，专利商标局局长应将下列有关该请求的文件传送给国际局：

（A）对该延伸保护请求审查后的驳回通知；

（B）针对该请求的异议申请的驳回通知；

（C）针对该请求的异议可能在 18 个月以后提出的通知。

（2）如果专利商标局局长根据（1）（C）段发出了可能存在异议的通知，专利商标局局长应在可能的情况下，在异议期开始后的七个月内或异议期结束之日起的一个月内（两者中较早的一个），向国际局传送基于异议的驳回通知，包括异议的所有理由。

（3）如果根据（1）或（2）段的规定，关于一项延伸保护请求的驳回通知已经发出，在这种情况下，除该通知中所列之驳回理由外的其他该请求的驳回理由，在（1）或（2）段规定期限结束之后，不能传送给国际局。

（4）如果（1）或（2）段规定的有关一项延伸保护请求的通知在该段所规定的期限内没有发给国际局，则该延伸保护请求不能被驳回，并且专利商标局局长应按照请求发给延伸保护的证明。

（d）为送达程序指定代理人

在回复有关一个商标的驳回通知时，该国际注册商标的所有人，应向美国专利商标局提交一份文件，指明一名美国居民的姓名和住所，以便在涉及该商标的相关程序中向其送达传票或通知。所述传票或通知将按最后提交的文件中指明的地址交付或邮递送达给该指定的人。如果按文件中的地址不能找到被指定人，或注册人没有向美国专利商标局提交文件指定一名美国居民的姓名和地址，以便在涉及该商标的相关程序中向其送达传票或通知，则所述传票或通知将送达专利商标局局长。

1141i. 延伸保护的效力

（a）延伸保护的颁布

除非基于本法第1141h条的延伸保护请求被驳回，专利商标局局长应当按照请求发给延伸保护注册证，并且在美国专利商标局的官方公告中公告该延伸保护的注册证。

（b）延伸保护的效力

自延伸保护的注册证根据（a）项的规定颁布之日起，

（1）该延伸保护具有与主注册簿上的注册同样的效力；

（2）该国际注册的所有人拥有与主注册簿上注册的所有人同样的权利和救济。

1141j. 在美国的延伸保护对作为其基础的国际注册的依附性

（a）国际注册撤销的效力

如果国际局通知美国专利商标局，一个国际注册在其部分或全部商品或服务上被撤销，则专利商标局局长应自该国际注册被撤销之日起在部分或全部商品或服务上撤销其在美国的延伸保护。

（b）国际注册没有续展的效力

如果国际局没有续展一项国际注册，则其在美国相关的延伸保护也将自国际注册期满之日起失效。

（c）一项延伸保护转为一个美国申请

根据马德里议定书第6（4）条的规定，一个国际注册在依照原属局的请求被国际局全部或部分撤销后，其所有人可以依据本法第1051条或第1126条的规定，在以国际注册为基础的延伸保护范围内，被撤销的任意商品和服务上，申请注册同样的商标。该申请应被视为在国际注册日或延伸保护请求在国际局登记之日提交的（无论适用哪个日期），并且，如果该延伸保护根据本法第 1141g 条的规定享有优先权，该申请应享有相同的优先权。只有当该申请在国际注册被部分或全部撤销之日起 3 个月内提出，且符合本法的所有要求，即适用于根据第 1051 条或第 1126 条的规定提交申请的所有要求，该申请才有权享有本项规定的权益。

1141k. 宣誓书和费用

（a）所需的宣誓书和费用

根据第 1141i 条的规定其注册证已经颁发的一项延伸保护应该在作为其基础的国际注册的有效期内一直有效，除非在下列日期，专利商标局局长撤销了商标的延伸保护：

（1）自专利商标局局长颁发延伸保护注册证起六年结束之时，除非在 6 年期满的前一年内，国际注册的所有人向专利商标局递交了（b）项规定的宣誓书并缴纳了专利商标局局长规定的费用；且

（2）自专利商标局局长颁发延伸保护注册证起至 10 年结束之时，及此后的每个十年期限结束之时，除非

（A）在 10 年期限届满之前的 6 个月内，国际注册的所有人向专利商标局递交了（b）项规定的宣誓书并缴纳了专利商标局局长规定的费用；或

（B）在 10 年期限届满之后的 3 个月内，国际注册的所有人向专利商标局递交了（b）项规定的宣誓书并缴纳了（A）段规定的费用及专利商标局局长规定的额外的费用。

（b）宣誓书的内容

（a）项所提到的宣誓书应列明延伸保护中所列举的该商标在商业中使用的或与之相关的商品或服务，并且该国际注册的所有人应随宣誓书附上能显示当前商标在商业中使用状况的样品或复制品，或说明能合理解释未使用原因的特殊情况而并非有任何放弃该商标的意图。有关宣誓书要求的专门通知，应附在每一个延伸保护的注册证后面。

（c）通知

专利商标局局长应通知提交宣誓书的国际注册的所有人其对该宣誓书的核准或驳回，如果是驳回，应通知驳回的理由。

（d）通知或传票的送达

该国际注册商标的所有人，应向美国专利商标局提交一份文件，指明一名美国居民的姓名和住所，以便在涉及该商标的相关程序中向其送达传票或通知。所述传票或通知将按最后提交的文件中指明的地址交付或邮递送达给该指定的人。如果按文件中的地址不能找到被指定人，或注册人没有向美国专利商标局提交文件指定一名美国居民的姓名和地址，以便在涉及该商标的相关程序中向其送达传票或通知，则所述传票或通知将送达专利商标局局长。

1141l. 延伸保护的转让

一项延伸保护，包括与该商标相联系的商誉，只能转让给缔约国或作为缔约方的国际组织的成员国的国民，或在其境内有住所的人，或在其境内有真实有效的工业或商业营业场所的人。

1141m. 不容置疑性

依据本法（第1141及其后的条款）的规定颁发延伸保护的商标，其依据第1065条规定连续使用的期限，不能早于专利商标局局长根据第1141i条的规定颁发延伸保护注册证的日期，但第1151n条的规定除外。

1141n. 延伸保护的权利

当一个美国注册和一个后来延伸保护至美国的注册，为同一个人所有，商标相同，商品和服务也一样，则该延伸保护拥有与在该延伸保护注册证颁发之前的注册一样的权利。

Lanham (Trademark) Act [1]

TABLE OF CONTENTS

---

〔1〕 资料来源于国家工商行政管理总局商标局中国商标网。

SUBCHAPTER I
THE PRINCIPAL REGISTER

Application for Registration; Verification

Application for Use of Trademarks

1051. — (a) (1) The owner of a trademark used in commerce may request registration of its trademark on the principal register hereby established by paying the prescribed fee and filing in the Patent and Trademark Office an application and a verified statement, in such form as may be prescribed by the Director, and such number of specimens or facsimiles of the mark as used as may be required by the Director.

(2) The application shall include specification of the applicant's domicile and citizenship, the date of the applicant's first use of the mark, the date of the applicant's first use of the mark in commerce, the goods in connection with which the mark is used, and a drawing of the mark.

(3) The statement shall be verified by the applicant and specify that—

(A) the person making the verification believes that he or she, or the juristic person in whose behalf he or she makes the verification, to be the owner of the mark sought to be registered;

(B) to the best of the verifier's knowledge and belief, the facts recited in the application are accurate;

(C) the mark is in use in commerce; and

(D) to the best of the verifier's knowledge and belief, no other person has the right to use such mark in commerce either in the identical form thereof or in such near resemblance thereto as to be likely, when used on or in connection with the goods of such other person, to cause confusion, or to cause mistake, or to deceive, except that, in the case of every application claiming concurrent use, the applicant shall—

(i) state exceptions to the claim of exclusive use; and

(ii) shall specify, to the extent of the verifier's knowledge—

(I) any concurrent use by others;

(II) the goods on or in connection with which and the areas in which each concurrent use exists;

(III) the periods of each use; and

(IV) the goods and area for which the applicant desires registration.

(4) The applicant shall comply with such rules or regulations as may be prescribed by the Director. The Director shall promulgate rules prescribing the requirements for the application and for obtaining a filing date herein.

Application for Bona Fide *Intention to Use Trademark*

(*b*) (1) A person who has a *bona fide* intention, under circumstances showing the good faith of such person, to use a trademark in commerce may request registration of its trademark on the principal register hereby established by paying the prescribed fee and filing in the Patent and Trademark Office an application and a verified statement, in such form as may be prescribed by the Director.

(2) The application shall include specification of the applicant's domicile and citizenship, the goods in connection with which the applicant has a *bona fide* intention to use the mark, and a drawing of the mark.

(3) The statement shall be verified by the applicant and specify—

(*A*) that the person making the verification believes that he or she, or the juristic person in whose behalf he or she makes the verification, to be entitled to use the mark in commerce;

(*B*) the applicant's *bona fide* intention to use the mark in commerce;

(*C*) that, to the best of the verifier's knowledge and belief, the facts recited in the application are accurate; and

(*D*) that, to the best of the verifier's knowledge and belief, no other person has the right to use such mark in commerce either in the identical form thereof or in such near resemblance thereto as to be likely, when used on or in connection with the goods of such other person, to cause confusion, or to cause mistake, or to deceive.

Except for applications filed pursuant to section 1126 of this title, no mark shall be registered until the applicant has met the requirements of subsections (c) and (d) of this section.

(4) The applicant shall comply with such rules or regulations as may be prescribed by the Director. The Director shall promulgate rules prescribing the requirements for the application and for obtaining a filing date herein.

Amendment of Application Under Subsection (b) to Conform
to Requirements of Subsection (a)

(c) At any time during examination of an application filed under subsection (b) of this section, an applicant who has made use of the mark in commerce may claim the benefits of such use for purposes of this chapter, by amending his or her application to bring it into conformity with the requirements of subsection (a) of this section.

Verified Statement that Trademark is Used in Commerce

(d) (1) Within six months after the date on which the notice of allowance with respect to a mark is issued under section 1063 (b) (2) of this title to an applicant under subsection (b) of this section, the applicant shall file in the Patent and Trademark Office, together with such number of specimens or facsimiles of the mark as used in commerce as may be required by the Director and payment of the prescribed fee, a verified statement that the mark is in use in commerce and specifying the date of the applicant's first use of the mark in commerce and those goods or services specified in the notice of allowance on or in connection with which the mark is used in commerce. Subject to examination and acceptance of the statement of use, the mark shall be registered in the Patent and Trademark Office, a certificate of registration shall be issued for those goods or services recited in the statement of use for which the mark is entitled to registration, and notice of registration shall be published in the Official Gazette of the Patent and Trademark Office. Such examination may include an examination of the factors set forth in subsections (a) through (e) of section 1052 of this title. The notice of registration shall specify the goods or services for which the mark is registered.

(2) The Director shall extend, for one additional 6-month period, the time for filing the statement of use under paragraph (1), upon written request of the applicant before the expiration of the 6-month period provided in paragraph (1). In addition to an extension under the preceding sentence, the Director may, upon a showing of good cause by the applicant, further extend the time for filing the statement of use under paragraph (1) for periods aggregating not more than 24 months, pursuant to written request of the applicant made before the expiration of the last extension granted under this paragraph. Any request for an extension under this paragraph shall be accompanied by a verified statement that the applicant has a continued *bona fide* intention to use the mark in commerce and specifying those goods or services identified in the notice of allowance on or in connection with which the applicant has a continued *bona fide* intention to use the mark in commerce. Any request for an extension under this paragraph shall be accompanied by payment of the prescribed fee. The Director shall issue regulations setting forth guidelines for determining what constitutes good cause for purposes of this paragraph.

(3) The Director shall notify any applicant who files a statement of use of the acceptance or refusal thereof and, if the statement of use is refused, the reasons for the refusal. An applicant may amend the statement of use.

(4) The failure to timely file a verified statement of use under paragraph (1) or an extension request under paragraph (2) shall result in abandonment of the application, unless it can be shown to the satisfaction of the Director that the delay in responding was unintentional, in which case the time for filing may be extended, but for a period not to exceed the period specified in paragraphs (1) and (2) for filing a statement of use.

Designation of Resident for Service of Process and Notices

(e) If the applicant is not domiciled in the United States the applicant may designate, by a document filed in the United States Patent and Trademark Office, the name and address of a person resident in the United States on whom may be served notices or process in proceedings affecting the mark. Such notices or process may be served upon the person so designated by leaving with that person or mailing to that person a copy thereof at the address specified in the last designation so filed. If the person so designated cannot be found at the address given in the last designation, or if the registrant does not designate by a document filed in the United States Patent and Trademark Office the name and address of a person resident in the United States on whom may be served notices or process in proceedings affecting the mark, such notices or process may be served on the Director.

Trademarks Registrable on the Principal Register;

Concurrent Registration

1052. No trademark by which the goods of the applicant may be distinguished from the goods of others shall be refused registration on the principal register on account of its nature unless it—

(*a*) Consists of or comprises immoral, deceptive, or scandalous matter; or matter which may disparage or falsely suggest a connection with persons, living or dead, institutions, beliefs, or national symbols, or bring them into contempt, or disrepute; or a geographical indication which, when used on or in connection with wines or spirits, identifies a place other than the origin of the goods and is first used on or in connection with wines or spirits by the applicant on or after one year after the date on which the WTO Agreement (as defined in section 3501 (9) of title 19) enters into force with respect to the United States.

(*b*) Consists of or comprises the flag or coat of arms or other insignia of the United States, or of any State or municipality, or of any foreign nation, or any simulation thereof.

(*c*) Consists of or comprises a name, portrait, or signature identifying a particular living individual except by his written consent, or the name, signature, or portrait of a deceased President of the United States during the life of his widow, if any, except by the written consent of the widow.

(*d*) Consists of or comprises a mark which so resembles a mark registered in the Patent and Trademark Office, or a mark or trade name previously used in the United States by another and not abandoned, as to be likely, when used on or in connection with the goods of the applicant, to cause confusion, or to cause mistake, or to deceive: Provided, That if the Director determines that confusion, mistake, or deception is not likely to result from the continued use by more than one person of the same or similar marks under conditions and limitations as to the mode or place of use of the marks or the goods on or in connection with which such marks are used, concurrent registrations may be issued to such persons when they have become entitled to use such marks as a result of their concurrent lawful use in commerce prior to

(1) the earliest of the filing dates of the applications pending or of any registration issued under this Act;

(2) July 5, 1947, in the case of registrations previously issued under the Act of March 3, 1881, or February 20, 1905, and continuing in full force and effect on that date; or

(3) July 5, 1947, in the case of applications filed under the Act of February 20, 1905, and registered after July 5, 1947. Use prior to the filing date of any pending application or a registration shall not be required when the owner of such application or registration consents to the grant of a concurrent registration to the applicant. Concurrent registrations may also be issued by the Director when a court of competent jurisdiction has finally determined that more than one person is entitled to use the same or similar marks in commerce. In issuing concurrent registrations, the Director shall prescribe conditions and limitations as to the mode or place of use of the mark or the goods on or in connection with which such mark is registered to the respective persons.

(*e*) Consists of a mark which

(1) when used on or in connection with the goods of the applicant is merely descriptive or deceptively misdescriptive of them,

(2) when used on or in connection with the goods of the applicant is primarily

geographically descriptive of them, except as indications of regional origin may be registrable under section 1054 of this title,

(3) when used on or in connection with the goods of the applicant is primarily geographically deceptively misdescriptive of them,

(4) is primarily merely a surname, or

(5) comprises any matter that, as a whole, is functional.

(*f*) Except as expressly excluded in subsections (*a*), (*b*), (*c*), (*d*), (*e*) (3), and (*e*)(5) of this section, nothing in this chapter shall prevent the registration of a mark used by the applicant which has become distinctive of the applicant's goods in commerce. The Director may accept as *prima facie* evidence that the mark has become distinctive, as used on or in connection with the applicant's goods in commerce, proof of substantially exclusive and continuous use thereof as a mark by the applicant in commerce for the five years before the date on which the claim of distinctiveness is made. Nothing in this section shall prevent the registration of a mark which, when used on or in connection with the goods of the applicant, is primarily geographically deceptively misdescriptive of them, and which became distinctive of the applicant's goods in commerce before December 8, 1993.

A mark which when used would cause dilution under section 1125 (*c*) of this title may be refused registration only pursuant to a proceeding brought under section 1063 of this title. A registration for a mark which when used would cause dilution under section 1125 (*c*) of this title may be canceled pursuant to a proceeding brought under either section 1064 of this title or section 1092 of this title.

Service Marks Registrable

1053. Subject to the provisions relating to the registration of trademarks, so far as they are applicable, service marks shall be registrable, in the same manner and with the same effect as are trademarks, and when registered they shall be entitled to the protection provided in this chapter in the case of trademarks. Applications and procedure under this section shall conform as nearly as practicable to those prescribed for the registration of trademarks.

Collective Marks and Certification Marks Registrable

1054. Subject to the provisions relating to the registration of trademarks, so far as they are applicable, collective and certification marks, including indications of regional origin, shall be registrable under this chapter, in the same manner and with the same effect as are trademarks, by persons, and nations, States, municipalities, and the like, exercising legitimate control over the use of the marks sought to be registered, even though not possessing an industrial or commercial establishment, and when registered they shall be entitled to the protection provided in this chapter in the case of trademarks, except in the case of certification marks when used so as to represent falsely that the owner or a user thereof makes or sells the goods or performs the services on or in connection with which such mark is used. Applications and procedure under this section shall conform as nearly as practicable to those prescribed for the registration of trademarks.

Use by Related Companies Affecting Validity and Registration

1055. Where a registered mark or a mark sought to be registered is or may be used legitimately by related companies, such use shall inure to the benefit of the registrant or applicant for registration, and such use shall not affect the validity of such mark or of its registration, provided such mark is not used in such manner as to deceive the public. If first use of a mark by a person is controlled by the registrant or applicant for registration of the mark with respect to the nature and quality of the goods or services, such first use shall inure to the benefit of the registrant or applicant, as the case may be.

Disclaimer of Unregistrable Matter

Compulsory and Voluntary Disclaimers

1056. — (a) The Director may require the applicant to disclaim an unregistrable component of a mark otherwise registrable. An applicant may voluntarily disclaim a component of a mark sought to be registered.

Prejudice of Rights

(*b*) No disclaimer, including those made under subsection (*e*) of section 1057 of this title, shall prejudice or affect the applicant's or registrant's rights then existing or thereafter arising in the disclaimed matter, or his right of registration on another application if the disclaimed matter be or shall have become distinctive of his goods or services.

Certificates of Registration

Issuance and Form

1057. — (*a*) Certificates of registration of marks registered upon the principal register shall be issued in the name of the United States of America, under the seal of the Patent and Trademark Office, and shall be signed by the Director or have his signature placed thereon, and a record thereof shall be kept in the Patent and Trademark Office. The registration shall reproduce the mark, and state that the mark is registered on the principal register under this chapter, the date of the first use of the mark, the date of the first use of the mark in commerce, the particular goods or services for which it is registered, the number and date of the registration, the term thereof, the date on which the application for registration was received in the Patent and Trademark Office, and any conditions and limitations that may be imposed in the registration.

Certificate as Prima Facie *Evidence*

(*b*) A certificate of registration of a mark upon the principal register provided by this chapter shall be *prima facie* evidence of the validity of the registered mark and of the registration of the mark, of the registrant's ownership of the mark, and of the registrant's exclusive right to use the registered mark in commerce on or in connection with the goods or services specified in the certificate, subject to any conditions or limitations stated in the certificate.

Application to Register Mark Considered Constructive Use

(*c*) Contingent on the registration of a mark on the principal register provided by this chapter, the filing of the application to register such mark shall constitute constructive use of the mark, conferring a right of priority, nationwide in effect, on or in connection with the goods or services specified in the registration against any other person except for a person whose mark has not been abandoned and who, prior to such filing—

(1) has used the mark;

(2) has filed an application to register the mark which is pending or has resulted in registration of the mark; or

(3) has filed a foreign application to register the mark on the basis of which he or she has acquired a right of priority, and timely files an application under section 1126 (*d*) of this title to register the mark which is pending or has resulted in registration of the mark.

Issuance to Assignee

(*d*) A certificate of registration of a mark may be issued to the assignee or the applicant, but the assignment must first be recorded in the Patent and Trademark Office. In case of change of ownership the Director shall, at the request of the owner and upon a proper showing and the payment of the prescribed fee, issue to such assignee a new certificate of registration of the said mark in the name of such assignee, and for the unexpired part of original period.

Surrender, Cancellation, or Amendment by Registrant

(*e*) Upon application of the registrant the Director may permit any registration to be surrendered for cancellation, and upon cancellation appropriate entry shall be made in the records of the Patent and Trademark Office. Upon application of the registrant and payment of the prescribed fee, the Director for good cause may permit any registration to be amended or to be disclaimed in part: Provided, That the amendment or disclaimer does not alter materially the character of the mark. Appropriate entry shall be made in the records of the Patent and Trademark Office and upon the certificate of registration or, if said certificate is lost or destroyed, upon a certified copy thereof.

Copies of Patent and Trademark Office Records as Evidence

(*f*) Copies of any records, books, papers, or drawings belonging to the Patent and Trademark Office relating to marks, and copies of registrations, when authenticated by the seal of the Patent and Trademark Office and certified by the Director, or in his name by an employee of the Office duly designated by the Director, shall be evidence in all cases wherein the originals would be evidence; and any person making application therefor and paying the prescribed fee shall have such copies.

Correction of Patent and Trademark Office Mistake

(*g*) Whenever a material mistake in a registration, incurred through the fault of the Patent and Trademark Office, is clearly disclosed by the records of the Office a certificate stating the fact and nature of such mistake, shall be issued without charge and recorded and a printed copy thereof shall be attached to each printed copy of the registration certificate and such corrected registration shall thereafter have the same effect as if the same had been originally issued in such corrected form, or in the discretion of the Director a new certificate of registration may be issued without charge. All certificates of correction heretofore issued in accordance with the rules of the Patent and Trademark Office and the registrations to which they are attached shall have the same force and effect as if such certificates and their issue had been specifically authorized by statute.

Correction of Applicant's Mistake

(*h*) Whenever a mistake has been made in a registration and a showing has been made that such mistake occurred in good faith through the fault of the applicant, the Director is authorized to issue a certificate of correction or, in his discretion, a new certificate upon the payment of the prescribed fee: Provided, That the correction does not involve such changes in the registration as to require republication of the mark.

Duration

In General

1058. — (*a*) Each registration shall remain in force for 10 years, except that the registration of any mark shall be canceled by the Director for failure to comply with the provisions of subsection (*b*) of this section, upon the expiration of the following time periods, as applicable:

(1) For registrations issued pursuant to the provisions of this chapter, at the end of 6 years following the date of registration.

(2) For registrations published under the provisions of section 1062 (*c*) of this title, at the end of 6 years following the date of publication under such section.

(3) For all registrations, at the end of each successive 10-year period following the date of registration.

Affidavit of Continuing Use

(b) *During the 1-year period immediately preceding the end of the applicable time period set forth in subsection (a) of this section, the owner of the registration shall pay the prescribed fee and file in the Patent and Trademark Office—*

(1) *an affidavit setting forth those goods or services recited in the registration on or in connection with which the mark is in use in commerce and such number of specimens or facsimiles showing current use of the mark as may be required by the Director; or*

(2) *an affidavit setting forth those goods or services recited in the registration on or in connection with which the mark is not in use in commerce and showing that any such nonuse is due to special circumstances which excuse such nonuse and is not due to any intention to abandon the mark.*

Grace Period for Submissions; Deficiency

(c) (1) *The owner of the registration may make the submissions required under*

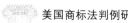

this section within a grace period of 6 months after the end of the applicable time period set forth in subsection (a) of this section. Such submission is required to be accompanied by a surcharge prescribed by the Director.

(2) If any submission filed under this section is deficient, the deficiency may be corrected after the statutory time period and within the time prescribed after notification of the deficiency. Such submission is required to be accompanied by a surcharge prescribed by the Director.

Notice of Affidavit Requirement

(d) Special notice of the requirement for affidavits under this section shall be attached to each certificate of registration and notice of publication under section 1062 (c) of this title.

Notification of Acceptance or Refusal of Affidavits

(e) The Director shall notify any owner who files 1 of the affidavits required by this section of the Commissioner's acceptance or refusal thereof and, in the case of a refusal, the reasons therefor.

Designation of Resident for Service of Process and Notices

(f) If the registrant is not domiciled in the United States, the registrant may designate, by a document filed in the United States Patent and Trademark Office, the name and address of a person resident in the United States on whom may be served notices or process in proceedings affecting the mark. Such notices or process may be served upon the person so designated by leaving with that person or mailing to that person a copy thereof at the address specified in the last designation so filed. If the person so designated cannot be found at the address given in the last designation, or if the registrant does not designate by a document filed in the United States Patent and Trademark Office the name and address of a person resident in the United States on whom may be served notices or process in proceedings affecting the mark, such notices or process may be served on the Director.

Renewal of Registration

Period of Renewal; Time for Renewal

1059. — (*a*) Subject to the provisions of section 1058 of this title, each registration may be renewed for periods of 10 years at the end of each successive 10-year period following the date of registration upon payment of the prescribed fee and the filing of a written application, in such form as may be prescribed by the Director. Such application may be made at any time within 1 year before the end of each successive 10-year period for which the registration was issued or renewed, or it may be made within a grace period of 6 months after the end of each successive 10-year period, upon payment of a fee and surcharge prescribed therefor. If any application filed under this section is deficient, the deficiency may be corrected within the time prescribed after notification of the deficiency, upon payment of a surcharge prescribed therefor.

Notification of Refusal of Renewal

(*b*) If the Director refuses to renew the registration, the Director shall notify the registrant of the Commissioner's refusal and the reasons therefor.

Designation of Resident for Service of Process and Notices

(*c*) If the registrant is not domiciled in the United States the registrant may designate, by a document filed in the United States Patent and Trademark Office, the name and address of a person resident in the United States on whom may be served notices or process in proceedings affecting the mark. Such notices or process may be served upon the person so designated by leaving with that person or mailing to that person a copy thereof at the address specified in the last designation so filed. If the person so designated cannot be found at the address given in the last designation, or if the registrant does not designate by a document filed in the United States Patent and Trademark Office the name and address of a person resident in the United States on whom may be served notices or process in proceedings affecting the mark, such notices or process may be served on the Director.

Assignment

1060. — (*a*) (1) A registered mark or a mark for which an application to register has been filed shall be assignable with the good will of the business in which the mark is used, or with that part of the good will of the business connected with the use of and symbolized by the mark. Notwithstanding the preceding sentence, no application to register a mark under section 1051 (*b*) of this title shall be assignable prior to the filing of an amendment under section 1051 (*c*) of this title to bring the application into conformity with section 1051 (*a*) of this title or the filing of the verified statement of use under section 1051 (*d*) of this title, except for an assignment to a successor to the business of the applicant, or portion thereof, to which the mark pertains, if that business is ongoing and existing.

(2) In any assignment authorized by this section, it shall not be necessary to include the good will of the business connected with the use of and symbolized by any other mark used in the business or by the name or style under which the business is conducted.

(3) Assignments shall be by instruments in writing duly executed. Acknowledgment shall be *prima facie* evidence of the execution of an assignment, and when the prescribed information reporting the assignment is recorded in the United States Patent and Trademark Office, the record shall be *prima facie* evidence of execution.

(4) An assignment shall be void against any subsequent purchaser for valuable consideration without notice, unless the prescribed information reporting the assignment is recorded in the United States Patent and Trademark Office within 3 months after the date of the assignment or prior to the subsequent purchase.

(5) The United States Patent and Trademark Office shall maintain a record of information on assignments, in such form as may be prescribed by the Director.

(*b*) An assignee not domiciled in the United States may designate by a document filed in the United States Patent and Trademark Office the name and address of a person resident in the United States on whom may be served notices or process in proceedings affecting the mark. Such notices or process may be served upon the person so designated by leaving with that person or mailing to that person a copy thereof at the address specified in the last designation so filed. If the person so designated cannot be found at the address given in the last designation, or if the assignee does not designate by a document filed in the United States Patent and Trademark Office the name and address of a person resident in the United States on whom may be served notices or process in proceedings affecting the mark, such notices or process may be served upon the Director.

Execution of Acknowledgments and Verifications

1061. Acknowledgments and verifications required under this chapter may be made before any person within the United States authorized by law to administer oaths, or, when made in a foreign country, before any diplomatic or consular officer of the United States or before any official authorized to administer oaths in the foreign country concerned whose authority shall be proved by a certificate of a diplomatic or consular officer of the United States, or apostille of an official designated by a foreign country which, by treaty or convention, accords like effect to apostilles of designated officials in the United States, and shall be valid if they comply with the laws of the state or country where made.

Publication

Examination and Publication

1062. — (a) Upon the filing of an application for registration and payment of the prescribed fee, the Director shall refer the application to the examiner in charge of the registration of marks, who shall cause an examination to be made and, if on such examination it shall appear that the applicant is entitled to registration, or would be entitled to registration upon the acceptance of the statement of use required by section 1051 (d) of this title, the Director shall cause the mark to be published in the Official Gazette of the Patent and Trademark Office; Provided, That in the case of an applicant claiming concurrent use, or in the case of an application to be placed in an interference as provided in section 1066 of this title the mark, if otherwise registrable, may be published subject to the determination of the rights of the parties to such proceedings.

Refusal of Registration; Amendment of Application; Abandonment

(*b*) If the applicant is found not entitled to registration, the examiner shall advise the applicant thereof and of the reasons therefor. The applicant shall have a period of six months in which to reply or amend his application, which shall then be reexamined. This procedure may be repeated until

(1) the examiner finally refuses registration of the mark or

(2) the applicant fails for a period of six months to reply or amend or appeal,

whereupon the application shall be deemed to have been abandoned, unless it can be shown to the satisfaction of the Director that the delay in responding was unintentional, whereupon such time may be extended.

Republication of Marks Registered under Prior Acts

(*c*) A registrant of a mark registered under the provisions of the Act of March 3, 1881, or the Act of February 20, 1905, may, at any time prior to the expiration of the registration thereof, upon the payment of the prescribed fee file with the Director an affidavit setting forth those goods stated in the registration on which said mark is in use in commerce and that the registrant claims the benefits of this chapter for said mark. The Director shall publish notice thereof with a reproduction of said mark in the Official Gazette, and notify the registrant of such publication and of the requirement for the affidavit of use or nonuse as provided for in subsection (*b*) of Section 1058 (*b*) of this title. Marks published under this subsection shall not be subject to the provisions of section 1063 of this title.

Opposition to Registration

1063. — (*a*) Any person who believes that he would be damaged by the registration of a mark upon the principal register, including as a result of dilution under section 1125 (c) of this title, may, upon payment of the prescribed fee, file an opposition in the Patent and Trademark Office, stating the grounds therefor, within thirty days after the publication under subsection (a) of section 1062 of this title of the mark sought to be registered. Upon written request prior to the expiration of the thirty-day period, the time for filing opposition shall be extended for an additional thirty days, and further extensions of time for filing opposition may be granted by the Director for good cause when requested prior to the expiration of an extension. The Director shall notify the applicant of each extension of the time for filing opposition. An opposition may be amended under such conditions as may be prescribed by the Director.

(b) Unless registration is successfully opposed—

(1) a mark entitled to registration on the principal register based on an application filed under section 1051 (a) of this title or pursuant to section 1126 of this title shall be registered in the Patent and Trademark Office, a certificate of registration shall be issued, and notice of the registration shall be published in the Official Gazette of the Patent and Trademark Office; or

(2) a notice of allowance shall be issued to the applicant if the applicant applied for registration under section 1051 (b) of this title.

Cancellation of Registration

1064. A petition to cancel a registration of a mark, stating the grounds relied upon, may, upon payment of the prescribed fee, be filed as follows by any person who believes that he is or will be damaged, including as a result of dilution under section 1125 (c) of this title, by the registration of a mark on the principal register established by this chapter, or under the Act of March 3, 1881, or the Act of February 20, 1905:

(1) Within five years from the date of the registration of the mark under this Act.

(2) Within five years from the date of publication under section 1062 (c) of this title of a mark registered under the Act of March 3, 1881, or the Act of

February 20, 1905.

(3) At any time if the registered mark becomes the generic name for the goods or services, or a portion thereof, for which it is registered, or is functional, or has been abandoned, or its registration was obtained fraudulently or contrary to the provisions of section 1054 of this title or of subsection (a), (b), or (c) of section 1052 of this title for a registration under this chapter, or contrary to similar prohibitory provisions of such prior Acts for a registration under such Acts, or if the registered mark is being used by, or with the permission of, the registrant so as to misrepresent the source of the goods or services on or in connection with which the mark is used. If the registered mark becomes the generic name for less than all of the goods or services for which it is registered, a petition to cancel the registration for only those goods or services may be filed. A registered mark shall not be deemed to be the generic name of goods or services solely because such mark is also used as a name of or to identify a unique product or service. The primary significance of the registered mark to the relevant public rather than purchaser motivation shall be the test for determining whether the registered mark has become the generic name of goods or services on or in connection with which it has been used.

(4) At any time if the mark is registered under the Act of March 3, 1881, or the Act of February 20, 1905, and has not been published under the provisions of subsection (c) of section 1062 of this title.

(5) At any time in the case of a certification mark on the ground that the registrant

(A) does not control, or is not able legitimately to exercise control over, the use of such mark, or

(B) engages in the production or marketing of any goods or services to which the certification mark is applied, or

(C) permits the use of the certification mark for purposes other than to certify, or

(D) discriminately refuses to certify or to continue to certify the goods or services of any person who maintains the standards or conditions which such mark certifies:

Provided, That the Federal Trade Commission may apply to cancel on the grounds specified in paragraphs (3) and (5) of this section any mark registered on the principal register established by this chapter, and the prescribed fee shall not be required. Nothing in paragraph (5) shall be deemed to prohibit the registrant from using its certification mark in advertising or promoting recognition of the certification program or of the goods or services meeting the certification standards of the registrant. Such uses of the certification mark shall not be grounds for cancellation under paragraph (5), so long as the registrant does not itself produce, manufacture, or sell any of the certified goods or services to which its identical certification mark is applied.

Incontestability of Right to Use Mark Under Certain Conditions

1065. Except on a ground for which application to cancel may be filed at any time under paragraphs (3) and (5) of section 1064 of this title, and except to the extent, if any, to which the use of a mark registered on the principal register infringes a valid right acquired under the law of any State or Territory by use of a mark or trade name continuing from a date prior to the date of registration under this chapter of such registered mark, the right of the registrant to use such registered mark in commerce for the goods or services on or in connection with which such registered mark has been in continuous use for five consecutive years subsequent to the date of such registration and is still in use in commerce, shall be incontestable: Provided, That—

(1) there has been no final decision adverse to registrant's claim of ownership of such mark for such goods or services, or to registrant's right to register the same or to keep the same on the register; and

(2) there is no proceeding involving said rights pending in the Patent and Trademark Office or in a court and not finally disposed of; and

(3) an affidavit is filed with the Director within one year after the expiration of

any such five-year period setting forth those goods or services stated in the registration on or in connection with which such mark has been in continuous use for such five consecutive years and is still in use in commerce, and the other matters specified in paragraphs (1) and (2) of this section; and

(4) no incontestable right shall be acquired in a mark which is the generic name for the goods or services or a portion thereof, for which it is registered.

Subject to the conditions above specified in this section, the incontestable right with reference to a mark registered under this chapter shall apply to a mark registered under the Act of March 3, 1881, or the Act of February 20, 1905, upon the filing of the required affidavit with the Director within one year after the expiration of any period of five consecutive years after the date of publication of a mark under the provisions of subsection (c) of section 1062 of this title.

The Director shall notify any registrant who files the above-prescribed affidavit of the filing thereof.

Interference; Declaration by Director

1066. Upon petition showing extraordinary circumstances, the Director may declare that an interference exists when application is made for the registration of a mark which so resembles a mark previously registered by another, or for the registration of which another has previously made application, as to be likely when used on or in connection with the goods or services of the applicant to cause confusion or mistake or to deceive. No interference shall be declared between an application and the registration of a mark the right to the use of which has become incontestable.

Interference, Opposition, and Proceedings for Concurrent Use Registration or for Cancellation; Notice; Trademark Trial and Appeal Board

1067. — (a) In every case of interference, opposition to registration, application to register as a lawful concurrent user, or application to cancel the registration of a mark, the Director shall give notice to all parties and shall direct a Trademark Trial and Appeal Board to determine and decide the respective rights of registration.

(*b*) The Trademark Trial and Appeal Board shall include the Director, the Commissioner for Patents, the Commissioner for Trademarks, and administrative trademark judges who are appointed by the Director.

Action of Director in Interference, Opposition, and Proceedings for Concurrent Use Registration or for Cancellation

1068. In such proceedings the Director may refuse to register the opposed mark, may cancel the registration, in whole or in part, may modify the application or registration by limiting the goods or services specified therein, may otherwise restrict or rectify with respect to the register the registration of a registered mark, may refuse to register any or all of several interfering marks, or may register the mark or marks for the person or persons entitled thereto, as the rights of the parties hereunder may be established in the proceedings: Provided, That in the case of the registration of any mark based on concurrent use, the Director shall determine and fix the conditions and limitations provided for in subsection (*d*) of section 1052 of this title. However, no final judgment shall be entered in favor of an applicant under section 1051 (*b*) of this title before the mark is registered, if such applicant cannot prevail without establishing constructive use pursuant to section 1057 (*c*) of this title.

Application of Equitable Principles in *inter partes* Proceedings

1069. In all *inter partes* proceedings equitable principles of laches, estoppel, and acquiescence, where applicable may be considered and applied.

Appeals to Trademark Trial and Appeal Board from Decisions of Examiners

1070. An appeal may be taken to the Trademark Trial and Appeal Board from any final decision of the examiner in charge of the registration of marks upon the payment of the prescribed fee.

Appeal to Courts

Persons Entitled to Appeal; *United States Court of Appeals for the Federal Circuit*; *Waiver of Civil Action*; *Election of Civil Action by Adverse Party*; *Procedure*

1071. — (a) (1) An applicant for registration of a mark, party to an interference proceeding, party to an opposition proceeding, party to an application to register as a lawful concurrent user, party to a cancellation proceeding, a registrant who has filed an affidavit as provided in section 1058 of this title, or an applicant for renewal, who is dissatisfied with the decision of the Director or Trademark Trial and Appeal Board, may appeal to the United States Court of Appeals for the Federal Circuit thereby waiving his right to proceed under subsection (b) of this section: Provided, That such appeal shall be dismissed if any adverse party to the proceeding, other than the Director, shall, within twenty days after the appellant has filed notice of appeal according to paragraph (2) of this section, files notice with the Director that he elects to have all further proceedings conducted as provided in subsection (b) of this section. Thereupon the appellant shall have thirty days thereafter within which to file a civil action under subsection (b) of this section, in default of which the decision appealed from shall govern the further proceedings in the case.

(2) When an appeal is taken to the United States Court of Appeals for the Federal Circuit, the appellant shall file in the Patent and Trademark Office a written notice of appeal directed to the Director, within such time after the date of the decision from which the appeal is taken as the Director prescribes, but in no case less than 60 days after that date.

(3) The Director shall transmit to the United States Court of Appeals for the Federal Circuit a certified list of the documents comprising the record in the Patent and Trademark Office. The court may request that the Director forward the original or certified copies of such documents during pendency of the appeal. In an *ex parte* case, the Director shall submit to that court a brief explaining the grounds for the decision of the Patent and Trademark Office, addressing all the issues involved in the appeal. The court shall, before hearing an appeal, give notice of the time and place of the hearing to the Director and the parties in the appeal.

(4) The United States Court of Appeals for the Federal Circuit shall review the decision from which the appeal is taken on the record before the Patent and Trademark Office. Upon its determination the court shall issue its mandate and opinion to the Director, which shall be entered of record in the Patent and Trademark Office and shall govern the further proceedings in the case. However, no final judgment shall be entered in favor of an applicant under section 1051 (*b*) of this title before the mark is registered, if such applicant cannot prevail without establishing constructive use pursuant to section 1057 (*c*) of this title.

Civil Action; *Persons Entitled to*; *Jurisdiction of Court*;
Status of Director; *Procedure*

(*b*) (1) Whenever a person authorized by subsection (*a*) of this section to appeal to the United States Court of Appeals for the Federal Circuit is dissatisfied with the decision of the Director or Trademark Trial and Appeal Board, said person may, unless appeal has been taken to said United States Court of Appeals for the Federal Circuit, have remedy by a civil action if commenced within such time after such decision, not less than sixty days, as the Director appoints or as provided in subsection (*a*) of this section. The court may adjudge that an applicant is entitled to a registration upon the application involved, that a registration involved should be canceled, or such other matter as the issues in the proceeding require, as the facts in the case may appear. Such adjudication shall authorize the Director to take any necessary action, upon compliance with the requirements of law. However, no final judgment shall be entered in favor of an applicant under section 1051 (*b*) of this title before the mark is registered, if such applicant cannot prevail without establishing constructive use pursuant to section 1057 (*c*) of this title.

(2) The Director shall not be made a party to an *inter partes* proceeding under this subsection, but he shall be notified of the filing of the complaint by the clerk of the court in which it is filed and shall have the right to intervene in the action.

(3) In any case where there is no adverse party, a copy of the complaint shall be served on the Director, and, unless the court finds the expenses to be unreasonable, all the expenses of the proceeding shall be paid by the party bringing the case, whether the final decision is in favor of such party or not. In suits brought

hereunder, the record in the Patent and Trademark Office shall be admitted on motion of any party, upon such terms and conditions as to costs, expenses, and the further cross-examination of the witnesses as the court imposes, without prejudice to the right of any party to take further testimony. The testimony and exhibits of the record in the Patent and Trademark Office, when admitted, shall have the same effect as if originally taken and produced in the suit.

(4) Where there is an adverse party, such suit may be instituted against the party in interest as shown by the records of the Patent and Trademark Office at the time of the decision complained of, but any party in interest may become a party to the action. If there be adverse parties residing in a plurality of districts not embraced within the same State, or an adverse party residing in a foreign country, the United States District Court for the District of Columbia shall have jurisdiction and may issue summons against the adverse parties directed to the marshal of any district in which any adverse party resides. Summons against adverse parties residing in foreign countries may be served by publication or otherwise as the court directs.

Registration as Constructive Notice of Claim of Ownership

1072. Registration of a mark on the principal register provided by this chapter or under the Act of March 3, 1881, or the Act of February 20, 1905, shall be constructive notice of the registrant's claim of ownership thereof.

SUBCHAPTER II THE SUPPLEMENTAL REGISTER

Supplemental Register

Marks Registrable

1091. — (a) In addition to the principal register, the Director shall keep a continuation of the register provided in paragraph (b) of section 1 of the Act of March 19, 1920, entitled "An Act to give effect to certain provisions of the convention for the protection of trademarks and commercial names, made and signed in the city of Buenos Aires, in the Argentine Republic, August 20, 1910, and for other purposes", to be called the supplemental register. All marks capable of distinguishing applicant's goods or services and not registrable on the principal register provided in this chapter, except thosedeclared to be unregistrable under subsections (a), (b), (c), (d), and (e)(3) of section 1052 of this title, which are in lawful use in commerce by the owner thereof, on or in connection with any goods or services may be registered on the supplemental register upon the payment of the prescribed fee and compliance with the provisions of subsections (a) and (e) of section 1051 of this title so far as they are applicable. Nothing in this section shall prevent the registration on the supplemental register of a mark, capable of distinguishing the applicant's goods or services and not registrable on the principal register under this chapter, that is declared to be unregistrable under section 1052 (e) (3) of this title, if such mark has been in lawful use in commerce by the owner thereof, on or in connection with any goods or services, since before December 8, 1993.

Application and Proceedings for Registration

(b) Upon the filing of an application for registration on the supplemental register and payment of the prescribed fee the Director shall refer the application to the examiner in charge of the registration of marks, who shall cause an examination to be made and if on such examination it shall appear that the applicant is entitled to registration, the registration shall be granted. If the applicant is found not entitled to registration the provisions of subsection (b) of section 1062 of this title shall apply.

Nature of Mark

(c) For the purposes of registration on the supplemental register, a mark may consist of any trademark, symbol, label, package, configuration of goods, name, word, slogan, phrase, surname, geographical name, numeral, device, any matter that as a whole is not functional, or any combination of any of the foregoing, but such mark must be capable of distinguishing the applicant's goods or services.

Publication; Not Subject to Opposition; Cancellation

1092. Marks for the supplemental register shall not be published for or be subject to opposition, but shall be published on registration in the Official Gazette of the Patent and Trademark Office. Whenever any person believes that he is or will be damaged by the registration of a mark on this register, including as a result of dilution under section 1125 (c) of this title, he may at any time, upon payment of the prescribed fee and the filing of a petition stating the ground therefor, apply to the Director to cancel such registration. The Director shall refer such application to the Trademark Trial and Appeal Board which shall give notice thereof to the registrant. If it is found after a hearing before the Board that the registrant is not entitled to registration, or that the mark has been abandoned, the registration shall be canceled by the Director. However, no final judgment shall be entered in favor of an applicant under section 1051 (b) of this title before the mark is registered, if such applicant cannot prevail without establishing constructive use pursuant to section 1057 (c) of this title.

Registration Certificates for Marks on Principal and
Supplemental Registers to Be Different

1093. The certificates of registration for marks registered on the supplemental register shall be conspicuously different from certificates issued for marks registered on the principal register.

Provisions of Chapter Applicable to Registrations on
Supplemental Register

1094. The provisions of this chapter shall govern so far as applicable applications for registration and registrations on the supplemental register as well as those on the principal register, but applications for and registrations on the supplemental register shall not be subject to or receive the advantages of sections 1051 (b), 1052 (e), 1052 (f), 1057 (b), 1057 (c), 1062 (a), 1063 to 1068, inclusive, 1072, 1115 and 1124 of this title.

Registration on Principal Register not Precluded

1095. Registration of a mark on the supplemental register, or under the Act of

March 19, 1920, shall not preclude registration by the registrant on the principal register established by this chapter. Registration of a mark on the supplemental register shall not constitute an admission that the mark has not acquired distinctiveness.

Registration on Supplemental Register not Used to Stop Importations

1096. Registration on the supplemental register or under the Act of March 19, 1920, shall not be filed in the Department of the Treasury or be used to stop importations.

SUBCHAPTER III GENERAL PROVISIONS

Notice of Registration; Display with Mark; Recovery of Profits
and Damages in Infringement Suit

1111. Notwithstanding the provisions of section 1072 of this title, a registrant of a mark registered in the Patent and Trademark Office, may give notice that his mark is registered by displaying with the mark the words "Registered in U. S. Patent and Trademark Office" or "Reg. U. S. Pat. & Tm. Off. " or the letter R enclosed within a circle, thus ®; and in any suit for infringement under this chapter by such a registrant failing to give such notice of registration, no profits and no damages shall be recovered under the provisions of this chapter unless the defendant had actual notice of the registration.

Classification of Goods and Services;
Registration in Plurality of Classes

1112. The Director may establish a classification of goods and services, for convenience of Patent and Trademark Office administration, but not to limit or extend the applicant's or registrant's rights. The applicant may apply to register a mark for any or all of the goods and services on or in connection with which he or she is using or has a *bona fide* intention to use the mark in commerce: Provided, That if the Director by regulation permits the filing of an application for the registration of a mark for goods or services which fall within a plurality of classes, a fee equaling the sum of the fees for filing an application in each class shall be paid, and the Director may issue a single certificate of registration for such mark.

Fees

Applications; *Services*; *Materials*

1113. — (*a*) The Director shall establish fees for the filing and processing of an application for the registration of a trademark or other mark and for all other services performed by and materials furnished by the Patent and Trademark Office related to trademarks and other marks. Fees established under this subsection may be adjusted by the Director once each year to reflect, in the aggregate, any fluctuations during the preceding 12 months in the Consumer Price Index, as determined by the Secretary of Labor. Changes of less than 1 percent may be ignored. No fee established under this section shall take effect until at least 30 days after notice of the fee has been published in the Federal Register and in the Official Gazette of the Patent and Trademark Office.

Waiver; *Indian Products*

(*b*) The Director may waive the payment of any fee for any service or material related to trademarks or other marks in connection with an occasional request made by a department or agency of the Government, or any officer thereof. The Indian Arts and Crafts Board will not be charged any fee to register Government trademarks of genuineness and quality for Indian products or for products of particular Indian tribes and groups.

Remedies; Infringement;
Innocent Infringement by Printers and Publishers

1114. — (1) Any person who shall, without the consent of the registrant—

(*a*) use in commerce any reproduction, counterfeit, copy, or colorable imitation of a registered mark in connection with the sale, offering for sale, distribution, or advertising of any goods or services on or in connection with which such use is likely to cause confusion, or to cause mistake, or to deceive; or

(b) reproduce, counterfeit, copy, or colorably imitate a registered mark and apply such reproduction, counterfeit, copy, or colorable imitation to labels, signs, prints, packages, wrappers, receptacles or advertisements intended to be used in commerce upon or in connection with the sale, offering for sale, distribution, or advertising of goods or services on or in connection with which such use is likely to cause confusion, or to cause mistake, or to deceive, shall be liable in a civil action by the registrant for the remedies hereinafter provided. Under subsection (b) hereof, the registrant shall not be entitled to recover profits or damages unless the acts have been committed with knowledge that such imitation is intended to be used to cause confusion, or to cause mistake, or to deceive.

As used in this paragraph, the term "any person" includes the United States, all agencies and instrumentalities thereof, and all individuals, firms, corporations, or other persons acting for the United States and with the authorization and consent of the United States, and any State, any instrumentality of a State, and any officer or employee of a State or instrumentality of a State acting in his or her official capacity. The United States, all agencies and instrumentalities thereof, and all individuals, firms, corporations, other persons acting for the United States and with the authorization and consent of the United States, and any State, and any such instrumentality, officer, or employee, shall be subject to the provisions of this chapter in the same manner and to the same extent as any non-governmental entity.

(2) Notwithstanding any other provision of this Act, the remedies given to the owner of a right infringed under this chapter or to a person bringing an action under section 1125 (a) or (d) of this title shall be limited as follows:

(A) Where an infringer or violator is engaged solely in the business of printing the mark or violating matter for others and establishes that he or she was an innocent infringer or innocent violator, the owner of the right infringed or person bringing the action under section 1125 (a) of this title shall be entitled as against such infringer or violator only to an injunction against future printing.

(B) Where the infringement or violation complained of is contained in or is part of paid advertising matter in a newspaper, magazine, or other similar periodical or in an electronic communication as defined in section 2510 (12) of title 18, the remedies of the owner of the right infringed or person bringing the action under section 1125 (a) of this title as against the publisher or distributor of such newspaper, magazine, or other similar periodical or electronic communication shall be limited to an injunction against the presentation of such advertising matter in future issues of such newspapers, magazines, or other similar periodicals or in future transmissions of such electronic communications. The limitations of this subparagraph shall apply only to innocent infringers and innocent violators.

(C) Injunctive relief shall not be available to the owner of the right infringed or person bringing the action under section 1125 (a) of this title with respect to an issue of a newspaper, magazine, or other similar periodical or an electronic communication containing infringing matter or violating matter where restraining the dissemination of such infringing matter or violating matter in any particular issue of such periodical or in an electronic communication would delay the delivery of such issue or transmission of such electronic communication after the regular time for such delivery or transmission, and such delay would be due to the method by which publication and distribution of such periodical or transmission of such electronic communication is customarily conducted in accordance with sound business practice, and not due to any method or device adopted to evade this section or to prevent or delay the issuance of an injunction or restraining order with respect to such infringing matter or violating matter.

(D) (i) (I) A domain name registrar, a domain name registry, or other domain name registration authority that takes any action described under clause (ii) affecting a domain name shall not be liable for monetary relief or, except as provided in subclause (II), for injunctive relief, to any person for such action, regardless of whether the domain name is finally determined to infringe or dilute the mark.

(II) A domain name registrar, domain name registry, or other domain name registration authority described in subclause (I) may be subject to injunctive relief only if such registrar, registry, or other registration authority has—

(*aa*) not expeditiously deposited with a court, in which an action has been filed regarding the disposition of the domain name, documents sufficient for the court to establish the court's control and authority regarding the disposition of the registration and use of the domain name;

(*bb*) transferred, suspended, or otherwise modified the domain name during the pendency of the action, except upon order of the court; or

(*cc*) willfully failed to comply with any such court order.

(ii) An action referred to under clause (i) (I) is any action of refusing to register, removing from registration, transferring, temporarily disabling, or permanently canceling a domain name—

(I) in compliance with a court order under section 1125 (*d*) of this title; or

(II) in the implementation of a reasonable policy by such registrar, registry, or authority prohibiting the registration of a domain name that is identical to, confusingly similar to, or dilutive of another's mark.

(iii) A domain name registrar, a domain name registry, or other domain name registration authority shall not be liable for damages under this section for the registration or maintenance of a domain name for another absent a showing of bad faith intent to profit from such registration or maintenance of the domain name.

(iv) If a registrar, registry, or other registration authority takes an action described under clause (ii) based on a knowing and material misrepresentation by any other person that a domain name is identical to, confusingly similar to, or dilutive of a mark, the person making the knowing and material misrepresentation shall be liable for any damages, including costs and attorney's fees, incurred by the domain name registrant as a result of such action. The court may also grant injunctive relief to the domain name registrant, including the reactivation of the domain name or the transfer of the domain name to the domain name registrant.

(v) A domain name registrant whose domain name has been suspended, disabled, or transferred under a policy described under clause (ii) (II) may, upon notice to the mark owner, file a civil action to establish that the registration or use of the domain name by such registrant is not unlawful under this chapter. The court may grant injunctive relief to the domain name registrant, including the reactivation of the domain name or transfer of the domain name to the domain name registrant.

(E) As used in this paragraph—

(i) the term "violator" means a person who violates section 1125 (a) of this title; and

(ii) the term "violating matter" means matter that is the subject of a violation under section 1125 (a) of this title.

Registration on Principal Register as Evidence of Exclusive Right to Use Mark; Defenses

Evidentiary Value; Defenses

1115. — (a) Any registration issued under the Act of March 3, 1881, or the Act of February 20, 1905, or of a mark registered on the principal register provided by this chapter and owned by a party to an action shall be admissible in evidence and shall be *prima facie* evidence of the validity of the registered mark and of the registration of the mark, of the registrant's ownership of the mark, and of the registrant's exclusive right to use the registered mark in commerce on or in connection with the goods or services specified in the registration subject to any conditions or limitations stated therein, but shall not preclude another person from proving any legal or equitable defense or defect, including those set forth in subsection (b), which might have been asserted if such mark had not been registered.

Incontestability; Defenses

(b) To the extent that the right to use the registered mark has become incontestable under section 1065 of this title, the registration shall be conclusive evidence of the validity of the registered mark and of the registration of the mark, of the registrant's ownership of the mark, and of the registrant's exclusive right to use the registered mark in commerce. Such conclusive evidence shall relate to the exclusive right to use the mark on or in connection with the goods or services specified in the affidavit filed under the provisions of section 1065 of this title, or in the renewal application filed under the provisions of section 1059 of this title if the goods or services specified in the renewal are fewer in number, subject to any conditions or limitations in the registration or in such affidavit or renewal application. Such conclusive evidence of the right to use the registered mark shall be subject to proof of infringement as defined in section 1114 of this title, and shall be subject to the following defenses or defects:

(1) That the registration or the incontestable right to use the mark was obtained fraudulently; or

(2) That the mark has been abandoned by the registrant; or

(3) That the registered mark is being used, by or with the permission of the registrant or a person in privity with the registrant, so as to misrepresent the source of the goods or services on or in connection with which the mark is used; or

(4) That the use of the name, term, or device charged to be an infringement is a use, otherwise than as a mark, of the party's individual name in his own business, or of the individual name of anyone in privity with such party, or of a term or device which is descriptive of and used fairly and in good faith only to describe the goods or services of such party, or their geographic origin; or

(5) That the mark whose use by a party is charged as an infringement was adopted without knowledge of the registrant's prior use and has been continuously used by such party or those in privity with him from a date prior to

(A) the date of constructive use of the mark established pursuant to section 1057 (c) of this title,

(B) the registration of the mark under this chapter if the application for registration is filed before the effective date of the Trademark Law Revision Act of 1988, or

(C) publication of the registered mark under subsection (c) of section 1062 of this title: Provided, however, That this defense or defect shall apply only for the area in which such continuous prior use is proved; or

(6) That the mark whose use is charged as an infringement was registered and used prior to the registration under this chapter or publication under subsection (c) of section 1062 of this title of the registered mark of the registrant, and not abandoned: Provided, however, That this defense or defect shall apply only for the area in which the mark was used prior to such registration or such publication of the registrant's mark; or

(7) That the mark has been or is being used to violate the antitrust laws of the United States; or

(8) That the mark is functional; or

(9) That equitable principles, including laches, estoppel, and acquiescence, are applicable.

Injunctive Relief

Jurisdiction; Service

1116. — (a) The several courts vested with jurisdiction of civil actions arising under this chapter shall have power to grant injunctions, according to the principles of equity and upon such terms as the court may deem reasonable, to prevent the violation of any right of the registrant of a mark registered in the Patent and Trademark Office or to prevent a violation under subsection (a), (c), or (d) of section 1125 of this title. Any such injunction may include a provision directing the defendant to file with the court and serve on the plaintiff within thirty days after the service on the defendant of such injunction, or such extended period as the court may direct, a report in writing under oath setting forth in detail the manner and form in which the defendant has complied with the injunction. Any such injunction granted upon hearing, after notice to the defendant, by any district court of the United States, may be served on the parties against whom such injunction is granted anywhere in the United States where they may be found, and shall be operative and may be enforced by proceedings to punish for contempt, or otherwise, by the court by which such injunction was granted, or by any other United States district court in whose jurisdiction the defendant may be found.

Transfer of Certified Copies of Court Papers

(*b*) The said courts shall have jurisdiction to enforce said injunction, as provided in this chapter, as fully as if the injunction had been granted by the district court in which it is sought to be enforced. The clerk of the court or judge granting the injunction shall, when required to do so by the court before which application to enforce said injunction is made, transfer without delay to said court a certified copy of all papers on file in his office upon which said injunction was granted.

Notice to Director

(*c*) It shall be the duty of the clerks of such courts within one month after the filing of any action, suit, or proceeding involving a mark registered under the provisions of this Act to give notice thereof in writing to the Director setting forth in order so far as known the names and addresses of the litigants and the designating number or numbers of the registration or registrations upon which the action, suit, or proceeding has been brought, and in the event any other registration be subsequently included in the action, suit, or proceeding by amendment, answer, or other pleading, the clerk shall give like notice thereof to the Director, and within one month after the judgment is entered or an appeal is taken the clerk of the court shall give notice thereof to the Director, and it shall be the duty of the Director on receipt of such notice forthwith to endorse the same upon the file wrapper of the said registration or registrations and to incorporate the same as a part of the contents of said file wrapper.

Civil Actions Arising Out of Use of Counterfeit Marks

(*d*) (1) (*A*) In the case of a civil action arising under section 1114 (1) (*a*) of this title or section 220506 of title 36, with respect to a violation that consists of using a counterfeit mark in connection with the sale, offering for sale, or distribution of goods or services, the court may, upon *ex parte* application, grant an order under subsection (*a*) of this section pursuant to this subsection providing for the seizure of goods and counterfeit marks involved in such violation and the means of making such marks, and records documenting the manufacturer, sale, or receipt of things involved in such violation.

(B) As used in this subsection the term "counterfeit mark" means—

(i) a counterfeit of a mark that is registered on the principal register in the United States Patent and Trademark Office for such goods or services sold, offered for sale, or distributed and that is in use, whether or not the person against whom relief is sought knew such mark was so registered; or

(ii) a spurious designation that is identical with, or substantially indistinguishable from, a designation as to which the remedies of this chapter are made available by reason of section 220506 of title 36;

but such term does not include any mark or designation used on or in connection with goods or services of which the manufacture or producer was, at the time of the manufacture or production in question authorized to use the mark or designation for the type of goods or services so manufactured or produced, by the holder of the right to use such mark or designation.

(2) The court shall not receive an application under this subsection unless the applicant has given such notice of the application as is reasonable under the circumstances to the United States attorney for the judicial district in which such order is sought. Such attorney may participate in the proceedings arising under such application if such proceedings may affect evidence of an offense against the United States. The court may deny such application if the court determines that the public interest in a potential prosecution so requires.

(3) The application for an order under this subsection shall—

(A) be based on an affidavit or the verified complaint establishing facts sufficient to support the findings of fact and conclusions of law required for such order; and

(B) contain the additional information required by paragraph (5) of this subsection to be set forth in such order.

(4) The court shall not grant such an application unless—

(A) the person obtaining an order under this subsection provides the security determined adequate by the court for the payment of such damages as any person may be entitled to recover as a result of a wrongful seizure or wrongful attempted seizure under this subsection; and

(B) the court finds that it clearly appears from specific facts that—

(i) an order other than an *ex parte* seizure order is not adequate to achieve the purposes of section 1114 of this title;

(ii) the applicant has not publicized the requested seizure;

(iii) the applicant is likely to succeed in showing that the person against whom seizure would be ordered used a counterfeit mark in connection with the sale, offering for sale, or distribution of goods or services;

(iv) an immediate and irreparable injury will occur if such seizure is not ordered;

(v) the matter to be seized will be located at the place identified in the application;

(vi) the harm to the applicant of denying the application outweighs the harm to the legitimate interests of the person against whom seizure would be ordered of granting the application; and

(vii) the person against whom seizure would be ordered, or persons acting in concert with such person, would destroy, move, hide, or otherwise make such matter inaccessible to the court, if the applicant were to proceed on notice to such person.

(5) An order under this subsection shall set forth—

(A) the findings of fact and conclusions of law required for the order;

(B) a particular description of the matter to be seized, and a description of each place at which such matter is to be seized;

(C) the time period, which shall end not later than seven days after the date on which such order is issued, during which the seizure is to be made;

(D) the amount of security required to be provided under this subsection; and

(E) a date for the hearing required under paragraph (10) of this subsection.

(6) The court shall take appropriate action to protect the person against whom an order under this subsection is directed from publicity, by or at the behest of the plaintiff, about such order and any seizure under such order.

(7) Any materials seized under this subsection shall be taken into the custody of the court. The court shall enter an appropriate protective order with respect to discovery by the applicant of any records that have been seized. The protective order shall provide for appropriate procedures to assure that confidential information contained in such records is not improperly disclosed to the applicant.

(8) An order under this subsection, together with the supporting documents, shall be sealed until the person against whom the order is directed has an opportunity to contest such order, except that any person against whom such order is issued shall have access to such order and supporting documents after the seizure has been carried out.

(9) The court shall order that service of a copy of the order under this subsection shall be made by a Federal law enforcement officer (such as a United States marshal or an officer or agent of the United States Customs Service, Secret Service, Federal Bureau of Investigation, or Post Office) or may be made by a State or local law enforcement officer, who, upon making service, shall carry out the seizure under the order. The court shall issue orders, when appropriate, to protect the defendant from undue damage from the disclosure of trade secrets or other confidential information during the course of the seizure, including, when appropriate, orders restricting the access of the applicant (or any agent or employee of the applicant) to such secrets or information.

(10) (A) The court shall hold a hearing, unless waived by all the parties, on the date set by the court in the order of seizure. That date shall be not sooner than ten days after the order is issued and not later than fifteen days after the order is issued, unless the applicant for the order shows good cause for another date or unless the party against whom such order is directed consents to another date for such hear-

ing. At such hearing the party obtaining the order shall have the burden to prove that the facts supporting findings of fact and conclusions of law necessary to support such order are still in effect. If that party fails to meet that burden, the seizure order shall be dissolved or modified appropriately.

(B) In connection with a hearing under this paragraph, the court may make such orders modifying the time limits for discovery under the Rules of Civil Procedure as may be necessary to prevent the frustration of the purposes of such hearing.

(11) A person who suffers damage by reason of a wrongful seizure under this subsection has a cause of action against the applicant for the order under which such seizure was made, and shall be entitled to recover such relief as may be appropriate, including damages for lost profits, cost of materials, loss of good will, and punitive damages in instances where the seizure was sought in bad faith, and, unless the court finds extenuating circumstances, to recover a reasonable attorney's fee. The court in its discretion may award prejudgment interest on relief recovered under this paragraph, at an annual interest rate established under section 6621 (a) (2) of title 26, commencing on the date of service of the claimant's pleading setting forth the claim under this paragraph and ending on the date such recovery is granted, or for such shorter time as the court deems appropriate.

Recovery for Violation of Rights
Profits, Damages and Costs; Attorney Fees

1117. — (a) When a violation of any right of the registrant of a mark registered in the Patent and Trademark Office, a violation under section 1125 (a) or (d) of this title, or a willful violation under section 1125 (c) of this title, shall have been established in any civil action arising under this chapter, the plaintiff shall be entitled, subject to the provisions of sections 1111 and 1114 of this title, and subject to the principles of equity, to recover

(1) defendant's profits,

(2) any damages sustained by the plaintiff, and

(3) the costs of the action. The court shall assess such profits and damages or cause the same to be assessed under its direction. In assessing profits the plaintiff shall be required to prove defendant's sales only; defendant must prove all elements of cost or deduction claimed. In assessing damages the court may enter judgment, according to the circumstances of the case, for any sum above the amount found as actual damages, not exceeding three times such amount. If the court shall find that the amount of the recovery based on profits is either inadequate or excessive the court may in its discretion enter judgment for such sum as the court shall find to be just, according to the circumstances of the case. Such sum in either of the above circumstances shall constitute compensation and not a penalty. The court in exceptional cases may award reasonable attorney fees to the prevailing party.

Treble Damages for Use of Counterfeit Mark

(b) In assessing damages under subsection (a) of this section, the court shall, unless the court finds extenuating circumstances, enter judgment for three times such profits or damages, whichever is greater, together with a reasonable attorney's fee, in the case of any violation of section 1114 (1) (a) of this title or section 220506 of title 36 that consists of intentionally using a mark or designation, knowing such mark or designation is a counterfeit mark (as defined in section 1116 (d) of this title), in connection with the sale, offering for sale, or distribution of goods or services. In such cases, the court may in its discretion award prejudgment interest on such amount at an annual interest rate established under section 6621 (a) (2) of title 26, commencing on the date of the service of the claimant's pleadings setting forth the claim for such entry and ending on the date such entry is made, or for such shorter time as the court deems appropriate.

Statutory Damages for Use of Counterfeit Marks

(c) In a case involving the use of a counterfeit mark (as defined in section 1116 (d) of this title in connection with the sale, offering for sale, or distribution of goods or services, the plaintiff may elect, at any time before final judgment is rendered by the trial court, to recover, instead of actual damages and profits under subsection (*a*), an award of statutory damages for any such use in connection with the sale, offering for sale, or distribution of goods or services in the amount of—

(1) not less than \$ 500 or more than \$ 100, 000 per counterfeit mark per type of goods or services sold, offered for sale, or distributed, as the court considers just; or

(2) if the court finds that the use of the counterfeit mark was willful, not more than \$ 1, 000, 000 per counterfeit mark per type of goods or services sold, offered for sale, or distributed, as the court considers just.

Statutory Damages for Violation of Section 1125 (*d*) (1)

(*d*) In a case involving a violation of section 1125 (*d*) (1) of this title, the plaintiff may elect, at any time before final judgment is rendered by the trial court, to recover, instead of actual damages and profits, an award of statutory damages in the amount of not less than \$ 1, 000 and not more than \$ 100, 000 per domain name, as the court considers just.

Destruction of Infringing Articles

1118. In any action arising under this Act, in which a violation of any right of the registrant of a mark registered in the Patent and Trademark Office, a violation under section 1125 (*a*) of this title, or a willful violation under section 1125 (*c*) of this title, shall have been established, the court may order that all labels, signs, prints, packages, wrappers, receptacles, and advertisements in the possession of the defendant, bearing the registered mark or, in the case of a violation of section 1125 (*a*) of this title or a willful violation under section 1125 (*c*) of this title, the word, term, name, symbol, device, combination thereof, designation, description, or representation that is the subject of the violation, or any reproduction, counterfeit, copy, or colorable imitation thereof, and all plates, molds, matrices, and other means of making the same, shall be delivered up and destroyed. The party seeking an order under this section for destruction of articles seized under section 1116 (*d*) of this title shall give ten days' notice to the United States attorney for the judicial

329

district in which such order is sought (unless good cause is shown for lesser notice) and such United States attorney may, if such destruction may affect evidence of an offense against the United States, seek a hearing on such destruction or participate in any hearing otherwise to be held with respect to such destruction.

Power of Court Over Registration

1119. In any action involving a registered mark the court may determine the right to registration, order the cancellation of registrations, in whole or in part, restore canceled registrations, and otherwise rectify the register with respect to the registrations of any party to the action. Decrees and orders shall be certified by the court to the Director, who shall make appropriate entry upon the records of the Patent and Trademark Office, and shall be controlled thereby.

Civil Liability for False or Fraudulent Registration

1120. Any person who shall procure registration in the Patent and Trademark Office of a mark by a false or fraudulent declaration or representation, oral or in writing, or by any false means, shall be liable in a civil action by any person injured thereby for any damages sustained in consequence thereof.

Jurisdiction of Federal Courts; State and Local Requirements that Registered Trademarks be Altered or Displayed Differently; Prohibition

1121. — (a) The district and territorial courts of the United States shall have original jurisdiction and the courts of appeal of the United States (other than the United States Court of Appeals for the Federal Circuit) shall have appellate jurisdiction, of all actions arising under this chapter, without regard to the amount in controversy or to diversity or lack of diversity of the citizenship of the parties.

(b) No State or other jurisdiction of the United States or any political subdivision or any agency thereof may require alteration of a registered mark, or require that additional trademarks, service marks, trade names, or corporate names that may be associated with or incorporated into the registered mark be displayed in the mark in a manner differing from the display of such additional trademarks, service marks, trade names, or corporate names contemplated by the registered mark as exhibited in the certificate of registration issued by the United States Patent and Trademark Office.

1121a. Transferred

Liability of United States and States,
and Instrumentalities and Officials Thereof

Waiver of Sovereign Immunity by the United States

1122. — (a) The United States, all agencies and instrumentalities thereof, and all individuals, firms, corporations, other persons acting for the United States and with the authorization and consent of the United States, shall not be immune from suit in Federal or State court by any person, including any governmental or nongovernmental entity, for any violation under this chapter.

Waiver of Sovereign Immunity by States

(b) Any State, instrumentality of a State or any officer or employee of a State or instrumentality of a State acting in his or her official capacity, shall not be immune, under the eleventh amendment of the Constitution of the United States or under any other doctrine of sovereign immunity, from suit in Federal court by any person, including any governmental or nongovernmental entity for any violation under this chapter.

Remedies

(c) *In a suit described in subsection (a) or (b) of this section for a violation described therein, remedies (including remedies both at law and in equity) are available for the violation to the same extent as such remedies are available for such a violation in a suit against any person other than the United States or any agency or instrumentality thereof, or any individual, firm, corporation, or other person acting for the United States and with authorization and consent of the United States, or a State, instrumentality of a State, or officer or employee of a State or instrumentality of a State acting in his or her official capacity. Such remedies include injunctive relief under section 1116 of this title, actual damages, profits, costs and attorney's fees under section*

1117 *of this title, destruction of infringing articles under section* 1118 *of this title, the remedies provided for under sections* 1114, 1119, 1120, 1124 *and* 1125 *of this title, and for any other remedies provided under this chapter.*

Rules and Regulations for Conduct of Proceedings in Patent and Trademark Office

1123. The Director shall make rules and regulations, not inconsistent with law, for the conduct of proceedings in the Patent and Trademark Office under this chapter.

Importation of Goods Bearing Infringing Marks or Names Forbidden

1124. Except as provided in subsection (*d*) of section 1526 of title 19, no article of imported merchandise which shall copy or simulate the name of any domestic manufacture, or manufacturer, or trader, or of any manufacturer or trader located in any foreign country which, by treaty, convention, or law affords similar privileges to citizens of the United States, or which shall copy or simulate a trademark registered in accordance with the provisions of this chapter or shall bear a name or mark calculated to induce the public to believe that the article is manufactured in the United States, or that it is manufactured in any foreign country or locality other than the country or locality in which it is in fact manufactured, shall be admitted to entry at any customhouse of the United States; and, in order to aid the officers of the customs in enforcing this prohibition, any domestic manufacturer or trader, and any foreign manufacturer or trader, who is entitled under the provisions of a treaty, convention, declaration, or agreement between the United States and any foreign country to the advantages afforded by law to citizens of the United States in respect to trademarks and commercial names, may require his name and residence, and the name of the locality in which his goods are manufactured, and a copy of the certificate of registration of his trademark, issued in accordance with the provisions of this chapter, to be recorded in books which shall be kept for this purpose in the Department of the Treasury, under such regulations as the Secretary of the Treasury shall prescribe, and may furnish to the Department facsimiles of his name, the name of the locality in which his goods are manufactured, or of his registered trademark, and thereupon the Secretary of the Treasury shall cause one or more copies of the same to be transmitted to each collector or other proper officer of customs.

False Designations of Origin, False Descriptions, and Dilution Forbidden

Civil Action

1125. — (*a*) (1) Any person who, on or in connection with any goods or services, or any container for goods, uses in commerce any word, term, name, symbol, or device, or any combination thereof, or any false designation of origin, false or misleading description of fact, or false or misleading representation of fact, which—

(*A*) is likely to cause confusion, or to cause mistake, or to deceive as to the affiliation, connection, or association of such person with another person, or as to the origin, sponsorship, or approval of his or her goods, services, or commercial activities by another person, or

(*B*) in commercial advertising or promotion, misrepresents the nature, characteristics, qualities, or geographic origin of his or her or another person's goods, services, or commercial activities,

shall be liable in a civil action by any person who believes that he or she is or is likely to be damaged by such act.

(2) As used in this subsection, the term "any person" includes any State, instrumentality of a State or employee of a State or instrumentality of a State acting in his or her official capacity. Any State, and any such instrumentality, officer, or employee, shall be subject to the provisions of this chapter in the same manner and to the same extent as any nongovernmental entity.

(3) In a civil action for trade dress infringement under this chapter for trade dress not registered on the principal register, the person who asserts trade dress protection has the burden of proving that the matter sought to be protected is not func-

tional.

Importation

(*b*) Any goods marked or labeled in contravention of the provisions of this section shall not be imported into the United States or admitted to entry at any customhouse of the United States. The owner, importer, or consignee of goods refused entry at any customhouse under this section may have any recourse by protest or appeal that is given under the customs revenue laws or may have the remedy given by this chapter in cases involving goods refused entry or seized.

Remedies for Dilution of Famous Marks

(*c*) (1) The owner of a famous mark shall be entitled, subject to the principles of equity and upon such terms as the court deems reasonable, to an injunction against another person's commercial use in commerce of a mark or trade name, if such use begins after the mark has become famous and causes dilution of the distinctive quality of the mark, and to obtain such other relief as is provided in this subsection. In determining whether a mark is distinctive and famous, a court may consider factors such as, but not limited to—

(*A*) the degree of inherent or acquired distinctiveness of the mark;

(*B*) the duration and extent of use of the mark in connection with the goods or services with which the mark is used;

(*C*) the duration and extent of advertising and publicity of the mark;

(*D*) the geographical extent of the trading area in which the mark is used;

(*E*) the channels of trade for the goods or services with which the mark is used;

(*F*) the degree of recognition of the mark in the trading areas and channels of trade used by the marks' owner and the person against whom the injunction is sought;

(*G*) the nature and extent of use of the same or similar marks by third parties; and

(*H*) whether the mark was registered under the Act of March 3, 1881, or the Act of February 20, 1905, or on the principal register.

(2) In an action brought under this subsection, the owner of the famous mark shall be entitled only to injunctive relief as set forth in section 1116 of this title unless the person against whom the injunction is sought willfully intended to trade on the owner's reputation or to cause dilution of the famous mark. If such willful intent is proven, the owner of the famous mark shall also be entitled to the remedies set forth in sections 1117 (*a*) and 1118 of this title, subject to the discretion of the court and the principles of equity.

(3) The ownership by a person of a valid registration under the Act of March 3, 1881, or the Act of February 20, 1905, or on the principal register shall be a complete bar to an action against that person, with respect to that mark, that is brought by another person under the common law or a statute of a State and that seeks to prevent dilution of the distinctiveness of a mark, label, or form of advertisement.

(4) The following shall not be actionable under this section:

(*A*) Fair use of a famous mark by another person in comparative commercial advertising or promotion to identify the competing goods or services of the owner of the famous mark.

(*B*) Noncommercial use of a mark.

(*C*) All forms of news reporting and news commentary.

Cyberpiracy Prevention

(*d*)(1)(*A*) A person shall be liable in a civil action by the owner of a mark, including a personal name which is protected as a mark under this section, if, without regard to the goods or services of the parties, that person—

(i) has a bad faith intent to profit from that mark, including a personal name which is protected as a mark under this section; and

(ii) registers, traffics in, or uses a domain name that—

(I) in the case of a mark that is distinctive at the time of registration of the domain name, is identical or confusingly similar to that mark;

(II) in the case of a famous mark that is famous at the time of registration of the domain name, is identical or confusingly similar to or dilutive of that mark; or

(III) is a trademark, word, or name protected by reason of section 706 of title 18 or section 220506 of title 36.

(B)(i) In determining whether a person has a bad faith intent described under subparagraph (A), a court may consider factors such as, but not limited to—

(I) the trademark or other intellectual property rights of the person, if any, in the domain name;

(II) the extent to which the domain name consists of the legal name of the person or a name that is otherwise commonly used to identify that person;

(III) the person's prior use, if any, of the domain name in connection with the *bona fide* offering of any goods or services;

(IV) the person's *bona fide* noncommercial or fair use of the mark in a site accessible under the domain name;

(V) the person's intent to divert consumers from the mark owner's online location to a site accessible under the domain name that could harm the goodwill represented by the mark, either for commercial gain or with the intent to tarnish or disparage the mark, by creating a likelihood of confusion as to the source, sponsorship, affiliation, or endorsement of the site;

(VI) the person's offer to transfer, sell, or otherwise assign the domain name to the mark owner or any third party for financial gain without having used, or having an intent to use, the domain name in the *bona fide* offering of any goods or services, or the person's prior conduct indicating a pattern of such conduct;

(VII) the person's provision of material and misleading false contact information when applying for the registration of the domain name, the person's intentional failure to maintain accurate contact information, or the person's prior conduct indicating a pattern of such conduct;

(VIII) the person's registration or acquisition of multiple domain names which the person knows are identical or confusingly similar to marks of others that are distinctive at the time of registration of such domain names, or dilutive of famous marks of others that are famous at the time of registration of such domain names, without regard to the goods or services of the parties; and

(IX) the extent to which the mark incorporated in the person's domain name registration is or is not distinctive and famous within the meaning of subsection (c) (1) of subsection (c) (1) of this section.

(ii) Bad faith intent described under subparagraph (A) shall not be found in any case in which the court determines that the person believed and had reasonable grounds to believe that the use of the domain name was a fair use or otherwise lawful.

(C) In any civil action involving the registration, trafficking, or use of a domain name under this paragraph, a court may order the forfeiture or cancellation of the domain name or the transfer of the domain name to the owner of the mark.

(D) A person shall be liable for using a domain name under subparagraph (A) only if that person is the domain name registrant or that registrant's authorized licensee.

(E) As used in this paragraph, the term "traffics in" refers to transactions that include, but are not limited to, sales, purchases, loans, pledges, licenses, exchanges of currency, and any other transfer for consideration or receipt in exchange for consideration.

(2) (A) The owner of a mark may file an *in rem* civil action against a domain name in the judicial district in which the domain name registrar, domain name registry, or other domain name authority that registered or assigned the domain name is located if—

(i) the domain name violates any right of the owner of a mark registered in the Patent and Trademark Office, or protected under subsection (a) or (c) of this section; and

(ii) the court finds that the owner—

(I) is not able to obtain*in personam* jurisdiction over a person who would have been a defendant in a civil action under paragraph (1) ; or

(II) through due diligence was not able to find a person who would have been a defendant in a civil action under paragraph (1) by—

(*aa*) sending a notice of the alleged violation and intent to proceed under this paragraph to the registrant of the domain name at the postal and e−mail address provided by the registrant to the registrar; and

(*bb*) publishing notice of the action as the court may direct promptly after filing the action.

(B) The actions under subparagraph (A) (ii) shall constitute service of process.

(C) In an *in rem* action under this paragraph, a domain name shall be deemed to have its *situs* in the judicial district in which—

(i) the domain name registrar, registry, or other domain name authority that registered or assigned the domain name is located; or

(ii) documents sufficient to establish control and authority regarding the disposition of the registration and use of the domain name are deposited with the court.

(D) (i) The remedies in an *in rem* action under this paragraph shall be limited to a court order for the forfeiture or cancellation of the domain name or the transfer of the domain name to the owner of the mark. Upon receipt of written notification of a filed, stamped copy of a complaint filed by the owner of a mark in a United States district court under this paragraph, the domain name registrar, domain name registry, or other domain name authority shall—

(I) expeditiously deposit with the court documents sufficient to establish the court's control and authority regarding the disposition of the registration and use of the domain name to the court; and

(II) not transfer, suspend, or otherwise modify the domain name during the pendency of the action, except upon order of the court.

(ii) The domain name registrar or registry or other domain name authority shall not be liable for injunctive or monetary relief under this paragraph except in the case of bad faith or reckless disregard, which includes a willful failure to comply with any such court order.

(3) The civil action established under paragraph (1) and the *in rem* action established under paragraph (2), and any remedy available under either such action, shall be in addition to any other civil action or remedy otherwise applicable.

(4) The *in rem* jurisdiction established under paragraph (2) shall be in addition to any other jurisdiction that otherwise exists, whether *in rem* or *in personam*.

International Conventions

Register of Marks Communicated by International Bureaus

1126. — (a) The Director shall keep a register of all marks communicated to him by the international bureaus provided for by the conventions for the protection of industrial property, trademarks, trade and commercial names, and the repression of unfair competition to which the United States is or may become a party, and upon the payment of the fees required by such conventions and the fees required in this chapter may place the marks so communicated upon such register. This register shall show a facsimile of the mark or trade or commercial name; the name, citizenship, and address of the registrant; the number, date, and place of the first registration of the mark, including the dates on which application for such registration was filed and granted and the term of such registration; a list of goods or services to which the mark is applied as shown by the registration in the country of origin, and such other data as may be useful concerning the mark. This register shall be a continuation of the register provided in section 1 (a) of the Act of March 19, 1920.

Benefits of Section to Persons Whose Country of Origin is Party to Convention or Treaty

(b) Any person whose country of origin is a party to any convention or treaty relating to trademarks, trade or commercial names, or the repression of unfair competition, to which the United States is also a party, or extends reciprocal rights to nationals of the United States by law, shall be entitled to the benefits of this section under the conditions expressed herein to the extent necessary to give effect to any provision of such convention, treaty or reciprocal law, in addition to the rights to which any owner of a mark is otherwise entitled by this chapter.

Prior Registration in Country of Origin; Country of Origin Defined

(c) No registration of a mark in the United States by a person described in subsection (b) of this section shall be granted until such mark has been registered in the country of origin of the applicant, unless the applicant alleges use in commerce.

For the purposes of this section, the country of origin of the applicant is the country in which he has a *bona fide* and effective industrial or commercial establishment, or if he has not such an establishment the country in which he is domiciled, or if he has not a domicile in any of the countries described in subsection (b) of this section, the country of which he is a national.

Right of Priority

(d) An application for registration of a mark under sections 1051, 1053, 1054, or 1091 of this title or under subsection (e) of this section, filed by a person described in subsection (b) of this section who has previously duly filed an application for registration of the same mark in one of the countries described in subsection (b) of this section shall be accorded the same force and effect as would be accorded to the same application if filed in the United States on the same date on which the application was first filed in such foreign country: Provided, that—

(1) the application in the United States is filed within six months from the date on which the application was first filed in the foreign country;

(2) the application conforms as nearly as practicable to the requirements of this chapter, including a statement that the applicant has a *bona fide* intention to use the mark in commerce;

(3) the rights acquired by third parties before the date of the filing of the first application in the foreign country shall in no way be affected by a registration obtained on an application filed under this subsection;

(4) nothing in this subsection shall entitle the owner of a registration granted under this section to sue for acts committed prior to the date on which his mark was registered in this country unless the registration is based on use in commerce.

In like manner and subject to the same conditions and requirements, the right provided in this section may be based upon a subsequent regularly filed application in the same foreign country, instead of the first filed foreign application: Provided, That any foreign application filed prior to such subsequent application has been withdrawn, abandoned, or otherwise disposed of, without having been laid open to public inspection and without leaving any rights outstanding, and has not served, nor thereafter shall serve, as a basis for claiming a right of priority.

Registration on Principal or Supplemental Register;

Copy of Foreign Registration

(e) A mark duly registered in the country of origin of the foreign applicant may be registered on the principal register if eligible, otherwise on the supplemental register in this chapter provided. Such applicant shall submit, within such time period as may be prescribed by the Director, a true copy, a photocopy, a certification, or a certified copy of the registration in the country of origin of the applicant. The application must state the applicant's *bona fide* intention to use the mark in commerce, but use in commerce shall not be required prior to registration.

Domestic Registration Independent of Foreign Registration

(f) The registration of a mark under the provisions of subsections (c)、(d), and (e) of this section by a person described in subsection (b) of this section shall be independent of the registration in the country of origin and the duration, validity, or transfer in the United States of such registration shall be governed by the provisions of this chapter.

Trade or Commercial Names of Foreign Nationals Protected Without Registration

(g) Trade names or commercial names of persons described in subsection (b) of this section shall be protected without the obligation of filing or registration whether or not they form parts of marks.

Protection of Foreign Nationals Against Unfair Competition

(*h*) Any person designated in subsection (*b*) of this section as entitled to the benefits and subject to the provisions of this chapter shall be entitled to effective protection against unfair competition, and the remedies provided herein for infringement of marks shall be available so far as they may be appropriate in repressing acts of unfair competition.

Citizens or Residents of United States Entitled to Benefits of Section

(*i*) Citizens or residents of the United States shall have the same benefits as are granted by this section to persons described in subsection (*b*) of this section.

Construction and Definitions;
Intent of Chapter

1127. In the construction of this chapter, unless the contrary is plainly apparent from the context—

The United States includes and embraces all territory which is under its jurisdiction and control.

The word "commerce" means all commerce which may lawfully be regulated by Congress.

The term "principal register" refers to the register provided for by sections 1051 to 1072 of this title, and the term "supplemental register" refers to the register provided for by sections 1091 to 1096 of this title.

The term "person" and any other word or term used to designate the applicant or other entitled to a benefit or privilege or rendered liable under the provisions of this chapter includes a juristic person as well as a natural person. The term "juristic person" includes a firm, corporation, union, association, or other organization capable of suing and being sued in a court of law.

The term "person" also includes the United States, any agency or instrumentality thereof, or any individual, firm, or corporation acting for the United States and with the authorization and consent of the United States. The United States, any agency or instrumentality thereof, and any individual, firm, or corporation acting for the United States and with the authorization and consent of the United States, shall be subject to the provisions of this chapter in the same manner and to the same extent as any nongovernmental entity.

The term "person" also includes any State, any instrumentality of a State, and any officer or employee of a State or instrumentality of a State acting in his or her official capacity. Any State, and any such instrumentality, officer, or employee, shall be subject to the provisions of this chapter in the same manner and to the same extent as any nongovernmental entity.

The terms "applicant" and "registrant" embrace the legal representatives, predecessors, successors and assigns of such applicant or registrant.

The term "Director" means the Under Secretary of Commerce for Intellectual Property and Director of the United States Patent and Trademark Office.

The term "related company" means any person whose use of a mark is controlled by the owner of the mark with respect to the nature and quality of the goods or services on or in connection with which the mark is used.

The terms "trade name" and "commercial name" mean any name used by a person to identify his or her business or vocation.

The term "trademark" includes any word, name, symbol, or device, or any combination thereof—

(1) used by a person, or

(2) which a person has a *bona fide* intention to use in commerce and applies to register on the principal register established by this chapter,

to identify and distinguish his or her goods, including a unique product, from those manufactured or sold by others and to indicate the source of the goods, even if that source is unknown.

The term "service mark" means any word, name, symbol, or device, or any combination thereof—

(1) used by a person, or

(2) which a person has a *bona fide* intention to use in commerce and applies to register on the principal register established by this chapter,

to identify and distinguish the services of one person, including a unique service, from the services of others and to indicate the source of the services, even if that source is unknown. Titles, character names, and other distinctive features of radio or television programs may be registered as service marks notwithstanding that they, or the programs, may advertise the goods of the sponsor.

The term "certification mark" means any word, name, symbol, or device, or any combination thereof—

(1) used by a person other than its owner, or

(2) which its owner has a *bona fide* intention to permit a person other than the owner to use in commerce and files an application to register on the principal register established by this chapter,

to certify regional or other origin, material, mode of manufacture, quality, accuracy, or other characteristics of such person's goods or services or that the work or labor on the goods or services was performed by members of a union or other organization.

The term "collective mark" means a trademark or service mark—

(1) used by the members of a cooperative, an association, or other collective group or organization, or

(2) which such cooperative, association, or other collective group or organization has a *bona fide* intention to use in commerce and applies to register on the principal register established by this chapter,

and includes marks indicating membership in a union, an association, or other organization.

The term "mark" includes any trademark, service mark, collective mark, or certification mark.

The term "use in commerce" means the *bona fide* use of a mark in the ordinary course of trade, and not made merely to reserve a right in a mark. For purposes of this chapter, a mark shall be deemed to be in use in commerce—

(1) on goods when—

(A) it is placed in any manner on the goods or their containers or the displays associated therewith or on the tags or labels affixed thereto, or if the nature of the goods makes such placement impracticable, then on documents associated with the goods or their sale, and

(B) the goods are sold or transported in commerce, and

(2) on services when it is used or displayed in the sale or advertising of services and the services are rendered in commerce, or the services are rendered in more than one State or in the United States and a foreign country and the person rendering the services is engaged in commerce in connection with the services.

A mark shall be deemed to be "abandoned" if either of the following occurs:

(1) When its use has been discontinued with intent not to resume such use. Intent not to resume may be inferred from circumstances. Nonuse for 3 consecutive years shall be *prima facie* evidence of abandonment. "Use" of a mark means the *bona fide* use of such mark made in the ordinary course of trade, and not made merely to reserve a right in a mark.

(2) When any course of conduct of the owner, including acts of omission as well as commission, causes the mark to become the generic name for the goods or services on or in connection with which it is used or otherwise to lose its significance as a mark. Purchaser motivation shall not be a test for determining abandonment under this paragraph.

The term "dilution" means the lessening of the capacity of a famous mark to identify and distinguish goods or services, regardless of the presence or absence of—

(1) competition between the owner of the famous mark and other parties, or

(2) likelihood of confusion, mistake, or deception.

The term "colorable imitation" includes any mark which so resembles a registered mark as to be likely to cause confusion or mistake or to deceive.

The term "registered mark" means a mark registered in the United States Patent and Trademark Office under this chapter or under the Act of March 3, 1881, or the Act of February 20, 1905, or the Act of March 19, 1920. The phrase "marks registered in the Patent and Trademark Office" means registered marks.

The term "Act of March 3, 1881," "Act of February 20, 1905," or "Act of March 19, 1920," means the respective Act as amended.

A "counterfeit" is a spurious mark which is identical with, or substantially indistinguishable from, a registered mark.

The term "domain name" means any alphanumeric designation which is registered with or assigned by any domain name registrar, domain name registry, or other domain name registration authority as part of an electronic address on the Internet.

The term "Internet" has the meaning given that term in section 230 (f) (1) of the title 47.

Words used in the singular include the plural and vice versa.

The intent of this chapter is to regulate commerce within the control of Congress by making actionable the deceptive and misleading use of marks in such commerce; to protect registered marks used in such commerce from interference by State, or territorial legislation; to protect persons engaged in such commerce against unfair competition; to prevent fraud and deception in such commerce by the use of reproductions, copies, counterfeits, or colorable imitations of registered marks; and to provide rights and remedies stipulated by treaties and conventions respecting trademarks, trade names, and unfair competition entered into between the United States and foreign nations.

National Intellectual Property Law Enforcement Coordination Council

Establishment

1128. — (*a*) There is established the National Intellectual Property Law Enforcement Coordination Council (in this section referred to as the "Council"). The Council shall consist of the following members—

(1) The Under Secretary of Commerce for Intellectual Property and Director of the United States Patent and Trademark Office, who shall serve as co-chair of the Council.

(2) The Assistant Attorney General, Criminal Division, who shall serve as co-chair of the Council.

(3) The Under Secretary of State for Economic and Agricultural Affairs.

(4) The Ambassador, Deputy United States Trade Representative.

(5) The Commissioner of Customs.

(6) The Under Secretary of Commerce for International Trade.

Duties

(b) The Council established in subsection (a) shall coordinate domestic and international intellectual property law enforcement among federal and foreign entities.

Consultation Required

(c) The Council shall consult with the Register of Copyrights on law enforcement matters relating to copyright and related rights and matters.

Non-Derogation

(d) Nothing in this section shall derogate from the duties of the Secretary of State or from the duties of the United States Trade Representative as set forth in section 2171 of title 19, or from the duties and functions of the Register of Copyrights, or otherwise alter current authorities relating to copyright matters.

Report

(e) The Council shall report annually on its coordination activities to the President, and to the Committees on Appropriations and on the Judiciary of the Senate and the House of Representatives.

Funding

(f) Notwithstanding section 1346 of title 31 or section 610 of this Act, funds made available for fiscal year 2000 and hereafter by this or any other Act shall be available for interagency funding of the National Intellectual Property Law Enforcement Coordination Council.

Cyberpiracy Protections for Individuals

IN GENERAL *Civil Liability*

1129. — (1) (*A*) Any person who registers a domain name that consists of the name of another living person, or a name substantially and confusingly similar thereto, without that person's consent, with the specific intent to profit from such name by selling the domain name for financial gain to that person or any third party, shall be liable in a civil action by such person.

Exception

(*B*) A person who in good faith registers a domain name consisting of the name of another living person, or a name substantially and confusingly similar thereto, shall not be liable under this paragraph if such name is used in, affiliated with, or related to a work of authorship protected under title 17, United States Code, including a work made for hire as defined in section 101 of title 17, and if the person registering the domain name is the copyright owner or licensee of the work, the person intends to sell the domain name in conjunction with the lawful exploitation of the work, and such registration is not prohibited by a contract between the registrant and the named person. The exception under this subparagraph shall apply only to a civil action brought under paragraph (1) and shall in no manner limit the protections afforded under the Trademark Act of 1946 (15 U. S. C. 1051 et seq.) or other provision of Federal or State law.

REMEDIES

(2) In any civil action brought under paragraph (1), a court may award injunctive relief, including the forfeiture or cancellation of the domain name or the transfer of the domain name to the plaintiff. The court may also, in its discretion, award costs and attorneys fees to the prevailing party.

DEFINITION

(3) In this subsection, the term "domain name" has the meaning given that term in section 45 of the Trademark Act of 1946 (15 U. S. C. 1127) .

EFFECTIVE DATE

(4) This subsection shall apply to domain names registered on or after November 29, 1999.

SUBCHAPTER IV
THE MADRID PROTOCOL
Definitions

1141. In this subchapter:

BASIC APPLICATION

(1) The term "basic application" means the application for the registration of a mark that has been filed with an Office of a Contracting Party and that constitutes the basis for an application for the international registration of that mark.

BASIC REGISTRATION

(2) The term "basic registration" means the registration of a mark that has been granted by an Office of a Contracting Party and that constitutes the basis for an application for the international registration of that mark.

CONTRACTING PARTY

(3) The term "Contracting Party" means any country or inter-governmental organization that is a party to the Madrid Protocol.

DATE OF RECORDAL

(4) The term "date of recordal" means the date on which a request for extension of protection, filed after an international registration is granted, is recorded on the International Register.

DECLARATION OF *BONA FIDE* INTENTION TO USE
THE MARK IN COMMERCE

(5) The term "declaration of *bona fide* intention to use the mark in commerce" means a declaration that is signed by the applicant for, or holder of, an international registration who is seeking extension of protection of a mark to the United States and that contains a statement that—

(A) the applicant or holder has a *bona fide* intention to use the mark in commerce;

(B) the person making the declaration believes himself or herself, or the firm, corporation, or association in whose behalf he or she makes the declaration, to be entitled to use the mark in commerce; and

(C) no other person, firm, corporation, or association, to the best of his or her knowledge and belief, has the right to use such mark in commerce either in the identical form of the mark or in such near resemblance to the mark as to be likely, when used on or in connection with the goods of such other person, firm, corporation, or association, to cause confusion, mistake, or deception.

EXTENSION OF PROTECTION

(6) The term "extension of protection" means the protection resulting from an international registration that extends to the United States at the request of the holder of the international registration, in accordance with the Madrid Protocol.

HOLDER OF AN INTERNATIONAL REGISTRATION

(7) A "holder" of an international registration is the natural or juristic person in whose name the international registration is recorded on the International Register.

INTERNATIONAL APPLICATION

(8) The term "international application" means an application for international registration that is filed under the Madrid Protocol.

INTERNATIONAL BUREAU

(9) The term "International Bureau" means the International Bureau of the World Intellectual Property Organization.

INTERNATIONAL REGISTER

(10) The term "International Register" means the official collection of data concerning international registrations maintained by the International Bureau that the Madrid Protocol or its implementing regulations require or permit to be recorded.

INTERNATIONAL REGISTRATION

(11) The term "international registration" means the registration of a mark granted under the Madrid Protocol.

INTERNATIONAL REGISTRATION DATE

(12) The term "international registration date" means the date assigned to the international registration by the International Bureau.

MADRID PROTOCOL

(13) The term "Madrid Protocol" means the Protocol Relating to the Madrid Agreement Concerning the International Registration of Marks, adopted at Madrid, Spain, on June 27, 1989.

NOTIFICATION OF REFUSAL

(14) The term "notification of refusal" means the notice sent by the United States Patent and Trademark Office to the International Bureau declaring that an extension of protection cannot be granted.

OFFICE OF A CONTRACTING PARTY

(15) The term "Office of a Contracting Party" means—

(A) the office, or governmental entity, of a Contracting Party that is responsible for the registration of marks; or

(B) the common office, or governmental entity, of more than 1 Contracting

Party that is responsible for the registration of marks and is so recognized by the International Bureau.

OFFICE OF ORIGIN

(16) The term "office of origin" means the Office of a Contracting Party with which a basic application was filed or by which a basic registration was granted.

OPPOSITION PERIOD

(17) The term "opposition period" means the time allowed for filing an opposition in the United States Patent and Trademark Office, including any extension of time granted under section 1063 of this title.

International Applications Based on United States Applications or Registrations

In General

1141a. — (a) The owner of a basic application pending before the United States Patent and Trademark Office, or the owner of a basic registration granted by the United States Patent and Trademark Office may file an international application by submitting to the United States Patent and Trademark Office a written application in such form, together with such fees, as may be prescribed by the Director.

Qualified Owners

(b) A qualified owner, under subsection (a), shall—

(1) be a national of the United States;

(2) be domiciled in the United States; or

(3) have a real and effective industrial or commercial establishment in the United States.

Certification of the International Application

Certification Procedure

1141b. — (a) Upon the filing of an application for international registration and payment of the prescribed fees, the Director shall examine the international application for the purpose of certifying that the information contained in the international application corresponds to the information contained in the basic application or basic registration at the time of the certification.

Transmittal

(b) Upon examination and certification of the international application, the Director shall transmit the international application to the International Bureau.

Restriction, Abandonment, Cancellation, or Expiration
of a Basic Application or Basic Registration

1141c. With respect to an international application transmitted to the International Bureau under section 1141b of this title, the Director shall notify the International Bureau whenever the basic application or basic registration which is the basis for the international application has been restricted, abandoned, or canceled, or has expired, with respect to some or all of the goods and services listed in the international registration—

(1) within 5 years after the international registration date; or

(2) more than 5 years after the international registration date if the restriction, abandonment, or cancellation of the basic application or basic registration resulted from an action that began before the end of that 5-year period.

Request for Extension of Protection Subsequent to
International Registration

1141d. The holder of an international registration that is based upon a basic application filed with the United States Patent and Trademark Office or a basic registration granted by the Patent and Trademark Office may request an extension of protection of its international registration by filing such a request—

(1) directly with the International Bureau; or

(2) with the United States Patent and Trademark Office for transmittal to the International Bureau, if the request is in such form, and contains such transmittal

fee, as may be prescribed by the Director.

Extension of Protection of an International Registration to the United States under the Madrid Protocol

1141e. — (a) In general. Subject to the provisions of section 68 [15 USCS § 1141h], the holder of an international registration shall be entitled to the benefits of extension of protection of that international registration to the United States to the extent necessary to give effect to any provision of the Madrid Protocol.

(b) If the United States is office of origin. Where the United States Patent and Trademark Office is the office of origin for a trademark application or registration, any international registration based on such application or registration cannot be used to obtain the benefits of the Madrid Protocol in the United States.

Effect of Filing a Request for Extension of Protection of an International Registration to the United States

1141f. — (a) Requirement for request for extension of protection. A request for extension of protection of an international registration to the United States that the International Bureau transmits to the United States Patent and Trademark Office shall be deemed to be properly filed in the United States if such request, when received by the International Bureau, has attached to it a declaration of *bona fide* intention to use the mark in commerce that is verified by the applicant for, or holder of, the international registration.

(b) Effect of proper filing. Unless extension of protection is refused under section 68 [15 USCS § 1141h], the proper filing of the request for extension of protection under subsection (a) shall constitute constructive use of the mark, conferring the same rights as those specified in section 7 (c) [15 USCS § 1057 (c)], as of the earliest of the following:

(1) The international registration date, if the request for extension of protection was filed in the international application.

(2) The date of recordal of the request for extension of protection, if the

request for extension of protection was made after the international registration date.

(3) The date of priority claimed pursuant to section 67 [15 USCS § 1141g] .

Right of Priority for Request for Extension of Protection to the United States

1141g. The holder of an international registration with a request for an extension of protection to the United States shall be entitled to claim a date of priority based on a right of priority within the meaning of Article 4 of the Paris Convention for the Protection of Industrial Property if—

(1) the request for extension of protection contains a claim of priority; and

(2) the date of international registration or the date of the recordal of the request for extension of protection to the United States is not later than 6 months after the date of the first regular national filing (within the meaning of Article 4 (*A*) (3) of the Paris Convention for the Protection of Industrial Property) or a subsequent application (within the meaning of Article 4 (*C*) (4) of the Paris Convention for the Protection of Industrial Property) .

Examination of and Opposition to Request for Extension
of Protection; Notification of Refusal

1141h. — (*a*) Examination and opposition.

(1) A request for extension of protection described in section 66 (*a*) [15 USCS § 1141f (*a*)] shall be examined as an application for registration on the Principal Register under this Act, and if on such examination it appears that the applicant is entitled to extension of protection under this title [15 USCS § § 1141 et seq.], the Director shall cause the mark to be published in the Official Gazette of the United States Patent and Trademark Office.

(2) Subject to the provisions of subsection (*c*) , a request for extension of protection under this title [15 USCS § § 1141 et seq.] shall be subject to opposition under section 13 [15 USCS § 1063] .

(3) Extension of protection shall not be refused on the ground that the mark has not been used in commerce.

(4) Extension of protection shall be refused to any mark not registrable on the Principal Register.

(*b*) Notification of refusal. If [,] a request for extension of protection is refused under subsection (*a*), the Director shall declare in a notification of refusal (as provided in subsection (*c*)) that the extension of protection cannot be granted, together with a statement of all grounds on which the refusal was based.

(*c*) Notice to International Bureau.

(1) Within 18 months after the date on which the International Bureau transmits to the Patent and Trademark Office a notification of a request for extension of protection, the Director shall transmit to the International Bureau any of the following that applies to such request:

(*A*) A notification of refusal based on an examination of the request for extension of protection.

(*B*) A notification of refusal based on the filing of an opposition to the request.

(*C*) A notification of the possibility that an opposition to the request may be filed after the end of that 18-month period.

(2) If the Director has sent a notification of the possibility of opposition under paragraph (1) (*C*), the Director shall, if applicable, transmit to the International Bureau a notification of refusal on the basis of the opposition, together with a statement of all the grounds for the opposition, within 7 months after the beginning of the opposition period or within 1 month after the end of the opposition period, whichever is earlier.

(3) If a notification of refusal of a request for extension of protection is transmitted under paragraph (1) or (2), no grounds for refusal of such request other than those set forth in such notification may be transmitted to the International Bureau by the Director after the expiration of the time periods set forth in paragraph (1) or (2), as the case may be.

(4) If a notification specified in paragraph (1) or (2) is not sent to the International Bureau within the time period set forth in such paragraph, with respect to a

request for extension of protection, the request for extension of protection shall not be refused and the Director shall issue a certificate of extension of protection pursuant to the request.

(*d*) Designation of agent for service of process. In responding to a notification of refusal with respect to a mark, the holder of the international registration of the mark may designate, by a document filed in the United States Patent and Trademark Office, the name and address of a person residing in the United States on whom notices or process in proceedings affecting the mark may be served. Such notices or process may be served upon the person designated by leaving with that person, or mailing to that person, a copy thereof at the address specified in the last designation filed. If the person designated cannot be found at the address given in the last designation, or if the holder does not designate by a document filed in the United States Patent and Trademark Office the name and address of a person residing in the United States for service of notices or process in proceedings affecting the mark, the notice or process may be served on the Director.

Effect of Extension of Protection

1141*i*. — (*a*) Issuance of extension of protection. Unless a request for extension of protection is refused under section 68 [15 USCS § 1141*h*], the Director shall issue a certificate of extension of protection pursuant to the request and shall cause notice of such certificate of extension of protection to be published in the Official Gazette of the United States Patent and Trademark Office.

(*b*) Effect of extension of protection. From the date on which a certificate of extension of protection is issued under subsection (*a*) —

(1) such extension of protection shall have the same effect and validity as a registration on the Principal Register; and

(2) the holder of the international registration shall have the same rights and remedies as the owner of a registration on the Principal Register.

Dependence of Extension of Protection to the United States

on the Underlying International Registration

1141*j*. — (*a*) Effect of cancellation of international registration. If the International Bureau notifies the United States Patent and Trademark Office of the cancellation of an international registration with respect to some or all of the goods and services listed in the international registration, the Director shall cancel any extension of protection to the United States with respect to such goods and services as of the date on which the international registration was canceled.

(*b*) Effect of failure to renew international registration. If the International Bureau does not renew an international registration, the corresponding extension of protection to the United States shall cease to be valid as of the date of the expiration of the international registration.

(*c*) Transformation of an extension of protection into a United States application. The holder of an international registration canceled in whole or in part by the International Bureau at the request of the office of origin, under article 6 (4) of the Madrid Protocol, may file an application, under section 1 or 44 of this Act [15 USCS § 1051 or 1126], for the registration of the same mark for any of the goods and services to which the cancellation applies that were covered by an extension of protection to the United States based on that international registration. Such an application shall be treated as if it had been filed on the international registration date or the date of recordal of the request for extension of protection with the International Bureau, whichever date applies, and, if the extension of protection enjoyed priority under section 67 of this title [15 USCS § 1141*g*], shall enjoy the same priority. Such an application shall be entitled to the benefits conferred by this subsection only if the application is filed not later than 3 months after the date on which the international registration was canceled, in whole or in part, and only if the application complies with all the requirements of this Act which apply to any application filed pursuant to section 1 or 44 [15 USCS § 1051 of 1126].

Affidavits and Fees

1141*k*. — (*a*) Required affidavits and fees. An extension of protection for which a certificate of extension of protection has been issued under section 69 [15 USCS § 1141*i*] shall remain in force for the term of the international registration upon which it is based, except that the extension of protection of any mark shall be canceled by the Director—

(1) at the end of the 6–year period beginning on the date on which the certificate of extension of protection was issued by the Director, unless within the 1–year period preceding the expiration of that 6–year period the holder of the international registration files in the Patent and Trademark Office an affidavit under subsection (*b*) together with a fee prescribed by the Director; and

(2) at the end of the 10–year period beginning on the date on which the certificate of extension of protection was issued by the Director, and at the end of each 10–year period thereafter, unless—

(*A*) within the 6–month period preceding the expiration of such 10–year period the holder of the international registration files in the United States Patent and Trademark Office an affidavit under subsection (*b*) together with a fee prescribed by the Director; or

(*B*) within 3 months after the expiration of such 10–year period, the holder of the international registration files in the Patent and Trademark Office an affidavit under subsection (*b*) together with the fee described in subparagraph (*A*) and the surcharge prescribed by the Director.

(*b*) Contents of affidavit. The affidavit referred to in subsection (*a*) shall set forth those goods or services recited in the extension of protection on or in connection with which the mark is in use in commerce and the holder of the international registration shall attach to the affidavit a specimen or facsimile showing the current use of the mark in commerce, or shall set forth that any nonuse is due to special circumstances which excuse such nonuse and is not due to any intention to abandon the mark. Special notice of the requirement for such affidavit shall be attached to each certificate of extension of protection.

(*c*) Notification. The Director shall notify the holder of the international registration who files 1 of the affidavits of the Director´s acceptance or refusal thereof and, in case of a refusal, the reasons therefor.

(*d*) Service of notice or process. The holder of the international registration of the mark may designate, by a document filed in the United States Patent and Trademark Office, the name and address of a person residing in the United States on whom notices or process in proceedings affecting the mark may be served. Such notices or process may be served upon the person so designated by leaving with that person, or mailing to that person, a copy thereof at the address specified in the last designation so filed. If the person designated cannot be found at the address given in the last designation, or if the holder does not designate by a document filed in the United States Patent and Trademark Office the name and address of a person residing in the United States for service of notices or process in proceedings affecting the mark, the notice or process may be served on the Director.

Assignment of an Extension of Protection

1141*l*. An extension of protection may be assigned, together with the goodwill associated with the mark, only to a person who is a national of, is domiciled in, or has a *bona fide* and effective industrial or commercial establishment either in a country that is a Contracting Party or in a country that is a member of an intergovernmental organization that is a Contracting Party.

Incontestability

1141*m*. The period of continuous use prescribed under section 15 [15 USCS § 1065] for a mark covered by an extension of protection issued under this title [15 USCS § § 1141 et seq.] may begin no earlier than the date on which the Director issues the certificate of the extension of protection under section 69 [15 USCS § 1141*i*], except as provided in section 74 [15 USCS § 1151*n*] .

Rights of Extension of Protection

1141*n*. When a United States registration and a subsequently issued certificate of extension of protection to the United States are owned by the same person, identify the same mark, and list the same goods or services, the extension of protection shall have the same rights that accrued to the registration prior to issuance of the certificate of extension of protection.